The Buddha

The Buddha

A Storied Life

Edited by

VANESSA R. SASSON AND KRISTIN SCHEIBLE

OXFORD
UNIVERSITY PRESS

OXFORD
UNIVERSITY PRESS

Oxford University Press is a department of the University of Oxford. It furthers the University's objective of excellence in research, scholarship, and education by publishing worldwide. Oxford is a registered trade mark of Oxford University Press in the UK and certain other countries.

Published in the United States of America by Oxford University Press
198 Madison Avenue, New York, NY 10016, United States of America.

Library of Congress Cataloging-in-Publication Data
Names: Sasson, Vanessa R., editor. | Scheible, Kristin, editor.
Title: The Buddha : a storied life / edited by Vanessa R. Sasson & Kristin Scheible.
Description: New York : Oxford University Press, 2024. |
Includes bibliographical references and index.
Identifiers: LCCN 2023032614 (print) | LCCN 2023032615 (ebook) |
ISBN 9780197649473 (paperback) | ISBN 9780197649466 (hardback) |
ISBN 9780197649497 (epub)
Subjects: LCSH: Gautama Buddha. | Buddhism—Origin. |
Buddhism—History. | Buddhism—Doctrines.
Classification: LCC BQ895.B828 2023 (print) | LCC BQ895 (ebook) |
DDC 294.3/63—dc23/eng/20230719
LC record available at https://lccn.loc.gov/2023032614
LC ebook record available at https://lccn.loc.gov/2023032615

DOI: 10.1093/oso/9780197649466.001.0001

Paperback printed by Marquis Book Printing, Canada
Hardback printed by Bridgeport National Bindery, Inc., United States of America

MIX
Paper | Supporting responsible forestry
FSC® C103567
FSC www.fsc.org

For John S. Strong

Contents

Contributors ix
Preface xiii
Learning from John Strong: Many Ways of Reading the Many Life Stories of the Buddha by Charles Hallisey xiii

Introduction: The Never-Ending Story 1
Vanessa R. Sasson and Kristin Scheible

1. The Vow That Starts the Story 14
Andy Rotman

2. Creative Tensions in the Past Lives of the Buddha 40
Naomi Appleton

3. The Final Birth 60
Reiko Ohnuma

4. A Timeless Love Story 82
Vanessa R. Sasson

5. A Great Departure 98
Kristin Scheible

6. Around the Tree of Awakening 119
Todd Lewis and Jinah Kim

7. The Buddha's Career: Teachings and Miracles 150
David Fiordalis

8. Sorrow and its Ending in the Buddha's Last Days 177
Maria Heim

9. The Buddha's Story Continues: Afterlives of the Relics 197
Stephen C. Berkwitz

10. Overstory: First There is a Buddha, Then There is No Buddha, Then There Is 215
John S. Strong

Bibliography 231
Index 247

Contributors

Naomi Appleton is Professor of Buddhist Studies and Indian Religions at the University of Edinburgh and Codirector of the Edinburgh Buddhist Studies network. Her primary research interest is the use of narrative in the construction, communication, and challenge of religious ideas in early India. She has a particular enthusiasm for *jātaka* stories, a genre she has studied since she was a postgraduate student first at Cardiff and then at Oxford. John Strong examined her doctorate on the subject in 2008, beginning one of the most important and nourishing academic associations of her career. She is the author of *Jātaka Stories in Theravāda Buddhism* (Ashgate 2010), *Narrating Karma and Rebirth* (Cambridge University Press 2014) and *Shared Characters in Jain, Buddhist and Hindu Narrative* (Routledge 2017) as well as a series of translations, articles, and edited collections on related themes.

Stephen C. Berkwitz is Professor and Department Head of Languages, Cultures, and Religions at Missouri State University. His research focuses on Sinhala Literature and Buddhist Culture in Sri Lanka from the medieval up to the contemporary periods. His books include *Buddhist Poetry and Colonialism: Alagiyavanna and the Portuguese in Sri Lanka* (Oxford University Press 2013), *The History of the Buddha's Relic Shrine: A Translation of the Sinhala Thūpavaṃsa* (Oxford University Press 2007), and *Buddhist History in the Vernacular: The Power of the Past in Medieval Sri Lanka* (Brill 2004). He coedited the *Routledge Handbook of Theravāda Buddhism* with Ashley Thompson (Routledge 2022). His current research interests include historical accounts of the Bodhi Tree and literary representations of Buddhist kingship. He has for many years enjoyed John's books and the informal conversations they have had at conferences.

David Fiordalis is Associate Professor of Religion at Linfield University in Oregon in the United States and Research Editor at 84000: Translating the Words of the Buddha. He received his doctorate from the University of Michigan, where Luis O. Gómez supervised his thesis on miracles and superhuman powers in Buddhist literature. While completing his dissertation, Fiordalis first met John Strong, who has since been a constant source of support and mentorship to him on this topic and many others. Fiordalis has published various articles, translations, and editions related to Buddhist narrative, poetry, and philosophy, including an edited volume on Buddhist philosophy as practice: *Buddhist Spiritual Practices: Thinking with Pierre Hadot on Buddhism, Philosophy, and the Path* (Mangalam, 2018).

Charles Hallisey is a student of Buddhist literatures whose areas of interest also include Buddhist ethics and moral anthropology, Buddhist scriptures, and the cultural history of Theravada Buddhism as well as the literary history of South Asia more generally. He teaches at Harvard Divinity School. John Strong and Charles Hallisey are both students of the late Frank E. Reynolds who taught them at the University of Chicago at different times, with John Strong one of Frank Reynolds's two most senior students. John Strong is an eminent scholar in his own right, for sure, but as a fellow student of Frank Reynolds, Charles Hallisey also has long valued John Strong's work as a "mesocosm" (a notion much loved by John Strong) to the thinking and insights of their teacher.

Maria Heim is George Lyman Crosby 1896 and Stanley Warfield Crosby Professor in Religion at Amherst College, and a Guggenheim fellow. She works on emotions in classical Indian thought and is the author of *Words for the Heart: A Treasury of Emotions from Classical India* (Princeton University Press 2022). She also works on Pali Buddhism and has written two books on the fifth-century Pali Buddhist thinker Buddhaghosa (*Voice of the Buddha*, Oxford University Press 2018, and *The Forerunner of All Things*, Oxford University Press 2014), and a short book on *Buddhist Ethics* (Cambridge University Press 2020). She was educated at Reed College and Harvard University. Much of what she knows about Buddha biographies have come from John Strong.

Jinah Kim is George P. Bickford Professor of Indian and South Asian art in the Department of History of Art and Architecture. She is the author of the *Receptacle of the Sacred: Illustrated Manuscripts and the Buddhist book cult in South Asia* (University of California Press 2013) and *Garland of Visions: Color, Tantra and a Material History of Indian Painting* (University of California Press 2021). She has also written numerous articles on text–image relationships, the art of the book in South Asia, the embodied artistic and ritual knowledge of artists and their patrons in South and Southeast Asian art, and the role of images in Indian Esoteric Buddhism. She cocurated an NEH-funded exhibition, *Dharma and Punya: Nepalese Ritual Art* (2019) with Todd Lewis and coedited the accompanying catalog published in 2019. She currently directs a digital humanities project on color and pigments in painting, "Mapping Color in History," with a searchable, open database for historical research on pigments. Her Buddhist Art courses always rely on John Strong's Buddha biography as an indispensable guide.

Todd Lewis is Distinguished Professor of Arts and Humanities and Professor of Religion at the College of the Holy Cross. His primary research since 1979 has been on Newar Buddhism in the Kathmandu Valley and the social history of Buddhism. Since completing his PhD (Columbia University 1984), Lewis has authored many articles on the Buddhist traditions of Nepal and a number of books. His translation, *Sugata Saurabha: A Poem on the Life of the Buddha by Chittadhar Hridaya of Nepal* (Oxford University Press 2010), received awards from the Khyentse Foundation and the Numata Foundation. His most recent publication with Jinah Kim, is *Dharma and Punya: Buddhist Ritual Art of Nepal* (Brill 2019). Throughout his career, Professor Lewis found the originality and interdisciplinarity of John Strong's work an inspiration to his own approach to Buddhist studies.

Reiko Ohnuma is Robert 1932 and Barbara Black Professor of Religion and Chair of the Department of Religion at Dartmouth College. Her scholarship focuses on South Asian Buddhist narrative literature preserved in Sanskrit and Pali, with a particular interest in the themes of embodiment, gender, and animality. She is the author of *Head, Eyes, Flesh,* *and Blood: Giving Away the Body in Indian Buddhist Literature* (Columbia University Press 2007); *Ties That Bind: Maternal Imagery and Discourse in Indian Buddhism* (Oxford University Press 2012); and *Unfortunate Destiny: Animals in the Indian Buddhist Imagination* (Oxford University Press 2017)—three books made better by the insightful comments (and masterful blurb-writing) of John Strong.

Andy Rotman is Sydenham Clark Parsons Professor of Religion, Buddhism, and South Asian Studies at Smith College. His publications include *Hungry Ghosts* (Wisdom Publications 2020), *Divine Stories: Translations from the Divyāvadāna, Part 1* and *Part 2* (Wisdom Publications 2008 and 2017), *Thus Have I Seen: Visualizing Faith in Early Indian Buddhism* (Oxford University Press 2009), and a coauthored volume, *Amar Akbar Anthony: Bollywood, Brotherhood, and the Nation* (Harvard University Press 2015). He has been engaged in textual and ethnographic work on religious and social life in South Asia for more than 25 years, and he owes an enormous debt of gratitude to John Strong.

Vanessa R. Sasson is a professor of Religious Studies in the Liberal Arts Department of Marianopolis College. She is also a research fellow at the University of the Free State and Research Member at CERIAS at UQAM. She is the author of *The Birth of Moses and the Buddha: A Paradigm for the Comparative Study of Religions* (Sheffield University Press 2007), which she would never have completed without John's generous help. She is the author of a number of articles and book chapters and has edited quite a few volumes over the years, the most recent being *Jewels, Jewelry, and Other Shiny Things in the Buddhist Imaginary* (University of Hawaiʻi Press 2021). The best part of the jewels volume was that John agreed to contribute. Sasson is the author of the novel, *Yasodhara and the Buddha* (Bloomsbury 2021), and its sequel, *The Gathering: A Story of the First Buddhist Women* (Equinox 2023).

Kristin Scheible is Professor of Religion and Humanities at Reed College and a scholar of South Asian religions. Her research focuses on rhetorical strategies employed in Pali and Sanskrit texts, especially in Pali historical narrative literature (vaṃsa). This work was launched while she read John Strong's draft for his *Relics of the Buddha* twenty years ago; he served on her dissertation committee at Harvard and continues to be her lodestar. Her first book, *Reading the Mahāvaṃsa: The Literary Aims of a Theravāda Buddhist History* (Columbia University Press 2016), explores the work-like dimension of the fifth and sixth century Sri Lankan Mahāvaṃsa, and destabilizes the dominant reading of this text as a political charter. She is currently researching the prolific use of agricultural metaphors in premodern Indic literature.

John S. Strong is Charles A. Dana Emeritus Professor of Religious Studies at Bates College in Lewiston, Maine. During his time at Bates, he held visiting professorships at the University of Peradeniya (1987), the University of Chicago (1995), Princeton (1997), Harvard (2002), and Stanford (2003) Universities. He is the author of a number of books including *Relics of the Buddha* (2004), *The Buddha: A Beginner's Guide* (2009), *Buddhisms: An Introduction* (2015), and *The Buddha's Tooth* (2021). He is happily retired, living in a house in the woods on a lake in Maine.

Preface

Learning from John Strong: Many Ways of Reading the Many Life Stories of the Buddha

I was reading two quite different things on the same day recently, one for "work" and one for ""pleasure," but it just so happened that each included comments about how most of us do not think enough about what it is that we do when we read. The first was a book by the Australian writer Gerald Murnane who said about himself, "I discovered early in life that the act of reading is much more complicated than most people seem to acknowledge."[1] The second was an essay by the American Sanskritist, Sheldon Pollock, who began an essay entitled "How We Read" with the observation that to ask about how we read may seem like a silly question to many, "since reading is something like walking, that we do without much thought once we learn how. Do we ask ourselves what it means to read when we sit down with our coffee and morning newspaper? Of course not, but we might well, because it is no straightforward matter."[2]

I suspect that these two comments came together so forcefully in my mind because I was thinking—far from the first time—about a statement that John Strong made three decades ago about Buddhist life worlds. "In my view, Buddhism, as it is popularly practiced," Strong said, "consists primarily of deeds done and stories told, that is, of rituals that regulate life both inside and outside the monastery, and of legends, myths, and tales that are recalled by, for, and about the faithful."[3] Strong elaborated on such stories "that are recalled by, for, and about the faithful," by adding that they

> can be thought of in terms of what Roger Bastide, in a very different context, called "belvedere phenomena," compilations of traditions that reveal a broader context, that enable one to see a whole surrounding countryside, in all of its various aspects (doctrinal, sociological, ritual, soteriological).[4]

I confess that I didn't particularly like this comment when I first read it, and John Strong has reminded me since that I told him so. If I try to understand now what I didn't like about it then, I think it was because I didn't know what a belvedere is and I didn't bother to look the word up in a dictionary. I simply—and wrongly—assumed that it was a fancy word for a place where one could see "a whole surrounding countryside," something like a scenic viewpoint on a highway where one pulls off to enjoy a vista for a few moments, only to get back into the car and continue on one's way. The metaphor struck me as naïve, possibly even suggesting that stories enabled one to "see," simply and directly, Buddhist life worlds as if they were right in front of one's eyes, like "a whole surrounding countryside," without any of the difficulties of historical or ethnographic reconstruction, and without any efforts of imagination, inference, and interpretation. It smacked of "positivism" to me, which at that time was a ready-at-hand term of abuse in certain sectors of the humane sciences. The contents of my reaction were not wrong. It is still the case today that no one should ever be complacent about under-acknowledging that, as Sheldon Pollock has put it, "sense-making becomes more complicated, becomes more of a problem requiring second-order reflection, the further in time and space the origins of the text are from the reader."[5] If the contents of my reaction were not wrong, my reaction was still misplaced.

I now think that my reaction, misplaced as it was, was wrong—seriously and arrogantly so. I saw just how wrong I was once I made the effort to look up the word "belvedere" in a dictionary. I learned that the English word is from Italian (literally "fair view" in Italian). In English, belvedere has a meaning that encompasses both "beautiful sight" and "fair view," that is, it is something beautiful to look at, in itself, and also something that turns one's attention to a larger scenic view. As an English word, it turns out that belvedere is an architectural term, a generic name for a built structure, whether self-standing or part of another building, that encourages one to tarry before something beautiful to look at. A belvedere is not the view itself, not what is seen from it, but it is the beautiful place from which one can see beautiful things.

On consideration of the term, I came to see the aptness and generative power of this architectural term as a metaphor for Buddhist stories. Moreover, the metaphor helps us to become alert to what can happen to us when we "enter" into the "built" spaces that Buddhists stories are. It is worthwhile to pause a bit to explore a belvedere as a metaphor for a Buddhist story as a way of helping us to become more self-conscious that reading "is no straightforward matter."[6]

Let's be sure to keep in mind that architectural belvederes are not merely scenic viewing places that are discovered, as if they are just "givens" in nature. They are always *built* spaces. They are built in ways that encourage us to linger within them and to get us to look out from within, their design even intended to guide us to see what is outside in particular ways. In other words, what we see from inside a belvedere is not only up to us. Once we get the hang of the belvedere's intended space, as we move about inside it to look out again and again, we end up seeing more and more of what we are intended to see. We also become self-conscious that we are seeing what we are seeing because of the belvedere's design, and as we become increasingly aware of being guided to see whatever we are seeing, we also become more aware of ourselves as viewers. That is to say, we look and we also know that we are looking.

There are thus three components to being in a belvedere: the "fair view," the beautifully designed building, and increasing self-awareness. When we think of a Buddhist story as a "belvedere phenomenon," we should expect that when we read the story something like the "fair view," the well-designed space, and the self-awareness will be part of our reading experience. It is probably the case that all stories well told are "belvedere phenomena," not just Buddhist ones. As the Australian writer Murnane says about stories more generally, "a story well told informs us not only that certain things may have happened but *what it is to know that one knows such things may have happened*."[7]

If we are lucky, we may come to a belvedere with someone else, someone who has brought us to it because of their own experience in it and with it. If we are still luckier, they share with us what they themselves have learned about how much there is to see, if only one tries to look from different angles and different positions. I remember one time many years ago sharing with Kenneth Morgan, my teacher at Colgate University, my appreciation of a Buddha image displayed at Chapel House there. After I had shared my own impressions, he asked me whether I had looked at the image seated on the floor eighteen inches to its left. I had not. When I did as he suggested, I was amazed. When someone who knows how to look guides us, we are enabled and enlarged.

Best of all, it can happen that as we become more and more self-conscious that we are being led to look in quite intentional ways, we start to try to see whether there are other intended, but unnoticed ways of seeing waiting for our discovery. To test this possibility, we try out different ways of moving inside the belvedere, searching for new possibilities from which to look outside. And as we do so, we can't help but appreciate and even admire all those who designed and built the belvedere, as well as those who discovered some of its best vantage points, and made it possible for us to enjoy them ourselves.

Let's not forget that we are thinking metaphorically here, that we are thinking about reading Buddhist stories, not entering actual buildings. What we have been exploring in the course of these imaginative reflections on architectural belvederes is about how to engage Buddhist stories and how to follow attentively writers, such as John Strong and the authors of the chapters in this volume, as they illuminate for us various ways of engaging Buddhist stories.

It is worth highlighting that we turned our attention in these reflections from beginning with what we see when we look out from a belvedere (toward "a whole landscape") to considering how we might see much more and much else by considering the various ways that we can move about within the belvedere. We end up looking around at what is possible inside just as much as we look outside. Similarly, there are many ways of reading Buddhist stories, getting inside them, and learning much more and much else from them. If reading Buddhist stories is like looking out from inside a belvedere, then learning how to read Buddhist stories well is like trying out and sharing different ways of moving about and positioning oneself within a belvedere, making it possible to see in many different ways.

We can illuminate the simile that reading Buddhist stories is like moving around the inside of a belvedere to discover different ways of looking out from within it, all the while becoming increasingly appreciative of just how well the viewing space is put together, with another metaphor about what we do when we read. In a beautiful essay, the American writer Toni Morrison suggests that when one reads, one experiences "one's own mind dancing with another's." In her essay, Toni Morrison refers to reading as "a very old-fashioned skill," but one that today is at risk because of "the danger to reading that our busied-up, education-as-horse-race, trophy-driven culture poses even to the entitled." Speaking of herself, Morrison says, "I need that intimate, sustained surrender to the company of my own mind while it touches another's—which is reading."[8] Toni Morrison's metaphor of reading as one mind dancing with another's helps us to see that when we allow our mind to dance with another's, to follow the lead of another, sometimes—and hopefully often—we find ourselves led to something that we want to remember, even something that we can't forget. It may be new ways of seeing ourselves or new possibilities for living. The Australian writer Murnane certainly experienced what Morrison helps us to see. He says what happens to us when we learn how to read in the manner that Morrison describes is that we learn many "things and much else while we read."[9]

I have been learning from John Strong for forty-five years. I heard him give a lecture in 1977 or 1978 at Harvard Divinity School, where I was then a student, about some of the Buddhist stories about the great Indian emperor, Aśoka. In the more than four decades since that first lucky chance to learn from John Strong, I have learned many things and much else from him. John Strong has introduced me to some of the best Buddhist stories I know, and he has been exceptionally generous in sharing with me and many others what he has learned about how much there is to see within and from a life story of the Buddha. He has encouraged by example others to try out the many possible ways of reading the many life stories of the Buddha, just as one might try out the different vantage points and angles of vision in a belvedere.

John Strong's lessons about the many possible ways of reading the many life stories of the Buddha can be distinguished as being of three kinds, using the three components of experiencing a belvedere that I named above: "fair views," beautifully designed buildings, and increasing self-awareness that encourages experimenting in unfamiliar ways of looking. All three are everywhere to be found in this book's chapters. Lingering with them and over them, attending to them as one reads, increases what one can see in the many life stories of the Buddha that have circulated for centuries across the Buddhist world globally.

What are the "fair views" of a "whole surrounding countryside" that are afforded whenever we read one of the many life stories of the Buddha? What are we trying to discern when we look out from within a life story of the Buddha? It is certainly not definite facts about the life of a historical person. In the first sentence of his book *The Buddha: A Beginner's Guide,* John Strong says bluntly, "Historically speaking, we know very little for certain about the life of Siddhārtha Gautama, the man who came to be known as "the Buddha."[10] Rather, in the "Introduction" to that same book, John Strong names three things to look for that exist outside in Buddhist life worlds from the inside of a life story: pilgrimage practices, aesthetic practices and art, and ritual. Sometimes such "fair views" help us to appreciate just why there are so many stories within the life story of the Buddha. About pilgrimage, John Strong says, pilgrimage "sites became established as the places where certain stories happened, [while] stories came to be told to explain the existence of certain sites." Attending to such a "fair view" helps us to see "the simultaneous and symbiotic growth of both the biographical and pilgrimage traditions."[11] Strong shows us that there is an analogous "fair view" with respect to the life stories of the Buddha and aesthetic practices and art:

> If there is a symbiosis in the relationship between the Buddha's biography and pilgrimage traditions, the same is true about its relationship to art. Simply put, what is recounted in story may affect what is sculpted in stone, just as what is sculpted in stone can influence what is recounted in story. There is nothing surprising in this; the impact of art on narrative is well-known.[12]

There is also a symbiotic relationship between ritual and the many life stories of the Buddha, in so far as "certain events in the life of the Buddha were directly correlated to particular ritual acts," such as monastic ordinations, while an awareness of ritual traditions, such as funerary rituals, can infuse a particular story with emotional depths and poignancy.[13] What is so exemplary in John Strong's understanding of the many life stories of the Buddha as belvedere phenomena is his emphasis on the reciprocal and symbiotic relation between what is inside a story and what is outside the story in pilgrimage, ritual, and art.

When we read the many life stories of the Buddha, how can we enter them as if they are "beautifully designed buildings?" What do we discern if we limit our attention only to what constitutes the form of a story? What can we discern if we limit our attention only to the manner in which the story is told? We can get started with some of the usual ways of reading any story. We look for the basic organizing elements that provide a tacit structure to a story, as in what John Strong calls “a Buddha-life blueprint” or what students of narratology call the *fabula* of a story. When we look for the manner in which a story is told, we note if it is rich in details or if its style is spare and direct. We can pause and ask what narrative function does a particular element play within a particular story. We can try to distinguish “layers” in the story, wondering whether these are evidence of the stages through which a life story came to assume the form it presently has or whether they have some other significance for the discerning reader. We can be on the lookout for patterns that emerge across stories, wondering what broader significance such patterns might have. For example, in the course of his reading a story about how the Buddha once left his community of monks to live alone in the forest, cared for by a wild elephant because the monks were so unbearably quarrelsome, John Strong suggestively wonders what this turn of events, an “architectural feature” of the story, might reveal: the Buddha’s going to live alone in the Pārileyyaka forest “is interesting for it is possible to detect within it a kind of nostalgia for solitude, for a simpler life, for peace and quiet.”[14]

When we read the many life stories of the Buddha, how can we be open to our increasing self-awareness to encourage us to experiment with diverse ways of reading. The English novelist, E. M. Forster is famous for the maxim “only connect,” which is found as an epigraph to his novel, *Howard’s End*. Forster’s maxim is a succinct and accurate statement of what I have learned from John Strong about the many ways of reading the many life stories of the Buddha: make sure that any particular way of reading you try always connects. The injunction to only connect is tacit in engaging Buddhist stories as belvedere phenomena: connect the inside of a story to what is going on outside it in a Buddhist life world. The injunction to only connect is at the heart of discovering the pleasures of a narrative insofar as one is able to trace the unitive connection between form and meaning within a story.

John Strong has taught me other ways of reading that exemplify this aspiration to only connect. He is a master of reading multiple versions of a story in ways that not only highlight the distinctive features of the different versions, but also the dense network of meanings that become visible only when one reads multiple versions of the same story together. Reading John Strong read and interpret the many life stories of the Buddha is to be reminded that it is important “to compare and contrast different versions of the same tale so as to reflect the many layers of meaning that different Buddhists came to find in the life of their founder.”[15] At the same time, John Strong also reminds when we read these many life stories, “we must avoid the risk of obscuring the unitive function that the Buddha’s life story has played throughout much of the Buddhist world.”[16]

Strong is also a master of connecting a suggestive detail in one story to illuminate a powerful meaning that is “not spelled out” in another, as, for example, when he mentions that a “queen in [a particular *jātaka*] story”

> is said to be having a hard time conceiving a son, who turns out to be the future Buddha. To my knowledge, no mention of such a difficulty is ever made in the accounts of the Buddha's mother, Mahāmāyā, conceiving him in his final life as Gautama, and yet the Somanassa tale causes us to think again about that final life.
>
> In light of it, it perhaps becomes more noteworthy that, in certain Pali commentaries, Mahāmāyā is presented as being in her mid-forties when she gives birth to the Buddha, a very advanced age, especially in ancient India, for becoming a first-time mother and possibly indicative of difficulties in conceiving. Such a thing, of course, is never spelled out in the lifestory of Gautama, and I do not want to overemphasize a detail which, in the *jātaka*, may serve no more than a narrative function, but . . . the *jātaka*s can sometimes act as a sort of reservoir for subconscious feelings about the Buddha, members of his family, or members of the *saṃgha*.[17]

There is one other way of reading the life stories of the Buddha that we should learn from John Strong. It also exemplifies the injunction to only connect when reading: we should be open to the possibility that particular stories within the life story of the Buddha as a whole will address us as persons, just as we find ourselves in our own lives. An example where we see John Strong reading in just such a way can be found in his *The Buddha* when he describes ritual reenactments in Burma of the Buddha teaching the *Abhidharma* to his deceased mother in heaven. A climax of the ritual re-enactment is a sermon from the Buddha, voiced by a monk crouching behind a statue of the Buddha "on the impossibility of fully repaying the debt one owes to one's mother." Strong concludes his discussion of this ritual re-enactment in the following way: "the message is clear: a mother's love and care know no bounds. Even the Buddha could not fully thank her for her kindness. Yet he tried, and so should we."[18]

These examples of different ways of reading that I have learned from John Strong are only a few of the many ways of reading the many life stories of the Buddha that I have learned from him. It will be obvious that the authors of this volume's chapters have learned from John Strong other ways of reading the many life stories of the Buddha. The general lesson is clear: we want to be able to read in different ways, always remembering to only connect.

The Australian writer Murnane was surely correct when he said that "a story well told informs us not only that certain things may have happened but *what it is to know that one knows such things may have happened*."[19] For those of us who have learned from John Strong how to read well-told stories well also know that, for us, he is an ineluctable part of "*what it is to know that one knows such things may have happened*."

Charles Hallisey

Notes

1. Gerald Murnane, *Last Letter to a Reader* (New York: And Other Stories, 2022 [Sydney: Giramondo, 2021]), 10.
2. Sheldon Pollock, "How We Read," in *Sensitive Reading: The Pleasures of Reading South Asian Literature in Translation* (Oakland: University of California Press, 2022), 44–45.
3. John S. Strong, *The Legend and Cult of Upagupta* (Princeton, NJ: Princeton University Press, 1992), xi.
4. Strong, *The Legend and Cult of Upagupta*, xii.
5. Pollock, "How We Read," 45.
6. Pollock, "How We Read," 45.
7. Murnane, *Last Letter to a Reader*, 14.
8. Toni Morrison, "The Dancing Mind," National Book Award Acceptance Speech, 1996.

   https://www.nationalbook.org/tag/the-dancing-mind/
9. Murnane, *Last Letter to a Reader*, 25.
10. John S. Strong, *The Buddha: A Short Biography* (London: Oneworld, 2001), 1.
11. Strong, *The Buddha*, 7.
12. Strong, *The Buddha*, 8.
13. Strong, *The Buddha*, 10.
14. Strong, *The Buddha*, 103.
15. Strong, *The Buddha*, xii.
16. Strong, *The Buddha*, 14.
17. Strong, *The Buddha*, 18.
18. Strong, *The Buddha*, 115.
19. Murnane, *Last Letter to a Reader*, 14.

Introduction

The Never-Ending Story

Vanessa R. Sasson and Kristin Scheible

How Does One Introduce the Buddha Biography?

On the one hand, the more one learns about the Buddha biography, the more impossible an introduction begins to seem. The Buddha biography is not a simple narrative following the life of the Buddha, moving from a clear beginning (birth) to a clear end (death and *parinirvāṇa*). It is a story that encapsulates myriad other stories. It is so vast and so layered, textured, and complicated with so many renditions, tellings, and retellings, that the more one learns about the ever-expanding Buddha biography, the more difficult it becomes to wrap our arms around any of it. An introduction to the Buddha biography soon becomes near impossible: we find ourselves surrounded by so many recensions, artistic manifestations, and versions from different parts of the world at once that we drown in its magnificent abundance. How exactly does one introduce something as vast and ubiquitous as that?

On the other hand, an introduction to the Buddha biography is one of the most primary and predictable discussions in the field; there is no Buddhism without the Buddha. The Buddha biography is introduced constantly, in classrooms and textbooks and sermons all around the world. In this sense, introducing the Buddha biography should be easy. The story is essential, waiting for us to tell it one more time.

Indeed, the Buddha biography is perhaps the strongest throughline, the most palpable thread connecting communities and ideas, that runs right through about 2,500 years of Buddhist history: it is the story of Siddhārtha Gautama, his birth, his early life as a prince, his awakening to become the Buddha, and his teaching career and death. This Buddha's life story is threaded through most texts in the vast corpus of Buddhist thought. If the Buddhist repertoire of sacred literature can fill, or even *be*, a library, the Buddha biography necessarily has a similar reach, and is evident on both the most reached-for and dustiest of shelves. Some Buddhist texts are entirely devoted to the Buddha biography, while others circulate independent scenes scattered between teachings. What we perceive as biography, then, is shuffled throughout the vast corpus of Buddhist

Vanessa R. Sasson and Kristin Scheible, *Introduction* In: *The Buddha*. Edited by: Vanessa R. Sasson and Kristin Scheible, Oxford University Press. © Oxford University Press 2024. DOI: 10.1093/oso/9780197649466.003.0001 writings in various ways, for various effects. Sometimes a scene emerges as the Buddha answers a question (which leads to the teaching conveyed by the text), or as he responds to a particular event. Perhaps the monks have asked him to elaborate on a legal matter, or a situation has arisen that has him contemplating a past-life narrative. Or nuns have gotten into trouble (as nuns sometimes do), and the Buddha is summoned. Whatever the situation may be, scenes of the Buddha's life unfold like the petals of a celestial *mandarva* flower, each one revealing another layer of this never-ending story. The more we learn about Buddhist texts, the more of the Buddha biography we encounter.

When it comes to engaging with this extraordinary abundance, few scholars have contributed as much as John S. Strong. From his work on the literary legends of Aśoka[1] and Upagupta[2] —both of which help us to understand the tradition's narrative trajectory—to his detailed study of particular moments in the Buddha's final life—such as his extraordinary work on the Buddha's relics,[3] or the mysterious perfumed chamber[4]—Strong's work quite simply has no intellectual parallel. In his recent work on the narratives that complicate the history (and historicity) of relics in Sri Lanka, he turns away from the historical to the "storical," moving away from historical reconstructions to examine the work of their "fictionality."[5]

One book has had a particularly important effect on the field. In 2001, Strong put together a concise book entitled *The Buddha: A Short Biography*.[6] Introductory in style, the book's language is accessible, the endnotes are limited, and the story is told with fluid ease. Many of us who teach Buddhism in colleges and universities have relied upon it. As introductory as it might seem, however, this little gem is probably the most cited of his works. Strong provides an overview of the Buddha biography in that book the way no one else can. Each time we return to it, we find ourselves amazed by all the information the book contains and the impact his storytelling has on our own thinking, teaching, and research.

When we heard of John Strong's retirement, we knew we had to do something to honor him. And it was his book, *The Buddha: A Short Biography*, that inspired us. A vivid retelling of the Buddha's story, it is just one iteration in a litany of retellings. But the best way to honor the force of the story, and the capacity of the storyteller, is to tell it some more. We therefore invited a group of scholars to reiterate the story of the Buddha's life one chapter at a time. We knew, however, that even a dream team of senior scholars could not match what Strong was able to produce on his own.

This book is an ode to John Strong's work and to his book, *The Buddha: A Short Biography*, in particular. Those of us who jumped into this project have all been inspired by John's work, and we all feel gratitude to him for the many ways he has encouraged the field of Buddhist Studies to grow. While we cannot speak for the others (beyond those few statements), we two editors feel that we would not be the scholars we are today without him. When we told him about this book and what we hoped to accomplish, we also admitted our concern that a book on the Buddha biography would be incomplete without him. Gracious as always, John agreed to join us in our adventure. He thus became part of a project that was designed to honor him, closing the book with a chapter that invites further exploration. We could not imagine it unfolding any other way.

The Buddha-Life Blueprint

While Strong's contributions to the study of the Buddha biography are many, his idea of a Buddha-life blueprint has become something of a classic, and it is the focus of our book.

The Buddha-life blueprint provides a metaperspective of the Buddha's life narrative. We can look at the Buddha biography up close and focus on the details of who Gautama Buddha was as an individual, or we can zoom out and see the Buddha biography as part of a much larger, even cosmic, narrative. The concept of *saṃsāra*, the "wandering on" cycle of births, lives, deaths, and rebirths, tells us that the universe (or multiple universes) cycles through time in a seemingly endless loop. A universe begins, trends for a bit, and then collapses, only to begin again. Every era in this almost interminable cycle eventually produces a buddha—a teacher—who achieves awakening and subsequently shares his insight with surrounding community members. That teacher eventually dies, and the community eventually disappears too (because everything is impermanent), but soon enough, another buddha arises, (re-)articulates those very same teachings (Dharma), galvanizes another community (Sangha), and infuses that tradition we recognize as Buddhism with life all over again. But then the teachings fade again, the community disperses, and once again everything is forgotten. But then *another* buddha arises and starts the system up again. And on the story goes.

These recurring buddhas share one important feature according to Strong: namely, that each buddha in this endless cycle has a virtually identical life story. Consider, for example, the *Mahāpadāna Sutta*: this text focuses on the story of a previous buddha named Buddha Vipassī whose life experiences parallel those of "our" buddha, Gautama's. The *Mahāpadāna Sutta* tells us when Buddha Vipassī lived, who his chief disciples were, and who were his parents. By introducing Vipassī, we are likewise provided with the outlines of many other buddha life stories: who *their* parents were, who their chief disciples were, and under what kinds of tree they were awakened.[7] What we quickly discover is that each of these previous buddhas had a similar narrative, that their biographies followed a set pattern, that buddhas always follow the same trail. The texts do not always agree on the details, but what Strong noticed is precisely this pattern. It reveals, as he says, "a biographical paradigm, a Buddha-life blueprint, which they, and all buddhas, follow."[8]

This blueprint is evident throughout a buddha's life, even before he achieves awakening, when he is a Buddha-to-be (a bodhisattva in Sanskrit; bodhisatta in Pali[9]). Many texts provide a list of events that a bodhisattva must experience on the way to becoming a buddha, such as the extraordinary circumstances for his birth, his particular relationship to others, the incitement to renounce and retreat to the forest, even a specific way to find a seat beneath a tree for meditation and awakening. The blueprint also details the miracles that all buddhas must perform, such as teaching the dharma to his mother in heaven and performing the "Twin Miracle" at Śrāvastī. The blueprint even directs the Buddha toward his final resting place in Kuśinagarī, where previous buddhas likewise died.

This shared biographical pattern was long overlooked by scholars in the field. As Strong has repeatedly noted in his writings, Buddhist studies struggles with an almost inevitable "bias toward individualism in the study of sacred biography,"[10] focusing on the Buddha as though he stood alone and could be separated out of the larger narrative. This bias is tempered when a reader understands the Buddhist biographical imperative to expand beyond a single lifetime. The road to awakening may seem to be an inner, psychological process, as well as a singular experience for a singular hero, but the Buddha's life narrative is in fact much broader in scope. Referring to Frank Reynolds's seminal work,[11] Strong recognized that a reader's "individualistic bias" can be mitigated by the appreciation of the karmic depth of a lifetime—the great expanse revealed in the "extended" Buddha biography. In other words, reading the Buddha as an individualized hero-type might seem logical and salient, but doing so obfuscates the work of many other beings in the stories of his final lifetime, the fact *of* his many previous lifetimes, and the pattern of the many previous (and future) buddhas as well.

It can, of course, be overwhelming to imagine a life story of such magnitude that transcends the agency of one individual and one time period. A means through this complexity is to think of the Buddha as having multiple lineages from which he emerges.[12] On the most basic level, the Buddha has an obvious human and biological lineage. He has a family tree of ancestors like anyone else. He is born to a specific mother in a specific time and place, and his story moves outward from there. But the Buddha's story is not limited by that one lineage. The Buddha can therefore claim a second lineage from which he emerges: a long continuum of past-life narratives that eventually culminate in his closing scene.

The Buddha biography does not begin with his birth in Lumbinī Grove some twenty-five hundred years ago.[13] Reiko Ohnuma's chapter tells the story of this final birth in Lumbinī, but this birth chapter is in fact the third chapter in this volume (and not the first). The Buddha's story is imagined as having begun long before his final birth, somewhere in the far distant past, with past-life narratives linking together like a chain across time. These stories of his many past lives (known as jātakas) are not, however, laid out chronologically. They do not appear in the literature in a linear fashion, but instead move in all directions, each one offering an almost unique perspective and serving its own narratological and doctrinal functions. As Naomi Appleton explains in her chapter in this volume:

> Sometimes the [past life] stories are presented as demonstrating the qualities required for buddhahood; sometimes they show the Buddha-to-be acting in morally dubious or foolish ways. Sometimes the stories don't really seem to be about the Buddha-to-be at all, but focus on other characters associated with him. Sometimes the fact that it is the Buddha telling the story seems more important than his behaviour within it.[14]

Whatever their purpose and however they might be used, past-life narratives function as an integral feature of the Buddha biography, even as they amplify the significance of his final life. The Buddha as an individual may have been born in a specific time and place, but his story is also the story of many lives lived, not just in the form of a prince or Buddha as we see him in his final birth, but in diverse animal and other forms that represent the variety of beings in the (Buddhist) cosmos.

The Buddha biography eventually extends even beyond his final-life narrative, after the individual Buddha's final death, when the story of his bodily relics picks up from where the rest of him leaves off. Stephen Berkwitz's chapter in this volume (Chapter 9) follows the Buddha biography into the future with stories about relics that sustain some of the Buddha's presence after his death. It is only when the long reel of the Buddha's life, from past-life narratives and into postdeath relics ones, are taken into consideration that one begins to appreciate the magnitude that is the Buddha narrative.

But there is more. The Buddha-life blueprint reveals the third and most magnificent of a buddha's lineages: the "buddha-lineage" itself. The Buddha is not a unique character. He is, as we have noted, just one buddha in a long line of predecessors. He is also just one buddha in a long line of successors, too. Every era produces a buddha (so some of the texts claim), and each one lives out a life that is structurally similar to the last—*this* is the Buddha-life blueprint.

Buddhas even cross paths with their successors in Buddhist narrative, so expansive is the genre. The Buddha of "our" era whose story we follow in this volume, is described in a number of sources as having met a previous buddha long ago. While this idea might be a bit dizzying to follow, it is nevertheless one of the most expansive features of the Buddha biography. Andy Rotman takes us through this feature in the opening chapter of this volume. In a past life long ago, before the Buddha-to-be was even the Buddha-to-be (because he had not vowed to become a buddha yet), he is born as the brahman Sumati/Sumedha. One day, he encounters the Buddha of that era—the Buddha Dīpaṅkara—and becomes "filled with faith" at the sight of him—a sight, Rotman tells us, that one "never tires of seeing."[15] A Pāli version reveals that this meeting occurred four *asaṅkheyya* (immeasurable time period) and 100,000 eons ago—an amazingly specific temporal calculation that heightens the sense of duration the bodhisattva's path takes.[16] This encounter, perhaps more than any other, best expresses the extraordinary lengths of time that characterize the Buddha biography.

This palpable lineage of past and future buddhas is what leads Strong to the conclusion that there is a Buddha-life blueprint that shapes and is shaped by the biography. This blueprint is, of course, not universally agreed upon, and variations reflect the interests of the communities responsible for them. Each text in the vast Buddhist repertoire that describes the blueprint (and its many elements), describes it a bit differently. But the concept of the blueprint is consistent and helps shape the Buddha narrative. David Fiordalis' chapter in this volume provides an example of how useful a blueprint can prove to be. His chapter (Chapter 7) tackles the Buddha's teaching career which spans more than four decades and contains any number of seemingly "pivotal" moments during that time. A comprehensive overview would be impossible. Fiordalis, therefore, looks to the Buddha-life blueprint for guidance, asking himself what the blueprint might be for the period of the Buddha's teaching career. From that question, his chapter emerges.

The bottom line, therefore, is this: buddhas share a structural biography. What happens in one buddha life story is likely to have happened (or will happen) in all the others. The details change, but the story repeats itself. Instead of being a one-dimensional, linear narrative about one individual, the Buddha's story proves to be much more complicated, with countless layers beneath the surface tying it all together. The Buddha-biography is, in other words, a paradigmatic narrative that plays out precisely as required.

Over and over and over again.

An Interconnected (Final) Life

When we take a step back and consider the Buddha biography as a whole, we encounter a tremendous narrative that cycles through huge expanses of time and space. But when we look more closely, the Buddha biography is also a story about an individual who struggles toward awakening after truly seeing the suffering in the world. The intimacy of this final narrative, the details of who he was, how he was raised, what he saw and how he left with his Great Departure—all of these are also important features of the Buddha biography. Indeed, we might well say that these details are the most beloved, because they are the details that make up his extraordinary final life.

But even in the midst of the details, even when we look closely at the Buddha's story and learn of his birth, his childhood, his experiences as a young man—even then, the story is far from simple. The one who will become Buddha Gautama arrives to the story with countless past-lives behind him, with a Buddha-lineage buttressing him, leading him to play a cosmic role even though he is an individual. Tensions therefore emerge in almost every scene of the Buddha biography, in almost every textual rendition, between this cosmic status and his individual reality. For instance, the Buddha-to-be is born of a human mother after a period of gestation—something that would mark him as being just like everyone else. And yet, as Ohnuma's chapter in this volume so beautifully articulates (Chapter 3), his birth is accompanied by a series of miraculous elements that sets his birth apart. Flowers fall from the sky, the earth trembles, and gods appear to receive him as he emerges from her womb.

But these miracles are just the tip of the iceberg. Ohnuma's chapter describes the many ways sources oscillate between the minutiae of one grounded moment and the cosmic vision of eternity. The Buddha's birth is described in some sources as miraculous and wonderful, each detail heightened with celestial enthusiasm, just as so many other heroic birth narratives operate throughout the world.[17] Other sources, however, engage a much wider lens. According to the *Gaṇḍavyūha Sūtra*, for example, the Buddha's mother's womb becomes a reflection of the entire cosmos. Māyā becomes the mother of *all* buddhas in this text—rather than just the individual mother of an individual son—her womb encompassing millions of buddhas who stride through her belly across huge expanses of space (while her body, Ohnuma explains, maintains an ordinary size). The mother of the Buddha therefore becomes the mother of all buddhas, and her womb becomes the cosmos itself. The Buddha biography thus expands to the point of immeasurability, perhaps inconceivability, and yet it remains the story of an individual buddha at the same time.

Tension is likewise revealed between the Buddha's individual agency and the requisite supporting cast of his surrounding community. Strong refers to this as a "lateral expansion" of the buddha life story, "the multiple and collective dimensions of certain common biographical events."[18] Widening the lens from the Buddha proper, then, includes the net of relationships that frame and support the Bodhisattva's experiences and life lessons. It might be tempting to give the Buddha all the credit, to imagine the Buddha as having the stage all to himself, but many other characters do, in fact, have parts to play. His immediate family members, his companions, even his arch-nemesis Devadatta, have all been with him through countless lifetimes. They land together in a final collective narrative with him. Other characters are not even human, but they feature with as much significance: the Mahābodhi tree beneath which he achieved awakening, Māra who taunts him and tries to shake his resolve, Kanthaka the glorious white horse who carries him out of the palace gates, and the guardian deities who watch his story from above and intervene when they feel a need to redirect—all of these characters *are* in fact characters, each one participating in the Buddha biography in their own way. We may want to imagine the Buddha as a solitary hero, charging into awakening all by himself, but the stage is always more populated than that.

To fully immerse ourselves in the great narrative that is the Buddha biography, we must therefore undo the still prevalent emphasis on the Buddha as an individual agent and as an ordinary human being. The goal for this book is to highlight the expansive, cosmic, miraculous, and deeply interconnected features of the Buddha biography, to move away from the limits of ordinary humanity so often associated with it and reveal the miraculous and integrated aspects of the Buddha's story as it regularly appears in the traditional sources. Each chapter in this volume works to highlight these tensions—the moments when the details of the everyday collide with the cosmic expanse, the scenes where the individual meets the collective, and the scenes when the collective returns to meet the individual again.

A Note About Method

Writing a book on the Buddha biography is not a simple task of following a narrative along a clear trajectory from beginning to end. The story itself is multifaceted, moving in so many directions, outwards and inwards, horizontally, vertically, and laterally all at once. There are, moreover, so many sources, so many versions, and so many individual fragments and scenes that any attempt at retelling the story (that is in itself a myriad of stories) will fail to capture it all. But here we take solace in being just another retelling in a litany of tellings that makes choices about what is told. Bernard Faure describes the Buddha biography as being like an accordion: each time the story is told, some scenes are expanded while others are compressed.[19] The Buddha's story does not move across time like an arrow and neither do we.

The story is, moreover, not limited to its many textual renditions. It shines through so many of the Buddhist arts—through painting, sculpture, architecture, music, dance, and more. When the vast and vital enduring practices of Buddhist pilgrimage and ritual are added to the repertoire, we realize that the

Buddha's story is threaded through every aspect of Buddhist life, informing it, shaping it, inspiring it—one telling at a time.

The story has been shaped by myriad historical and geographical contexts—it has been a central conduit that has helped Buddhism spread across the globe in various genres. From images on stūpas (memorial mounds that are sites of pilgrimage and worship) marking the significant sites of the historical Buddha's life, to Sir Edwin Arnold's *Light of Asia* (1879), to Osamu Tezuka's celebrated serial manga *Buddha* (1972–1983), to Bernardo Bertolucci's Hollywood film (starring Keanu Reeves as Siddhārtha Gautama) *The Little Buddha* (1993), the story in its many folds has helped galvanize interest in Buddhist faith, tradition, and practices.

We therefore had to make a few choices if we were to manage this material in one volume. First, we had to decide on a structure. We quickly agreed that the chapters would be stacked chronologically, creating a skeletal structure that moves from a (seemingly beginningless) beginning to an (endless) end. With this, we had the structure set—one that reveals well the Buddha-life blueprint. But the structure of this book, like so many Buddhist texts, does not reveal the whole story. Inside each chapter, multidirectionality abounds. The table of contents might suggest linear logic, but readers will discover a much more complicated geometry beneath the surface with the narrative moving in multiple directions all at once.

We chose, moreover, to focus on texts for this book, which makes sense for a cohort of textual scholars. And of the myriad Buddhist texts available, we chose to focus on South Asian ones. This book is, after all, inspired by John Strong, who is himself a scholar of South Asian texts. Those of us most influenced by his work are likewise scholars of South Asian literature, so it seemed a natural continuum to follow.

But the decision was based on more than that. Buddhist literature can be fantastically intimidating. The entire corpus of Buddhist writing is a library unto itself, and the Buddha biography, in parts or in whole, is peppered through it all. The range of source material is well beyond what any of us can write about. We therefore had to limit the sources we were willing to negotiate. We agreed, however, that we did not want to be exclusively focused on texts. Each chapter therefore includes at least one South Asian image to ground and complement the discussion. There are also a number of references to pilgrimage and ritual, so readers might gain a sense of the enduring, lived relevance of the Buddha's life story beyond the written word.

As a group-authored book, we also encountered a methodological challenge in our individual chapters. Each contributor in this volume works with Buddhist materials in a particular way. How do we collectively narrate the flow of the Buddha's story when we are each trained differently? Sasson, for example, has a strong narrative voice. In her chapter in this volume, she does not examine one scene of the Buddha biography, but instead follows the Bodhisattva's relationship with his wife through their many lives together as a never-ending story all its own. Todd Lewis and Jinah Kim, by contrast, focus on visual representations of the Buddha biography, the sights of the sites significant to his very awakening. Maria Heim performs a close reading of one text focused on the Buddha's death. How do we bring together all of these different styles, sources, and methodologies at once?

John Strong, once again, became our muse. While he himself has his own methodology and style, one of his great gifts has been his ability to work with scholars from across the field. Every contributor to this volume has a story about his generosity as a colleague—how he welcomed their research, encouraged them, or expressed appreciation for their ideas. John routinely weaves together material from diverse sources to lead a reader to new insights (who else might begin a conclusion to a book on the Buddha with the iconic 1960s Scottish musician Donovan?[20]). Multivocality even within our chapters preserves some of the heteroglossic richness of the biographical traditions, while likewise revealing our own intellectual diversity. We therefore decided not to try to force ourselves to fit into a singular methodological box, but instead trust ourselves as authors to utilize the salient tools from our own hermeneutical toolkit. Instead of being a problem to resolve, our methodological diversity thus serves to reflect the field as it actually is. There is, after all, no one way to "do" Buddhist Studies properly, so diversity must be our response.

The Never-Ending Story

This short introduction has emphasized the expansive nature of the Buddha's life story. Not only is the material of the Buddha biography textually expansive, with a never-ending collection of narratives, but it is expansive in structure, with a story that never really quite comes to an end. The Buddha as an individual dies, but his death is not the end of the story. The presence of the Buddha endures, his power reverberating in images and stūpas, conveyed through his Dharma (teachings), and perpetuated by his Sangha (community) so that his story does not seem to end even after his body is gone. He continues on in his relics, until they, too, come to their own extinction. But even the end of his relics does not quite seem to be the end of the story. As in the image of the Bodhisattva's Great Departure that Kristin Scheible examines in Chapter 5, where he is not depicted in bodily form, the Buddha's absence invites an ongoing presence to be actualized in the repetition and reiteration of his life story.

In his closing chapter to this volume (Chapter 10), John Strong articulates this ongoing paradox of the Buddha-biography when he playfully taunts us with, "first there is a buddha, then there is no buddha, then there is, . . . then there isn't, . . . then there is, . . . then there isn't."[21] As infuriating as this might seem, how else does one engage with a Buddha that is never quite here and never quite gone? The paradox is captured by the epithet the Buddha often uses to refer to himself: "Tathāgata," which in Sanskrit means either "Thus Come One" (*tathā-āgata*) or "Thus Gone One" (*tathā-gata*), or both at the same time. Even after he dies, and even when his relics die, even when all the *stūpas* and Buddha images disappear, we can rest assured that the story will go on, because another embodiment of awakening promises to be right around the corner. Buddhism may preach impermanence, but the Buddha's impermanence is not so clear.

This never-ending quality of the Buddha-biography is perhaps best articulated in a story that Maria Heim shares with us in her chapter in this volume. In her discussion of the Buddha's death, we learn about the Varavāraṇā—a little crowd of beautiful deities in the far-away heavens who are especially determined to honor the Buddha with a garland at his funeral.[22] Apparently, the Varavāraṇā started making this celestial garland the moment they heard that the Buddha would descend into his mother's womb. Eager to express their devotion, they began to weave, but the Varavāraṇā could not finish the garland nearly as quickly as they had hoped, so they decided to offer it when he was born instead. Unfortunately, the celestial garland was *still* not finished when he emerged from his mother's womb, so the Varavāraṇā decided to offer it at the next major moment in a future buddha's life: they would offer it on the day the future Buddha renounced.

But, as we might well expect at this point, the garland was *still* not ready even then. The Varavāraṇā did not, however, despair. Nor did they chastise themselves for perpetually missing the mark. They just chose the next turning point in the anticipated Buddha-life blueprint and decided to offer it when he achieved awakening. But they were *still* threading their garland when he achieved awakening! And they were still threading it when he gave his first sermon, when he performed the Twin Miracle at Śrāvastī, when he descended from Trāyastriṃśa heaven, and even when he renounced his "life-impetus" just before his death. At every pivotal moment in the Buddha biography, our dedicated deities hoped to present the Buddha with their gift, but they never managed. Their work was never done. They only relented when the Buddha died. At that point, they could no longer delay; it was time to offer their celestial garland, despite the fact that it remained unfinished. The Varavāraṇā were valiant in their efforts, dedicated dearly to their cause, but the garland proved to be just too vast for them. There were too many threads to weave. They eventually had to accept that they would never reach the end.

Like them, we will never reach the end of the Buddha biography. There will always be more texts to discover, more tellings and performances and possibilities to enjoy. There will, moreover, always be more teachers to listen to and learn from. The story is far from over and we hope, in some ways at least, that it will remain that way. May this introduction entice readers to enjoy the story and want to learn it a bit more.

Notes

We thank Maria Heim for being a great supporter of this book through every stage of the process. We thank her especially for providing us with invaluable feedback on this introduction.

1. John S. Strong, *The Legend of King Aśoka: A Study and Translation of the Aśokāvadāna* (Princeton, NJ: Princeton University Press, 1983).
2. John S. Strong, *The Legend and Cult of Upagupta: Sanskrit Buddhism in North India* (Princeton, NJ: Princeton University Press, 1992).
3. Strong has a number of publications in this area alone. Included among these are his two books, *Relics of the Buddha* (Princeton, NJ: Princeton University Press, 2004); and *The Buddha's Tooth: Western Tales of a Sri Lankan Relic* (Chicago: University of Chicago Press, 2021).
4. "Gandhakuṭī: The Perfumed Chamber of the Buddha." *History of Religions* 16 (1977): 390–406.
5. John S. Strong, *The Buddha's Tooth: Western Tales of a Sri Lankan Relic* (Chicago: University of Chicago Press, 2021), 4.
6. John S. Strong, *The Buddha: A Short Biography* (London: Oneworld Publications, 2001).
7. The *Mahāpadāna Sutta* is sutta 14 of the Dīgha Nikāya. For an English translation, see Maurice Walshe, trans., *The Long Discourses of the Buddha: A Translation of the Dīgha Nikāya* (Boston: Wisdom Publications, 1987).
8. Strong, *The Buddha*, 12.
9. Authors in this volume use both Pali and Pāli; it is the Middle Indic language used in the literature of the Theravāda. Just as "Sanskrit" is now a common word in English to describe the classical and sacred South Asian language more technically called *saṃskṛtam*, "Pali" is often used for Pāli. One could deploy a decolonial caveat for using either variation; at the end of the day, both render the word from various South Asian scripts into Latin script compatible with the English language.
10. John S. Strong, "A Family Quest: The Buddha, Yaśodharā, and Rāhula in the *Mūlasarvāstivāda Vinaya*," in *Sacred Biography in the Buddhist Traditions of South and Southeast Asia*, ed. Juliane Schober (Honolulu: University of Hawai'i Press, 1997), 114.
11. Frank E. Reynolds, "The Many Lives of the Buddha," in *The Biographical Process*, ed. Frank E. Reynolds and Donald Capps (The Hague: Mouton, 1976), 37–61.
12. Strong, *The Buddha*, 35.
13. Dating the Buddha of "our" era is a tricky affair. While most scholars are content to date the Buddha to the fifth century BCE, traditional sources provide a range of

potential dates, from 961 BCE to 486 BCE, according to Bernard Faure, *Les mille et une vies du bouddha* (Paris: Seuil, 2018), 74. For an overview of some of the debates surrounding the Buddha's dates, see Heinz Bechert, ed. *When Did the Buddha Live? The Controversy on the Dating of the Historical Buddha* (Delhi: Sri Satguru Publications, 1995). Herein, we round out the Buddha's dates to being approximately twenty-five hundred years ago.

14. See Naomi Appleton in this volume, Chapter 2.
15. See Andy Rotman, Chapter 1 in this volume.
16. N. A. Jayawickrama, trans., *The Story of Gotama Buddha (Jātaka Nidānakathā)* (Oxford: The Pali Text Society, 2000), 5.
17. This is the argument brought forward in Otto Rank, *The Myth of the Birth of the Hero: A Psychological Interpretation of Mythology*, trans. F. Robins and S. E. Jelliffe (New York: Johnson Reprint Incorporation, [1914] 1970), namely, that the heroes of most traditions are eventually provided with heroic beginnings.
18. Strong, "A Family Quest," 114.
19. Bernard Faure, *Les mille et une vies du bouddha*, 97.
20. Donovan's 1996 album is, however, titled "Sutras," and contains songs like "The Way" and "Nirvana."
21. See Strong, Chapter 10, in this volume.
22. Yang-Gyu An, trans., *The Buddha's Last Days: Buddhaghosa's Commentary on the Mahāparinibbāna Sutta* (Oxford: The Pali Text Society, 2005), 141–143.

1
The Vow That Starts the Story

Andy Rotman

Figure 1.1 The Buddha-to-be meets Dīpaṅkara Buddha; Swat Valley, Pakistan, ca. second century CE.

"Dīpaṅkara Jātaka" Pakistan, Swat Valley, ca. second century CE. Schist with gold leaf, 8 3/4" × 8 3/8." (22.2 × 21.3 cm). The Metropolitan Museum of Art, New York. Open Access, www.metmuseum.org/art/collection/search/49809.

Andy Rotman, *The Vow That Starts the Story* In: *The Buddha*. Edited by: Vanessa R. Sasson and Kristin Scheible, Oxford University Press. © Oxford University Press 2024. DOI: 10.1093/oso/9780197649466.003.0002

Introduction

The Buddha's story is generally said to begin not with his birth as Prince Gautama but instead during a previous birth, many eons ago, when as a learned brahmin he made a vow before the Buddha Dīpaṅkara (Illuminator) that he too would one day become a buddha, and Dīpaṅkara Buddha foretold that in the distant future this would come to pass. Fig. 1.1 shows the iconic moment when the Buddha-to-be offered flowers to Dīpaṅkara Buddha, placed his head at the latter's feet as an act of veneration, spreading out his hair for Dīpaṅkara to step on, and made his historic vow. This inaugurated his own path as the Bodhisattva destined to become the buddha known as Śākyamuni (Sage of the Śākyans).

The story exists in many permutations, both in literature and in art, with the name of the Buddha-to-be differing in various sources—Sumedha in Pāli texts, Sumati or Megha in Sanskrit ones—and the particulars of the story differing as well.[1] In Pāli, the story of the vow is a late addition to the Buddhist canon. Dīpaṅkara Buddha, in fact, is completely absent from the canonical discourses of the Buddha (*sutta*), making "it virtually certain that traditions concerning this buddha did not gain general currency until several centuries after Śākyamuni Buddha's death."[2] Later, however, there is a proliferation of accounts, such that the story of the vow "is by no means only a single narrative."[3] What is often referred to as "Sumedha's Story" (*Sumedhakathā*) is quite diverse, with different lineages of the story going through multiple revisions and iterations.[4] For example, in the introduction to the Pāli commentary on the *Jātakas*—stories of Śākyamuni Buddha's past lives—there is an attempt to synthesize various accounts of Śākyamuni's life into a cohesive story. As the author of the commentary explains at the beginning of his synthesis, "the story of Sumedha should be narrated here. Even though it occurs in full in the *Buddhavaṃsa* (*Chronicle of Buddhas*)"—a late addition to the Pāli canon that chronicles the life of Śākyamuni Buddha and the twenty-four buddhas who preceded him—"on account of the fact that it is handed down in metrical form, it is not quite clear. Therefore we shall narrate it with frequent statements explaining the stanzas."[5]

In Sanskrit, there are two principal versions of the vow story, each of which is preserved in a text that primarily consists of narratives from the monastic code of conduct (*vinaya*) of a particular Buddhist community. Nevertheless, even though the two versions of the story share similar origins, they differ significantly in the details, especially in their framing narratives. One version is preserved in the *Divyāvadāna* (*Divine Stories*), which is mostly a compendium of narratives excerpted from the monastic code of conduct of the Mūlasarvāstivādins. This version occurs within "The Story of Dharmaruci" (*Dharmaruci-avadāna*), which begins with the travails of a monstrously large sea creature. Just as the veritable leviathan is about to devour a boatload of merchants, he hears an invocation of the Buddha's name and vows to refrain from eating. Soon he dies and is reborn as a human with an insatiable appetite named Dharmaruci (Relishing the Dharma), who eventually goes forth as a monk and attains the awakening of an arhat. The Buddha then recounts how he and Dharmaruci had previously met three times, long ago during the respective eras of three different buddhas. It is during his account of their time together with Dīpaṅkara Buddha that he tells how he made his vow for future buddhahood.[6] The other version is preserved in the *Mahāvastu* (*Great Chapter*), which recounts the story of Śākyamuni Buddha over many eons and is a section of the monastic code of conduct of the Mahāsāṃghika-Lokottaravādins. That version occurs within an extended account of the life of Dīpaṅkara Buddha. Only after the episode of the vow is there mention of the story of Dharmaruci and the various times the Buddha-to-be and Dharmaruci met, and this is done in brief as a precursor to the story of the buddha named Maṅgala (Auspicious).[7]

One oddity in tracking versions of the vow story is that its earliest extant renderings likely occur not as texts but as images. There are many sculptures of the vow story from the first centuries of the Common Era from the northwest region of the Indian subcontinent then known as Gandhāra, just like the one at the beginning of this chapter. Gandhāran art mostly features images from Śākyamuni Buddha's lifetime, in particular his birth, his departure from the palace to pursue life as an ascetic, and his passing into final nirvāṇa, with far fewer representations of events from his previous births. The vow story is the major exception. Of the roughly 180 representations of past-life stories in Gandhāran art, nearly 130 of them depict the vow story, "a dominance not matched anywhere else in the world of Buddhist arts."[8] And while scenes from the other past-life stories are typically depicted on Buddhist stūpas—moundlike monuments for Buddhist holy figures—"in small panels in subsidiary positions, such as 'stair risers' on the steps leading up the pathway for circumambulation," scenes of the vow are often given pride of place, appearing directly on stūpas in panel reliefs.[9] It seems that the vow story not only originated in Gandhāra but was an important element of Gandhāran art and ritual practice.

Yet the vow story, which is so well represented in Gandhāran art, barely exists in Gandhāran literature. The version of the story preserved in "The Story of Dharmaruci" is a notable exception.[10] In fact, there is "little or no overlap between previous-birth stories as they are represented in Gandhāran texts and art, much to the chagrin of art and literary historians alike."[11] And yet this lack of overlap, especially at such an early moment in the vow story's development, is certainly intriguing. In particular, why might the vow story have generated so many images and yet been recorded in so few texts? Did the textual version of the vow story somehow present a problem? And what role might the images of the story have played in Buddhist rituals? Furthermore, why has the vow story become so important, both in text and art, for Buddhists across the globe during the past two millennia? In an effort to answer these questions, we will first consider the vow story preserved in "The Story of Dharmaruci" in the *Divyāvadāna*.

The Vow Story in "The Story of Dharmaruci"

The vow story in "The Story of Dharmaruci," which makes up about one-quarter of the tale, recounts what transpired when the future Śākyamuni Buddha and Dharmaruci met during the dispensation of Dīpaṅkara Buddha, and how the karmic consequences of their deeds and the karmic connections among characters continued to affect their lives throughout the eons. It also addresses key themes, such as the value of seeing a buddha, cultivating faith, giving offerings, and making vows, as well as the inexorability of karma. Yet the story has a number of peculiarities, especially around the character of the marginalized young woman who, by the power of a vow, will marry the future Prince Gautama in countless lifetimes. "The Story of Dharmaruci" is an *avadāna*, a genre of Buddhist past-life stories that monastic "jurist-cum-storytellers" followed to create legal documents for the Buddhist community that were also compelling narratives.[12] With this in mind, we will both retell the vow story and offer a detailed commentary, attuned to the way the text relates to other law codes and how it might have challenged devotees who wanted to use this account to model the quest for spiritual perfection.

Vow Story, Part 1

The story begins with Dīpaṅkara Buddha arriving in Dīpāvatī (Full of Light), the prosperous capital of King Dīpa (Light), and King Dīpa inviting Dīpaṅkara to enter. The king also invites a neighboring ruler, King Vāsava, to come and join him in honoring Dīpaṅkara. Meanwhile, King Vāsava, who has just finished performing a twelve-year-long sacrifice, is arranging to celebrate its completion by giving away five great gifts—a golden water-pitcher, a golden bowl, a four-jeweled bed, five hundred *kārṣāpaṇa* coins,[13] and a virgin bride bedecked with jewelry—to the brahmin most adept at reciting the sacred scriptures known as the Vedas.[14] Two young brahmins, Sumati (Very Wise) and Mati (Wise), who have just completed their study of the Vedas and were thinking that they should now honor their teacher with a gift and hear about King Vāsava's plan. Confident that none can surpass them in learning and recitation, they set out for the sacrificial grounds in King Vāsava's kingdom.

In the meantime, a deity informs King Vāsava that two young brahmins are coming, and that he should give the five gifts to Sumati. When the young brahmins arrive, King Vāsava offers the five gifts to Sumati, who accepts the first four gifts but rejects the gift of a bride, explaining that he is a celibate follower of the religious life. The rejected young woman experiences love at her first sight of Sumati and directly asks him to accept her in marriage, and once again he declines. Since the king has offered the young woman as a gift, he won't accept her back—such are the rules, which we'll discuss in what follows. The young woman is now on her own. She becomes a devotee of Dīpaṅkara Buddha, and in exchange for all her jewelry, she gets a flower seller to give her a daily allotment of blue waterlilies[15] that she can use to honor Dīpaṅkara.

Meanwhile Sumati goes to his teacher and offers him the four gifts. The teacher accepts three of the gifts but gives him back the five hundred coins. That night Sumati has ten dreams. He asks a nearby sage to interpret them, and instead the sage encourages him to go to Dīpāvatī and ask Dīpaṅkara Buddha for his help.

In the interim, King Vāsava accepts King Dīpa's invitation to honor Dīpaṅkara Buddha and arrives in Dīpāvatī along with eighty thousand ministers. King Dīpa begins to make arrangements for Dīpaṅkara Buddha to enter the city after seven days and be honored appropriately. To this end, he arranges for all the flowers in his kingdom to be collected.

On the day that Dīpaṅkara Buddha is scheduled to enter Dīpāvatī, the young woman goes to the flower seller to gather her daily allotment of blue waterlilies so that she can honor him. The flower seller explains that the king has gathered all the available flowers. The young woman asks him to check the lily pond once again, and seven blue waterlilies have miraculously appeared. The flower seller plucks the waterlilies and gives them to the young woman, who hides them in a waterpot and sets off for the city to see Dīpaṅkara.

Sumati has also arrived in Dīpāvatī, and realizing that he can't see Dīpaṅkara and not honor him with an offering, he begins searching for flowers, but he can't find any. He then meets up with the young woman, and by the power of his merit, the blue waterlilies that she has hidden rise up out of her waterpot. Sumati then offers her the five hundred coins he has previously been gifted in exchange for the waterlilies. The young woman vehemently declines:

> "Back then you didn't want to accept me," the young woman said to Sumati, "and now you're begging me for waterlilies. I won't give them to you!" With that, she then said to the young brahmin Sumati, "What will you do with them?"
>
> "I will honor the Lord Buddha," Sumati said.
>
> "But what use are *kārṣāpaṇa* coins to me?" the young woman asked. "I'll give these waterlilies to the Buddha, unless as a result of giving them to you, you'll seek me as your wife in every rebirth to come—that is, at the time of giving this

gift to the Buddha, you make the following fervent aspiration: 'May she be my wife in every rebirth to come.'"

"We're both intent on giving. Both of us would sacrifice our own family members, even our own flesh," Sumati said.

"Make the fervent aspiration!" the young woman said to Sumati. "Afterward, you may offer me to whomever you wish." After the young woman had said this, she gave five waterlilies to Sumati and took two herself. Then she uttered this verse:

> When you make a fervent aspiration,
> having accepted the Buddha as your guide,
> then I shall be your wife,
> a constant companion in the dharma.[16]

Commentary, Part 1

Let's pause in the retelling of the story to highlight some key features of the characters and the narrative. Sumati is a brahmin schooled in traditional Brahmanical Hinduism. He has studied the Vedas, which one traditionally memorizes so that they can be recited for ritual purposes, and he maintains the vow of celibacy (*brahmacarya*), which is appropriate for a young student.[17] In the Vedic world that he inhabits, the ideal religious person is a married householder, so it is likely that he would one day abandon his vow of celibacy, get married, settle down, and have children.[18] As best we can tell, Sumati has neither heard nor accepted Buddhist teachings before being told to seek out the Buddha to interpret his dreams.

The position of the young woman, who remains nameless in the story, is much less clear. Since the king can give her away in marriage, he is apparently her legal guardian—there is no mention of a father—suggesting that she is one of the king's servants. But the king gives her away prematurely, likely assuming that a brilliant Vedic student would want such a woman as a bride and wouldn't want to rebuff the king's generosity. But Sumati refuses her, citing his continued adherence to a vow of celibacy. Once the young woman has been given in marriage, she can't be taken back, at least not according to Brahmanical rules of marriage.[19] In this given-but-not-accepted state, she abides in a kind of legal limbo, neither wife nor daughter nor widow nor any other conventional role. Women were generally expected to be under the protection of a male guardian, usually husband, father, or son.[20] Brahmanical sources classified such unprotected women as "independent and wanton" (*svairiṇī*), grouping them together with prostitutes, perverts, and slaves, and treating them as social outcastes.[21] While the young woman here has sufficient independence to directly ask Sumati to marry her, it's unclear if she could ask anyone else to marry her. Instances of a young woman choosing her own husband—called a *svayaṃvara*, or "choosing for oneself"—are rare in early Indian materials.[22] Perhaps she is simply double checking to make sure that Sumati hasn't changed his mind.

Could it be that Sumati felt the same stirrings of love upon seeing her that she felt upon seeing him? Apparently not. Sumati rejects her, and as a brilliant Vedic scholar, he would presumably have known enough about Brahmanical marriage practices to know that his refusal to marry the young woman would place her in a precarious situation.[23] His decision to continue pursuing his own spiritual path as a bachelor would likely lead the young woman to suffer. And the young woman, as we shall see, seems to know this as well.

After being rejected by Sumati, the young woman—now homeless, stigmatized, and on her own—tries to create some security and respectability for herself. She removes the jewelry with which she has been adorned in preparation for marriage—even though the jewelry, according to the lawbooks, belongs to King Vāsava and not to her[24]—and approaches a flower seller with a proposition: she will give him the jewelry if, in return, he gives her a daily supply of blue waterlilies "for honoring the Lord." With that agreement in place, the young woman becomes a "servant of the Lord" (*devaśuśrūṣikā*). The term "servant" (*śuśrūṣaka*) is noteworthy here, for it is a technical term in Brahmanical law texts that encompasses both "workers" and "slaves," each with various subtypes.[25] The term is rare in Buddhist materials, and it seems to be used here to place the young woman in a matrix of servitude. She has apparently shifted her "service" (*śuśrūṣā*) from one "Lord"—the king—to another "Lord"—Dīpaṅkara.[26] The young woman has no legal obligations to Dīpaṅkara, for he is neither her employer nor her guardian, and yet the text is expressing some sense of continuity with regard to the woman's position. The young woman begins to make daily offerings of flowers to Dīpaṅkara, and within a week she becomes for him a "lay attendant" (*upasthāyikā*). Although she now has a form of refuge, she does not seem satisfied with her situation, and judging by her response to Sumati's offer of money, her main problems aren't financial. She yearns for an additional "Lord"—Sumati—in this lifetime and in countless lifetimes to come. It seems that she never wants to be unprotected again.

Important to the story is the concept of "merit" (*puṇya*)—that is, the good karma one accrues as a result of performing virtuous deeds. After the flower seller tells the young woman that the king has collected every flower in the city, she asks the flower seller to double check the lily pond: "If, because of my meritorious deeds, there are once again blue waterlilies in the lily pond that haven't been plucked, then get them for me." The flower seller complies and finds that seven blue waterlilies have suddenly appeared in the lily pond. The text explains that this has happened "by the power of Sumati's merit," and not, as we might expect, the young woman's merit. The flower seller is hesitant to pick the flowers and give them to the young woman because all flowers in the city are to be given to the king. But she explains to him, "It's because of my meritorious deeds that they have appeared. So give whatever you pick to me." The flower seller acquiesces, with the reasoning that the flowers rightfully belong to whoever had the merit that caused the flowers to miraculously appear.

Our ability to identify the karmic cause of any event is undermined by "the opacity, phenomenologically speaking, of karma."[27] Ordinary humans can't simply look inside themselves or look into others and know their karmic accounting. Buddhist literature, however, is alive with deities who have special forms of insight, like knowing the karma of others, that they use to intervene strategically in human affairs. A deity knows that Sumati is "of the highest standing" (*mahattamapada*) and informs King Vāsava to offer him the gifts from the sacrifice, thus assuring that they will be given to the most worthy recipient and, knowingly or not, help Sumati on his way to becoming a bodhisattva. According to the karmic logic of the story, the young woman, who is a devotee/servant of Dīpaṅkara Buddha and offers him flowers every day, has likely accrued significant merit from these offerings. And she is right that enough merit has the power to make additional flowers magically appear. But she is wrong in thinking that the merit that did so in this case was hers. One's karmic condition is opaque, which means that anyone you "might meet, no matter how apparently lacking in qualities, could be on the verge of some great attainment."[28] Even the person who just rejected you in marriage—twice.

Both Sumati and the young woman place far more value on being able to offer Dīpaṅkara Buddha flowers on this day than on accruing wealth. Sumati has searched diligently for flowers, visiting the homes of various flower sellers and wandering from garden to garden, but he hasn't come across a single flower. When he finally runs into the young woman and the waterlilies miraculously rise up from her waterpot, he says, "Give me those waterlilies. And take these five hundred *kārṣāpaṇa* coins from me as a reward." This is a significant amount of money. Elsewhere in the *Divyāvadāna* it is said that five hundred *kārṣāpaṇa* coins is how much it takes to feed the entire community of monks led by the Buddha.[29] Sumati's request to the young woman is rather blunt, especially since the last time they met he refused her request for marriage. He asks her to accept the money for the flowers as a "reward," more like "ransom" or "pay off" (*niṣkraya*), as though she were holding the flowers hostage.[30] His lack of politeness might be why the young woman rejects his offer so vociferously. Sumati is still young and chaste, very smart if not very worldly, and he isn't yet a bodhisattva. But he is right that the young woman has appropriated something that isn't hers, for the flowers are a product of Sumati's merit and, by her own logic, thus belong to him. The young woman is both enamored and angered by Sumati, and yet she also recognizes that he will make great progress on the spiritual path in future lifetimes. As a dedicated spiritual practitioner, she wants to partner with him on that journey and share in that success. But she also wants to make sure that she always has the protection of a husband.

Crucial as well to the story is the concept of "fervent aspiration" (*praṇidhāna*)—an aspirational vow or solemn resolution that functions as a wish and commitment toward some future goal. After rejecting Sumati's offer of a cash payment for the flowers, she proposes a different kind of remuneration, and she is very specific. She will give Sumati the waterlilies if, in return, at the moment of offering the flowers to Dīpaṅkara, he makes a fervent aspiration that she will be his wife in every rebirth to come. The ability to make a fervent aspiration is usually dependent on having accumulated a stockpile of merit that one can "cash in" to make the vow. One can accumulate merit, for example, by making offerings to Buddhist saints or shrines—or, if you're fortunate, the Buddha himself—and this merit can then function as the purchasing power for a fervent aspiration, such that one can transform a present wish into a future reality. The young woman wants Sumati to make a gift of the waterlilies to Dīpaṅkara, which would likely earn him a lot of merit, and immediately cash in the merit to make a fervent aspiration. Sumati affirms his commitment to giving—suddenly sounding like the bodhisattva in his future rebirths who makes gifts even of his own body for the sake of awakening[31]—but the young woman only wants him to commit to the fervent aspiration she requested. Then he can give her away to whoever he wants. She then utters an enigmatic verse, promising that when Sumati accepts the Buddha as his guide and makes a fervent aspiration, then she will be his lawful wife and companion in the dharma.

Vow Story, Part 2

After the young woman utters that verse, the story—without recording Sumati's response—chronicles how King Dīpa beautifies Dīpāvatī and then, accompanied by King Vāsava and their respective ministers, welcomes Dīpaṅkara Buddha and his community of monks into the city. Dīpaṅkara makes use of his magical power so that both kings and their vast cabinets of ministers, each of whom carry a hundred-ribbed umbrella, think that they alone have been honored with holding an umbrella over Dīpaṅkara. At the threshold to the city, Dīpaṅkara focuses his mind and puts down his foot, which causes a gentle earthquake and host of miracles, with the blind, deaf, mute, and crippled suddenly able to see, hear, speak, and walk. Hundreds of thousands of beings make offerings of flowers, incense, and perfume to Dīpaṅkara. Sumati and the young woman, holding their waterlilies, try to get close enough to Dīpaṅkara to make their offerings, but they are engulfed by the enormous crowd. Dīpaṅkara, realizing that Sumati would earn more merit from his offering than anyone in the crowd, magically creates a rainstorm that disperses the crowd.

Sumati and the young woman can now see Dīpaṅkara, and at his sight, both are filled with faith. Sumati tosses his five waterlilies toward Dīpaṅkara, and owing to the latter's power, they magically circle around his head. The young woman tosses her two waterlilies toward Dīpaṅkara, and they magically circle around his ears. The rain has turned the area muddy, so Sumati now approaches Dīpaṅkara, spreads out the locks of his matted hair and utters a verse:

> If I am to become a buddha for the sake
> of awakening others, O awakener to wisdom,
> may you tread with your feet on my matted hair,
> which will bring an end to birth and old age.[32]

Dīpaṅkara then places his feet on Sumati's matted hair. His brother Mati—who has been absent from the story since the two brothers visited King Vāsava at his sacrificial grounds—is present to see this and angrily addresses Dīpaṅkara, reprimanding the latter for trampling on his brother's hair like an animal. Dīpaṅkara doesn't address Mati; instead, he foretells Sumati's future:

> You will be freed from human existence, liberated,
> powerful, a teacher for the benefit of the world,
> the scion of the Śākyas with the name Śākyamuni,
> best in the three worlds and a light for the universe.

At the moment of this foretelling, Sumati rises high up into the air, his matted hair falls off, and more distinguished matted hair appears in its place. A large crowd of people sees Sumati floating in the air and makes this fervent aspiration: "When he attains supreme knowledge, may we become his disciples." The young woman also makes a fervent aspiration, reciting two verses, the first being the one she had previously uttered when she gave the five waterlilies to Sumati and the second one being this:

> When you are perfectly awakened,
> the best instructor in the world,
> at that time, when it comes,
> I will be your disciple.

King Dīpa then picks up Sumati's hair that has fallen to the ground and gives it to King Vāsava, at the latter's request. King Vāsava counts up the hairs, and finding that there are eighty thousand, gives one hair each to his eighty thousand ministers, who bring them back to their respective territories and make shrines for them.

Sumati then addresses Mati, acknowledging that he has been foretold to become a buddha and wondering what Mati has set his mind on attaining. Mati explains that he has been spiritually damaged, as he spoke words of anger at Dīpaṅkara. The two then go forth as monks in Dīpaṅkara's order. Sumati learns the Buddhist scriptures and endears himself to the other monks with his righteousness. After his death, he is reborn among the gods of the Tuṣita heaven. As for Mati, after his death, he is born in the realms of hell.

Śākyamuni Buddha, the narrator of the tale, then identifies the characters in the story. The people of Dīpāvatī are now the citizens of Śrāvastī, where Dharmaruci was born and where Śākyamuni delivered this discourse. The young woman is now Yaśodharā, who had been Śākyamuni's wife when he was still Prince Gautama. Mati is now Dharmaruci. And Sumati is none other than Śākyamuni himself.

Commentary, Part 2

King Dīpa goes to great lengths to make his capital, Dīpāvatī, beautiful for Dīpaṅkara Buddha's arrival. Then he is joined by King Vāsava and his ministers, each of whom holds for Dīpaṅkara a ceremonial umbrella, which is part of the paraphernalia for both gods and kings. Dīpaṅkara is neither god nor king, but his power is such that even kings honor and serve him. And Dīpaṅkara's power is considerable. He uses of his "magical power" (*ṛddhi*)—a set of superhuman abilities acquired through spiritual practice—to instill thoughts in two kings and their ministers such that they all think that they are personally attending to him. And when he concentrates his mind and places his foot on the threshold to the city, the whole earth trembles and miraculous cures and occurrences abound. The sick become healthy, the angry become loving, elephants trumpet, horses neigh, bulls bellow, musical instruments make beautiful sounds without being touched, and so on. Such is the power that all buddhas possess, the text explains. Perhaps this is why King Dīpa wanted him to enter his kingdom.

Sumati and the young woman want to offer their waterlilies to Dīpaṅkara, but they are engulfed by an enormous crowd who want to honor him with their own offerings, so they can't get close enough to do so. Knowing that Sumati will earn more merit from his offering than anyone else in the crowd, and that the ritual of offering requires that he be close enough to clearly see Dīpaṅkara, Dīpaṅkara creates a rainstorm that forces the crowd to flee. Now Sumati can see Dīpaṅkara—"a sight one never tires of seeing,"[33] according to the text—and he is "filled with intense faith."

Throughout the *Divyāvadāna* and the monastic code of conduct of the Mūlasarvāstivādins, buddhas, along with saints, stūpas, and images of buddhas, are described as instilling "faith" (*prasāda*) in those who see them. And faith usually leads those individuals to make an offering, a kind of giving back to whoever instilled faith in them. This sort of giving, which is initiated by faith and directed to a virtuous object, earns the giver enormous amounts of merit.[34] In this case, Sumati sees an object that instills faith, experiences intense faith, and then makes an offering of five waterlilies, giving back to Dīpaṅkara. Dīpaṅkara then exercises his power so that the waterlilies magically circumambulate his head, following him wherever he goes, no doubt generating even more merit for Sumati with each auspicious round they make. The young woman likewise sees Dīpaṅkara, is filled with faith, and offers him two waterlilies, which Dīpaṅkara causes to magically circumambulate his ears.[35]

Sumati and the young woman become filled with faith at the sight of Dīpaṅkara, which is likely an experience of religious conversion for the former and religious confirmation for the latter. As an outpouring of faith, they each make an offering to Dīpaṅkara, which probably earns them enormous reserves of merit. A buddha, as John Strong explains, "is seen as a vast and fertile 'field of merit' (*puṇyakṣetra*) where devotees can 'plant' their meritorious deeds. Thus any good (or bad) action directed toward him, no matter how petty it may seem, can have positive (or negative) karmic results beyond all expectations."[36] As recipients of merit that is "beyond all expectations," Sumati and the young woman experience a radical change in their karmic destinies.

Sumati then approaches Dīpaṅkara, bows down, and spreads out the locks of his matted hair on the muddy ground before him. By placing his head at the latter's feet, Sumati is performing a common ritual act for honoring another while also expressing one's own humility and submission. And by placing his hair on the ground, Sumati allows Dīpaṅkara to rise above the mud just like a blue waterlily, radiant and undefiled.[37] Sumati then utters a verse, explaining if he is to become a buddha then Dīpaṅkara will tread on his hair, which prompts Dīpaṅkara to stand on Sumati's dreadlocks. Matted hair is one of the defining marks of non-Buddhist renunciants, as opposed to the shaven heads of Buddhist monastics, and for Dīpaṅkara to stand on Sumati's matted hair is a visual representation of Buddhism's dominance over these other traditions.[38] Sumati, it might be said, has fully submitted to Dīpaṅkara's authority.

Notice that Sumati does not follow the conditions explicitly set out by the young woman. She said that she would give him the waterlilies only if he made this fervent aspiration: "May she be my wife in every rebirth to come." In fact, Sumati doesn't even make a fervent aspiration; he only "utters a verse" (*gāthāṃ bhāṣate*), requesting that Dīpaṅkara confirm his future buddhahood by treading on his hair. It seems that Sumati, at least from the perspective of the young woman, has reneged on their agreement.[39] And he hasn't made the fervent aspiration that becomes so crucial and canonical in later retellings of Śākyamuni's journey to buddhahood. Nevertheless, Dīpaṅkara confirms Sumati's request with a "foretelling" (*vyākaraṇa*)—often translated as "prediction" but which functions here as a "confirmation of the future," as buddhas have full knowledge of all aspects of karmic causality. Sumati will be the buddha named Śākyamuni. His journey as a bodhisattva has begun.

After Dīpaṅkara's foretelling, Sumati rises into the air and his matted hair falls off and new matted hair appears in its place, affirming Sumati's continued status as a non-Buddhist renunciant.[40] The fallen hair contains eighty thousand strands, and each one of King Vāsava's eighty thousand ministers takes a single strand, brings it back to his homeland, and creates a "shrine" (*caitya*) for it. In many Buddhist traditions, hairs of a buddha are a common form of bodily relic and are thought to be capable of empowering shrines and stūpas. Yet, in this case, the hairs don't belong to the living buddha who is present, Dīpaṅkara. Instead, they belong to Sumati, a buddha-to-be, but who hasn't yet gone forth as a Buddhist monk and who hasn't begun studying Buddhist scripture.[41] The hairs seem to be a kind of "contact relic"—an object, following John Strong, "that the Buddha owned or used or with which he was closely associated."[42] Sometimes such contact relics include the Buddha's footprints, for in some cases a buddha was thought to have transformed a place into a shrine simply by standing there.[43] It seems that by standing on Sumati's matted hair, Dīpaṅkara has imbued it with his own power.

At the sight of Sumati's miraculous behavior, a large crowd makes a fervent aspiration that they will be disciples of the future buddha to be known as Śākyamuni. Then the young woman makes her fervent aspiration in two verses. The second verse repeats the aspiration of the large crowd: she too wants to be a disciple of Śākyamuni Buddha. The first verse is restatement of what she uttered previously when she gave Sumati the five waterlilies:

> When you make a fervent aspiration,
> having accepted the Buddha as your guide,
> then I shall be your wife,
> a constant companion in the dharma.[44]

When the young woman first utters this verse, it functions as a kind of wishful thinking. She hopes that in exchange for the waterlilies, Sumati will make a fervent aspiration, saying "May she be my wife in every rebirth to come." He can then offer her to someone else in marriage, but she will be his wife in all of his future lives until he reaches buddhahood. But Sumati never makes that fervent aspiration. Unlike the young woman and the large crowd—glossed later as "hundreds and thousands of beings"—he makes no fervent aspiration at all. Now the young woman recites the verse as her own fervent aspiration. She might not be his "companion in the dharma" (*sahadharmacāriṇī*)—that is, his legal wife and partner in religious practice—in every lifetime to come, but she will be eventually, at least once and maybe more. It is unclear, in other words, when the "then" in "then I shall be your wife" will be.

The young woman's fervent aspiration apparently comes true. The *Jātakas* record at least thirty-two lifetimes that she and the Bodhisattva share together before his birth as Gautama.[45] And in the *Buddhacarita* (*Life of the Buddha*), Aśvaghoṣa's poetic biography of the Buddha from the first or second century CE, Yaśodharā is Gautama's legal wife and she explicitly refers to herself as his "companion in the dharma." Yaśodharā, however, uses the expression not as a wish but as a lament. Gautama has just abandoned her for a life as a renunciant, and she is befuddled:

> He wants to practice dharma and yet abandons me,
> his companion in dharma, leaving me with no protector.
> How can he ever find dharma when what he wants is
> to practice austerities without a companion in dharma?[46]

Yaśodharā, after many eons and countless lifetimes, finally gets what she wished for. It just doesn't last. Once again she will be without a "Lord" and protector. But then her second fervent aspiration comes true; she gets to be a disciple of her former husband after he becomes "perfectly awakened, the best instructor in the world." Having shared a complicated, eons-long history, Gautama and Yaśodharā now come together as Buddha and disciple, and according to at least some accounts, Yaśodharā goes on to achieve the awakening of an arhat.[47] Vanessa Sasson tells us more about this shared history in Chapter 4 of this volume.

Vow Story, Some Lessons

So what are some of the lessons of this version of the vow story? To summarize: Buddhas are very powerful, and while ordinary humans might accrue enough merit, say, to make flowers arise from a waterpot, they are not miracle workers, capable of causing earthquakes, rainstorms, and healing the sick, and they aren't fertile "fields of merit" that allow others to vastly magnify the karmic consequences of their deeds. Buddhas are so powerful, in fact, that the Buddhist path is open to the powerless, like women who exist on the margins of society with no protector, and to non-Buddhists who have never heard Buddhist teachings. The practice offered is simple: see a buddha, let faith arise, make an offering, and accrue merit, and then use the accrued merit to make a fervent aspiration.

Noteworthy here is that the Buddha-to-be is still an ordinary human, although a Vedic scholar "of the highest standing" and capable of earning more merit from a single offering than anyone else who crowded around Dīpaṅkara. The story isn't a hagiography of the Buddha-to-be, unlike later versions of the story. It's the story of a smart, high-standing young brahmin, who hasn't yet cultivated wisdom or compassion to the fullest extent—his interactions with the young woman are a case in point—but who is sufficiently meritorious and fortunate to come before a buddha and make a vow for buddhahood. It is the story, in short, not of greatness attained but of a path to greatness begun.

Noteworthy, too, is that the Buddha-to-be doesn't succeed on his own; he has lots of help. His is not "the solo quest of a solitary seeker," to build on John Strong's insight; it is "at least in part, a family affair."[48] And it is also a community affair and a cosmic affair, with diverse participants working in conjunction with one another. There is the teacher who trained Sumati in the Vedas; King Vāsava who gave him postsacrificial gifts; the deity who informed King Vāsava of his standing; the young woman who gave him the blue waterlilies; Dīpaṅkara who scattered the crowd so he could see; and the eighty thousand ministers and citizens of Dīpāvatī who will follow Sumati through the eons, joining him when he finally attains buddhahood. As John Strong notes, "karma is not only individual, it is collective as well, and as a result, karmic biographies treat . . . ongoing karmic nexuses."[49] The Buddha-to-be's story, in other words, is the interconnected biography of a multitude.

So—to return to the questions from the beginning of this chapter—why might this vow story have been recorded in so few texts in ancient Gandhāra? One can only conjecture, but perhaps there was a problem with genre. The vow story in "The Story of Dharmaruci" is part of an avadāna, and as expected with the genre, it tells of the power of buddhas and how ordinary humans can avail themselves to that power; it provides interconnected karmic biographies; and it also engages legal issues. In this case, the legal issues gesture to general concerns about women's independence, which were important for both Buddhist and Brahmanical communities,[50] but they are pursued through the peculiar case of a given-but-not-accepted woman and her quest for security and fulfillment. Perhaps the focus on the young woman's clever audacity and the legal issues regarding women's independence were regarded as an impediment to the story, for these plot lines are much less prominent in later tellings. Or perhaps the Buddha-to-be isn't represented as sufficiently heroic or self-sacrificing, for most past-life stories of Śākyamuni Buddha focus on the countless difficult deeds that the Buddha-to-be, once he became a bodhisattva, performed during the three eons it took him to attain buddhahood. Or perhaps because what follows the vow story in the "The Story of Dharmaruci" is an account of Dharmaruci's rebirth during the time of Krakucchanda Buddha, when he committed incest, matricide, patricide, and killed an arhat, and audiences might not have liked the juxtaposition of these various episodes.[51] Or maybe it's just that visual versions of the vow story work better for what the Buddhists in ancient Gandhāra wanted to accomplish.

The Vow Story in Gandhāran Art and Practice

So—to address that last question—what might Buddhists in Gandhāra have wanted visual versions of the vow story to do? And how did they represent the story, highlighting certain scenes and characters and eliding others, to accomplish those goals? As a test case, let's briefly consider the image at the start of this chapter, which features a relief panel of the vow story from a Buddhist stūpa in Gandhāra.

Like many visual representations of the vow story from Gandhāra, this sculpture depicts the story in what has been called the "conflated narrative mode," with multiple scenes from the story represented while "the figure of the protagonist is conflated instead of repeated from one scene to the next."[52] In this case, Dīpaṅkara—the protagonist of the sculpture—appears once, the young woman appears twice, and the Buddha-to-be appears three times. First, the Buddha-to-be appears standing just left of center, looking into Dīpaṅkara's eyes. He has a water-pitcher in his left hand and five waterlilies in his right hand, which is raised to indicate that he is tossing the waterlilies toward Dīpaṅkara as an offering. Second, he appears prostrate, having spread out his hair for Dīpaṅkara to step on, with his head at Dīpaṅkara's right foot, which he also holds with his right hand. Third, he appears in the upper left corner floating miraculously in the air, with his hands clasped in front of him as a sign of respect. The young woman appears once standing next to the Buddha-to-be, and like him, she has a water pot in her left hand, lotuses in her right hand, and she looks into Dīpaṅkara's eyes. Unlike him, she smiles and clutches the lotuses to her chest, not yet ready to offer them. At the far left she appears again, head bowed with hands respectfully clasped in front of her. Dīpaṅkara appears only once, just right of center, his head encircled both by a halo and the waterlilies that he has been offered to him, and he gazes back at the Buddha-to-be who stands before him. Dīpaṅkara's right hand is in the "fear not" gesture (*abhayamudrā*), which is a common hand gesture for buddhas in Gandhāran art, and his right foot stands firmly on the hair of the Buddha-to-be who lies prostrate beneath him.[53]

This is a barebones version of the vow story, without kings or ministers or crowds of people, without any refence to Dharmaruci or the various times they met, and with no hint of the marriage subplot.[54] What is central to this account is Dīpaṅkara, who is a large and singular presence and the only figure marked with a divine halo. He is the proverbial star of the show.[55] Before him are two figures engaged in five separate acts of veneration in an "overlapping manner of presentation [that] undermines temporal succession."[56] Sequential acts are represented as happening simultaneously—what might be thought of as a synchronic view of diachronic time[57]—demonstrating the continuity and interconnectedness of our actions, and the salvific power of placing a buddha at the center of them. One might view this sculpture as a model for action: if you get the chance to be in the presence of a buddha, perform acts of veneration—seeing, bowing, giving respect, making offerings, prostrating, or even touching—which will produce unprecedented karmic results.

Reflecting on the vow story as both text and image, how might individuals in Gandhāra who came to Buddhist shrines and saw sculptures like the one above have responded to them? Judging by texts from that period, Buddhist shrines, especially those empowered by a buddha's relics, were considered to be functionally equivalent to living buddhas. As John Strong explains,

> The relics [of a buddha] are alive, own property, perform miracles, inspire devotees, are filled with various buddha qualities, in exactly the same way that the Buddha is. This does not mean that they *are* the Buddha, that they make *him* present. Rather they are themselves present in the same way that he is, they can act like him, they are a substitute for him in his absence.[58]

In addition, images of a buddha were thought to channel or invoke that buddha's presence, especially iconic images of a buddha but likely narrative images portraying events in his life as well.[59] Furthermore, Gandhāra was closely connected with Dīpaṅkara and home to pilgrimage sites associated with his life, including the place where he accepted flowers from the Buddha-to-be and predicted his future awakening.[60]

In other words, it's quite likely that individuals went on pilgrimage to Buddhist shrines in Gandhāra and treated those shrines and the images of buddhas that adorn them as living buddhas and as powerful objects for giving gifts, earning merit, and making vows, especially when those shrines and images were of Dīpaṅkara Buddha. We find the suggestion of something similar in the *Avadānaśataka* (*One Hundred Stories*), which was likely compiled by a Mūlasarvāstivādin monk in Gandhāra sometime in the early centuries of the Common Era.[61] Each of the stories in the sixth decade (nos. 61–70) follows a similar pattern, with an individual encountering a stūpa for Vipaśyin Buddha and being inspired to make a vow to attain the awakening of an arhat, and then eons later, during the time of Gautama Buddha, finally attaining arhatship.[62] As John Strong observes,

> the text seems to go out of its way to make the point that what is being venerated here is not the living body of the buddha Vipaśyin but his stūpa, that is, his relics . . . In the *Avadānaśataka*, then, both the enshrined relics of a past buddha (e.g. in the Vipasyin chapter) or a past buddha in person (e.g. in other chapters) are equally effective in inspiring devotees on the way to arhatship.[63]

Most Buddhist communities, including the Mūlasarvāstivādins, insist that one must be in the presence of a living buddha to make a vow to become a buddha,[64] but one could apparently make other kinds of vows before a buddha-as-shrine or buddha-as-image. Presumably one could make a vow to attain the awakening of an arhat, as in the *Avadānaśataka*, or a vow to be reborn as a disciple of a future buddha, as with the great crowd of people in the vow story in "The Story of Dharmaruci." This innovation, following John Strong, opened up new avenues for religious practice:

> The authors of the *Avadanasataka*, like Buddhists today, were living in post-parinirvāṇa times, in an age when there was no buddha present. The soteriological pattern they inherited and propounded was one that stressed the importance of meeting the Buddha in order to embark on the path to enlightenment. But meeting the Buddha in person is impossible in a buddhaless time. The solution that was adopted, then, was to leave open the possibility of meeting the Buddha in his relics, and being inspired by them. Thus, in the *Avadānśataka*, relics, in the absence of a buddha, make soteriology possible, but they do not apparently open all soteriological paths; the relics are functionally equivalent to living buddhas in bringing individuals to future *arhatship*, but not in bringing them to future *buddhahood* (or pratyekabuddhahood).[65]

There is a lesson here about the Buddha and the Buddhist tradition: they are alive with possibility! For more than two millennia, Buddhism has evolved in historical and "storical" fashion, with events and stories reworked and represented to preserve traditions while also transforming them.[66] Solutions are innovated, in literature and art, in recitation and ritual, and possibilities are explored even as limitations are acknowledged. Sculptures of the vow story in Gandhāra offer one such solution.[67] To put it another way: The Buddha is dead. Long live the Buddha!

Notes

For their help and support with this chapter, my thanks to Donald R. Davis, Jr., Carole DeSanti, M. G. Dhadphale, Oskar von Hinüber, Timothy Lenz, Jessie Pons, Janna White, James Wilson, Monika Zin, the other authors in this volume, and most especially John Strong—scholar, sage, and friend.

"Dīpaṅkara Jātaka" Pakistan, Swat Valley, ca. second century CE. Schist with gold leaf, 8 3/4" × 8 3/8." (22.2 × 21.3 cm). The Metropolitan Museum of Art, New York. Open Access, www.metmuseum.org/ art/collection/search/49809.

1. Junko Matsumura has an excellent series of articles on the Dīpaṅkara legend in both southern and northern literary traditions. See Junko Matsumura, "The Sumedhakathā in Pāli Literature and Its Relation to the Northern Buddhist Textual Tradition," *Journal of the International College for Postgraduate Buddhist Studies* 14 (2010): 101–133; Junko Matsumura, "The Story of the Dīpaṃkara Prophecy in Northern Buddhist Texts: An Attempt at Classification," *Journal of Indian and Buddhist Studies (Indogaku bukkyōggaku kenkyū)* 59, no. 3 (2011): 1137–1146; Junko Matsumura, "An Independent Sūtra on the Dīpaṃkara Prophecy: Tibetan Text and English Translation of the *Ārya-Dīpaṃkara-vyākaraṇa nāma Mahāyānasūtra*," *Journal of the International College for Postgraduate Buddhist Studies* 15 (2011): 81–141; and Junko Matsumura, "The Formation and Development of the Dīpaṃkara Prophecy Story: The *Ārya-Dīpaṃkaravyākaraṇa-nāma-mahāyānasūtra* and its Relation to Other Versions," *Journal of Indian and Buddhist Studies (Indogaku bukkyōggaku kenkyū)* 60, no. 3 (2012): 1204–1213.
2. Jan Nattier, "Dīpaṃkara," in *Encyclopedia of Buddhism*, vol. 1, ed. R. E. Buswell (New York: Macmillan, 2004), 230. See too Bhikkhu Ānālayo, "Compassion in the *Āgamas* and *Nikāyas*," *Dharma Drum Journal of Buddhist Studies* 16 (2015): 6.
3. Matsumura, "The Sumedhakathā in Pāli Literature and Its Relation to the Northern Buddhist Textual Tradition," 124.
4. Scholars often refer to the vow story as the "Dīpaṅkara Jātaka"—as the image that begins this chapter is titled by The Metropolitan Museum of Art—or, more accurately, as the "so-called Dīpaṅkara Jātaka," for the Buddha-to-be's encounter with Dīpaṅkara is not actually included in the Pāli *Jātaka* collection. For more on the genre classification of the vow story, see the section entitled "*Jātaka* or not?" in Tianshu Zhu's "Revisiting the Dīpaṃkara Story in Gandharan Buddhist Art," in *Connecting the Art, Literature, and Religion of South and Central Asia: Studies in Honour of Monika Zin*, ed. Ines Konczak-Nagel, Satomi Hiyama, and Astrid Klein (New Delhi: Dev Publishers and Distributors, 2022), 420.
5. *Jātaka*, vol. 1, 2; translated in N. A. Jayawickrama, *The Story of Gotama Buddha (Jātaka-nidāna)* (Oxford: Pali Text Society, 1990), 3–4.
6. *Divyāvadāna* 246.5–254.2; translated in John Strong, *The Experience of Buddhism: Sources and Interpretations*, 2nd edition (Belmont, CA: Wadsworth/Thomson Learning, 2002), 19–23; and Andy Rotman, *Divine Stories: Translations from the Divyāvadāna, Part 2* (Boston: Wisdom Publications, 2017), 24–34. For more on "The Story of Dharmaruci" (*Dharmaruci-avadāna*), see Jonathan Silk, *Riven by Lust: Incest and Schism in Indian Buddhist Legend and Historiography* (Honolulu: University of Hawai'i Press, 2009). And for more on the *Divyāvadāna* and its historical development, see Andy Rotman, *Divine*

Stories: Translations from the Divyāvadāna, Part 1 (Boston: Wisdom Publications, 2008), 1–30; and Camillo A. Formigatti, "Walking the Deckle Edge: Scribe or Author? Jayamuni and the Creation of the Nepalese *Avadānamālā* Literature," *Buddhist Studies Review* 33, nos. 1–2 (2016): 101–140.

7. *Mahāvastu* 231–248; translated in J. J. Jones, *The Mahāvastu: Translated from the Buddhist Sanskrit*, vol. 1 (London: Pali Text Society, 1949), 188–203. For more on the *Mahāvastu*, as well as its relationship to the logic and structure of the overall text, see Vincent Tournier, *La formation du "Mahāvastu" et la mise en place des conceptions relatives à la carrière du "bodhisattva"* (Paris: École française d'Extrême-Orient, 2017). A version of the vow story is also preserved in the monastic code of conduct of the Dharmaguptakas, who have been instrumental in fostering Buddhism throughout East Asia, but that version of the vow story is only available in Chinese. For a translation, see André Bareau, "Le Dīpaṃkarajātaka des Dharmaguptaka," in *Mélanges de Sinologie offerts à Monsieur Paul Demiéville*, vol. 1 (Paris: Presses universitaires de France, 1966), 1–16.
8. David Jongeward, Timothy Lenz, and Jessie Pons, "The Buddha's Previous Births: Gandhāran Stories in Birchbark and Stone" (Unpublished Manuscript), 44. See too Jason Neelis, "Making Places for Buddhism in Gandhāra: Stories of Previous Births in Image and Text," in *The Geography of Gandhāran Art*, ed. Wannaporn Rienjang and Peter Stewart, Proceedings of the Second International Workshop of the Gandhāra Connections Project, University of Oxford, 22nd–23rd March, 2018 (Oxford: Archaeopress Publishing, 2019), 176–179.
9. Jason Neelis, "Aspiring Narratives of Previous Births in Written and Visual Media from Ancient Gandhāra," *Postscripts* 10 (2019): 113.
10. Two different manuscripts of "The Story of Dharmaruci" are preserved in the so-called Gilgit Manuscripts from Gandhāra, but the portion that contains the vow story is incomplete and it hasn't yet been edited or translated. See Noriyuki Kudo, ed., *Gilgit Manuscripts in the National Archives of India Facsimile Edition, vol. 3: Avadānas and Miscellaneous Texts* (New Delhi: National Archives of India & Tokyo: The International Research Institute for Advanced Buddhology, Soka University, 2017), folios 85r, 85v, 86r [= Cowell and Neil, *Divyāvadāna*, 249.30–251.20, 251.23–253.19, 253.21–252]). Kabita Das Gupta transliterated the text in 1984, but it was never published. A very similar version of "The Story of Dharmaruci" is found in the *Divyāvadāna*, although the dating of that version is tricky, as the *Divyāvadāna* is a much later compilation. Interestingly, "The Story of Dharmaruci" is not included in the monastic code of conduct of the Mūlasarvāstivādins, and it isn't preserved in any Tibetan or Chinese translations, so no alternative versions of the text exist for corroboration.
11. Jongeward, Lenz, and Pons, "The Buddha's Previous Births," 39.
12. Juan Wu, "The *Cīvaravastu* of the Mūlasarvāstivāda *Vinaya* and Its Counterparts in Other Indian Buddhist Monastic Law Codes: A Comparative Survey," *Journal of Indian Philosophy* 50, no. 4 (2020): 581–618. For more on these legal-storytelling avadānists, see John Strong, "The Buddhist Avadānists and the Elder Upagupta," in *Tantric and Taoist Studies in Honor of R.A. Stein*, ed. Michel Strickmann, Mélanges chinoises et bouddhiques 22 (Brussels: Institut belge des hautes études chinoises, 1985), 862–881. The Sanskrit *avadāna* is not to be confused with the Pāli *apadāna*—a

kind of autobiographical poem about a religious adept of the early Buddhist community. For a translation of the apadāna about Dhammaruci (the Pāli name for Dharmaruci), see Jonathan S. Walters, *Legends of the Buddhist Saints (Apadānapāli)* (Walla Walla, WA: Jonathan S. Walters and Whitman College, 2017), 805–809. It is also available digitally at http://apadanatranslation.org.

13. A *kārṣāpaṇa* is a kind of coin used in ancient India, usually of copper or silver, although gold ones also circulated.
14. These "five great gifts" (*mahāpradāna*) seem to be a variant of the "great gifts" (*mahādāna*) described in Brahmanical law texts. As Maria Heim notes, "The *mahādānas* are first and foremost about royal display and largesse, bestowed primarily by kings upon brahmans." Maria Heim, *Theories of the Gift in South Asia: Hindu, Buddhist, and Jain Reflections on Dāna* (New York and London: Routledge, 2004), 113.
15. These flowers in the story are referred to variously as *nīlotpala, nīlapadma,* and *nīlotpalapadma* (*Divyāvadāna* 248.21–25), making it clear that the flowers are "blue" (*nīla*) but unclear whether they are "lotuses" or "waterlilies," as the terms *utpala* and *padma* are used imprecisely in Sanskrit. In this case, however, the meaning is clear, as blue lotuses don't exist in nature and blue waterlilies most certainly do. As Jürgen Hanneder explains, "There is no blue lotus, only a blue waterlily; Sanskrit terms with the literal meaning 'blue lotus' (*nīlāmbuja*, etc.) denote the blue waterlily (for an explanation, see Hanneder 2002)." Jürgen Hanneder, "Some Common Errors Concerning Water-Lilies and Lotuses," *Indo-Iranian Journal* no. 50 (2007): 162, citing Jürgen Hanneder, "The Blue Lotus: Oriental Research between Philology, Botany and Poetics?" *Zeitschrift der Deutschen Morgenländischen Gesellschaft* 152 (2002): 295–308.
16. Rotman, *Divine Stories: Translations from the Divyāvadāna, Part 2*, 28–29 (slightly modified).
17. Considering that Sumati has matted hair (*jaṭa*), he might be a *jaṭila*—a type of ascetic known for possessing matted hair, as well as for living in hermitages in the wilderness and maintaining sacred fires. These ascetics, who were usually depicted favorably in Buddhist texts, sometimes lived celibate lives and sometimes got married. For more on the *jaṭila*, see Patrick Olivelle, *The Āśrama System: The History and Hermeneutics of a Religious Institution* (New York: Oxford University Press, 1993), 21–22.
18. The ideal religious person within the Vedic world pursues a path such as this: "A twice-born man, following his vedic initiation, studies the Vedas at the house of his teacher; after returning home he marries a suitable wife and establishes his sacred fires; he begets offspring, especially sons, by his legitimate wife; and during his entire life offers sacrifices, recites the Veda, offers food and water to his deceased ancestors, gives food to guests and mendicants, and offers food oblations to all creatures" (Olivelle, *The Āśrama System*, 55).
19. See *Mānavadharmaśāstra*, 9.47 (translated on p. 192) and *Yājñavalkya Dharmaśāstra*, 1.65 (translated on p. 23). See also Ludo Rocher, "In Defense of Jimutavahana," *Journal of the American Oriental Society* 96, no. 1 (1976): 107–109.
20. The *Mānavadharmaśāstra* 9.3–4 (translated on p. 190), one of the most famous Brahmanical law books, dating from the third to fifth century CE, makes this

explicit: "Day and night men should keep their women from acting independently; for, attached as they are to sensual pleasures, men should keep them under their control. Her father guards her in her childhood, her husband guards her in her youth, and her sons guard her in old age; a woman is not qualified to act independently."

21. See, for example, *Nāradasmṛti* 12.77 (translated on vol. 2, 158). For more on such women and the ways that Brahmanical materials disparaged them and viewed them as a threat, see Stephanie Jamison, "Women 'Between the Empires' and 'Between the Lines,'" in *Between the Empires: Society in India 300 BCE to 400 CE*, ed. Patrick Olivelle (New York: Oxford University Press, 2006), 191–214.
22. See Stephanie Jamison's research on the position of women in early India, and her attempt to answer the question, "Does a maiden, in the absence of other guardian[s], 'own' herself sufficiently to give herself away?" Stephanie Jamison, *Sacrificed Wife/Sacrificer's Wife: Women, Ritual, and Hospitality in Ancient India* (New York: Oxford University Press, 1996), 247. See too Hanns-Peter Schmidt, *Some Women's Rites and Rights in the Veda* (Poona: Bhandarkar Oriental Research Institute, 1987), 76–109; and Mari Johanna Jyväsjärvi, "Fragile Virtue: Women's Monastic Practice in Early Medieval India" (PhD dissertation, Harvard University, 2011), 48–108.
23. For more on Brahmanical marriage practices and how they affect women, see Jamison, *Sacrificed Wife/Sacrificer's Wife*, 207–250.
24. According to *Mānavadharmaśāstra* 9.92 (translated on p. 194), "A girl who chooses a husband on her own must not take with her any ornament coming from her father or mother or given by her brothers; if she takes it, it is theft." See too Jamison, *Sacrificed Wife/Sacrificer's Wife*, 239–240.
25. According to *Nāradasmṛti* 5.2 (translated on vol. 2, 10), there are five types of servant (*śuśrūṣaka*), which include four types of laborer (*karmakara*)—students, apprentices, wage-earners, and overseers—and a fifth type that consists of fifteen kinds of slave (*dāsa*). Sumati would have been classified as a student-laborer; the young woman, before being offered in marriage, would likely have been classified as a slave. See also Uma Chakravarti, "Of Dasas and Karmakaras: Servile Labour in Ancient India," in *Chains of Servitude: Bondage and Slavery in India*, eds. Utsa Patnaik and Manjari Dingwaney (Madras: Sangam Books, 1985), 35–75; and Donald R. Davis, Jr., "Slaves and Slavery in the *Smṛticandrikā*," *The Indian Economic and Social History Review* 57, no. 3 (2020): 302.
26. The young woman's use of "Lord" (*deva*) is ambiguous and suggestive, as the term can refer to the king, one's husband, the Buddha, or some deity. Kings are usually "Lord" (*deva*) to their subjects, and buddhas are usually "Blessed One" (*bhagavān*) to their devotees. Yet the young woman repeatedly uses "Lord" to refer to Dīpaṅkara Buddha, perhaps suggesting a similarity in her relationship to both and her continued state of dependence.
27. Charles Hallisey and Anne Hansen, "Narrative, Sub-Ethics, and the Moral Life: Some Evidence from Theravāda Buddhism," *Journal of Religious Ethics* 24, no. 2 (1996): 320.
28. Sara McClintock, "Ethical Reading and the Ethics of Forgetting and Remembering," in *A Mirror Is for Reflection: Understanding Buddhist Ethics*, ed. Jake H. Davis (New York: Oxford University Press, 2017), 199.

29. *Divyāvadāna* 303; translated in Rotman, *Divine Stories: Translations from the Divyāvadāna, Part 2*, 101.
30. Gregory Schopen, *Buddhist Nuns, Monks, and Other Worldly Matters: Recent Papers on Monastic Buddhism in India* (Honolulu: University of Hawai'i Press, 2014), 145–146. See too *Divyāvadāna* 94; translated in Rotman, *Divine Stories: Translations from the Divyāvadāna, Part 1*, 181.
31. See *Reiko Ohnuma, Head, Eyes, Flesh, and Blood: Giving Away the Body in Indian Buddhist Literature* (New York: Columbia University Press, 2007).
32. This verse is open to multiple readings. See Rotman, *Divine Stories: Translations from the Divyāvadāna, Part 2*, 355, note 73.
33. For more on "sights one never tires of seeing" (*asecanakadarśana*), see Andy Rotman, *Thus Have I Seen: Visualizing Faith in Early Indian Buddhism* (New York: Oxford University Press, 2009), 84–85.
34. For more on seeing, faith, and giving, see Rotman, *Thus Have I Seen*, 65–148.
35. The young woman's reaction at seeing Sumati is much like her reaction—and Sumati's as well—at seeing Dīpaṅkara. Both Sumati and Dīpaṅkara are described with the multivalent term *prāsādika*, for the former instills love and the latter instills faith. For more on these different senses of *prāsādika* and how they connect, see Rotman, *Thus Have I Seen*, 67–70.
36. John Strong, *The Legend of King Aśoka* (*Aśokāvadāna*) (Princeton, NJ: Princeton University Press, 1989), 57.
37. This metaphor is made explicit in "The Story of Mākandika" (*Divyāvadāna* 520; translated in Rotman, *Divine Stories: Translations from the Divyāvadāna, Part 2*, 248), when Śākyamuni Buddha explains:

    And just as a blue waterlily in muddy water
    is in no way defiled by mud,
    in just this way, brahmin, I live in the world,
    totally separate from sense pleasures.

38. For more on the significance of matted hair and shaven heads in South Asia, see Gananath Obeyesekere, *Medusa's Hair: An Essay on Personal Symbols and Religious Experience* (Chicago: University of Chicago Press, 1981), 33–51; and Patrick Olivelle, "Hair and Society: Social Significance of Hair in South Asian Traditions," in *Hair: Its Power and Meaning in Asian Cultures*, ed. Alf Hiltebeitel and Barbara D. Miller (New York: State University of New York Press, 1998), 11–49.
39. Sumati also never asks Dīpaṅkara for help in interpreting his dreams, which was the sole reason, according to the text, that he set out to meet Dīpaṅkara.
40. There are many stories of Śākyamuni Buddha exercising his power such that a new initiate will suddenly appear as a monk—with his head shaved, bowl, and water pot in hand, wearing monastic robes, and so on—but here Sumati loses his matted hair only to have it return. Sumati will eventually have his head shaved and become a Buddhist monk but at present he is still a lay follower.
41. Even at the end of his life, Sumati doesn't show himself to be worthy of a shrine. After Sumati dies, he is reborn in the Tuṣita heaven, signifying that he has made considerable spiritual progress. Yet, there are numerous accounts in the *Divyāvadāna* and the monastic code of conduct of the Mūlasarvāstivādins of individuals being reborn in the Tuṣita heaven, and they are not rewarded with shrines. For example, in "The Story

of a Woman Dependent on a City for Alms" (*Nagarāvalambikā-avadāna*) a leprous beggar woman sees the venerable Mahākāśyapa, experiences faith, and then offers him some rice gruel along with her rotten finger, which happens to fall in. From that single deed, she earns enough merit to be reborn among the gods in Tuṣita heaven. According to many Buddhist texts, the Bodhisattva is destined to be born once again in the Tuṣita heaven, as bodhisattvas are always born there before taking their final birth in the human realm and attaining buddhahood.

42. John Strong, *Relics of the Buddha* (Princeton, NJ: Princeton University Press, 2004), 8. See too Andy Rotman, "The Power of Proximity: Creating and Venerating Shrines in Indian Buddhist Narratives," in *Buddhist Stūpas in South Asia: Recent Archaeological, Art-Historical, and Historical Perspectives*, eds. Jason Hawkes and Akira Shimada (Delhi: Oxford University Press. 2009), 51–62. For more on the status of the Buddha-to-be's matted hair, see Strong, *Relics of the Buddha*, 55–56.
43. Strong, *Relics of the Buddha*, 72, 87–89.
44. *Divyāvadāna* 250.3–4 and 252.21–22,

    praṇidhiṃ yatra kuryās tvaṃ buddham āsādya nāyakaṃ
    tatra te 'haṃ bhavet patnī nityaṃ sahadharmacāriṇī

    This verse is open to a number of interpretations, and my sense of the meaning of the verse has changed since I published my translation of "The Story of Dharmaruci." There I translated the verse differently each time it appeared, struggling to make sense of it (Rotman, *Divine Stories: Translations from the Divyāvadāna, Part 2*, 29, and 32). John Strong, reading against the grammar, created this sensible translation: "When you fulfill your resolve to become a buddha, a guide, then I would be your wife, your constant companion in the Dharma." Strong, *The Experience of Buddhism*, 23.
45. See Sarah Shaw, "Yaśodharā in *Jātakas*," *Buddhist Studies Review* 35, nos. 1–2 (2018): 261–278.
46. *Buddhacarita* 8.61 (translation on p. 231). Stephanie Jamison (*Sacrificed Wife/Sacrificer's Wife*, 218) discusses how the term *sahadharmacāriṇī* might be indicative of "a marriage of mutual agreement, like the Gandharva marriage, arising not from lust as in the latter type, but from a mutually felt desire to embark on ritual responsibilities. The emphasis on the word *saha* 'joint' might then indicate that the marriage was originally conceived as an equal venture, a partnership between two independent parties." This seems like the kind of marriage the young woman in our story would want.
47. Jonathan S. Walters, "*Apadāna: Therī-apadāna*: Wives of the Saints: Marriage and Kamma in the Path to Arahantship," in *Women in Early Buddhism: Comparative Textual Studies*, ed. Alice Collett (Oxford: Oxford University Press, 2014), 182–190.
48. John Strong, "A Family Quest: The Buddha, Yaśodharā and Rāhula in the Mūlasarvāstivāda Vinaya," in *Sacred Biography in the Buddhist Traditions of South and Southeast Asia*, ed. Juliane Schober (Honolulu: University of Hawai'i Press, 1997), 122.
49. Strong, *A Family Quest*, 114.
50. Stephanie Jamison ("Women 'Between the Empires' and 'Between the Lines,'" 206) contends "that part of the impetus for the intensely misogynist sentiments" in Brahmanical law texts "comes from the challenge posed by this new female type, the independent *and* religiously unorthodox woman," exemplified by the Buddhist

nun and characters like the young woman in our story. Damchö Diana Finnegan describes the ways that women "are far from powerless victims in the narratives of the [monastic code of conduct of the Mūlasarvāstivādins] . . . yet the forms of agency they do recover for themselves . . . [are] profoundly shaped by the social institutions and practices that treat them as objects of exchange." Damchö Diana. Finnegan, "'For the Sake of Women, Too': Ethics and Gender in the Narratives of the *Mūlasarvāstivāda Vinaya*" (PhD dissertation, University of Wisconsin, 2009), 145. Finnegan documents this struggle between empowerment and objectification, especially in the section of her work entitled "Women are Gifts Men Give to Each Other" (144–163).

51. Jonathan Silk, "The Story of Dharmaruci: In the *Divyāvadāna* and in Kṣemendra's *Bodhisattvāvadānakalpalatā*," *Indo-Iranian Journal* 51 (2008): 137–185.
52. Vidya Dehejia, "On Modes of Visual Narration in Early Buddhist Art," *The Art Bulletin* 72, no. 3 (1990): 384.
53. Although the Metropolitan Museum of Art identifies the Buddha-to-be in this sculpture as "Megha"—his name in the *Mahāvastu*—this representation of the vow story accords more closely with the version in "The Story of Dharmaruci" than the one in the *Mahāvastu*. In the *Mahāvastu*, the Buddha-to-be "puts down his water-pitcher to one side, spreads out his animal-skin garment, prostrates himself at the feet of Lord Dīpaṅkara, and while wiping clean the soles of Dīpaṅkara's feet with his own hair," sets forth his intention to become a buddha (*Mahāvastu*, vol. 1, 238; cf. trans. Jones, *The Mahāvastu*, vol. 1, 194). In this image, when the Buddha-to-be offers lotuses to Dīpaṅkara, he doesn't appear to be wearing an animal skin (*ajina*), and when he lies prostrate, he doesn't appear to have spread out anything on the ground or to be using his hair to wipe clean Dīpaṅkara's feet. For a detailed description of this piece, see Kurt A. Behrendt, *The Art of Gandhara in the Metropolitan Museum of Art* (New Haven, CT: Yale University Press, 2007), 34–35.
54. It is noteworthy that in the upper right corner of the sculpture stands a figure even larger and taller than Dīpaṅkara. It is the muscular protector deity known as Vajrapāṇi, holding a telltale "thunderbolt" (*vajra*) in his "hand" (*pāṇi*). His presence "is enigmatic, however, because he does not appear in text accounts; he is known only from reliefs, where he never participates in the narrative story" (Behrendt, *The Art of Gandhara in the Metropolitan Museum of Art*, 35). This suggests that the sculptor wasn't merely transcribing a text account into visual form, jettisoning extraneous elements; instead, images like this one "have their own logic, which is usually constituted by the artist having engaged with texts, written or oral, with varying degrees of fidelity and creativity, depending on the artist's skill and intent, and then indulging in some measure of artistic exigency and license, depending on the medium and moment." Andy Rotman, *Hungry Ghosts* (Somerville: Wisdom Publications, 2021), 44.
55. Tianshu Zhu notes that "the number one unique feature, which separates the iconography of the Dīpaṃkara story from other jātakas [in Gandhāra], is an anthropomorphic representation of a Buddha. Iconographies of other jātakas do not contain a Buddha image. Depictions of the Dīpaṃkara story in essence is [*sic*] an iconography of a standing Buddha." As such, they are "more like shrine images for worship than

illustrations of the Buddha's life." Tianshu Zhu, "Revisiting the Dīpaṃkara Story in Gandharan Buddhist Art," 417, 424.

56. Dehejia, "On Modes of Visual Narration in Early Buddhist Art," 384.
57. Such a representation of time aligns—whether by design or by chance—with the philosophical position of the Sarvāstivādins who, as their name indicates, "teach" (*vādin*) that "all" (*sarva*) "exists" (*asti*). More specifically, they maintain that all things continue to exist throughout the three periods of time: past, present, and future. For more on Sarvāstivāda philosophy, see Charles Willemen, Bart Dessein, and Collet Cox, *Sarvāstivāda Buddhist Scholasticism* (Leiden: Brill, 1998), 19–35.
58. Strong, *Relics of the Buddha*, 4. See too Schopen, *Bones, Stones, and Buddhist Monks*, 114–147.
59. An image of the Buddha can "come to re-present the Buddha in a way that is obviously religiously real." John Strong, *The Legend of King Aśoka (Aśokāvadāna)* (Princeton, NJ: Princeton University Press, 1989), 108. For more on the ways that images of a buddha can function as living entities, see Rotman, *Thus Have I Seen*, 177–195. For more on Buddhist narratives in visual form, see Naomi Appleton, ed., *Narrative Visions and Visual Narratives in Indian Buddhism* (Sheffield: Equinox Publishing, 2022), especially 6–11.
60. The Chinese pilgrims Faxian and Xuanzang both visited such a site—in the fifth and seventh centuries, respectively—and recorded their observations. See James Legge, *A Record of Buddhistic Kingdoms* (New York: Paragon, 1965), 38, and Li Ronxi, *The Great Tang Dynasty Record of the Western Regions* (Berkeley, CA: Numata Center for Buddhist Translation and Research, 1996), 56.
61. Rotman, *Hungry Ghosts*, 4.
62. *Avadānaśataka* 155–174; translated in Léon Feer, *Avadana-Çataka: Cent légendes (bouddhiques)*, Annales du Musée Guimet 18 (Paris: E. Leroux, 1891), 233–258.
63. Strong, *Relics of the Buddha*, 31–32.
64. David Drewes, "The Problem of Becoming a Bodhisattva and the Emergence of the Mahāyāna," *History of Religions* 61, no. 2 (2021): 145–172.
65. Strong, *Relics of the Buddha*, 32.
66. John S. Strong, *The Buddha's Tooth: Western Tales of a Sri Lankan Relic* (Chicago: University of Chicago Press, 2021), 4.
67. One can find other solutions in the paintings of the vow story in the Buddhist cave complexes at Kucha and Turfan in Western China, or in art of Myanmar, or in festivals in Nepal. See, for example, Ines Konczak, "Praṇidhi-Darstellungen an der Nördlichen Seidenstraße: Das Bildmotiv der Prophezeiung der Buddhaschaft Śākyamunis in den Malereien Xinjiangs" (PhD Dissertation, Ludwig-Maximilians-Universität, 2014); Tianshu Zhu, "Reshaping the Jātaka Stories: From Jātakas to Avadānas and Praṇidhānas in Paintings at Kucha and Turfan," *Buddhist Studies Review* 29, no. 1 (2012): 57–83; Carolina Bodner, "Depictions of the Narrative of the Buddha Dipankara and the Hermit Sumedha in the Art of Burma/Myanmar" (MA thesis, Northern Illinois University, 2009); and Andrea Wollein, "Bhaktapur Revisited: Dīpaṅkara Buddha's Life in a Hindu City," *European Bulletin of Himalayan Research* 53 (2019): 108–141.

2

Creative Tensions in the Past Lives of the Buddha

Naomi Appleton

Figure 2.1 The story of the otters and the jackal depicted in stone relief at the early stūpa site of Bharhut, Madhya Pradesh. A holy man (the Buddha-to-be) watches as a jackal outwits some otters who are arguing over a fish. Image from Alexander Cunningham, *The Stûpa of Bharhut: A Buddhist Monument Ornamented With Numerous Sculptures Illustrative of Buddhist Legend and History in the Third Century B.C.* (London: W.H. Allen and Co, 1879), plate XLVI.

Figure 2.1 shows us a stone relief at a stūpa site at Bharhut in present-day Madhya Pradesh. Bharhut offers our earliest evidence of Buddhist narrative art, perhaps from as early as the second or first century BCE. In particular, the site contains several dozen jātaka stories, or stories of the past lives of the Buddha, depicted on pillars, railings and coping stones that surround the central reliquary mound. This particular depiction is easily recognizable to those who know the story: A

Naomi Appleton, *Creative Tensions in the Past Lives of the Buddha* In: *The Buddha*. Edited by: Vanessa R. Sasson and Kristin Scheible, Oxford University Press. © Oxford University Press 2024. DOI: 10.1093/oso/9780197649466.003.0003 man sits watching some animals near a river, his hair and clothes indicating that he is an ascetic dwelling in the forest. On the other side of the river, two otters are arguing over the fair division of a fish they have caught. They ask a passing jackal to adjudicate, which he does, but he takes the majority of the fish as his fee, and leaves just the head and tail to the otters. The jackal is depicted twice: first adjudicating, and then nonchalantly wandering off with his prize. The ascetic who observes the animals is understood to be the Buddha in a past life, qualifying the story for inclusion in the jātaka genre.

Jātaka stories are some of the most famous and beloved narratives of the Buddhist world. They include tales of heroic self-sacrifice, such as the Buddha's past life as a hare who jumped into a fire to offer himself as a meal to a holy man, or the human lifetime in which he fed his body to a starving tigress to prevent her from eating her own cubs.[1] They also include animal fables, such as the story of the otters depicted above, or the time the Buddha was born as a woodpecker and helped a lion by removing a splinter from his throat, only to be met with ingratitude in return.[2] And there are great works of romance and epic poetry, adventure tales and quests, such as that of the Buddha's past-life as the wise minister Vidhura who is won at dice by a demon with a magical flying horse and taken to the realm of the nāgas (snake-deities), from which he must secure his safe return.[3]

The telling of jātaka stories is attested from images carved in stone from as early as a few centuries after the death of the Buddha, and they continue to be a bedrock of literature, art, and performance across vast swathes of the Buddhist world up to the present day. The stories appear in a range of different texts, in different languages and belonging to different monastic lineages and geographical areas. The largest and best-known text, the great Pāli collection belonging to the Theravāda school (the *Jātakatthavaṇṇanā* or *Jātakatthakathā* to give its full title), contains nearly 550 stories, and Sanskrit literature provides several hundred more, with more still preserved in other Asian languages. Even more are hinted at from the visual art at early Indian Buddhist sites, since the images don't always match up with extant literature, suggesting other stories circulated orally or in texts now lost. The genre was naturally expansive because any story could become a jātaka through identifying a character as the Buddha-to-be;[4] the genre includes stories of local heroes as well as of characters more famous from Hindu epic traditions.

The different contexts in which the stories appear suggest different understandings of what the genre is and is for. Sometimes the stories are presented as demonstrating the qualities required for buddhahood; sometimes they show the Buddha-to-be acting in morally dubious or foolish ways. Sometimes the stories don't really seem to be about the Buddha-to-be at all, but focus on other characters associated with him. Sometimes the fact that it is the

Buddha telling the story seems more important than his behavior within it.[5] Rarely do the texts or artistic contexts imply a chronology or progress; these stories are not a linear biographical account.[6]

With so many stories offered as teachings of the Buddha, about his past and the intertwined pasts of others, it is easy to become overwhelmed by the size and complexity of the literature. Very little can be said about jātakas that will reliably apply across the many texts and material contexts that contain them. This is the case even if we exclude those stories in which the Buddha-to-be experienced encounters with *buddha*s of the past, such as the story of the encounter with Dīpaṅkara Buddha discussed in Chapter 1.[7] In many ways it is the diversity that also makes the genre so interesting, however, since it provides a multitude of creative opportunities for authors and compilers (and indeed artists and site-planners) working with the stories. Creative tensions are found when you look at different textual collections or artistic sites, but very often they are also found within single contexts, sometimes even within the possible interpretations of a single story. Narrative is a rich way to explore human concerns, in part because a story is able to carry a tension or paradox without offering a straightforward resolution. Collections of stories—whether in written form or visual form—add extra layers of intrigue, with the possibility of one story seeming to contradict the previous, or exhibiting an entirely different conception of what it means to be on the way to buddhahood.

In this chapter I will be exploring two creative tensions within the jātaka genre that capture some of the richness that they add to the Buddha's life story. The first of these is the tension between the widely held notion that jātaka stories illustrate the Buddha's long path to perfection, and the reality that many of the stories have far more worldly or even imperfect concerns. The second tension is between the focus of the stories on building up a community around the Buddha, benefiting from their connections with him, and his ultimate transcendence of all ties. Since jātakas are as much a visual tradition as a literary one, I will also briefly touch upon how visual jātakas often seem to be playing with the same themes and questions. As chapters elsewhere in this volume attest, these two creative tensions can also be seen in other areas of the Buddha's life story, where perfection balances humanity and community balances the notion of an exemplary individual. In thinking about their applicability to the past lives of the Buddha in particular, they can also be seen as being part of a bigger tension, between stability and flexibility in the Buddhist understanding of what jātakas are and do.

Perfection and Imperfection

Probably the most famous jātaka story across the Buddhist world concerns the Buddha's past birth as a prince called Vessantara (in Pāli, or Viśvantara in

Sanskrit).[8] Prince Vessantara was incredibly generous. It is said that even on the day of his birth he asked his mother for something to give away. (This was one of a few occasions on which he spoke immediately after birth, another being his final birth, as discussed in the next chapter.) When he was of age, Vessantara was married and fathered a son and daughter. He was also given the kingship. However, things started to unravel when representatives from a neighboring kingdom came to ask Vessantara if they could take away a particularly important state elephant. This elephant was understood to bring rain and good fortune, and the neighboring kingdom was suffering from a severe drought. Vessantara happily gave the elephant away. The citizens were not impressed by this, and petitioned Vessantara's father to exile his son in order to prevent any more of the state wealth being lost.

Reluctantly, Vessantara's father agreed, but negotiated for Vessantara to enjoy one more day as king before his exile. During this day, Vessantara gave away huge quantities of wealth, and people came from far and wide to receive gifts. He then left the city in a carriage with his wife and children, but not far out of the city someone asked for the horses, which Vessantara gladly gave; deities took the form of golden deer to pull the carriage in their stead. A little further along someone asked for the carriage, and so the family proceeded on foot, Vessantara and his wife carrying their children in their arms. They took up residence in the forest, in hermit huts built by the gods.

Figure 2.2 *Vessantara Jātaka* as illustrated on a stone gateway by the stūpa at Sanchi, Madhya Pradesh, one of the earliest Buddhist sites to survive. At the center of the narrative, and of the depiction, is Vessantara's gift of his two small children, while his wife (depicted above him) is kept away by wild animals. Photograph courtesy of James Hegarty.

Vessantara's generosity did not end with his exile, however; the story's most famous and uncomfortable scene takes place in the forest one day, while his wife is off collecting fruits. A beggar seeks out Vessantara and requests his children as slaves. Vessantara agrees and the children are tied up and taken away, without even having the chance to say goodbye to their mother. Shortly afterwards, Vessantara gives his wife away, though this time the recipient turns out to be the king of the gods in disguise, and he immediately returns the gift.

Vessantara's gifts are widely considered to be the paramount demonstration of generosity; indeed they illustrate the perfection of generosity or giving, one of ten perfections (*pāramī* or *pāramitā* in Pāli and Sanskrit) required for buddhahood. This story, among others, contributes to a widely held idea that jātaka stories illustrate the Buddha-to-be's pursuit of key qualities required for his eventual attainment of buddhahood. Vessantara's readiness to give is taken as a sign of his readiness for buddhahood, a state he achieves—according to Theravāda tradition—a mere two lifetimes later. In this first section of the chapter we will ask to what extent the association with perfection underscores the *jātaka* genre, and how this association offers creative opportunities for the use of the stories in a variety of contexts.

The jātaka genre is often described as illustrating the perfections as pursued by the Buddha-to-be across multiple lifetimes. In the Pāli tradition we usually find ten perfections listed: generosity, morality, renunciation, wisdom, vigor, forbearance, truthfulness, resolve, loving-kindness, and equanimity. Sanskrit lists that become associated with Mahāyāna traditions, including those found in the Perfection of Wisdom texts, generally contain six: generosity, morality, forbearance, vigor, meditation, and wisdom. In other Mahāyāna *sūtra* texts, four more are added to align with the ten stages of the bodhisattva path: skillful means, aspiration, power, and knowledge.[9] Stories about generosity are particularly prominent across the genre, with Vessantara's great gifts challenged for prominence by Sanskrit jātaka stories preoccupied with bodily gift-giving or self-sacrifice.

Although the perfections are clearly important to the presentation of jātakas in many texts, their alignment with stories is rarely straightforward. The *Cariyāpiṭaka*, a late-canonical Pāli collection, appears to offer stories aligned with perfections, but features a different list to the ten that became the Theravāda standard: ten stories address generosity and ten morality, then the remaining fifteen appear spread between addressing renunciation, determination, truth, loving kindness, and equanimity. Similarly, the most famous Sanskrit collection, Ārya Śūra's *Jātakamālā*, has ten stories about generosity, ten about morality, ten that could be addressing forbearance, and then another four stories with no obvious pattern. While later legends suggest the author meant to compose ten stories about each of the ten (Mahāyāna) perfections, there is nothing in the text itself to suggest this.[10] Meanwhile the earliest Chinese *jātaka* text, the *Liudu ji jing* (T152), presents itself as a collection of stories illustrating each of the six perfections, yet the stories themselves often have little to do with the chapter to which they have been assigned, and the tales betray evidence of a variety of origins.[11] Hence the framing of texts as illustrative of a standard list of buddha-qualities, though clearly important to conceptions of the genre, breaks down very easily on closer inspection of the texts.

The influence of the idea that jātakas are about the perfections may in part be due to the fact that it is how the great Pāli *Jātakaṭṭhavaṇṇanā*, which has often been taken as the paradigmatic or classic jātaka text, introduces itself. Despite this framing, few of its almost 550 stories exhibit any real interest in the perfections.[12] Even in the final ten stories of that collection, which themselves form a distinct textual unit that is explicitly mapped onto the ten perfections in Theravāda tradition, the particular qualities exhibited are rather hard to discern, and several of the stories seem to run counter to one another's values. We find a multitude of perspectives here, that include celebrations of honesty and the use of trickery to escape unwanted fates, famed acts of generosity and the strategic gaining of wealth, extraordinary commitment to renunciation and the equally committed pursuit of just forms of kingship.

For example, in the Buddha's past life as Prince Temiya we learn that kingship is inherently bad and should be avoided at all costs, as the young man does everything in his power to escape the throne, and instead ends up presiding over a large community of renouncers in the forest. As King Nimi, however, he rules well, without accruing bad karma, and is rewarded with a tour of the heavens and hells before—later in life—deciding to renounce and pass the throne to his son. Meanwhile as Janaka he takes great pains to gain his rightful kingdom and then even greater pains to leave it behind, pursuing this time a very solitary form of renunciation that leaves no room for worldly ties at all, in direct contrast to the renunciation of Temiya. In the famous story of the Buddha's past life as Prince Vessantara with which we began this section, we see him exiled for over-generous kingship, but later return triumphant to the city to rule, supported by enough divine donations to ensure that his generous nature will no more endanger his citizens; the story has a delightful structure as each gift (including, in case you were concerned, his children) is returned to leave us back where we started.[13] Tensions between different ideals are thus evident even within this small sample of stories; the mapping of stories to particular qualities is clearly a later tradition, albeit a highly significant one.[14]

It is clear that jātaka stories, even when presented as being about the Buddha's acquisition of the perfections required for buddhahood, often have other concerns. Rather than see this as a problematic inconsistency, I would argue that this tension offers creative opportunities: the genre may be "about" perfection, but the stories themselves need not be, at least not in every text. After all, hundreds of stories about a perfect being might not have much value for their thoroughly imperfect audiences. Let us explore three aspects of this creative tension between perfection and imperfection in the jātaka genre.

The Perfect Buddha and His Past-life Imperfections

One of the most obvious ways in which imperfection can be accommodated in the jātaka genre is through the understanding that, in some stories, the

Buddha-to-be is very far from his destination. Many of the stories in the great Pāli collection, for example, portray the Buddha-to-be as interested in the pursuit of wealth or power, through clever means including outwitting others. In the famous story of the monkey and the crocodile, a crocodile's wife wants the monkey's heart to eat, and so the crocodile tricks the monkey into riding on his back in the water, completely defenseless. In order to escape, the monkey (the Buddha in the past) tells the crocodile that his heart is hanging in a tree for safe keeping and thereby escapes back to dry land in the pretense of fetching it. This is clearly a lie, yet it is presented as perfectly reasonable, indeed even laudable, since it results in the monkey's escape. The distance from the perfection of truth here is not a problem because the Buddha-to-be is still on the path and not yet subject to the same standards as a Buddha.[15] Likewise, stories can show the Buddha-to-be making mistakes, following bad advice, pursuing things that he will later reject, and these are all part of the extraordinarily long backstory of the Buddha. The alternation between first-person and third-person narration in the *Jātakatthavaṇṇanā* carefully navigates the Buddha's identity with and separation from his past lives, as Sarah Shaw has shown.[16]

In addition to showing the Buddha-to-be as frequently engaged in mundane matters in the larger collections, there is also an important subset of stories, namely those about the *imperfections* of the Buddha in his past lives that are identified as the karmic causes of misfortunes or illnesses that the Buddha experiences in his final lifetime. As some (though certainly not all) texts are keen to remind us, even the Buddha experiences the karmic consequences of his past deeds, and these can include bad experiences such as physical suffering. For example, several texts portray the Buddha explaining the karmic causes of his final illness, perhaps a form of dysentery that led to his death: this was the result of a past life as a doctor, in which he deliberately gave a patient a medicine that made him more ill; John Strong, among others, has done important work in making such stories better known.[17]

This idea that the Buddha can still be affected by his bad karma even until his final lifetime was taken for granted by some Buddhist textual communities and used to demonstrate the importance of maintaining a concern for karma and merit-making. An interesting text in this regard is the *Avadānaśataka*, the fourth chapter of which contains ten stories of the Buddha's past lives in times of no *buddha*s (albeit not explicitly labeled jātaka). In this collection, stories of two bad deeds and their consequences feature among other stories of karmic results that are more positively framed. For example, we learn that the Buddha remained healthy and free from illness because of a past life in which he sacrificed his life in order to be reborn as a great medicinal fish that would then save his citizens. We also learn that he hurt his mother in a past life and suffered terrible karmic consequences as a result. Mixing up the karmic stories in this way emphasizes the idea that the Buddha is still tied to karmic results both good and bad; even though he has attained buddhahood he is still—until death—subject to the same karmic laws that affect us all.

Indeed, this collection of stories goes even further with an unusual narrative device. The Buddha who tells the stories of his past deeds is portrayed as distinctly human: he sweeps his own hermitage, helps a monk with his sewing, and teaches the importance of respect for one's parents. This human portrayal of the Buddha is quite out of character with the rest of the *Avadānaśataka*, which is full of descriptions of the Buddha's supernormal powers and overpowering physical perfection. The down-to-earth final-life activities of the Buddha in this chapter are thrown into contrast with his past lives, for example, as a man willing to sacrifice his life for the sake of a teaching and as a king who makes great bodily gifts to save his citizens. In other words, this particular text uses a very human portrayal of the Buddha to counterbalance the extraordinary perfection of his past lives. This is the reverse of the strategy in which the perfection of the Buddha is counterbalanced by the imperfection of his past lives. Yet while it is a different literary approach, it speaks to the same concerns around balancing the Buddha's perfection with the audience's awareness of their own imperfection.

The Perfect Buddha and the Imperfections of Others

Another way in which jātaka stories can address this balance is through characters other than the Buddha-to-be. Many jātaka stories are not only *not about the perfections*, but are also *not about the Buddha's past lives*. Although he always features, he can be a character on the sidelines, observing or teaching rather than participating in the action. In such stories, the Buddha's revelation of the story to his audience demonstrates his perfect storytelling abilities, and his perfect vision of the past, and this is more important than anything he does in the past lifetime.

For example, in the jātaka of the dung beetle (*Gūthapāṇa Jātaka*, *Jātakatthavaṇṇanā* 227), a dung beetle drinks some leftover alcohol at an abandoned camp site and then climbs up a pile of fresh dung. The dung squishes, and the now drunken dung beetle declares that the earth cannot bear his weight! An elephant maddened by rut charges into the clearing, sees the piles of dung, and charges out again. The dung-beetle, presumably still under his inebriated delusion of grandeur, thinks the elephant has run away from him, and challenges him to a duel. The elephant unceremoniously adds to the pile with his own dung, thereby killing the beetle.

There is a clear Buddhist message here about the importance of not getting drunk, either by literal drink, or by the powers of lust that overcome the elephant and make him act rashly. The dung-beetle dies because of his drunkenness, and the elephant kills because of his; once karma has taken its course it is likely that the latter will have experienced the worse consequences. The moral message here might be clear, and one could relate it to the perfection of wisdom, which certainly requires a clear mind, or to the perfection of morality, with avoidance of harm at its core. However, these animals are very far from perfection, and the Buddha-to-be is nowhere to be seen, identified at the end of the story as a tree-deity who witnesses the events. He does nothing in the story, and says nothing, the two verses being taken up by the two protagonists. Clearly this is not a story that demonstrates the Buddha's long path to perfection; rather it is a comic moral fable, with a memorable lesson about the evils of drink. This lesson is given by the fully perfected Buddha, whose great clarity of vision makes it possible to see the past.

The story of the dung-beetle may be unusual in barely featuring the Buddha-to-be at all, but many other jātaka stories, especially in the great Pāli collection, have him only in a bit part. The story of the jackal and the otters mentioned earlier, for example, has the Buddha-to-be simply as an observer, and the sources don't even agree over whether he observed the actions as a tree deity (in the *Jātakatthavaṇṇanā* occurrence) or an ascetic (in the Bharhut depiction, see Figure 2.1). Sidelining the Buddha's character is not necessary to this approach to balancing his perfection with an interest in imperfection, however; even in those stories in which he plays a central role, other characters may have an important place in how an audience member relates to the story. We will return to this possibility below.

Perfection: Path or Destination?

A third way in which the perfection of the Buddha can be balanced with the imperfection of other people is by presenting perfection as a spectrum, on which each audience member can find their own place. For example, while few Buddhists would be able to give away their children as Vessantara does in his magnificent—if morally contentious—display of generosity, or tear out their own eyes as King Sivi does in another story, lower forms of gift-giving are widely practiced. Indeed, these include explicit echoes of these great gifts, in the form of children "given" to the monastery for ordination, and mass commitment to donation of corneas after death.[18] Likewise, giving up everything and pursuing a life of solitary meditation in the forest like Janaka might be beyond the reach of most Buddhists, but a gentler form of renunciation in a monastic environment, or an even gentler giving up of attachment to material wealth, is very much within the norm of Buddhist practice. Likewise we can all remember the dangers of clouding the mind with drink, even if we may be far from the clarity of vision embodied by the Buddha.

This understanding of the perfections as a spectrum offers a challenge to our terminology, since it is difficult to think about a Buddhist being "a bit perfect" or indeed an awakened person being "more than perfect." Other terms have been suggested as alternative translations for the underlying *pāramitā*, most notably "excellence," which was argued for by Steven Collins in his final work.[19] To pursue "excellence in giving" is certainly a better way of thinking about practice that might be inspired by the exemplary generosity of the Buddha in his past lives. However, to my mind the fact that one can always be "more excellent" is an argument against the choice; the Buddha achieves something that is beyond the norm, and this notion of "beyond" (*pāra*) or "most excellent" (*parama*) is key to the traditional etymologies offered for the term. In addition, it is uncomfortable English to talk of the lists of excellences. Instead, I would advocate for keeping the established translation, but remembering that striving for perfection takes extraordinary effort across many lifetimes, and that any progress in the right direction is worthy of celebration. In many cases it is the pursuit of perfection that underlies the stories more than its achievement (though with some notable exceptions).

The idea that the Buddha was not always perfect, and the idea that beings who are currently imperfect can aspire to improve, are of course highly compatible notions. The jātakas, as stories about the Buddha before he becomes the Buddha, offer a unique opportunity for Buddhist authors and compilers to explore the extent to which the Buddha's path is exemplary and the extent to which others might find a place on it for themselves. With the addition of multiple characters there are multiple ways of using stories to teach, entertain, and provoke reflection. It is the role of the Buddha's companions and community that are at the center of our second creative tension.

Community Assembled, Transformed, and Transcended

It is already clear that jātaka stories are not just about a single awesome individual working toward buddhahood. Rather, the stories are about the Buddha's interactions with others, both before his awakening (during his multiple past lives) and after his awakening (as the prompts for telling the stories of the past). Even the stories that maintain a strong focus on the pursuit of the perfections need other characters: after all, the perfections can only be practiced by the Buddha-to-be in relation to his encounters with others, and indeed several stories see him crying out for an opportunity to, for example, give a great gift. In addition, jātakas often have a focus on the building of community. Key followers of the Buddha, including members of his family, his senior monastic followers, and even his nemesis, are reborn with him in lifetime after lifetime, demonstrating and developing karmic bonds with the person who will be at the center of their experience. As John Strong has highlighted in his work, and as several other chapters in this volume affirm, karma involves bonds between individuals, and so any biography is of a karmic nexus rather than a single person.[20]

Once again, this tendency plays out differently in different texts. Some *jātaka* collections, such as the *Jātakamālā* texts, only identify the character that is the Buddha in the past because their focus is more strongly on celebrating his individual pạth; other characters are not generally identified. The *Jātakatthavaṇṇanā*, in contrast, is particularly keen to tell us which characters appear alongside the Buddha in the stories. The Buddha's parents, wife, and son are very often his parents, wife, and son in past lives too. His trusty attendant Ānanda accompanies him through many adventures, often as a hapless but well-intentioned character (and twice as female, in a rare gender variance suggestive of a critique of his advocacy for female Buddhist followers). The nun Uppallavaṇṇā, famed for her supernormal powers, had previous rebirths as a goddess. The Buddha's cousin and adversary Devadatta made multiple attempts on his life in the past. And so the list goes on.

This sense of a community travelling together toward an endpoint is further reinforced by the related genre of *avadāna* (in Sanskrit, or *apadāna* in Pāli). Although this genre can be tricky to define, in most cases such narratives offer stories of karmically potent encounters and their results. For example, we learn about the past-life encounters that key liberated followers of the Buddha had with past *buddhas* or with stūpas. Their own liberation—and their "luck" in being reborn in a time and place conducive to hearing the Buddha's teachings—is linked to their own gifts, as seeds planted in a powerful field of merit. Other stories in the genre concern encounters people have with the Buddha of our time, and his predictions of their future attainment of liberation. Such stories are of course related to those in which the Buddha has his own past-life encounters with other *buddhas*, the paradigmatic example of which was explored in the previous chapter. Working together, these different narrative genres build up a network of encounters, extending into the past and the future, with the Buddha as a central node. Community is key to the Buddha's multilife path.

Transforming the Community

I noted at the beginning of this chapter that we would be excluding stories of encounters with past *buddhas* from our analysis. The contrasts between such stories and the classical jātaka genre explored here are important to understand.

In times of past *buddha*s the Buddha has only to make a modest offering such as food or a flower, as is the case for the encounters of other beings with such powerful fields of merit in the past. It is only in times of no *buddha*s, as in the classical jātaka genre, that he has to go to extreme lengths in pursuit of the perfections, including sacrificing his family members and his own life. There is a deliberate contrast here, and it suggests that the result of these great deeds is that he is able to become a Buddha and provide an easier path for others.

Reiko Ohnuma has gone so far as to argue that this underscores the very definition of Buddhist narrative genres: "By means of the *jātakas*, the bodhisattva is lauded and exalted for the magnificent lengths he went to during his past lives—but by means of the *avadāna*s, ordinary Buddhists receive the message that such magnificent lengths are now *unnecessary* thanks to the presence of Buddhism in the world as a powerful field of merit."[21] According to this interpretation, we need not imitate the Buddha's perfection because his perfection has made our ordinary deeds, such as giving food to the monastery, more efficacious. As such, the perfection of the Buddha-to-be in his past lives is a celebration of heroic deeds, but not a roadmap to achieving buddhahood ourselves. Instead, liberation can come from more mundane deeds—even what we might term devotional deeds—such as offering gifts to the monastery or to Buddha-images or stūpas.

While this interpretation might be seen as more in line with non-Mahāyāna thinking, where arhatship is the mainstream goal, the notion that the Buddha's achievement transformed the path of others can also be seen in traditions that advocate following the path to buddhahood. Mahāyāna jātaka stories develop the Sanskritic tradition of celebrating the Bodhisattva's repeated bodily sacrifice.[22] Yet the idea that all Buddhists might therefore need to do such terrifying things as chop off their own head or pluck out their eyes was dealt with in different creative ways. For example, Natalie Gummer has shown that some Mahāyāna texts portray themselves "as aesthetic, dramatic forms of sacrifice, rituals of recitation that obviate the violence . . . of the bodhisattva's self-sacrifice."[23] So even where perfection for the Buddha would appear to imply—in Mahāyāna contexts—that all Buddhists must also sacrifice their bodies and family members, jātaka literature is not quite so straightforward in its reception. Instead, the texts portray the Buddha teaching alternative paths of practice, ones that don't require the same level of perfection. The Buddha's own perfection is so powerful that his whole community benefits through completely transformed prospects of their own.

Transcending the Community

Being bound to the Buddha is clearly beneficial for the many followers who thereby attain their own liberation, or for audience members seeking rebirth in the presence of future awakened teachers. However, the building of a community of followers is naturally accompanied by the Buddha's departure from them. The "Great Departure," when the Buddha-to-be in his final life leaves his wife and child and goes off on his quest, is echoed in many jātaka stories about the importance of renunciation, including the Vessantara story discussed earlier. Just like Vessantara, who regains his wife and children by the end of the narrative, the Buddha too is reunited with his wife and son, who both join his monastic community and achieve liberation from rebirth like he does. Yet this liberation is also, necessarily, a solitary attainment, and one that can only be reached through transcending attachments. Sometimes jātaka stories seem particularly keen to explore this tension.

A good example is the way jātaka stories are used in the *Mahāvastu*, a buddhological and biographical text belonging to the lost Mahāsāṅghika-Lokottaravāda school of Indian Buddhism, and dating perhaps to the early centuries CE. In this text, most of the stories of the Buddha's past lives are presented at relevant moments in the account of his final life, and most relate parallel events that took place in the past. For example, the section of the *Mahāvastu* that recounts the youth of the Buddha-to-be in his final lifetime includes multiple stories of his past-life encounters with his wife Yaśodharā. Some of these are romances: we learn that the Buddha chose her in the past too, and that he went to great lengths to woo her in several past lives, including the famous story of Prince Sudhana who fell in love with the *kinnarī* Manoharā that is discussed in Chapter 4, and another famous tale of the wise minister Mahauṣadha who had to work hard to win his equally wise wife Amarā.[24] Such stories hint at the depth of affection between husband and wife, and remind us that the Buddha's life story is about more than just one figure. However, they add no sense of progress to his life story—only repetition.

Some of the other stories relate to specific details of the final-life encounter. For example when Yaśodharā is displeased with his gifts, the Buddha recounts a past life in which the two of them were living in exile in the wilderness, and he offered her a dead lizard to eat. She refused to cook it, and so he cooked and ate it while she was out and then claimed it had run away! Later, when their fortunes improved, he lavished her with gifts but she never got over the lizard episode, and could not be pleased.[25] A few stories later, we learn of how, after the Buddha-to-be renounced to pursue awakening, both Devadatta and Sundara-Nanda propositioned Yaśodharā but she refused them. In a past life, we learn, the three men were animals seeking the affection of the tigress who had won a contest to be monarch. Once again she (Yaśodharā in a past life) chose the Buddha-to-be (a lion) despite the best efforts of the other two (an elephant and a bull).[26]

The *Mahāvastu* stories add to the sense that the Buddha's multilife story is inherently bound up with other people; his path is individual but also communal. However, there is another strong sense that comes from the *Mahāvastu* presentation of these jātaka stories: a sense of repetition that is set in contrast to the motion—in the final-life story that frames the jātakas—toward an end-point. Steven Collins has written about the idea that nirvana functions like a full stop (or period) at the end of a sentence, providing the "sense of an ending" that offers "satisfactory closure, where the mere breaking-off of life occasioned by death cannot."[27] While Collins related this idea specifically to Pāli literature, the same analysis could be used more broadly of the jātaka genre: nirvana provides the end-point of the long multilife experience of a being trapped in *saṃsāra*, and the presence of this sense of closure—in the Buddha's life story more broadly—creates a productive tension with the proliferation of his past-life stories. Put another way, the Buddha-to-be tells stories of the tiresome repetition of bonds and relationships and experiences in order to highlight just how liberating it is to achieve awakening, as well as just how much patience and dedication it takes to get there.

This analysis is strengthened by another cluster of stories a little later in the *Mahāvastu*, when we learn of the past-life efforts of the Buddha to escape from Māra, the overlord of the cycle of rebirth. In a series of jātakas that elsewhere usually have Devadatta cast in the villainous role, the Bodhisattva is a bird seeking to escape a fowler, a turtle seeking to escape his captor, and a monkey seeking to escape a crocodile. Sometimes he escapes alone, and other times he helps his followers too, such as coordinating the escape of his flock of birds, or instructing his troop of monkeys to use straws when drinking from a pond in order to avoid disturbing the dangerous water-demon who lives there.[28] Escape in these contexts is very much a physical escape from captivity or immediate danger, and Māra in these past lives is not yet Māra the overlord of *saṃsāra*. The last quest—liberation from the cycle of rebirth—requires a slightly different cast, but is (so the stories imply) more or less a repetition of the same efforts. Yet as the stories suggest, by achieving escape from rebirth, the Buddha also escapes ever having to be born again as an animal, and will never be captured or tortured or pursued again. Nirvana is the *only* true escape from suffering. These jātaka stories of the *Mahāvastu* rarely show any interest in the progress made toward buddhahood, but rather they offer us a vision into the tiresome repetition of life after life.[29]

Playing with the ambiguity of rebirth—the possibilities of good rebirth, the advantages of being karmically bound to the Buddha, but also the need to escape karmic bonds—is yet another creative approach to the jātaka genre. Once again it is particularly visible in specific texts, but also in some sense underpins the genre more broadly.

Creativity in Visual Jātakas

These two creative tensions are not the only ways in which jātaka literature addresses Buddhist concerns, but they offer a good range of evidence for the advantages of the genre's diversity and flexibility. Even more advantages can be seen when we bring visual and material evidence into the conversation. As just one example, let us briefly consider the role of jātaka images at the earliest stūpa sites of Bharhut and Sanchi, and how this relates to the strategies and concerns just explored.

Figure 2.3 A full stone gateway at the Sanchi stūpa, showing the distance from the ground and the obvious difficulty of viewing any image in detail. Jātaka stories feature on the gateway crossbars (as in Figure 2.2) and in scenes on the pillars, and at other sites also medallions decorating the railings. While jātaka stories are commonly depicted, they feature amongst other decorative themes including episodes from the Buddha's final lifetime. Photograph courtesy of James Hegarty.

The sites of Bharhut and Sanchi offer our earliest evidence for the jātaka genre (earlier than any extant texts), with multiple stories depicted on the stone railings and gateways, and—at Bharhut—often accompanied by inscriptions that aid our identification of the stories and attest to the label "jātaka." These stories surround the stūpa or reliquary mound that contains bodily relics of the Buddha. So what is the relationship between the stories and the site?

To begin with, the Buddha's perfections are clearly related to his relics; as several texts remind us, the Buddha's body is the culmination of his past deeds. In the "Discourse on the Marks" (*Lakkhaṇa Sutta*) of the *Dīgha Nikāya*, one of the oldest collections of Buddhist teachings preserved by the Theravāda tradition, we learn how each of the famous thirty-two marks of a great man are linked to past deeds. For example, multiple lifetimes living without anger are revealed as the karmic cause of the Buddha's golden complexion, while avoiding harm to other beings resulted in him having an exceptionally good sense of taste.[30] Indeed, John Strong has even argued that the Buddha's relics represent the transformation (and in some sense continuation) of his lineage of past-lives.[31] Hence narrative depictions at stūpa sites hint at how the Buddha's body became so powerful that even the relics remaining after his death are worthy of being enshrined.

Importantly, this interpretation has merit regardless of the exact stories depicted, which—we might note—betray no explicit concern with perfections, though they do tend to focus on exemplary or heroic deeds. The ability of visual jātaka stories to carry competing associations is—as with textual jātakas—in part because of their framing. As Robert Brown pointed out long ago, and as Figure 2.3 demonstrates, at stūpa sites stories themselves are rarely very easy to "read" in their visual forms. Often they are highly conflated, or depicted in scenes arranged in a nonlinear way, or else depicted high overhead or in other inaccessible spaces. Their presence, it would seem, is a lot more important than the ability of any visitors to interact with them.[32] There is a possibility that storytelling guides offered interpretations of particular stories, but the overall impression is likely to be one of amazement at the repeated heroism of the being enshrined at the center of the site. At the same time, the stories sit outside the stūpa in the accessible areas. Perhaps this reinforces the idea of the stories being relatable: visitors can learn from the tales of his past, even as they struggle to respond to the perfection of his final form with anything other than awe.

Bringing the related narrative genres into the discussion adds yet more dimensions. Many stories in the *avadāna* or *apadāna* genre are about the powerful benefits of making an offering to a stūpa. Simple deeds such as this are, as we have seen, efficacious precisely because of the extraordinary perfection of the Buddha, pursued over multiple lifetimes. Through all these interconnected stories, including those of the Buddha's own encounters with past *buddhas*, we find ourselves drawn into a vast network of interconnected beings, in which our own devotional encounters might themselves bear fruit in the future. As Jonathan Walters has emphasized, this network has a place for us all: we too can make an offering to a stūpa and make an aspiration to meet a *buddha* in the future, or even to become one ourselves, and this might well be the reason past-life narratives feature so prominently at stūpa sites.[33]

Although much more could and should be said about visual jātakas in early Buddhism, even this brief exploration has shown that it is not only in their verbal and literary forms that jātaka stories offer creative and flexible explorations of who the Buddha is, how he got there, and what this means for others. Imperfect beings can benefit from visiting a site imbued with the perfection of the Buddha and perform devotional activities that guarantee their own place in the community that he has made possible.

Concluding Thoughts

If there is one takeaway message from this chapter, it is that the diversity and flexibility of the jātaka genre allows the stories to work in lots of different ways at once. Jātaka stories are both about the Buddha as an individual and also about the path to buddhahood. They are about the perfections required for buddhahood but also about many imperfections experienced on the way. They are about buddhahood but also about comic animals and human folly. They illustrate the perfected storytelling abilities of an all-seeing teacher, who tells stories about his own lives that sometimes have more to say about other people. They are about an individual path pursued with absolute dedication, but also about the community built up in the process through repeated interactions, as well as the ultimate need to transcend all ties. As a naturally expansive narrative genre, jātakas are able to be many things at once, and to carry and explore tensions and competing priorities, without seeking to resolve or systematize them.

While we may now appreciate the rich creative opportunities offered by the jātaka genre both within and across different texts, and in both verbal and visual contexts, where does that leave us in this account of the Buddha's life story? Far from being a simple chronological or biographical account, jātakas offer an exploration of key Buddhist ideas through varied literary and visual strategies.

We can easily get lost among the moral fables, adventure quests, epic poems, and celebrations of repeated self-sacrifice. But even the scale of the genre can be seen as a lesson in itself: the exhaustion of trying to achieve an exhaustive knowledge of all of the Buddha's past lives helps us to experience the fatigue of the endless round of rebirth and see that sharply contrasted with the experience of awakening. For after this seemingly endless series of lifetimes, after actions and experiences both extraordinary and utterly ordinary, at last the Buddha-to-be is ready for his final birth.

Notes

I would like to thank the editors and other contributors to this volume, Brian Black, and the audience at the Chinese jātakas workshop (Heidelberg, 2022) for their comments on an earlier version of this chapter. I would also like to take this opportunity to thank John Strong for his example, mentorship, and collegiality over the many years I have had the pleasure of knowing him.

1. Versions of the hare story can be found in *Jātakatthavaṇṇanā* 316, Ārya Śūra's *Jātakamālā* 6, Haribhaṭṭa's *Jātakamālā* 4, *Avadānaśataka* 37, and *Cariyāpiṭaka* 10, among other places. The story is often associated with the belief that the moon contains the image of a hare, placed there by the god Śakra in recognition of the hare's great deed. The tigress story is the first in Ārya Śūra's *Jātakamālā*, as well as being found in many other sources, though not in the classical Pāli tradition. References are to story numbers found in the *Jātakatthavaṇṇanā* edition by Fausboll and translation by Cowell, the two Jātakamālā translations by Khoroche, the *Avadānaśataka* translation by Appleton, and the *Cariyāpiṭaka* translation by Horner. Most translations, or at least summaries, are also available on https://jatakastories.div.ed.ac.uk along with editions of the original text.
2. For the former see *Jātakatthavaṇṇanā* 400, and for the latter *Jātakatthavaṇṇanā* 308 and number 34 of Ārya Śūra's *Jātakamālā*.
3. Best known as the *Vidhurapaṇḍita Jātaka*, *Jātakatthavaṇṇanā* 545.
4. I tend to use Buddha-to-be when talking about the Buddha in his past lives in recognition of the fact that the term Bodhisattva/Bodhisatva (in Sanskrit) or Bodhisatta (in Pāli) is not commonly used in *jātaka* stories.
5. On what the *jātaka*s tell us about the Buddha who tells them, see Naomi Appleton, "The Buddha as Storyteller: The Dialogical Setting of Jātaka Stories," in *Dialogue in Early South Asian Religions: Hindu, Buddhist, and Jain Traditions*, ed. Laurie Patton and Brian Black (Farnham: Ashgate, 2015), 99–112; and Eviatar Shulman, "Contemplating the Buddha in the *Jātakas*," *Religions of South Asia* 12, no. 1 (2018): 9–33.
6. Despite the fact that they are rarely presented as a chronological account, I would argue that it is still helpful to think of jātaka stories as biographical, in contrast to Eviaṭar Shulman, who argues that *jātaka*s are not biographical since "[t]he focus is on what makes a Buddha, on his very nature and being, not on the sequence of events that trace the life history of the particular being who later became the Buddha" (Shulman, "Contemplating," 15). While I agree with Shulman's emphasis on the "buddhological" dimension of the genre, it is worth remembering that biography is never a dispassionate account of a series of events; rather it is always selective, and seeks to explain how events shaped a particular outcome, such as an achievement or personality. As such, to say that the jātaka genre is part of the Buddha's sacred biography is to say that it tells us something about "what makes the Buddha" as well as, potentially, "what makes a *buddha*," and it need not do so in a straightforward or chronological way.
7. There are three reasons for excluding stories of the Buddha's encounters with past *buddhas* from our discussion of the jātaka genre: First, the most interesting example has already been discussed in the previous chapter, and other tales of such encounters tend to become rather formulaic and dry as the genre expands. Second, classical understandings of the jātaka genre tend to consider it to comprise stories of the Buddha's past lives specifically in times of no past *buddha*; stories involving past *buddhas* are usually separated off into different chapters or texts, or different

modes of art, and not usually designated jātaka. Third, jātaka stories defined as past-life episodes in times without any *buddhas* in the world are more than extensive and diverse enough to offer sufficient challenge for a single chapter!

8. For an excellent set of papers exploring this crucial narrative see Steven Collins, ed., *Readings of the Vessantara Jātaka* (New York: Columbia University Press, 2016). The story is not only important as a great work of Buddhist literature; it also underpins a variety of ritual, festive and pilgrimage activities.
9. For a discussion of how the lists of perfections might relate see Naomi Appleton, *Jātaka Stories in Theravāda Buddhism: Narrating the Bodhisatta Path* (Farnham: Ashgate, 2010), 98–103.
10. See discussion in the introduction to Peter Khoroche, trans., *Once the Buddha Was a Monkey: Ārya Śūra's Jātakamālā* (Chicago: University of Chicago Press, 1989). The text dates to around the fourth century CE.
11. My understanding of this text is thanks to the ongoing translation work of Janine Nicol, yet to be published.
12. See Appleton, *Jātaka Stories*, Chapter 3.
13. On this see Shi Huifeng (Matthew Orsborn), "Chiastic Structure of the *Vessantara Jātaka*: Textual Criticism and Interpretation Through Inverted Parallelism," *Buddhist Studies Review* 32, no. 1 (2015): 143–159.
14. See discussion in Appleton, *Jātaka Stories*, 71–78; and Naomi Appleton and Sarah Shaw, trans., *The Ten Great Birth Stories of the Buddha: The Mahānipāta of the Jātakatthavaṇṇanā* (Chiang Mai: Silkworm Press, 2015), 4–7.
15. Variations on this story are found in *Cariyāpiṭaka* 27, and *Jātakatthavaṇṇanā* 57, 208, and 342. The presentation of this story in the "truth" section of the *Cariyāpiṭaka* is a peculiarly brazen denial that any lie was involved at all; see discussion in Appleton, *Jātaka Stories*, 66.
16. Sarah Shaw, "And That Was I: How the Buddha Himself Creates a Path between Biography and Autobiography," in *Lives Lived, Lives Imagined: Biography in the Buddhist Traditions*, ed. Lindạ Covill, Ulrike Roesler, and Sarah Shaw (Boston: Wisdom Publications, 2010), 15–47. The choices over narrative voice are yet another important distinction between different jātaka collections.
17. The explanation cited here is given in John S. Strong, "Explicating the Buddha's Final Illness in the Context of his Other Ailments: the Making and Unmaking of some *Jātaka* Tales," *Buddhist Studies Review* 29, no. 1 (2012): 17–33. See also John S. Strong, *The Buddha: A Short Biography*. Oxford: Oneworld, 2001, 32–34. For a discussion of the more contentious reception of this idea in the Theravāda tradition see Jonathan S. Walters, "The Buddha's Bad Karma: A Problem in the History of Theravāda Buddhism," *Numen* 37, no. 1 (1990): 70–95.
18. This influence in Sri Lankan contexts is documented in Bob Simpson, "Impossible Gifts: Bodies, Buddhism and Bioethics in Contemporary Sri Lanka," *The Journal of the Royal Anthropological Institute* 10, no. 4 (2004): 839–859.
19. Steven Collins, *Wisdom as a Way of Life: Theravāda Buddhism Reimagined* (New York: Columbia University Press, 2020), 5–7.

20. John S. Strong, "A Family Quest: The Buddha, Yaśodharā, and Rāhula in the *Mūlasarvāstivāda Vinaya*," in *Sacred Biography in the Buddhist Traditions of South and Southeast Asia*, ed. Juliane Schober (Honolulu: University of Hawai'i Press, 1997), 114. On lateral karmic bonds see also Jonathan S. Walters "Stūpa, Story and Empire: Constructions of the Buddha Biography in Early Post-Aśokan India" in the same volume.
21. Reiko Ohnuma, *Head, Eyes, Flesh, and Blood: Giving Away the Body in Indian Buddhist Literature* (New York: Columbia University Press, 2007), 43.
22. This focus is clear in the *Jātakamālā* traditions, for example, but considerably less prominent in the Pāli understanding of the genre. See Ohnuma, *Head, Eyes* for a thorough discussion of the Sanskrit narratives addressing this theme.
23. Natalie Gummer, "Sacrificial Sūtras: Mahāyāna Literature and the South Asian Ritual Cosmos," *Journal of the American Academy of Religion* 82, no. 4 (2014): 1091.
24. *Mahāvastu* volume 2, 91–111, and 80–87. References to the *Mahāvastu* are to volume and page number in the translation by J. J. Jones. See also the edition by Senart.
25. *Mahāvastu* volume 2, 61–64.
26. *Mahāvastu* volume 2, 66–69.
27. Steven Collins, *Nirvana: Concept, Imagery, Narrative* (Cambridge University Press, 2010), 110–111.
28. There are in fact two clusters of stories told about the defeat of Māra: *Mahāvastu* volume 2, 224–240, and volume 2, 372—volume 3, 31.
29. There are other references to the Buddha's past lives in the *Mahāvastu* that have a focus on progress, however; see discussion in Naomi Appleton, "The Story of the Path: Indian *Jātaka* Literature and the Way to Buddhahood," in *Mārga: Paths to Liberation in South Asian Buddhist Traditions*, ed. C. Pecchia and V. Eltschinger (Vienna: Austrian Academy of Sciences Press, 2020), 79–98.
30. The large *Prajñāpāramitā Sūtra* and other Mahāyāna texts also offer similar sorts of analyses: see discussion in Strong, *The Buddha*, 31–32.
31. John S. Strong, "The Buddha as Ender and Transformer of Lineages," *Religions of South Asia* 5, no. 1–2 (2011): 171–188. On the lineages of the Buddha see also Frank E. Reynolds, "Rebirth Traditions and the Lineages of Gotama: A Study in Theravāda Buddhology," in *Sacred Biography in the Buddhist Traditions of South and Southeast Asia*, ed. Juliane Schober (Honolulu: University of Hawai'i Press, 1997), 19–39.
32. The classic work on this is Robert L. Brown, "Narrative as Icon: The *Jātaka* Stories in Ancient Indian and Southeast Asian Architecture," in *Sacred Biography in the Buddhist Traditions of South and Southeast Asia*, ed. Juliane Schober (Honolulu: University of Hawai'i Press, 1997), 64–109. For a collection of more recent scholarship on the function of jātakas and other Buddhist narratives in art see Naomi Appleton, ed., *Narrative Visions and Visual Narratives in Indian Buddhism* (Sheffield: Equinox, 2022).
33. See discussion in Walters, "Stūpa, Story and Empire."

3
The Final Birth

Reiko Ohnuma

Figure 3.1 Queen Māyā gives birth to the future Buddha from her right side, as a tree branch magically bends down to offer her support. Gandhāra, second to third century CE; courtesy of National Museum of Asian Art, Washington, DC.

Near the conclusion of the bodhisattva career discussed in the previous chapter, we come to a crucial moment: thousands of lifetimes have been lived, gifts have been given and moral deeds performed, the necessary perfections cultivated and fulfilled, innumerable previous buddhas worshipped and adored, the bodhisattva path traversed—and at last, the time comes for the future Buddha to take his final birth, the birth in which he will put an end to *all* birth, the birth in which he will live out his final life as Prince Siddhārtha and then succeed in becoming the buddha of our age, the Buddha Śākyamuni. The final birth of the Buddha indeed marks a momentous event in the narrative of the Buddha's life story.

Reiko Ohnuma, *The Final Birth* In: *The Buddha*. Edited by: Vanessa R. Sasson and Kristin Scheible, Oxford University Press. © Oxford University Press 2024. DOI: 10.1093/oso/9780197649466.003.0004

But the depiction of the Buddha's final birth poses a seemingly insurmountable problem: Buddhism is a profoundly human-centered tradition, and Buddhist doctrine dictates that all buddhas are *human beings*—they must have a human birth and emerge from a human mother. For it is only by seeing the Buddha as a fellow human being that his followers can have faith that they, too, are able to achieve the spiritual goal that he preached. And yet, the bodies of human women and the human processes of pregnancy, gestation, and giving birth were powerfully associated with Indian cultural notions of impurity, pain, and suffering. The first of the Buddha's Four Noble Truths—the Noble Truth of Suffering (*duḥkha*)—*begins* by proclaiming that "birth is suffering."[1] In fact, for Buddhism, birth from a woman's body is not merely an *example* of suffering; it is, as Amy Langenberg has shown, a "root metaphor for suffering"—the very quintessence of the suffering that entraps all benighted beings within the realm of *saṃsāra*.[2] So how could the future Buddha—a pure and holy being who reveals the path to the eradication of all suffering—be himself subject to the suffering and indignity of birth from a human woman? The *Lalitavistara*, a third to fourth century CE Sanskrit biography of the Buddha, states the problem succinctly: "Bodhisattvas are born in the realm of human beings," it first asserts, "for gods do not turn the Wheel of the Dharma."[3] But, "How, indeed, could the bodhisattva, who rises above all worlds, who is pure and free from any foul odors, who is a jewel among beings—how could he . . . remain for ten months in a foul-smelling human body, in the womb of his mother?"[4] How could the sacred figure of the Buddha be depicted as dwelling in the filthy substances of a woman's womb and then emerging from a woman's vagina? In short, as Michael Radich has noted, "Buddhism was embarrassed by the fact that the Buddha had a mother."[5]

One major way this problem was solved was by depicting the mother, the son, and the process of birth itself in a miraculous, highly sanitized, and wholly purified manner—a manner that departs, in virtually every way, from the ordinary birth-giving process (much as we also find in the miraculous conception and virgin birth of Jesus Christ). In other words, the gendered notions surrounding the impurity of the female, birth-giving body are simply avoided by depicting the Buddha's mother as a woman who is utterly unlike any other human woman, and by depicting the Buddha's birth as the very opposite of any ordinary human birth. Since both I and others have written about this topic at some length before, I will here deal with it only in a cursory fashion.[6]

For the purposes of this chapter, I am more interested in exploring a second solution to the problem, which is to dislocate and decenter the singular focus on "mother and son" by turning the birth into a *cosmic* and *universal* event, one that encompasses the entire hierarchy of living beings and reverberates outward in all directions of space, as well as moving both backward and forward in time—backward to recall the eons-long bodhisattva career of which the birth is only a culmination, and forward to foreshadow virtually the entire trajectory of the Buddha's final life. From this perspective, the birth is not merely a "birth"; indeed, it becomes like a multifaceted jewel reflecting light in every direction and encompassing infinite parameters of time and space—as well as becoming a universal law or blueprint adhered to by *all* buddhas without exception, a cosmic pulsation that regularly moves through the universe. In this way, the birth is transformed from an unseemly human event into something cosmic, mythic, and universal—something that could not possibly be tainted by human impurity and suffering.[7]

In this chapter, I will first recount the Bodhisattva's birth with a focus on mother and son, and then shift my focus to all the features of the birth story that move beyond the mother–son dyad and render it virtually irrelevant.

A brief note about my sources and methodology: In the discussion below, I freely weave together many of the standard elements of the Buddha's birth-narrative, as depicted in a range of important early-to-middle-period South Asian sources on the Buddha's life story, including the *Mahāpadāna Sutta, Acchariyabbhuta Sutta, Nidānakathā, Buddhacarita, Mahāvastu, Lalitavistara, Saṅghabhedavastu* of the *Mūlasarvāstivāda Vinaya,* and *Abhiniṣkramaṇa Sūtra.*[8] It should be understood that the resulting portrait is a composite that is not exactly replicated in any single source alone, and that would not have been available, in exactly this form, to any single historical reader. Is this a valid way to "read" the episode of the Buddha's birth? I believe that it is.

Here, I am drawing inspiration from the poet and scholar of Indian literature A. K. Ramanujan (now deceased). In speaking of the hundreds of versions of the Rāmāyaṇa epic that have crisscrossed their way across ancient and modern South and Southeast Asia—with each "telling" offering a slightly different view of the story—Ramanujan once observed that the Rāmāyaṇa is not just a series of "texts" or "stories" or "versions." Instead, it is a set of cultural resources—what he termed a "pool of signifiers"—that each individual version dips into to bring out a "unique crystallization."[9] Each "version" has its own, unique internal logic and necessity, but relies for its ability to convey meaning on the overall "pool" from which it draws. I find this to be a most felicitous image for thinking about the Buddha's life story. In my account of the Buddha's birth, I offer my own "unique crystallization" that hopefully also conveys some sense of the larger "pool of signifiers" from which all Buddha-biographies draw.

Finally, in constructing my account, I have chosen to deemphasize the matter of which detail comes from which source in favor of a more flowing narrative that will hopefully immerse and bathe the reader in the mind-bending swirl that constitutes the Buddha's final birth.

Mother, Son, and the Perfect Birth

Keeping our focus first on the mother, the son, and the birth-giving process itself, let us quickly recount the basic story of the Bodhisattva's final birth, emphasizing the many ways in which it erases and subverts all the negative connotations normally surrounding pregnancy, gestation, and birth.

To begin with: How were these processes ordinarily seen? In the standard Buddhist understanding, the conception of a child occurs when the mother and father come together in sexual intercourse, the mother is in her fertile period, and a *gandharva* or "intermediate-state being" with the appropriate karma is present at the scene. In some sources, it also involves a rather twisted Oedipal scenario in which the male *gandharva,* as he watches the act of sex, lusts after his future mother and wants to eradicate his future father, while the female *gandharva* lusts after her future father and wants to eradicate her future mother. From the very beginning of the process, then, conception is embroiled in lust, incestuous passion, jealousy, and the messy act of sex.

Once conception has occurred, the embryo/fetus embarks on its long road of suffering. Indian descriptions of the "suffering of the womb" (*garbha-duḥkha*) and the "suffering of birth" (*janma-duḥkha*) describe the mother's womb as a dark, cramped, and airless space in which the fetus constantly suffers, being submerged in feces and urine and experiencing torment whenever its mother moves or eats the wrong food.[10] In the *Visuddhimagga,* Buddhaghosa compares the fetus to "a worm in rotting fish or rotting curds or a cesspool," trapped within a womb that is "exceedingly loathsome and full of foul odors and fetid smells," where it undergoes "extreme suffering, being cooked like a pudding in a bag by the heat produced by [its] mother's womb, being steamed like a lump of dough, unable to bend, stretch, etc."[11]

But as awful as it is to be trapped in a dark and filthy womb, being expelled from the womb is no picnic either, for birth is depicted as an extremely painful passage through the narrow canal of the vagina and a violent expulsion into the cold air outside, with the startled infant dropping "like a worm . . . which falls down upon the ground from a foul-smelling sore."[12] Moreover, according to many Hindu sources at least, it is precisely because of the enormous suffering experienced during the harrowing passage through the birth-canal that the ordinary infant is said to lose the knowledge of karma and the memory of its previous lives that a fully developed fetus was believed to have possessed. Thus, rather than being born with an awareness of the past, such an infant is born as a *bāla* (both "fool" and "child") who "does not know who he is, whence he has come, to whom he belongs, by what form of bondage he has been bound, what he should do, what he should not do, what he should eat, what he should not eat, what he should drink, what he should not drink, what is truth, what is falsehood, what is knowledge, what is ignorance."[13] Filthy, startled, and stupefied, the newborn baby falls down onto the dirty ground, where its body is immediately "set upon by 80,000 parasitical worms that colonize and nibble at every organ, bone, and tissue."[14]

This is what it means to be born. It is thus no wonder that the ultimate goal of nirvana was often described as becoming "one who is unborn (*ajāta*), has destroyed birth (*khīṇā jāti*), has abandoned the flow of births (*jātisaṃsāro pahīno*), and escaped birth (*jātiyā parimuccati*)."[15] As the Buddha concludes (in the *Garbhāvakrānti Sūtra*): "In the same way that even a little vomit stinks . . . even the momentary conception of a tiny life is suffering."[16]

The strength of these cultural conceptions of filth, impurity, and suffering surrounding the pregnant and birth-giving female body will be brought into high relief as we now consider the birth of the future Buddha, which departs from this gloomy picture on virtually every point. In the first place, the status of Queen Māyā as the Bodhisattva's mother is neither a random accident of sex nor a result brought about by ordinary karmic processes. Instead, it is a conscious *choice* on the part of the future Buddha, one of the four or five considerations he makes, "mindful and deliberate,"[17] at the end of his previous life as a deity in the Tuṣita Heaven (where all bodhisattvas reside in their next-to-last existences) about when and where he will take his final, human rebirth. In addition to choosing such things as the caste, the country, and the family into which he will be born, he also chooses Māyā to be his mother because she adheres to a daunting list of thirty-two specific qualities of both physical and moral perfection: she is beautiful, pure, chaste, and virtuous—"free from all of the faults of womankind"[18]—and "she alone is fit to be the mother of the Great Sage and has served as the bodhisattva's mother in no fewer than five hundred births."[19]

The conception of the Bodhisattva, in most biographies, is not associated with the sexual act, for "bodhisattvas certainly don't come from their mothers and fathers, but are, in fact, self-produced and originate from their own qualities."[20] In place of sexual intercourse, the conception is generally depicted as taking the form of an auspicious dream Māyā has in which a noble, six-tusked white elephant comes to her and appears to enter her right side. Brahmin soothsayers then interpret the dream to mean that a noble son will be born to King Śuddhodana. His body will bear the thirty-two marks of a Great Man (*mahāpuruṣa*), which indicate only two possible future destinies: If he remains within the world, he will become a Universal Emperor (*cakravartin*), but if he leaves the world and "goes forth" into homelessness, then he will become a fully awakened buddha. The conception itself is depicted as a divine and cosmic procession, for as the Bodhisattva departs from his divine abode in the Tuṣita Heaven and descends to take up his place within Queen Māyā's womb, the earth trembles, the whole world fills with light, throngs of deities come to stand guard over mother and son, and thirty-two miracles occur—the blind can see, the deaf can hear, and the lame can walk; flowers burst into bloom, rivers stop running, and musical instruments resound without being played.

Throughout the pregnancy, the Bodhisattva inhabits the auspicious right side of Māyā's womb and never moves over to the left. He has plenty of room to sit upright and cross-legged, and his movements within the womb cause his mother no discomfort, nor do her movements cause any discomfort to him. Unlike other embryos, which develop gradually over time by feeding on the mother's blood, the Bodhisattva, from the very beginning, is "complete with all major and minor limbs and not lacking any of his faculties"[21]—a sort of perfect, homunculus buddha already. Even more remarkable, Māyā can *see* the Bodhisattva within her womb, "just as if a pure and genuine lapis lazuli jewel, beautifully cut into an octagon, clear, bright, flawless, and perfect in every way, were strung on a blue, yellow, red, white, or orange thread,"[22] and a man with good eyesight could determine the color of the thread. Māyā's womb, in other words, is full of radiant light and as perfectly transparent as a crystal. Within the womb, the Bodhisattva remains "unsmeared by the filth of the womb, the filth of semen, the filth of blood, or any other impurity"[23]—either because "his body is anointed with oils and washed clean"[24] by the gods, or because he never even comes into direct physical contact with his mother's flesh, spending the entire pregnancy comfortably encased within a beautiful "jeweled sanctum"[25] within the womb. Throughout the pregnancy, Maya is perfectly virtuous and chaste, for "it is the rule that while the blessed Bodhisattva abides in his mother's womb, his mother's mind is not fixated upon men, nor is it affected by sensual desire."[26] Both conception and pregnancy, in his case, have been utterly removed from any association with flesh, bodily fluids, or sex.

When the time comes for her to give birth, Māyā sets out for her natal home of Devadaha in an elaborate procession, only to make a stop, halfway, in the beautiful Lumbinī Grove, full of flowers, plants, and trees in full blossom. It is here that the birth will take place, characterized by many wonderful qualities that are common to all bodhisattvas in their last existences. Here, we can turn to a sculptural frieze from Gandhāra (Figure 3.1) for a visual rendition of many of the features also found in the texts: Māyā gives birth standing up and with no pain whatsoever, her body arranged in a graceful pose. Directly above her stands a bountiful and auspicious tree, and when she reaches up to take a hold of one of its branches, the branch magically bends down to support her. Immediately to Māyā's right, we can see that the baby is received on a soft cloth by deities (rather than falling onto the ground like a worm). Although he is perfectly clean, "two showers of water fall down from the sky—one cool and one warm—to bathe the bodhisattva."[27] The earth quakes again; more miracles occur; gods and supernatural beings shower flowers down from the sky and play heavenly musical instruments (represented in Figure 3.1 by the two figures at the top of the scene).

Most significantly, the Bodhisattva does not emerge from his mother's vagina; instead, as charmingly illustrated in Figure 3.1, "mindful and deliberate, the bodhisattva, without injuring his mother, appears from her right side."[28] This ensures not only that the Bodhisattva can avoid the impurity of the mother's vagina—and the association with sexuality that the vagina immediately calls to mind—but also that he is spared from the harrowing and painful passage down the vaginal canal, and is thus born with full knowledge, memory, and awareness (rather than as a stupefied child). Māyā's body, moreover, is "uninjured and unscarred," her womb is "unobstructed and whole,"[29] there are no unpleasant bodily fluids, and her side is not rent by the Bodhisattva passing through: "When she gives birth to the most excellent of men, why does the side of the Conqueror's mother not split open, and why does she have no pain? Because Tathāgatas appear in a form that is made of mind; thus, her side does not split open, nor does she have any pain."[30]

Nevertheless, she does die seven days later—again, a rule for all buddhas' mothers—*not* because of giving birth, but rather, because "it would not be appropriate for one who has carried an excellent [being] like [him] to engage in sexual intercourse later on."[31] Her womb, in fact, is compared to a sacred shrine containing relics that cannot later be corrupted by the ordinary, polluting processes of sex, pregnancy, and giving birth. In short, Māyā performs her birth-giving function in a highly idealized manner, and then quickly exits the scene. Even the name Māyā itself—which means "illusion"—suggests a near-erasure of any real biological mother.[32]

This highly idealized depiction of a purified birth-giving mother is matched by that of her precocious newborn son—for immediately upon being born, the Bodhisattva is fully conscious and aware. He stands firmly on his own two feet, without any assistance; takes seven steps (sometimes in one direction, sometimes in all four), with lotus flowers magically blossoming under his feet at each step; and makes his famous proclamation: "For awakening I am born, for the welfare of the world! This is the last coming-into-existence for me!"[33] Far from being a helpless, screaming newborn roughly manhandled by the midwife, the Bodhisattva is born awake and capable, with perfect knowledge, clarity, and insight. In this way, the birth of the future Buddha illustrates a stark and point-by-point opposition to all the associations of filth, impurity, pain, and suffering that ordinarily surround the reproductive bodies of women and the processes of conception, gestation, and birth.

Beyond Mother and Son

I turn my attention now to a second way of solving the problem posed by the Buddha's birth, which is to depict the birth as something that utterly transcends the mother–son dyad and ultimately reflects and encompasses *everything*. I have in mind here something like the famous Buddhist metaphor of Indra's Net (*indrajāla*), as depicted in the Mahāyāna *Avataṃsaka Sūtra* and later Chinese Huayan texts. The metaphor of Indra's Net has been summarized as follows:

> [A]bove the palace of Indra, the king of the gods, is spread an infinitely vast, bejeweled net. At each of the infinite numbers of knots in the net is tied a jewel that itself has an infinite number of facets. A person looking at any single one of the jewels on this net would thus see reflected in its infinite facets not only everything in the cosmos but also an infinite number of other jewels, themselves also reflecting everything in the cosmos; thus, every jewel in this vast net is simultaneously reflecting, and being reflected by, an infinite number of other jewels.[34]

The Buddha's birth is like a jewel in Indra's Net: only with blinders on can we see it as merely a single jewel, rather than as an endless mirror that reflects, replicates, and illuminates every other jewel in the net simultaneously. Or, perhaps another way of conveying this idea is through John Strong's insightful description of Buddhist stories as "belvedere phenomena"—that is, phenomena that are not only beautiful in and of themselves, but also perfectly sited to "enable one to see a whole surrounding countryside, in all its various aspects," taking time to enjoy the view.[35] The Buddha's birth is such a belvedere, using a presumed focus upon mother and son to allow for an expansive view that ultimately encompasses the entire universe. Numerous details involved in the birth narrative have the effect of decentering a single mother–son pair and diffusing our focus outward in all directions, until it vanishes into empty space.

Let me begin with the category of *time* and the placement of the birth into cosmic rather than historical time. Whereas ordinary conception and birth are highly unpredictable and somewhat random in terms of their timing (subject to the vagaries of innumerable causes and conditions), the Buddha's birth exhibits an extreme *regularity* in its timing and is bound within several intricate and interlocking networks of time. First, as a deity in the Tuṣita Heaven, the Bodhisattva *chooses* the proper time to be born, based upon the waxing and waning lifespans of human beings as each cosmic eon proceeds. As a rule, bodhisattvas do not enter their final rebirth near the beginning of a cosmic eon, when the human lifespan exceeds 80,000 years—"for at such a time, beings do not recognize birth, old age, and death,"[36] which makes it impossible for them to comprehend the Dharma. Likewise, bodhisattvas also do not enter their final rebirth near the end of a cosmic eon, when the human lifespan is below 100 years—"for at such a time, beings are excessive in the afflictions,"[37] which again renders them unsavable. Thus, a bodhisattva takes his final rebirth when the human lifespan is below 80,000 years but above 100 years, with the Buddha Śākyamuni choosing to take his final birth at the lowest end of this spectrum, when the human lifespan is roughly 100 years. Buddhahood cannot appear at just any time; it must be in tune with the overall rhythm of the cosmos and the waxing and waning fortunes of the human race.

The cosmos itself seems to be aware of this timing, for there are said to be three "tumultuous uproars"[38] made by deities that regularly take place in the universe: one occurs one hundred thousand years before the dawn of a new cosmic eon; a second occurs one thousand years before the appearance of a buddha; and a third occurs one hundred years before the appearance of a Universal Emperor. Thus, exactly one thousand years before the future Buddha is born, the four World Guardian deities wander around the universe and proclaim: "Listen up, People! One thousand years from now, a buddha will appear in the world!"[39] The world is thus *ready* for the birth to occur. The Bodhisattva lives out "his entire natural lifespan"[40] of four thousand years as a deity in the Tuṣita Heaven—he does not die prematurely—and then announces, twelve years ahead of time, his impending descent into the human realm.[41] He chooses a mother whose remaining lifespan is exactly ten lunar months and seven days, and his conception occurs when the stars and the planets are properly aligned—"just at the right moment, on the fifteenth day of the month, when the moon is full and in conjunction with the constellation Puṣya."[42] The pregnancy lasts for exactly ten months; the moment of birth is again aligned with the stars, taking place "under the asterism of Visākha";[43] and the mother dies seven days later—this is the rule. Thus, in stark contrast to the accidental timing of ordinary pregnancy and birth, the birth of the future Buddha must occur within multiple constraints relating to the cosmic march of time, space, stars, and planets. In this way, it transcends the profane realm of mere history to become something mythic and universal.

But as regular and rule-bound as the moment of birth may be, it is far from being just a single moment, for it also refracts both backward and forward in time—backward to invoke the eons-long bodhisattva career that precedes it, and forward to foreshadow the entirety of the Buddha's final life. The long bodhisattva career preceding the birth is invoked in several clever ways throughout the process of birth itself. As we already saw in Naomi Appleton's chapter (Chapter 2), the newborn Bodhisattva's proclamation upon being born, for example, has its echoes in the distant past—"for in three different lifetimes did the bodhisattva utter a proclamation as soon as he emerged from his mother's womb: in his lifetime as Mahosadha, in his lifetime as Vessantara, and in this lifetime, as well."[44] This pattern of repeated newborn proclamations, invoking two of the major jātakas (previous life stories of the Buddha), has the effect of recalling the bodhisattva career as a whole.[45] Similarly, the various miracles that occur at the moment of the future Buddha's conception are sometimes described as the karmic result of specific deeds he performed in his previous lives. Why, at the moment of conception, did divine flowers shower down from the sky? Because, as a bodhisattva, he repeatedly "gave away gifts and precious sons and daughters."[46] Why did the realm of hungry ghosts suddenly gain access to food and drink? Because, as a bodhisattva (specifically, in his lifetime as King Śibi), he "weighed out his own flesh and gave it away on behalf of a cherished bird."[47] Why did the newborn baby's body bear the thirty-two distinctive marks of a Great Man (*mahāpuruṣa*)? Because each mark is the karmic result of a specific type of meritorious deed performed in his previous lives.[48] Thus, the elements of the birth are not singular, one-time events; instead, they are reflections of the entire bodhisattva path that leads up to the final life.

Even more than invoking events in the past, the moment of birth also looks forward in time to foreshadow the whole of the Buddha's final life; the final life, in fact, seems to be *predestined* by the birth itself. One major way this is done is through the tradition of the "conatals" (*sahajāta*), or those beings and entities that come into existence at *exactly the same moment* as the future Buddha's birth, most of which are destined to play important roles later on in his life. Often, there is a standard set of seven such conatals, which are clearly meant as a parallel to the seven "treasures" of a Universal Emperor (*cakravartin*):

> At the very same time as our bodhisattva was born in the Lumbinī Grove, the queen (Rāhula's mother), the elder Ānanda, the minister Channa, the minister Kāḷudāyī, the king of horses Kanthaka, the great Bodhi tree, and the four vases of treasure also came into existence . . . These seven are called the co-natals.[49]

In brief, the queen—"Rāhula's mother"—is the woman who will become the Bodhisattva's wife; Channa (in Sanskrit, Chandaka) is the attendant who will help him renounce the world; Kanthaka is the horse on which he will escape from the palace; the Bodhi tree is the tree underneath which he will attain awakening to become the Buddha; Kāḷudāyī is a royal minister who will bring about a reconciliation between the Buddha and the family he has abandoned; Ānanda is the Buddha's cousin and faithful monastic attendant; and, finally, the four vases of treasure are a general symbol of the auspiciousness that will characterize both his worldly and his spiritual endeavors.[50] The moment of the Buddha's birth thus simultaneously gives rise to crucial players in his household life as a married prince, his Great Renunciation, his attainment of buddhahood, and his monastic career—in short, crucial players in the whole of his final life. In some cases, the number of conatals is multiplied by making each of these figures (Rāhula's mother, Chandaka, etc.) merely the foremost of a group of hundreds or thousands of similar figures—all born at the same time—thus providing the newborn Bodhisattva with an entire human community to await his dispensation in the future.[51] Even the surrounding political environment that will impact the Buddha's future career as a teacher is put into place at his birth, for in one text the conatals also include four important future kings: King Prasenajit of Śrāvastī, King Bimbisāra of Rājagṛha, King Udayana of Kauśāṃbī, and King Pradyota of Ujjayanī—all of whom are said to be born at this very moment "by the power of the bodhisattva" alone.[52] It is as if an entire *world* or *environment* dedicated to furthering the Buddha's dispensation springs up into existence at the very moment of his birth.

The conatals are far from being the birth-story's only invocation of future events, however. Sometimes, each miracle that occurs upon the Bodhisattva's birth is described as being a foreshadowing of one of the spiritual qualities to be attained by the Buddha later in his life. Thus, the light that spreads throughout the universe at the moment of birth is "one of the signs of [the] Buddha's future conquest over the powers of darkness and sin."[53] The seven steps he takes as a newborn baby are a foreshadowing of the seven "limbs of awakening" (*bodhyaṅga*) he will attain under the Bodhi tree. His proclamation at the moment of birth—"Now then I have arrived at my last birth; no more shall I enter into the womb to be born; now shall I accomplish the end of my being, and become [a] Buddha"—will reach its fulfillment in a parallel proclamation he makes upon becoming a buddha—"Now I have finished my births; I have completed my course; I have done all that I had to do; there is no further form of life for me to assume."[54] His surveying of the four quarters of the universe stands for the "four fearlessnesses" (*vaiṣāradya*) he will later attain as a buddha. The two streams of water that fall from the sky to bathe him stand for the meditative powers of calm (*śamatha*) and insight (*vipaśyana*) he will later master as an ascetic. The golden seat brought by deities for the baby to sit upon foreshadows the lotus throne he will occupy as a buddha. The trees and flowers bursting into bloom stand for the blooming faith his later disciples will experience when they first hear the Dharma.[55] And so on. And so on.

Once again, the stars and planets are sometimes involved in such foreshadowing—for just as the constellation of Uttarāsāḷha reigned over his conception in his mother's womb, it will similarly reign over his Great Departure, his First Sermon, and his famous "Twin Miracle" at Śrāvastī; likewise, just as the constellation of Visākha reigned over the moment of his birth, it will similarly reign over his attainment of buddhahood and the moment of his death or *parinirvāṇa*.[56] Even mundane human relations are used to point forward toward future events: Of the eight soothsaying brahmins who interpret the thirty-two marks on the body of the newborn Bodhisattva, one of them, together with the sons of four more, will later become the first five disciples to hear the Dharma from the newly awakened Buddha (in Pāli, the so-called *pañcavaggiya* or "Group of Five").[57] Thus, each element of the birth-narrative is precisely positioned within the cosmic network of time, as well as pointing both backward into the past and forward into the future, reflecting in all directions—like a jewel in Indra's Net.

What is true for the category of *time*, moreover, is equally true for the category of *space*. The birth may occur in a single, small location—the beautifully blooming Lumbinī Grove, on the road between Kapilavastu and Devadaha—but it reverberates both vertically and horizontally to encompass the whole of space. In vertical terms, the birth narrative is marked by a consistent emphasis on movement both upward and downward, traversing the vertical levels of the universe. Deities move *downward* from the heavens to enter the human realm, for when the Bodhisattva departs from the Tuṣita Heaven to take his place in Māyā's womb, "thousands of deities accompanied him and were reborn in the sixteen great provinces of Jambudvīpa, in the great householding families of Brahmins, Kshatriyas, and merchants"[58] down on earth. Likewise, humans move *upward* from the surface of the earth: Five hundred *pratyekabuddhas* rise up into the sky and attain final *nirvāṇa* to make way for the appearance of a buddha;[59] meanwhile, Queen Māyā dreams of rising up into the sky and climbing a great mountain peak,[60] or she dreams that deities come down from the heavens and transport her up into the Himalayan mountains and bathe her with celestial waters "to remove her human imperfections."[61] Thus, gods descend to become humans, and humans seem to rise like gods. Upon the baby's birth, water magically bubbles *upward* from the ground for Māyā to perform her ritual ablutions, and similarly streams *downward* from the heavens to bathe the newborn child.[62] We are even provided with a cosmic *axis mundi* image, for "on the very night that the bodhisattva descended into his mother's womb, a lotus flower rose upward for sixty-eight million yojanas, beginning from the subterranean waters, cleaving through the great earth, and extending upward to the world of Brahmā"[63]—bearing a drop of nectar that would sustain the Bodhisattva throughout his entire gestation, as if he were drinking the universe itself. The effects of the birth similarly reverberate through each of the hierarchically arranged realms of rebirth—for upon the Bodhisattva's conception:

> Fire in all the hells was extinguished. Hunger and thirst in the realm of hungry ghosts were appeased. Animals lost their fear. Disease vanished among all sentient beings. All sentient beings became happy. Horses neighed and elephants trumpeted sweetly. All musical instruments played themselves, without being struck. Among human beings, bracelets and other jewelry rattled. All the directions became clear.[64]

The birth reverberates both upward and downward, traversing a cosmic ladder that extends throughout the universe.

In horizontal terms, as well, the birth narrative displays a consistent emphasis on depicting the birth as an event that extends *outward* in all directions of space. One way this is done is through repeated invocations of the four cardinal directions—north, south, east, and west—which, when taken together, are a convenient way to indicate absolute horizontal omnipresence. Thus, as soon as the Bodhisattva is conceived, the four World Guardian (*lokapāla*) deities who preside over the four directions of space immediately come to stand guard over the Bodhisattva and his mother.[65] During the pregnancy, Māyā experiences a pregnancy craving (*dohada*) to "drink water from the four great oceans" that lie in the north, south, east, and west.[66] Once the Bodhisattva is born, he surveys all four quarters of the universe, sees that there is nobody equal to him anywhere, and makes his famous proclamation. In some texts, in fact, he takes his famous seven steps not only in one direction, but in all four, with a proclamation whose wording is directly tied to each specific direction:

> This is the eastern (*pūrva*) direction, and I will be foremost (*pūrvaṃgama*) in attaining Nirvana! This is the southern (*dakṣiṇa*) direction, and I will be worthy of veneration (*dakṣiṇīya*) by the entire world! This is the western (*paścima*) direction, and this will be my final (*paścima*) birth! This is the northern (*uttara*) direction, and I will rescue (*uttariṣyāmi*) beings from the round of Samsara![67]

These repeated invocations of the four cardinal directions—sometimes expanded to ten directions through the addition of the four intermediate directions, upward, and downward[68]—effectively suggest that the Buddha's birth is an event of *omnipresence.*

An alternative way of suggesting omnipresence is also employed, and that is by depicting a force or a phenomenon that is truly capable of extending *everywhere,* seeping in through every tiny little gap or crack. Here, virtually all of the biographical sources are in agreement on two standard miracles that characterize both the moment of conception and the moment of birth. One is a tremendous *earthquake* that shakes the entire universe down to its very foundations: "As soon as the bodhisattva descended [into his mother's womb]," we are told, "this great earth trembled, shook, and quaked violently six times, and this earthquake was thrilling, delightful, joyful, appealing, agreeable, pleasing, attractive, enchanting, graceful, calming, and not frightening—for as the earth quaked, it did not harm any life, whether animal or plant."[69] Despite not hurting a single living thing, this is an earthquake that extends to *everywhere,* leaving nothing unmoved or unshaken.

The second image used is that of *light*—not just any light, but a cosmic, blazing radiance that extends in all directions and illuminates the entire universe. At both the moment of conception and again at the moment of birth:

> The entire world explodes with a blazing light. Even those blindingly dark and gloomy places that exist in the intermediate spaces between the worlds, and that do not shine with light in spite of the great power and strength of the sun and the moon—at that time, even those spaces explode with a blazing light.[70]

In fact, the unfortunate beings who exist in these dark and gloomy interstices, who normally "cannot even see their own arm extended [in front of them],"[71] suddenly become aware of each other's presence and greet each other cheerfully. Both the image of the *earthquake* and the image of radiant *light* effectively disperse the singular event of the birth until it permeates the entire cosmos.

The earth trembles, rumbles, and quakes. Light spreads outward in all directions, turning around corners and seeping into tiny cracks. Time itself is extended, stretching backward into the past and forward into the future. Gods and supernatural beings of all types enact a cosmic display of heavenly flowers, perfumes, and music, while animals stop preying upon one another, hell-beings are relieved of their suffering, and women's bracelets rattle of their own accord. The Buddha's birth may seem like a singular event that takes place in one specific time and place, but its true nature is timeless and omnipresent, blanketing the planet, the stars, and the galaxy that lies beyond. Far from involving just a single individual, moreover, the birth is an eminently collective and communal event.

At this point, we have moved very far indeed from the image of a single pregnant female body giving birth to a screaming newborn child.

The Many Jewels of Indra's Net

If the Buddha's birth can be usefully compared to a jewel in Indra's Net, then it is also worth remembering that the net contains not merely a single jewel, but an infinite number of similar jewels, each one perfectly reflecting the images of all the others, in an endless, cosmic, funhouse mirror. In other words, Śākyamuni Buddha is not the only buddha: There were infinite buddhas in the past, there will be infinite buddhas in the future, and—at least in the Mahāyāna tradition—there are infinite buddhas existing in the present, in innumerable worlds throughout space. Each one of these buddhas is "born"—and each birth is a perfect reflection of all others. Thus, the birth of "our" Buddha is not unique; instead, it follows the basic pattern marking the births of *all* buddhas without exception. The contributors to this volume are indebted to John Strong's insight that there is "a biographical paradigm, a Buddha-life blueprint" that all buddhas follow and that is constitutive of buddhahood itself.[72] The birth is a crucial element of this "Buddha-life blueprint," and this constitutes yet another way in which the

Buddha Śākyamuni's birth is decentered as a particular, human, historical event, and recast as a universal, cosmic pattern.

One major way this is done is through the constant repetition of the phrase *dharmatā khalu* (in Sanskrit), which might be translated as: "Now, it is the rule that . . ." Through repetitive invocations of this phrase (or its variants), each element of the birth-narrative, rather than being unique to the Buddha Śākyamuni alone, becomes an ironclad *rule* necessarily followed by all buddhas without exception. Perhaps the earliest instance of this pattern can be seen in the *Mahāpadāna Sutta* of the Theravāda Pāli Canon, which recounts the birth-story not of the Buddha Śākyamuni, but rather, of the previous Buddha Vipassī. In the course of narrating Vipassī's birth, the text relates fifteen different features of the birth, beginning each feature with—"It is the rule that . . ." (*dhammatā esā*)—and ending each feature with—"That is the rule" (*ayam ettha dhammatā*).[73] Thus, "it is the rule" for all buddhas that: light fills the cosmos when they are conceived; the earth quakes; the four World Guardian deities protect the Bodhisattva and his mother; his mother remains pure throughout the pregnancy; she is pregnant for exactly ten months; she gives birth standing up; the newborn is received first by deities; he is cleansed by two streams of water from the sky; and this cycle continues. These are not merely events that *happened;* instead, they are *rules* that the universe is compelled to follow, over and over again. We are told that they happened in the case of the previous buddha, Vipassī, but we *know* that they also happened in the case of "our" Buddha, Śākyamuni, and that they *will* happen in the case of the future buddha Maitreya—and every buddha yet to come. In this sense, the birth of any buddha is transformed from a singular, random event into a regular rhythm of the cosmos—a cosmic pulsation that repeatedly rocks the universe and will do so for all eternity. Though the use of *dharmatā khalu* (or its equivalents) is perhaps particularly characteristic of the *Mahāpadāna Sutta,* it is widely scattered throughout other Buddha-biographies, as well. In fact, it is difficult to point to any single feature of the Buddha Śākyamuni's birth and say definitively that it was true of *his birth alone*.

A similar, but slightly different, strategy is found in the *Acchariyabbhuta Sutta* (also from the Theravāda Pāli Canon),[74] which systematically enumerates all of the "wonderful and marvelous qualities" (*acchariya-abbhuta-dhamma*) of the Buddha's birth—with the suggestion that such "wonderful and marvelous qualities" characterize the births of *all* buddhas and are thus destined to repeat themselves in an endless, cosmic loop. Finally, a third strategy of universalizing the Buddha's birth takes the form of a set list of deeds that every buddha must perform in the course of his final existence. In the Pāli commentarial tradition, for example, there is a standard list of thirty such deeds, the first five of which pertain to the manner of a buddha's birth:

> Now we will explain those features that are common to all buddhas. There are thirty features altogether that are common to all buddhas—namely: (1) a bodhisattva in his final existence enters his mother's womb mindfully; (2) he sits in his mother's womb cross-legged and facing outward; (3) the bodhisattva's mother gives birth standing up; (4) he emerges from his mother's womb only in a grove; (5) he stands on a golden cloth, faces the north, takes seven steps, surveys the four directions, and roars the lion's roar [etc.].[75]

In a Mahāyāna tradition that was later to have much influence in Tibet, on the other hand, there is a standard list of "twelve deeds of a buddha" (*dvadaśa-buddha-kārya*) performed by the "emanation body" (*nirmāṇa-kāya*) of every buddha—of which the first three deeds are (1) descending from Tuṣita Heaven, (2) entering his mother's womb, and (3) being born in the Lumbinī Grove.[76] Such lists—constituting the "Buddha-life blueprint"—have the effect of further generalizing the Buddha's birth, transforming it from a singular, biological event into a universal, cosmic, and rule-bound pattern—a jewel in Indra's net, perfectly reflecting all other jewels.

This tendency to erase the human particularity of Śākyamuni Buddha by immersing him into an endless ocean of identical buddhas can be further highlighted by briefly looking at a text in which it seems to reach its absolute culmination—the *Gaṇḍavyūha Sūtra*,[77] a Mahāyāna sūtra that takes place in a magical and ephemeral landscape with no real connection to historical time or space. Here, we are told that everything existing in all universes was reflected within Māyā's single abdomen; the complete vision of the Bodhisattva's eons-long bodhisattva career was reflected within every one of Māyā's pores; and Māyā gave birth not only to this bodhisattva, but to "bodhisattvas equal in number to the atoms and dust-particles in inexpressible tens of hundreds of thousands of millions of billions of buddha-fields."[78] As Māyā herself explains, "My body rose above all worlds, and my womb became as vast as the realm of space, yet it did not exceed a normal human size."[79] Billions of bodhisattvas and buddhas inhabited her womb simultaneously, and "all of them walked around with strides as big as three thousand world-systems, with strides as big as world-systems equal in number to the atoms and dust-particles in an inexpressible number of buddha-fields . . . and yet, even receiving so many multitudes, my womb did not grow any larger, nor did my body become any different from a regular human body."[80] Though we may identify Māyā as the mother of Śākyamuni, specifically, she will, in fact, be the mother "of all the Tathāgata Arhat Saṃyaksambuddhas of this eon . . . within this million-billion-fold world-system . . . [and] for millions of eons in the future, in all Jambudvīpas in all world-systems . . . throughout this entire ocean of world-systems."[81]

With this cosmic, phantasmagorical vision of the Buddha's nativity, the problem with which we began—the problem posed by attributing to the Buddha *a human birth*—seems to shimmer for a moment, like an illusion, before dissipating into empty space.

The Impossibility of the Buddha's Birth

I cannot help but wonder, however, whether the problem has really been solved. Once the mother, the son, and the process of birth itself have been made into something that is utterly *unlike* any ordinary form of birth giving, and once the birth has been turned into a cosmic event that extends to the outer reaches of the universe, do we still have a buddha who is *human,* and who illustrates the *human problem of suffering* for which Buddhism aims to provide an answer? Does the story still speak to the man wracked by illness or the mother who has lost a child? Does an ordinary, average human still believe that they, too, can do what the Buddha did? Or, has the Buddha been transmogrified to such an extent that his human relatability is diminished and even erased?

The *Lalitavistara*—which, as we saw, was so eloquent in posing the fundamental problem—finally seems to doubt whether the solution really works. For just after relating the many miraculous features of the Buddha's birth, it has the Buddha issue a dire warning about the future:

> Ānanda, in the future, there will be certain monks who are uncultivated in body, uncultivated in mind, uncultivated in moral discipline, uncultivated in wisdom, foolish, ignorant, conceited, arrogant, stuck-up, unrestrained, with scattered thoughts, full of doubt, full of uncertainty, unfaithful, a stain among the *śramaṇas,* charlatans among the *śramaṇas!* They will not believe that the bodhisattva's descent into the womb was pure in this way. They will gather together privately and say amongst themselves: "Look, the bodhisattva entered his mother's womb and mingled with feces, urine, and bodily fluids. This is undignified! What kind of superhuman power is this? And people *say* that he emerged from his mother's right side unsmeared by the filth of the womb—how is that possible?"[82]

The text thus seems to recognize a potential conflict between the Buddha's basic humanity and the miraculous nature of his birth: How can both be true simultaneously?

Nevertheless—the text goes on to assure us—such a conflict exists in the minds of evil and foolish monks alone. The problem with these monks, the Buddha says, is their ignorant assumption of the fundamental *legibility* of the figure known as the Buddha. "It does not even occur to those foolish men"—the Buddha notes—"that this being is inconceivable, that he cannot be measured by them!"[83] Ultimately, then, it is clear what stance we *ought* to take when we consider the birth of the Buddha from the womb of a human woman: "Ānanda," the Buddha implores, "do not measure the Tathāgata! Why not? Ānanda, the Tathāgata is immeasurable, profound, expansive, and impossible to fathom!!"[84]

Notes

1. As stated in the *Dhammacakkappavattana Sutta* (Bhikkhu Bodhi, trans., *The Connected Discourses of the Buddha: A New Translation of the Saṃyutta Nikāya,* 2 vols. [Somerville, MA: Wisdom Publications, 2000], ii, 1844).
2. Amy Paris Langenberg, *Birth in Buddhism: The Suffering Fetus and Female Freedom* (London: Routledge Press, 2017), 33.
3. P. L. Vaidya, ed., *Lalitavistara*, Buddhist Sanskrit Texts, No. 1 (Darbhanga: Mithila Institute, 1958), 64.
4. Vaidya, *Lalitavistara,* 47.
5. Michael Radich, *The Mahāparinirvāṇa-mahāsūtra and the Emergence of Tathāgatagarbha Dotrine*, Hamburg Buddhist Studies, No. 5 (Hamburg: Hamburg University Press, 2015), 143.
6. See the following: Reiko Ohnuma, *Ties That Bind: Maternal Imagery and Discourse in Indian Buddhism* (Oxford: Oxford University Press, 2012), 66–85 (from which portions of the discussion below have been drawn); Vanessa R. Sasson, "A Womb with a View: The Buddha's Final Fetal Experience," in *Imagining the Fetus: The Unborn in Myth, Religion, and Culture*, ed. Vanessa R. Sasson and Jane Marie Law, American Academy of Religion Cultural Criticism Series (Oxford: Oxford University Press, 2009), 55–72; Langenberg, *Birth in Buddhism,* 96–106; Radich, *Mahāparinirvāṇa-mahāsūtra,* 105–157; and Minoru Hara, "A Note on the Buddha's Birth Story," in *Indianisme et bouddhisme: mélanges offerts à Mgr Étienne Lamotte* (Louvain-la-Neuve: Université Catholique de Louvain, Institut Orientaliste, 1980), 143–157.
7. Here, it is instructive to compare the episode of the Buddha's birth to the episode of his death or *parinirvāṇa,* which has quite a different tone. See Maria Heim's chapter (Chapter 8) in this volume.
8. Unless otherwise noted, all translations from Pāli and Sanskrit are my own. All of these texts can be dated from the third century BCE to the sixth century CE and constitute some of the most well-known and widespread biographies of the Buddha from South Asia. The *Mahāpadāna Sutta* is No. 14 in the *Dīgha Nikāya* collection of the *Sutta Piṭaka* of the Theravāda canon in Pāli; English translation in Maurice Walshe, *The Long Discourses of the Buddha: A Translation of the Dīgha Nikāya* (Boston: Wisdom Publications, 1987), 199–221. The *Acchariyabbhuta Sutta* is No. 123 in the *Majjhima Nikāya* collection of the *Sutta Piṭaka* of the Theravāda canon in Pāli; English translation in Bhikkhu Ñāṇamoli, *The Middle Length Discourses of the*

Buddha: A New Translation of the Majjhima Nikāya (Boston: Wisdom Publications, 1995), 979–984. The *Nidānakathā* is the introduction to the *Jātakaṭṭhakathā*, Buddhaghosa's commentary on the *Jātaka*, the tenth text in the *Khuddaka Nikāya* collection of the *Sutta Piṭaka* of the Theravāda canon in Pāli; English translation in N. Jayawickrama, *The Story of Gotama Buddha (Jātaka-nidāna)* (Oxford: Pali Text Society, 1990). The *Buddhacarita* is a poetic biography of the Buddha composed in courtly Sanskrit by Aśvaghoṣa; English translation in Patrick Olivelle, *Life of the Buddha by Aśvaghoṣa*, Clay Sanskrit Library (New York: New York University Press and JJC Foundation, 2008). The *Mahāvastu* is an extensive biography of the Buddha from the Lokottaravāda school of early Buddhism, composed in Buddhist Hybrid Sanskrit; English translation in J. J. Jones, *The Mahāvastu*, 3 vols., Sacred Books of the Buddhists, Nos. 16, 18, and 19 (London: Routledge & Kegan Paul, [1949–1956] 1973–1978). The *Lalitavistara* is a Mahāyāna biography of the Buddha composed in Sanskrit; English translation in Gwendolyn Bays, *The Voice of the Buddha: The Beauty of Compassion (Lalitavistara)*, 2 vols. (Berkeley: Dharma Publishing, 1983). The *Saṅghabhedavastu* is one of the portions of the *Mūlasarvāstivāda Vinaya* still extant in Sanskrit (no full English translation available). Finally, the *Abhiniṣkramana Sūtra* (*Fo benxing ji jing*, T190) is a Chinese translation of a Sanskrit biography of the Buddha (no longer extant in Sanskrit); English translation in Samuel Beal, *The Romantic Legend of Śākya Buddha: A Translation of the Chinese Version of the Abhiniṣkramaṇasūtra* (Delhi: Motilal Banarsidass, [1875] 1985).

9. A. K. Ramanujan, "Three Hundred Rāmāyaṇas: Five Examples and Three Thoughts on Translation," in *Many Rāmāyaṇas: The Diversity of a Narrative Tradition in South Asia*, ed. Paula Richman (Berkeley: University of California Press, 1991), 46.
10. See Hara, "Note on the Buddha's Birth Story," which gathers together some typical passages on both *garbha-duḥkha* and *janma-duḥkha*. See also Langenberg, *Birth in Buddhism*, 65–69; and Robert Kritzer, "Life in the Womb: Conception and Gestation in Buddhist Scripture and Classical Indian Medical Literature," in *Imagining the Fetus: The Unborn in Myth, Religion, and Culture*, ed. Vanessa R. Sasson and Jane Marie Law, American Academy of Religion Cultural Criticism Series (Oxford and New York: Oxford University Press, 2009), 73–89.
11. C. A. F. Rhys Davids, ed., *The Visuddhi-magga of Buddhaghosa*, 2 vols. (London: Pali Text Society, 1920-21), ii, 500.
12. From the *Viṣṇu Purāṇa*, cited in Hara, "Note on the Buddha's Birth Story," 149.
13. This passage comes from Kauṇḍinya's *Pañcārthabhāṣya*, a commentary on the *Pāsupatasūtra*, as cited in Hara, "Note on the Buddha's Birth Story," 148. Here, it should be noted that traditional sources routinely assume a male fetus.
14. Langenberg, *Birth in Buddhism*, 39 (paraphrasing a passage from the *Garbhāvakrānti Sūtra*).
15. Langenberg, *Birth in Buddhism*, 33.
16. Translated in Langenberg, *Birth in Buddhism*, 38.
17. Pāli *sato sampajāno* (Vilhelm Trenckner, ed., *The Majjhima Nikāya*, 4 vols. [London: Pali Text Society, 1888–1925], iii, 118–124). This phrase is used repeatedly throughout the *Acchariyabbhuta Sutta* (*Majjhima Nikāya* No. 123) to emphasize the

conscious and deliberate manner in which the Bodhisattva behaves throughout the entire birth-taking process.

18. Skt. *apagatamātṛgrāmadoṣāyāḥ* (Vaidya, *Lalitavistara*, 17).
19. Vaidya, *Lalitavistara*, 20.
20. Émile Senart, ed., *Mahāvastu avadānaṃ. Le Mahāvastu: Texte sanscrit publié pour la première fois et accompagné d'introductions et d'un commentaire*, 3 vols. (Paris: Société Asiatique, 1882–1897), i, 145.
21. Pāli *sabbaṅgapaccaṅgiṃ ahīnindriyaṃ* (*Mahāpadāna Sutta, Dīgha Nikāya* No. 14) (T. W. Rhys Davids and William Stede, eds., *The Dīgha Nikāya*, 3 vols. [London: Pali Text Society, 1890–1911], ii, 13).
22. *Mahāpadāna Sutta* (*Dīgha Nikāya* No. 14) (Rhys Davids and Stede, *Dīgha Nikāya*, ii, 13).
23. Raniero Gnoli, ed., *The Gilgit Manuscript of the Saṅghabhedavastu, Being the 17th and Last Section of the Vinaya of the Mūlasarvāstivādin*, Serie Orientale Roma, Vol. XLIX, 1 (Rome: Istituto per il Medio ed Estremo Oriente, 1977), 42.
24. Senart, *Mahāvastu avadānam*, ii, 16.
25. Skt. *ratnavyūha* (Vaidya, *Lalitavistara*, 47).
26. Gnoli, *Gilgit Manuscript of the Saṅghabhedavastu*, 43.
27. Gnoli, *Gilgit Manuscript of the Saṅghabhedavastu*, 45.
28. Senart, *Mahāvastu avadānam*, ii, 20.
29. Senart, *Mahāvastu avadānam*, ii, 23.
30. Senart, *Mahāvastu avadānam*, ii, 20.
31. Senart, *Mahāvastu avadānam*, ii, 3.
32. For a discussion of this point, see Gananath Obeyesekere, "The Goddess Pattini and the Lord Buddha: Notes on the Myth of the Birth of the Deity," *Social Compass* 20, no. 2 (1973): 226.
33. E. H. Johnston, ed. and trans., *The Buddhacarita or Acts of the Buddha, by Aśvaghoṣa*, new enlarged ed. (Delhi: Motilal Banarsidass, [1936] 1984), pt. 1: 2, v. 1.15.
34. Robert E. Buswell, Jr., and Donald S. Lopez, Jr., eds., *The Princeton Dictionary of Buddhism* (Princeton, NJ: Princeton University Press, 2013), 372–373 (*s.v.*, Indrajāla).
35. John Strong, *The Legend and Cult of Upagupta: Sanskrit Buddhism in North India and Southeast Asia* (Princeton, NJ: Princeton University Press, 1992), xii.
36. *Nidānakathā* (V. Fausboll, ed., *The Jātaka Together with Its Commentary, Being Tales of the Anterior Births of Gotama Buddha*, 6 vols. and Index [London: Trübner, 1875–97], i, 48).
37. *Nidānakathā* (Fausboll, *Jātaka Together with Its Commentary*, i, 48).
38. Pāli *halāhala* (*Nidānakathā*) (Fausboll, *Jātaka Together with Its Commentary*, i, 47).
39. *Nidānakathā* (Fausboll, *Jātaka Together with Its Commentary*, i, 48).
40. Pāli *yāvatāyukaṃ* (*Accariyabbhuta Sutta, Majjhima Nikāya* No. 123) (Trenckner, *Majjhima Nikāya*, iii, 120).
41. Vaidya, *Lalitavistara*, 11.
42. Vaidya, *Lalitavistara*, 43.
43. From the *Madhuratthavilāsinī*, commentary on the *Buddhavaṃsa* (I. B. Horner, trans., *The Clarifier of the Sweet Meaning [Madhuratthavilāsinī], Commentary on*

the Chronicle of Buddhas [Buddhavaṃsa] by Buddhadatta Thera [London: Pali Text Society, 1978], 429).

44. *Nidānakathā* (Fausboll, *Jātaka Together with Its Commentary*, i, 53).
45. In the Pāli *Jātakatthavaṇṇanā* collection, the Bodhisattva's previous life story as Prince Mahosadha is told in *Jātaka* No. 546 (*Mahā Ummagga Jātaka*), and his previous life story as Prince Vessantara is told in *Jātaka* No. 547 (*Vessantara Jātaka*). Both stories belong to a special group of ten *jātakas* (collectively referred to as the *Mahānipāta*), which are not only the final ten *jātakas* in the Pāli collection, but also understood to be the final ten lives of the Bodhisattva career, and the ten lives in which the Bodhisattva fulfilled each of the ten moral virtues or "perfections" (*pāramitā*) that are required for the attainment of buddhahood. For a translation and study of this special group of ten *jātakas*, see Naomi Appleton and Sarah Shaw, trans., *The Ten Great Birth Stories of the Buddha: The Mahānipāta of the Jātakatthavaṇṇanā* (Bangkok: Chulalongkorn University Press and Chiang Mai: Silkworm Books, 2015).
46. Vaidya, *Lalitavistara*, 40.
47. Vaidya, *Lalitavistara*, 40.
48. As related at length in the *Lakkhaṇa Sutta* (*Dīgha Nikāya* No. 30) (English translation in Walshe, *Long Discourses of the Buddha*, 441–460).
49. *Nidānakathā* (Fausboll, *Jātaka Together with Its Commentary*, i, 54).
50. For a discussion of the seven conatals, see, for example, Horner, *Clarifier of the Sweet Meaning*, xliii-xlix. See also Vanessa R. Sasson, "A Buddhist Love Story: The Buddha and Yaśodharā," *Buddhist Studies Review* 37, no. 1 (2020): 55–58. Ānanda is sometimes replaced in the list by a royal elephant.
51. For example, in the *Abhiniṣkramaṇa Sūtra*, the conatals include 500 Śākya princesses, of whom Yaśodharā (the equivalent of Rāhula's mother) is best; 500 children born to King Śuddhodana's concubines, of whom Chandaka is the best; 500 foals born from the royal stud horse, of whom Kanthaka is the best; and so forth. See Beal, *Romantic Legend of Śākya Buddha*, 53–54.
52. Gnoli, *Gilgit Manuscript of the Saṅghabhedavastu*, 46.
53. *Abhiniṣkramaṇa Sūtra* (Beal, *Romantic Legend of Śākya Buddha*, 43).
54. *Abhiniṣkramaṇa Sūtra* (Beal, *Romantic Legend of Śākya Buddha*, 44).
55. All of these foreshadowings are related in the *Abhiniṣkramaṇa Sūtra* (Beal, *Romantic Legend of Śākya Buddha*, 43–45).
56. From the *Madhuratthavilāsinī*, commentary on the *Buddhavaṃsa* (Horner, *Clarifier of the Sweet Meaning*, 429).
57. *Nidānakathā* (Fausboll, *Jātaka Together with Its Commentary*, i, 56–57).
58. Senart, *Mahāvastu avadānam*, ii, 2.
59. *Abhiniṣkramaṇa Sūtra* (Beal, *Romantic Legend of Śākya Buddha*, 25–26).
60. Gnoli, *Gilgit Manuscript of the Saṅghabhedavastu*, 40.
61. *Nidānakathā* (Fausboll, *Jātaka Together with Its Commentary*, i, 50).
62. Both details occur, for example, in the *Buddhacarita* (vv. 1.16 and 1.23) (Olivelle, *Life of the Buddha by Aśvaghoṣa*, 7–9).
63. Vaidya, *Lalitavistara*, 48.
64. *Nidānakathā* (Fausboll, *Jātaka Together with Its Commentary*, i, 51).

65. This is common to many of the biographical sources, including the *Mahāpadāna Sutta, Accariyabbhuta Sutta, Nidānakathā, Saṅghabhedavastu* (of the *Mūlasarvāstivāda Vinaya*), and *Abhiniṣkramaṇa Sūtra.*
66. Gnoli, *Gilgit Manuscript of the Saṅghabhedavastu,* 43.
67. Gnoli, *Gilgit Manuscript of the Saṅghabhedavastu,* 45.
68. For example, in the *Nidānakathā* and *Mahāvastu.*
69. Senart, *Mahāvastu avadānam,* ii, 10.
70. Gnoli, *Gilgit Manuscript of the Saṅghabhedavastu,* 41.
71. Gnoli, *Gilgit Manuscript of the Saṅghabhedavastu,* 41.
72. John Strong, *The Buddha: A Short Biography* (London: Oneworld Publications, 2001), 10–14.
73. *Mahāpadāna Sutta* (*Dīgha Nikāya* No. 14) (Rhys Davids and Stede, *Dīgha Nikāya,* ii, 12–15).
74. *Acchariyabbhuta Sutta* (*Majjhima Nikāya* No. 123) (Trenckner, *Majjhima Nikāya,* iii, 118–24).
75. *Madhuratthavilāsinī* (commentary on the *Buddhavaṃsa*) (Horner, *Clarifier of the Sweet Meaning,* 298).
76. Buswell and Lopez, *Princeton Dictionary of Buddhism,* 930 (*s.v.*, twelve deeds of a buddha).
77. For an English translation, see Thomas Cleary, trans., *Entry into the Realm of Reality. The Text. A Translation of the Gandavyuha, the Final Book of the Avatamsaka Sutra* (Boston: Shambhala, 1989).
78. P. L. Vaidya, ed., *Gaṇḍavyūhasūtra,* 2nd ed., Buddhist Sanskrit Texts, Vol. 5. (Darbhanga, India: Mithila Institute, 2002), 294.
79. Vaidya, *Gaṇḍavyūhasūtra,* 345.
80. Vaidya, *Gaṇḍavyūhasūtra,* 346.
81. Vaidya, *Gaṇḍavyūhasūtra,* 348.
82. Vaidya, *Lalitavistara,* 64.
83. Vaidya, *Lalitavistara,* 64.
84. Vaidya, *Lalitavistara,* 65.

4
A Timeless Love Story

Vanessa R. Sasson

Figure 4.1 The Bodhisattva and Yaśodharā sit on small thrones with their hands on a table or reaching into a bowl on the table; relief panel from Aziz Dheri, Pakistan, approximately third century CE; courtesy of Peshawar Museum. A special thanks to the curator, Mohammad Asif Raza, who went above and beyond in helping me track this image down.

Figure 4.1 is from a stūpa settlement in Aziz Dheri, Pakistan, and was produced around the third century CE.[1] According to Nasim Khan, the male figure on the left is probably the young prince Siddhārtha, the future Buddha. He has his hand on the table (or in a bowl on the table) in front of him. The female figure on the right is probably Yaśodharā, the prince's wife. She too has her hand on the table (or in a bowl on the table). It is not clear what they are doing—possibly playing a game or they are engaged in some kind of ritual. It may even depict a marriage rite. Regardless of what they are doing, though, what is particularly intriguing is that the two figures are seated on thrones of the same height. Yaśodharā is shorter,

Vanessa R. Sasson, *A Timeless Love Story* In: *The Buddha*. Edited by: Vanessa R. Sasson and Kristin Scheible, Oxford University Press. © Oxford University Press 2024. DOI: 10.1093/oso/9780197649466.003.0005 so she has a stool beneath her feet, but otherwise the thrones are nearly identical. The artist could have lowered Yaśodharā's throne and placed her feet directly on the ground, but it was apparently more important that her throne match his in height. The artist could have likewise left her legs dangling in mid-air, but that too was apparently out of the question. Yaśodharā is therefore depicted directly opposite her husband (or husband-to-be) on a throne just like his, with her feet firmly planted. Just like him.

This image is not the only one to represent Siddhārtha and Yaśodharā so equally. Many Gandhāran images feature the two together this way.[2] I may therefore not be wrong to read something into their matching thrones. According to a number of early textual sources, the Bodhisattva was married to Yaśodharā for lifetimes. They shared a trajectory, they shared their final rebirth together, and then they shared their householder lives together, too. We may therefore say that the two of them were partners (a contemporary term, perhaps, but one that speaks to this relationship well), with their life stories deeply intertwined.[3] The intimacy of their relationship is evident throughout these narratives, and it may be evident again here in one of the earliest images we have of the two of them together.

(Past-Life) Wedding Bells

The Buddha's relationship to the one we will call Yaśodharā begins lifetimes ago.[4] As Naomi Appleton demonstrates in her chapter, stories of the Buddha's past lives—known as jātaka tales—are popular throughout the Buddhist world. We have jātakas in every language, length, and style. Jātaka stories are not only preserved in writing; they are also performed, recited, and painted on temple walls. They are beloved stories that tell us about the Buddha and his relationships long before he was perfected.

The Buddha's relationship to Yaśodharā features in many of these. Their relationship is not consistently characterized: sometimes he chases her; sometimes she chases him; sometimes it is something else altogether. The point, for our purposes, is that she is regularly featured in the jātakas, participating in his multilife journey, standing beside him, married to him, and functioning as his partner while they move together from one lifetime to the next. For the purposes of this chapter, we must consider at least one of these past-life stories before immersing ourselves in the final narrative. As every chapter in this volume highlights, the Buddha's biography extends well beyond the limits of his final life story. It stretches far into the past, innumerable lifetimes ago, as far back as when he was reborn as the brahman Sumati (see Andy Rotman's chapter) and perhaps even earlier than that. To explore the Buddha's relationship with Yaśodharā, we must dabble at least for a moment in this ancient history, when the two of them found each other in other lives.

Of the many jātakas where Yaśodharā features, one of the most beloved is the *Kinnarī Jātaka* (also known as the *Jātaka of Sudhana and Manoharā*). It belongs to some of the earliest Buddhist collections recorded while appearing in later collections as well. It is carved into the extraordinary Indonesian stūpa that is Borobudur; it is painted on the cave walls of Ajanta in India and is the subject of both popular and ritual performances throughout Southeast Asia. The *Kinnarī Jātaka* (as we shall refer to it here) is, in other words, one of Buddhism's most popular tales.[5] It is a great adventure story that includes romance, palace politics, terrifying ogres, beautiful bird princesses, and a signet ring that helps save the day. In this tale, our two protagonists, the Bodhisattva and Yaśodharā, are passionately intertwined, in some versions falling madly in love at first sight.

The story does not always begin the same way (it is quite an elaborate tale), but it invariably leads to the kidnapping of one of the most evasive creatures of the Buddhist imagination: the half-bird, half-human, magical kinnarī. According to the Sanskrit account of the Kinnarī *Jātaka* preserved in the *Divyāvadanā*, this kinnarī is none other than Princess Manoharā, the daughter of the kinnara king, who is "exquisitely formed, lovely to look at, beautiful, with a perfect complexion."[6] Her breasts are described as being like golden melons, her lips are red like rubies, and her limbs are like plantain stalks. She is, moreover, draped in exquisite fabrics and decorated with jewels that chime with every step. Manoharā is, in other words, a devastating magical beauty.

The reason she is kidnapped varies, depending on the version one reads. According to the version preserved in the *Mahāvastu*, she is captured to fulfill the requirements of a great sacrifice. A king is made to believe that he will be guaranteed success in the afterlife if he makes a sacrifice of every type of living being in his domain. Since kinnarīs are included in the list, he captures Manoharā and sends her to be slaughtered in his great heap.

The Bodhisattva in this past-life narrative is a prince named Sudhana. He lives in a neighboring kingdom and is invited to witness the great sacrificial event next door. The moment he lays eyes on the captured kinnarī, however, Prince Sudhana falls madly in love. Indeed, according to the *Mahāvastu*, it is love at first sight for them both: he develops "a noble love for her, and she . . . a love for [him]."[7] Prince Sudhana cannot bear to see her killed, so he throws himself at the king's feet and makes a passionate argument for her release. The king is soon convinced and sets the kinnarī free. Prince Sudhana thus walks away from the event with the beautiful kinnarī by his side. Cue the credits—it looks like it's time for happily ever after.[8]

But Buddhist storytelling rarely concludes so quickly. The prince and Manoharā move into the palace and are now quite literally in their honeymoon phase. The prince becomes so wrapped up in his wedded bliss, that he neglects his royal obligations. His relationship to the kinnarī turns into a political liability. When a complaint is made to the king about his lovesick son, the king decides to have the kinnarī sent away. While the prince is looking elsewhere, Manoharā is escorted out of the palace dressed in all her finery. She flies away reluctantly, looking back repeatedly to see if she might catch one last glimpse of her husband. When Prince Sudhana later learns of his wife's eviction, he drops everything and sets off in search of her. The Buddha-to-be is dedicated to getting his wife back, no matter the cost.

Now begins the adventure part of the story, with monkey kings and mystical seers. The Paññāsa version includes ogres and giant pythons too. In every account, the prince sets off into the great unknown, navigating fantastical terrain in the hopes of reaching the golden city that lies hidden on a Himalayan mountaintop. As Joel Tatelman says in the introduction to his translation, "a film version [of this segment] would tax the special-effects technologies of even the wealthiest modern studios"[9] because the many descriptions are so elaborate. Eventually, however, Prince Sudhana reaches the magical kingdom. He makes himself known to Manoharā (by slipping a signet ring into her bathing jar), and so impresses her father, the kinnara king, with his extraordinary abilities, that Prince Sudhana is invited to live happily ever after with his wife there.

We might once again imagine that we have finally reached the happily-ever-after moment, but we are not there just yet. We have one last scene to cover before the story ends: after many years of frolicking in their magical paradise, Prince Sudhana realizes how homesick he has become. He approaches the kinnara king with a request to return to the human world and the request is granted. That very night, while the two are fast asleep, magical beings pick up the couple's bed and carry them to the prince's native city. When they wake up the next morning, Prince Sudhana and Manoharā find themselves back in the city the prince once called home. And now, *finally*, they are ready to live happily ever after.

Although this jātaka is just one of many, the *Kinnarī Jātaka* beautifully expresses how tied our two protagonists have been for lifetimes. They fall madly in love the moment they lay eyes on each other, and then the Bodhisattva spends the rest of the narrative fighting for her. He saves her from a sacrificial fire, travels for years to get her back after losing her, and then stays with her in a magical kingdom, far from home, until he is finally prepared to return. The story is not the same in every rendition, but the story consistently emphasizes a powerful bond between the two characters. Yaśodharā and the Bodhisattva are tied to each other in past lives, just as they are tied to each other in their last life together. It is a pattern that is repeated in many narratives, a cyclical feature of their shared story, reminding us once again that the Buddha biography is so much bigger than just his final scene. It may be focused on him as an individual as he cycles his way toward awakening, but the Buddha biography is ultimately cosmic in dimension, expanding not only horizontally, but laterally as well, incorporating as it does all those beings who cycle through time with him.

But a word of caution before we close: the *Kinnarī Jātaka* as we have discussed it here is a wonderful adventure that provides us with a glimpse into the Bodhisattva's past. The role it plays in Buddhist textual history is, however, different in each telling. Jātaka stories typically open with frame narratives, and these frame narratives often tell us (ahead of time) about the story and what it means. Someone might ask the Buddha a question, or a situation might arise that leads the Buddha to respond with a story about the past. In the *Mahāvastu* version of the story, the Buddha frames the *Kinnarī Jātaka* with a discussion about how hard he worked to "win" Yaśodharā before he married her: "this was not the first occasion that I won Yaśodharā after much fatigue," he explains. "There was another occasion also on which she was won by me after great fatigue, great patience, and great exertion."[10] Then the Buddha tells the story of the *Kinnarī Jātaka*, which reveals the extraordinary lengths the Buddha made in the past to marry his bride.

The purpose of the *Kinnarī Jātaka* is, as far as the *Mahāvastu* version is concerned, to demonstrate the Buddha's commitment to Yaśodharā—a rather romantic explanation for a romantic tale. But in other renditions of the story, the frame story reveals something quite different. The Paññāsa version, for example, opens with a story about a lovesick monk. The Buddha learns of this lovesick monk who has shirked his responsibilities and responds with the following teaching: "desire for women is the cause of evils that are hard to prevent. Sages in the past have had problems as a result of desire of women, causing them to neglect their wealth, their parents, and even their own life, causing great hardship on account of sensual feelings like this."[11] The point of telling the story of the *Kinnarī Jātaka*, in this case, is to warn monks away from women, because they can cause even wise men to neglect their families. A similar justification is provided by the *Jātakamālā* version of this story. Here it opens with the statement: "on earth, it seems to me, that man is happy who never feels affection. For once it arises, it is like an enemy and with it arises dreadful unhappiness."[12] The affection the prince felt for the beautiful kinnarī princess is not something to admire, according to these accounts. The Bodhisattva's behavior in the *Kinnarī Jātaka* is behavior to avoid instead. Even the wisest among us—those destined for Buddhahood—risk being led astray when women are involved.

As we have seen throughout this book, the Buddha's biography is forever expanding and transforming itself. Stories mean one thing here and are interpreted differently there. The tone changes, details are added or stripped away, an entirely different lesson is conveyed. The jātakas generally agree that the Buddha and Yaśodharā were together for lifetimes, but what the nature of their relationship was, what it meant, what it became, how it was understood, what lessons one might learn—this is different in every jātaka, and in every telling.[13]

Wedding Bells (One Last Time)

When the Bodhisattva is reborn for the last time, astrologers are summoned for a reading of his chart. There are, as always, multiple versions of this important scene in the Buddha biography, but ultimately the story leads to a complicated astrological reading: the king is told that the young prince will either become a great wheel-turning king or he will become a religious teacher. Obviously, the king has no interest in watching his son become a religious teacher. He needs his son to take the throne. He therefore devises a plan that he believes will ensure that his son chooses a life of kingship. He raises his son with almost obscene extravagance, hoping that this will render him addicted to pleasure and will steer him away from the contemplative life. The *Sukhamalasutta*, for example, tells us that the Bodhisattva is "delicately brought up" with no fewer than three palaces placed at his disposal (one for every season).[14] The *Mahāvastu* describes one of these as being like a heavenly realm, with its upper chamber "gleaming like a brilliant mountain-top in the sky."

> On the front of the mansion were pinnacles resplendent with silver and its corners gleamed like the flame of the sacrificial fire. The inner apartments were fair like pellucid shells. They sparkled like brilliant little suns or like moon-shaped ornaments . . . There were seen arched portals of gold like burning fire . . . On the ground with its heaps of jewels and piles of other splendours a lion sits and starts with fear at the rising sun which it has seen.[15]

In other words, the prince is drenched in splendor throughout his youth, the hope being that it will keep the Bodhisattva tied to materialism.[16]

The prince, however, exhibits an undeniably contemplative nature. No matter how many beautiful things (or people) he is surrounded with, the Bodhisattva remains "absorbed in deep thought, without desire for any sensual things."[17] According to the *Lalitavistara*, the king's ministers express no small measure of concern (similar to the concern we saw in the *Kinnarī Jātaka* when he became so immersed in his wedded bliss). They therefore approach the king and remind him of the astrological prediction made at his son's birth. If the king does not respond soon, the prince risked becoming a religious teacher, and what they needed was a future king.

The ministers recall that a wheel-turning king is always equipped with seven treasures: "the precious wheel, the precious elephant, the precious horse, the precious wife, the precious jewel, the precious steward, and the precious minister."[18] Presumably, the prince already has the horse and the elephant, the steward, and the minister. He may even have the precious jewel and the wheel (although nothing is said about that here). What he is missing in his repertoire as potential king is the wife. According to the *Lalitavistara*, they therefore recommend a royal marriage: "he will discover pleasure and not renounce," they explain. "In that way the line of our universal monarchy will not be cut, and we will be irreproachably respected by all the kings of the realm."[19]

This statement in the *Lalitavistara* tells us a few things. We learn that the prince needs a wife because he cannot become a wheel-turning king without one. And we learn that a wife is meant to anchor the Bodhisattva to the experience of pleasure. In other words, a wife is meant to achieve what a life of splendor could not. Moreover, the text claims that the monarchic lineage will be ensured once the Bodhisattva is married (assuming that a son is born to the couple). But perhaps most important of all, a wife—say the ministers—would give the throne much needed credibility. After all, what would other kings say if the Śākya throne was occupied by an unmarried man? A wife, we now realize, solves a whole host of problems with one quick rite.

The king brings the idea to his son and the Bodhisattva responds in a way that should be familiar to us by now: he consults the Buddha-life blueprint before coming to a decision. According to the *Lalitavistara*, the Bodhisattva yet again considers what previous Buddhas had done in such circumstances before he decides his own life trajectory, and sure enough, he sees that previous buddhas were also married before they achieved awakening. It is therefore fitting that he first be married too. This tells us that a wife solves more than just social and political concerns. A wife, according to the *Lalitavistara*, also helps the Bodhisattva fit the blueprint. If he is to become a buddha in the future, he requires a wife now, with cosmic concerns melding seamlessly into mundane realities.

The prince, however, will not accept just any wife. He is the future Buddha, an exceptional being in the cosmos who will perform exceptional feats. He needs an exceptional wife by his side for this part of the story. He therefore presents his father with a list of requirements that his future wife would have to meet: she would have to be perfectly pure in beauty, birth, and family,[20] young but without vanity, fond of renunciation, generous and disciplined,[21] without pride, conceit, or hostility, and she must not lust after other men, even in her dreams. She should lie with her husband, free from carelessness,[22] be loving like a sister,[23] but also as adept as a courtesan in the arts of love. She should be obedient, and she should be as guileless as a mother.[24] In other words, his future wife must fulfill every fantasy and play every possible role a woman can play. She should be a mother, a sister, a lover, and a wife.[25] The prince ends his demands with the exclamation, "Find me, O father, a wife like this!"[26]

The *Lalitavistara* is the only early biography that presents us with such a list. But this list of requirements highlights something that many of our early sources point to in other ways: namely, that the future Buddha's wife must be almost as exceptional as he is. Indeed, it is safe to say that most of his family members fall into a similar category. For the early Buddhist writers, to be reborn as a member of the Buddha's family is an exquisite honor. To be reborn as his mother, father, future wife, or son is to have an intimate relationship with a great being. Only great beings can merit an honor like that.

A priest is sent out to look for a woman who will meet all the prince's requirements. When he arrives at Yaśodharā's door, he hands her the letter that explains the purpose of his visit and she immediately recognizes herself in the description. "Since I have all of these suitable qualities," she says to the priest, "may this handsome and gentle prince be my husband!" She then urges the priest to hurry because otherwise, she may end up with "an inferior, ordinary man."[27] Yaśodharā seems just as intent on marrying a great being as he appears to be intent on marrying someone like her.

And now we reach one of the greatest (and most Cinderella-like) scenes of the Buddha's biography: a scene I have called "the Choosing" in my writing elsewhere.[28] The king learns about Yaśodharā, but before he accepts her as a bride for his son, he wants to see how the prince responds to her (a wise parental move). The king therefore summons all the maidens in the land to present themselves to the prince—Yaśodharā included among them. Will the prince notice her?

According to the *Lalitavistara*, the women line up expectantly, but the prince barely glances at any of them. He simply hands each one a gift (a "thank you for coming" gesture) and sends them on their way. But when Yaśodharā steps forward, the tone of the narrative shifts. He comments on how late she is (she is last to arrive!). Then he takes a ring from his own finger and places it on hers. In the *Mahāvastu* version of this story, she responds to his gift with the fabulously audacious question, "is this all I'm worth?"[29] The *Lalitavistara* tells us that, while all the other women could barely look at the prince due to his blinding presence, Yaśodharā was able to stare at him "with unblinking eyes."[30]

She is, without a doubt, the Bodhisattva's match.

An Untrained Prince

It seems as though the story is now well onto its predetermined course. The couple that has been together for lifetimes, that took rebirth together as conatals (see

Ohnuma's chapter in this volume), is now ready to marry again. He has chosen her, she fits the requirements, and onward we go into a future of wedded bliss.

But a few texts pause here to raise a question they are eager to resolve: as we saw earlier in his narrative, the Bodhisattva was shielded from every kind of suffering throughout his youth. He was raised in opulent luxury and was never forced to work. Does this mean that the prince is lacking in real-world attributes? Did he ever learn to wield a sword? Does he know anything about the traditional arts? What kind of a husband would such a prince really be?

According to the *Lalitavistara*, the one to raise these concerns is Yaśodharā's father. He approaches the king and says,

> The noble boy has grown up in the palace in ease and comfort. Yet our family rule is such that a girl can only be granted to someone who is skilled in the arts, and not to a man who lacks these skills. The prince is not skilled in the arts since he does not know the maneuvers of swordsmanship, archery, combat, or wrestling. How can I give away my daughter to someone who lacks such skills?[31]

The *Mahāvastu* is even more cutting in its account. Here, Yaśodharā's father says, "I cannot give Yaśodharā to the young prince. Because the lad has grown up among the women, he has not advanced at all in the arts, in archery, in elephant-riding, in handling bow and sword and in kingly accomplishments. In short, the prince has made no progress at all."[32] These words are astounding! How can a royal subject challenge the king on something so intimate as his parenting without facing immediate and violent repercussions?

The *Jātakanidāna* provides us with an alternative version of this moment that strikes me as more reasonable. In this account, Yaśodharā's father does not say any of this directly to the king. Instead, a thread of local gossip reaches the king's ears. People are wondering if the prince has the skills required to rule.[33] The king has no choice but to deal with the accusations. If he does not, he risks jeopardizing the throne's reputation.

Whether these concerns reach the king directly or through the age-old grapevine, the result is the same: the future Buddha must prove his prowess publicly if the throne is to be preserved.[34] A competition is therefore announced: whoever wins the competition (with its many events) will receive Yaśodharā as a bride. The Bodhisattva presents himself. And as we might well expect, he wins it all.

The Departure

We now reach the climax of the story. After searching for his bride throughout the kingdom, after choosing her publicly (and dismissing every other woman who was waiting in line), and then fighting for her on the field in every category imaginable; after marrying her and spending the next few years living with her as husband and wife; after all that, the Bodhisattva is going to leave Yaśodharā. He will see the Four Sights and realize he does not want to be a householder after all.

We have multiple accounts of what happens when he comes to this decision. In the *Buddhacarita* account, the prince approaches his father and asks for permission to take his leave. "I desire the wandering life," he says. "Separation is appointed for this man."[35] The king is devastated. The *Buddhacarita* tells us that the king begins to shake, "like a tree struck down by an elephant" and is choked with tears.[36] He begs his son not to leave and makes a series of impassioned arguments, hoping to change his son's mind. He tells him that it is too difficult to live a life of renunciation at such an early age, because the senses are strong and easily excited. But the prince is determined. He is the future Buddha, and he knows it. "Don't hold me back," the Bodhisattva declares earnestly, "for it is not right to obstruct a man who's trying to escape from a burning house."[37]

In other accounts, the prince does not approach his father about his departure. Instead, he goes to see his wife who we learn has just given birth to their son. The *Jātaknidāna* describes the Bodhisattva standing at the door to his wife's room where she is sleeping with their newborn son, her hand resting on him. A lamp is fed with scented oil and her bed is covered with flowers. The prince stands on the threshold and looks at his child. He then thinks to himself, "If I remove the queen's hand, and take my son into my arms she will wake up and that will prevent my journey."[38] He therefore decides not to approach; he turns around and walks away.

One of John Strong's most important contributions to the field (there are, admittedly, many) is his discussion of this scene as it appears in yet another account: the *Saṅghabhedavastu* of the *Mūlasarvāstivāda Vinaya*. According to this version of the story, the prince goes to see his wife prior to his Great Departure, but not to see his sleeping newborn son. Rather, in this account, "the Great Departure marks not the birth but the conception of the Buddha's son, for far from not waking his wife on his way out the door, the Bodhisattva decides to make love to her."[39] The reason for this, according to the text, is explicit: "lest others say that the prince Śākyamuni was not a man (*apamān*—a eunuch) and that he wandered forth without 'paying attention' to Yaśodharā..."[40]

There are, in other words, quite a few accounts of this moment, but whatever the version, at the end of the scene the Bodhisattva makes his departure. According to the *Jātakanidāna*, he gallops off into the night. Just before the palace slips out of view, he stops to look back one last time. He looks at the palace where he spent his youth and turns away from it, as though it is nothing more than "a blob of spit."[41] He then races toward the forest where he will finally become the Buddha he was always meant to be.

Interconnected Lives

We might expect the storytellers to train their lens on the aspiring Buddha and follow him into the forest at this point. After innumerable lifetimes of effort, the Bodhisattva is finally on the very cusp of awakening. The ten-thousand universes are on the edge of their seats. It is the moment we have been waiting for.

But before the storytellers make their own departure from palace life, many of them take a moment to tell us about those the Bodhisattva left behind. And the picture is grim. According to the *Mahāvastu*, for example, Gotamī (the Bodhisattva's stepmother) cries so many tears that her eyes are covered with scales, and she becomes blind.[42] Kanthaka the horse is so overcome with grief that he dies broken-hearted. In the *Buddhacarita*, even the kingdom looks devastated, looking more like a jungle than the sparkling fairy tale it used to be.[43] Everyone, in other words, experiences the prince's departure as a profound loss, but perhaps no one more so than his wife (who is now a widow), Yaśodharā.

The *Buddhacarita* tells us that when she learns of his departure, Yaśodharā's eyes become red with fury. Her voice is choked "by the bitterness of despair."[44] She accuses Channa the chariot driver and Kanthaka the horse of betrayal. She calls Channa "a heartless man" and soaks him in sarcastic rebuke.[45] In the *Mahāvastu's* telling, she throws her arms around Kanthaka's neck as she sobs. Then she asks that valiant horse, "where have you taken the prince? What offence have I given you and Chandaka that you take the prince away when I was sleeping blissfully? I and the sixty thousand women of the palace are bereaved."[46] Yaśodharā's suffering is not shielded from us. On the contrary, her suffering is placed center stage for the audience to witness directly. Her suffering, we now realize, is part of the Buddha's story too. It reveals a paradox that lies at the heart of the Buddha's narrative: although the Bodhisattva's Great Departure is cause for joyous celebration (the wheel of Dharma is about to be set in motion), it is also the cause of tremendous suffering. The Bodhisattva is on a quest to solve the question of suffering, and yet he creates suffering all along the way.[47]

Throughout the Buddha biography, Yaśodharā stands beside her husband, living out a parallel existence. She competes against the women of the kingdom during the Choosing, just as he competes against the men during the competition.[48] She embodies suffering by giving birth, while he wrestles with suffering as he considers the Four Sights. And if we follow the *Saṅghabhedavastu*'s version, she gives birth just as he attains awakening. Throughout their shared narrative, spanning multiple lifetimes, the two live out their lives together, alongside each other, very similar to the image this chapter opened with, as they sit on parallel thrones.

In the *Lalitavistara*, this point is made with explicit intent. After their wedding, Yaśodharā is asked to veil herself, but she refuses, arguing that noble beings shine perpetually, while those who commit evil never shine, no matter what they wear. Why should she cover her face when her thoughts are pure, she asks. The king is so impressed with her response that he declares, "just as my son is adorned with good qualities, his bride too is radiant with her own good qualities. That these two pristine beings have come together, is just like butter and clarified butter."[49] Yaśodharā does not have to wear the veil.

Despite this extraordinary symmetry, the Bodhisattva chooses to make his Great Departure without her. After innumerable lifetimes together, after sitting on parallel thrones, the Bodhisattva abandons Yaśodharā and charges into the forest on his own. Perhaps she is left behind to remind us of what saṃsāra looks like—he is the picture of awakening, and she provides us with a picture of life without it (symmetry gone amiss?). Or maybe he knew that she would eventually follow when it was the right time for her (just not yet?)[50] Most likely, awakening was a journey he simply had to take alone. The point, however, is that his quest would not have been possible without her.

Indeed, the Buddha would not have had a story at all were it not for the many other characters in his life playing their parts. The Buddha's story is built around relationships, each character participating in the great narrative that is the Buddha biography. As Strong so insightfully argues, the Buddha's story is not just a "solo quest of a solitary seeker."[51] It is also a collective narrative, intertwined as it is with so many others.

Throughout this book, we have highlighted the ongoing tension present in the Buddha biography between the microcosm and the macrocosm. The Buddha operates in this world as an individual, and yet he is also a manifestation of something much greater. His story spans lifetimes, moving backward into the past, soaring far into the unknowable future, extending to other buddhas and their stories in all directions. It is a cosmic narrative, as much as it is the story of an individual on a quest.

When we consider his relationship to Yaśodharā, however, we see the macrocosm reflected in a different way: the Buddha's story is linked to hers, connected with hers. Even lived out in parallel. The Buddha's story cannot be told without telling her story and the story of all the others who participated. Each character gently pulls on the web that ties them all together, maintaining a tension between them all. The Buddha biography is the story of the Buddha, but the story of the Buddha belongs to all the characters in it—human, animal, plant, cosmic. It is, quite simply, not his story alone.

Notes

1. M. Nasim Khan and M. A. Durrani discuss this image in their article, "Playing with Rings: Siddhārtha and Yaśodharā: A Relief Panel from Aziz Dheri Revisited," *Ancient Pakistan* 21 (2021): 35–47. In his encyclopedic collection entitled, *The Sacred and the Secular*, Nasim Khan details the archaeological work done at Aziz Dheri and explains that, while some of the images found at Aziz Dheri can be precisely dated, several sculptures (like this one) are missing the necessary stratigraphic information. A precise chronology for these pieces is therefore impossible (3:2–13), but he dates this relief as "post-Kushan," which brings me to a date of approximately third century CE. See his collection, *The Sacred and the Secular: Investigating the Unique Stūpa and Settlement Site of Aziz Dheri, Peshawar Valley, Khyber Pakhtunkhwa, Pakistan* (Peshawar: M. Nasim Khan, 2010), 3: 2–13.
2. See Nasim Khan and Durrani, "Playing with Rings," for a series of similar reliefs.
3. In the *Buddhacarita*, Yaśodharā speaks of herself as the Buddha's *sahadharmacāriṇī*, which Olivelle translates as "partner in dharma" (8.60). See Patrick Olivelle, trans., *The Life of the Buddha by Ashvaghosha*. Clay Sanskrit Library (New York: New York University Press and JJC Foundation, 2008).
4. The Bodhisattva's wife goes by a few names. Sometimes she is referred to as Bimbā, sometimes as Yaśodharā, sometimes just as Rāhulamātā (Rāhula's mother). This has led to two possible interpretations: either the Bodhisattva had multiple wives (a reasonable conclusion given the context), or he had one wife who was known by different names. I think both interpretations are reasonable (and perhaps both are true). For the purposes of this chapter, I will assume one principal wife, and since this one wife is most often known as Yaśodharā, I will call her Yaśodharā here. For discussion of these various names and her possible history, see N. Péri, "Les femmes de Cākya-muni," *Bulletin de l'école Française de l'Extrême Orient* 18, no. 2 (1918): 1–37; and André Bareau, "Un personnage bien mysterieux: L'épouse du Buddha," in *Indological and Buddhist Studies, Volume in Honour of Professor J. W. de Jong on his Sixtieth Birthday*, ed. L. A. Hercus et al., 31–59 (Canberra: Australian National University, 1982).
5. According to Jaini, "no other Buddhist story seems to have enjoyed such wide popularity with the possible exception of the *Vessantara Jātaka* and the *Suvaṇṇasaṅkhajātaka*" (534). He provides an extensive list of alternative versions of the *Kinnarī Jātaka*, from early Sanskrit to Tibetan, Chinese, Siamese, and Khotanese. See Padmanabh S. Jaini, "The Story of Sudhana and Manoharā: An Analysis of the Texts and the Borobudur Reliefs," *Bulletin of the School of Oriental and African Studies, University of London* 29, no. 3 (1966): 533–558.
6. Joel Tatelman, trans., *Heavenly Exploits (Buddhist Biographies from the Dīvyavadāna)*. Clay Sanskrit Library (New York: New York University Press and JJC Foundation, 2005), 251–253.
7. J. J. Jones, trans., *The Mahāvastu* (London: The Pali Text Society, 1976), 2:95.
8. The *Mahāvastu* version of the narrative, which I am following here, creates a strong impression of mutual adoration. The Bodhisattva and Manoharā are described as falling in love with each other. Other versions of the story, though, are much more

one-sided in their telling. In the *Divyāvadanā* account, the Bodhisattva receives Manoharā as a gift from a hunter who has captured her. He takes her back to the palace where "he frolicked, dallied and took his pleasure with her" (Tatelman, *Heavenly Exploits,* 255). How *she* felt about his taking "his pleasure with her" is not recorded. Similarly in the Paññāsa account, where the Bodhisattva seems to decide everything about their relationship. She is kidnapped by a hunter and then transferred to him like a piece of property without a voice. The prince then brings her back to the palace, marries her, and makes love to her (Tatelman, *Heavenly Exploits,* 10). Manoharā does not speak in any of these early scenes, so we do not know if she consented to any of it. These important differences reveal much about the different accounts, their writers, and their audiences. For a translation of the Paññāsa version of the story, see Chris Baker and Pasuk Phongpaichit, *From the Fifty Jātaka: Selections from the Thai Paññāsa Jātaka* (Bangkok: Silkworm, 2019).

9. Tatelman, *Heavenly Exploits*, 21.
10. Jones, *The Mahāvastu*, 2:91.
11. Baker and Phongpaichit, *From the Fifty Jātaka*, 2.
12. Peter Khoroche, trans., *Once A Peacock, Once an Actress: Twenty-Four Lives of the Bodhisattva from Haribhaṭṭa Jātakamālā* (Chicago: University of Chicago Press, 2017), 147.
13. For an excellent discussion of the relationship between the Bodhisattva and Yaśodharā in the jātakas, see Sarah Shaw, "Yasodharā in the Jātakas," *Buddhist Studies Review* 35, nos. 1–2 (2018): 261–278.
14. *Sukhamalasutta* AN 3.39; i 145. For an English translation, see Bhikkhu Bodhi, trans., *The Numerical Discourses of the Buddha: A Translation of the Aṅguttara Nikāya* (Boston: Wisdom, 2012).
15. Jones, *The Mahāvastu,* 2:33–34. For more on this sense of splendor in the Buddha's biography, see Vanessa R. Sasson, "Jeweled Renunciation: Reading the Buddha's Biography," in *Jewels, Jewelry, and Other Shiny Things in the Buddhist Imaginary*, ed. Vanessa R. Sasson (Honolulu: University of Hawai'i Press, 2021), 65–85 .
16. The splendor the Bodhisattva is raised with is not just there to entrap him. According to the *Buddhacarita*, it is also the product of his own merit, which the Bodhisattva brings with him at his birth. A great being brings great things, so the text implies. See Olivelle, *Life of the Buddha by Aśvaghoṣa*.
17. Olivelle, *Life of the Buddha*, 4.62.
18. Dharmachakra Translation Committee, *The Play in Full (Lalitavistara)* (84000: Translating the Words of the Buddha, n.d.), 12.1.
19. Dharmachakra Translation Committee, *The Play in Full*, 12.1.
20. Dharmachakra Translation Committee, *The Play in Full*, 12.8.
21. Dharmachakra Translation Committee, *The Play in Full*, 12.9.
22. Dharmachakra Translation Committee, *The Play in Full*, 12.11.
23. Dharmachakra Translation Committee, *The Play in Full*, 12.8.
24. Dharmachakra Translation Committee, *The Play in Full*, 12.15.
25. The *Lalitavistara* is fond of such lists. As Ohnuma's chapter in this volume reveals, a similar list of attributes is required of the Bodhisattva's mother. Just before he takes

his final rebirth, the Bodhisattva scans the ten-thousand universes for the one woman who would meet all of them. As Gotamī reminds us in her *apadāna*, "the name, 'Mother of the Buddha' is the hardest [name] to obtain (262)." So much is expected of her right from the start. In the same way, only one woman could have been the Bodhisattva's bride according to this account. See Jonathan S. Walters for a translation (*Legends of the Buddhist Saints: Apadānapāli*, 2017), available for free at http://apadanatranslation.org/.

26. Dharmachakra Translation Committee, *The Play in Full*, 12.15.
27. Dharmachakra Translation Committee, *The Play in Full*, 12.20.
28. Vanessa R. Sasson, *Yasodhara and the Buddha* (London: Bloomsbury Academic, 2021).
29. Jones, *The Mahāvastu*, 2:70.
30. Dharmachakra Translation Committee, *The Play in Full*, 12.24.
31. Dharmachakra Translation Committee, *The Play in Full*, 12.25.
32. Jones, *The Mahāvastu*, 2:70.
33. N. A. Jayawickrama, trans., *The Story of Gotama Buddha (Jātaka Nidānakathā)* (Bristol: Pali Text Society, 2011), 78.
34. This question was of concern not only to early writers. In Ambedkar's biography of the Buddha, this concern is resolved by eliminating the possibility of an accusation altogether. In Ambedkar's narrative, the Bodhisattva is politically initiated at the age of twenty and spends the next eight years participating in government. He was therefore always fit to be king, and no one could accuse him otherwise. See B. R. Ambedkar, *The Buddha and his Dhamma: A Critical Edition*, eds. Akash Singh Rathore and Ajay Verma (New Delhi: Oxford University Press, 2011).
35. Olivelle, *Life of the Buddha*, 5.28.
36. Olivelle, *Life of the Buddha*, 5.29.
37. Olivelle, *Life of the Buddha*, 5.38.
38. Jayawickrama, *The Story of Gotama Buddha*, 83.
39. John S. Strong, "A Family Quest: The Buddha, Yaśodharā, and Rāhula in the Mūlasarvāstivāda Vinaya," in *Sacred Biography in the Buddhist Traditions of South and Southeast Asia*, ed. Juliane Schober (Honolulu: University of Hawai'i Press, 1997), 115.
40. Strong, "A Family Quest," 115.
41. Jayawickrama, *The Story of Gotama Buddha*, 63.
42. Jones, *The Mahāvastu*, 3:116.
43. Olivelle, *Life of the Buddha*, 8.6.
44. Olivelle, *Life of the Buddha*, 8.31.
45. Olivelle, *Life of the Buddha*, 8.33.
46. Jones, *The Mahāvastu*, 2:182.
47. For more on this topic, see Vanessa R. Sasson, "A Buddhist Love Story: The Buddha and Yaśodharā," *Buddhist Studies Review* 37, no. 1 (2020): 53–72.
48. I thank a student for this insight. I had never noticed this parallel (of Yaśodharā competing against the women just as he competes against the men) until a student

at Chapman University, Grace Chamberlain, pointed it out to me in our discussion in class.

49. Dharmachakra Translation Committee, *The Play in Full*, 12.81.
50. In several texts, Yaśodharā eventually becomes a nun in the Buddha's order. She does not have any verses in the *Therigātha*, but she is well represented in the *Apadāna* where she is said to have been honored by one hundred thousand other nuns (*Apadāna*, 958).
51. Strong, "A Family Quest," 122.

5
A Great Departure

Kristin Scheible

Figure 5.1 The Buddha's Great Departure from Kapilavastu; the Great Stūpa at Sanchi, Eastern Gateway, middle architrave; courtesy of Kevin Standage.

Here, we pick up the story of the youthful prince Siddhārtha Gautama beginning to grow weary, and wary, of the privilege and problem that is royal life within the capital of the Śakyas, Kapilavastu. We will consider the quickening of events during this ultimate life in the more expansive Buddha life story, where his growing disillusionment and repeated experiences of *duḥkha* (disease) prime him for his awakening. We will see that "incitements" to leave home and "encouragements" to aim for full awakening spring from a variety of sources outside of himself. There are nudges from a whole host of supernatural beings (gods, *nāgas*, *yakṣas*, *gandharvas*, demigods, *garuḍas*, *kinnaras*, and *mahoragas*) and his "conatals," those beings and objects like his horse and groom that were born on the same day he was. Deities conspire to present visions of old age, sickness, death, and renunciation to prod the prince's mounting awareness of his impending journey. Catching sight of sleeping, drooling women in disarray provides a tableau of the instability and unsatisfactoriness of bodies, and life in general. An enthusiastic female bystander utters a verse of admiration that he (mis)interprets as a blessing urging him onward toward renunciation, the so-called Great Departure from his privileged life to pursue awakening. The scene of the Bodhisattva's unfolding renunciation culminates in the dramatic event of the

Kristin Scheible, *A Great Departure* In: *The Buddha*. Edited by: Vanessa R. Sasson and Kristin Scheible, Oxford University Press. © Oxford University Press 2024. DOI: 10.1093/oso/9780197649466.003.0006

Great Departure, visually captured in Figure 5.1, but it also invokes practice runs and dress rehearsals both during his life as the Prince Siddhārtha Gautama, and in his many previous lifetimes. The road to awakening—the performance of his lifetime(s)—is so often characterized as a solitary endeavor, yet when we soften our sharp focus on the hero Buddha-to-be, we recognize the impressive influence of a cast of various others on his story.

Gateway to Departure and Awakening

All sorts of characters crowd the focal image that opens this chapter. It is located on a gateway, one of the four entrances that frame one's approach to the Great Stūpa at Sanchi in Madhya Pradesh, India. The gateways at the four cardinal directions invite onlookers and pilgrims to regard the stūpa itself, a built memorial mound and site for relics that affirms the absence of the physical Buddha. Recollection of the Buddha (the contemplative practice *buddhānusmṛti*), is, indeed, what the various iterations of the Buddha's life story, both carved in stone and narrated in story, do as well. The decorated surfaces of the gateway arches illustrate the importance of the events in the Buddha's life story, whether they animate scenes from the story or depict stūpas of previous buddhas or depict processions and worship of the stūpa long after the Buddha's *parinirvāṇa*.

The four gates each have three arched and decorative architrave panels that entice the viewer. On the eastern gateway, the upper architrave presents stūpas of the most recent past buddhas, and the lower architrave illustrates the visit of the great king Aśoka (r. 268–232 BCE) to the Bodhi Tree. Sandwiched between these visions of the past before–Gautama Buddha and future after–Gautama Buddha, the central architrave (our focus) is a cacophonous collage of bodies and structures detailing the events around the Bodhisattva's Great Departure. Our image decorates the front of the panel; on its reverse is the *sambodhi*, the Buddha's awakening, underscoring the complementarity of a deliberate departure narrative and the culminating event of awakening.[1] There is no *sambodhi* without renunciation, and no renunciation without something to renounce.

It is difficult to pinpoint just where the story of his Great Departure really begins, as is the question of where his life story begins. The Great Departure is a momentous event in the Buddha-life blueprint, a requisite item on the lists of requirements for Buddhahood that various Buddhist traditions maintain, and is told in a stand-alone way in the heart of the Pali canon (the *Ariyapariyesanasutta*, or "Sermon on the Noble Quest").[2] Yet one could argue for many points of departure and inclinations toward buddhahood that give shape to his extended life story, a series of trial runs. Is the initial departure when he left his palace after the birth of his son, Rāhula? Or much earlier, when the Bodhisattva resided in the Tuṣita heaven and chose his place and family to take his final birth? When Sumedha (Sumati), four *asaṅkheyya* (immeasurable time period) and 100,000 eons ago, made his vow to become a buddha like Dīpaṃkara, the buddha of his day?[3] Or even before that, when, as Sumedha, he noted that his parents wouldn't even take one *kahāpaṇa* (small copper coin) to their grave, so he might as well set his mind on renunciation?[4] As John Strong poses the problem,

> Given the possibility of an infinity of previous lives, when did Gautama's aspiration for buddhahood actually begin? When he first *thought* about becoming a buddha? When he first *said* that that was his intention? When he first actually *did* something physically and had that action confirmed by a past buddha? At the same time, within this very questioning there is a recognition of a down-to-earth pattern. For all of its traipsing through incalculable aeons, there is a simple message in this scheme for ordinary Buddhists who might be interested in embarking on the Buddhist path: first you think about it, then you talk about it, then you do something about it.[5]

Every scene seems to have a dress rehearsal, whether in the same or in a previous lifetime, where thinking and speaking precede the doing.[6]

Our architrave preserves the structure of the overarching story, both in a narrow sense of the Great Departure story, and simultaneously of the broader, expansive life story. This condensed visual form of the sweeping life story captures the prince's movement from being a spectacle himself, to formulating observations from having seen the sights of the world, to cultivating a renunciant's introspection that then leads to a buddha's insight. The Great Departure is both an event, a fabula within the bigger story of the Buddha's extended lifetime, and a way to refer to the entire story of the Buddha's move from privileged, fawned-over prince, to awakening, to *parinirvāṇa*. It can be challenging, however, for an interpreter to keep the story of the Bodhisattva's renunciation straight, with its fits and starts and turns, and many movable pieces that are not presented in a consistent temporal or narrative form through the varied biographical traditions. The architrave before us freezes one form of the story, juxtaposing selected scenes and episodes of a larger, more complicated story. It frames the way we see the story unfold, highlighting only some elements and absenting others altogether. Yet the story of the Great Departure is recognizable, and even in this abbreviated bas-relief form it conjures the entire narrative.

The Great Departure scene is, in some ways, a type of *mise en abyme*, where the story of the departure from the palace, beginning with city sights and spectacle and ending with insight set apart from the others in the forest, structurally replicates the whole story. Our perspective is controlled, held in sharp focus by the cuts in the stone. And yet every textual version of the story similarly freezes the elements, the individual scenes or fabulae, creating the illusion that there is a set recipe. This is another dimension of a narrative like the Buddha's life story—it is more like a favorite recipe passed down through the generations: a cultural crucible, source of nourishment, a blueprint flexible enough to accommodate local tastes and preferences, yet still recognizable as what it is. One strategy we engage in reading this scene, then, is seeing the parts and the whole both as representations of a particular scene, and as reminders of the bigger frame story, the entire narrative arc of Siddhārtha Gautama's life from exceptional childhood in the palace bustle to the solitary practice of insight after renunciation.

Figure 5.2 Detail of Figure 5.1 at the far left: upper balconies filled with voyeurs as the (absent) Bodhisattva leaves the palace; the Great Stūpa at Sanchi, Eastern Gateway, middle architrave; courtesy of Kevin Standage.

The architrave image is "read" left to right. On the far left of Figure 5.2 is the Śakyan capital city Kapilavastu, with upper balconies bursting with eager voyeurs of the spectacle below, an auspicious start to this portion of the story. Aśvaghoṣa's *Buddhacarita* captures the framing effect of the adoration we see in the frieze:

> As they looked down at the prince on the road,
> the women, it seemed, longed to come down to earth;
> as they looked up at him with their necks stretched,
> the men, it seemed, longed to go up to heaven.
> Seeing that prince so resplendent
> with beauty and sovereign splendor,

"Blessed is his wife!" those women murmured,
with pure hearts, and for no other reason.[7]

At this moment in the story, the prince has not left the palace for good—he has simply slipped out to see what he can see, even as he is himself the center of attention. In the image, the prince is not actually depicted in corporeal form, either; while he is slipping out to see what he can see, we can't actually see him. We can be sure he is there in the story, as the fly-whisk bearer, horse, and royal umbrella are present to hold his place.

Siddhārtha is not the only element missing in this tableau. This image also does not physically represent certain events commonly told in the biographical literature, the "germs of awareness and questioning,"[8] that led the prince to leave the palace, such as the Four Sights. Most textual renditions explicitly focus on the Four Sights—the old man, sick man, dead man, and renunciant—but these are not part of the tableau here. But as the saying goes, "absence of presence does not mean the presence of absence." In other words, the lack of physical representation does not mean the full story is not a part of this scene; the absence of a figural image of the main character Siddhārtha proves this point! Let's stray from the image for a moment to retell this missing story.

The Four Sights

A very common story within the story that is not explicitly depicted in the gateway image from Sanchi is the iconic story of the Four Omens, or Sights—old man, sick man, dead man, and renunciant—that catalyze the prince's desire to leave. Some tellings are compact (the *Lalitavistara* has all four sights in one excursion), some are iterative (*Jātakanidāna* narrates excursions on consecutive days[9]), and the *Buddhacarita* separates the three first sights from the fourth (we will meet the fourth sight, the mendicant, at the *jambu* tree later). As the sights are about Siddhārtha's increasing ability to see, and in turn awaken, we will tell the story as it theatrically unfolds in the *Buddhacarita*, which captures some of the spectacle that Siddhārtha himself becomes as he leaves the city to see more of the world, a sight depicted in the gateway frieze.[10]

Inclined to sightsee, to see what's out in the world, the prince sets out "as citizens from all sides gaped at him, a road strewn with eyes like blue lotus halves, eyes open wide with curiosity."[11] Ladies clamber for a view from upper stories: "commotion then reigned in those balconies, as they thronged pressing against each other, ornaments on their bodies jingling loud, their earrings aflutter with the jostling."[12] He's aware of the spectacle, and that he is on display: "Seeing for the first time the royal highway, so crowded with respectful citizens, dressed in clean and dignified clothes, the prince rejoiced somewhat and thought he was in some way born again."[13]

Significantly, it isn't just the citizens watching. The gods "create" an old man to place in Siddhārtha's sightline, "in order to induce the son of the king to go forth."[14] In other words, by conjuring the depredations of old age, the prince might become disenchanted and renounce the world. Then, "his gaze unwavering directed solely on that man,"[15] the Bodhisattva sees the first of the four sights, the old man, and questions his charioteer about what it is he is witnessing.

He may seem ignorant, but he is primed for this experience, "hearing about old age he became deeply perturbed (*saṃvivije*),"[16] and his distressed emotional state disrupts his singular focus on the old man. In his averted vision, the peripheral gaze, he sees sharp contrast with the surrounding happy people:

> He sighed deeply and shook his head,
> he fixed his eyes on that old man,
> and, seeing the people full of joy,
> dejected (*saṃvigna*), he uttered these words:
> "Old age thus strikes down without distraction,
> Memory, beauty, and manly valor;
> And yet people do not become distraught (*saṃvega*),
> Seeing such a man with their very eyes."[17]

The sight of the old man shocks him, the contrast between the suffering of the old man and the joy of the crowds of people shocks him, and he is moved to wonder why such a sight does not shock the people.

In the *Jātakanidāna*, the scene is private, "The Bodhisatta and the charioteer only were able to see [them]." And in the conjuring of the old man by deities in this text, there is added weight to the sense of blueprint because the deities seem to be following a plan. The deities think, "Prince Siddhattha's time for Enlightenment is drawing near; let us show him the Omens," as if the Omens (sights) are a predetermined and expected event.[18] The *Buddhacarita*, by contrast, establishes a sense of pattern in the Bodhisattva's actions. After seeing the old man, the prince quickly retreats to the palace, only to repeat the adventure with subsequent excursions where he sees a sick man, and then a dead man. Each sight follows a precise blueprint—the Bodhisattva moves out of the palace, encounters a sight, has an insight, and returns to the palace—only for it to happen again. This seems like a paradigm, a blueprint for lifetimes within *saṃsāra*—one experiences, and sees, and learns much, only to be reborn to do it all again. Within this one lifetime, the blueprint is seemingly disrupted when the prince does not return to the palace as he did in his practice runs, but instead sends his horse and groom back alone—the scene that is our focus for this chapter.

We might recall the blueprint aspect of the Four Sights, and how, as fabulae, they are framed in the canonical material within a lesson from Gautama Buddha himself. In the *Mahāpadāna Sutta* (Dīgha Nikāya 14), the Buddha recounts not his own vision of the four sights, but that of a former buddha, Vipassī.[19] Like Gautama, Vipassī was born into a royal family, and events surrounding his birth were just like those of Gautama's—extraordinary, but "normal" for a buddha-to-be. Like Gautama, he was presented to seers to interpret the thirty-two marks of a *māhapuruṣa* (great man). But Vipassī ("well-seeing, gifted with insight") was well-named because he was clairvoyant, unblinking, and able to see at great distance whether it was day or night. Like Gautama, when he no longer derived pleasure from seeing his female musicians perform, he left the palace to sightsee four times, although these visits occurred thousands of years apart (Vipassī lived to be 80,000 years old). He, too, encountered the Four Sights of the old man, sick man, corpse, and mendicant.[20] The sights inspired his renunciation, where he, too, was awakened and encouraged by Brahmā to teach. The life stories are essentially the same; Gautama, as a buddha, is not unique, and in relating the story of a past buddha, the blueprint is made visible.[21]

So central and vividly portrayed in various written versions of the Buddha's life story, the episode where the Bodhisattva sees and reflects on the four sights—an old man, sick man, corpse, and renunciant—is surprisingly absent in the early visual record, and it is absent here.[22] But it looms large in the literary record. The perception and impact of these three natural, inescapable states stick with the prince, and prime him to see things in a new light. The sights steer him through his awakening and set the scene for the first noble truth (that all life is *duḥkha*: dis-ease, and suffering). What troubles him (*saṃvega*) gets under his skin. The *saṃvega*-inducing visions are extraordinary in the eyes of the Bodhisattva/beholder; the sights grip him, and he can't unsee them. And most significantly, the excursions are precursors and practice runs for the Great Departure to come.

Accidental Teachers: Kisāgotamī and the Dancing Girls

Other events, too, portend the Great Departure, and others other than the Four Omens help prime the Buddha-to-be for the quest of his lifetime(s). In the *Jātakanidāna*, the events following "the four omens"[23] and immediately preceding the Great Departure entail lessons learned from women, like those leaning over the balconies in Kapilavastu. While these stories are not explicitly revealed on our Sanchi architrave, we can perhaps read a synoptic reference into the presence of the women depicted on the palace balconies. Kisāgotamī, a

Kṣatriya (royal) woman poised in an upper balcony, watches the prince process out of the palace, and . . .

> beholding the majestic beauty of the bodhisatta as he paraded the city streets, gave utterance to the following statement of joy, being exceedingly pleased by his appearance:
>
> > Tranquilled indeed is the mother, tranquilled is the father, and tranquilled is the woman who has a lord like him.[24]

The verse she utters is a famous passage that makes its way into multiple texts as part of the intertextual, pastiche reading world of Buddhists. What we and readers through time know is something Kisāgotamī within the text does not because the *Jātakanidāna*'s narrator weaves commentary directly into the narrative of the text: *Nibbuta*, "tranquilled," in a polysemous way conjures another meaning, "to extinguish," like a lamp. And so the Buddha-to-be comes to a very different comprehension of her utterance, perhaps prefiguring his altered mindset to come, where his mind is set on awakening rather than the elements of life in the palace:

> When the fires of attachment, hatred and delusion are extinguished, and the cares of all defilements such as those arising from arrogance and dogmatic beliefs are allayed, then only is one tranquilled. A worthy saying she has put into my hearing; and I go about seeking Nibbāna. It is meet that this very day I should give up household life, go forth, and become a religious mendicant in order to seek Nibbāna.[25]

The polysemous phrase allows for two simultaneously true meanings of the uttered phrase, enabling misaligned understandings. The misunderstanding between the two characters is not the prince's alone. It is a double misunderstanding, or rather, an understanding of the higher truth, that provides the narrative catalyst for the Buddha-to-be's imminent departure. He has no more need of the royal jewels around his neck, having already lodged the thought of awakening. Struck by the "worthy saying," he tosses her the necklace as "a teacher's fee," and she is thrilled; framed by her lower understanding of the exchange she thinks that this gesture means the prince is in love with her. By removing the mark of his princely status, he foreshadows the removal of his jeweled top-knot during his imminent Great Departure. He misunderstands her, and then she misunderstands his gift; the true gift will be his Buddhahood made possible by his renunciation.

The Buddha-to-be is now on a mission; he cannot shake the Four Sights when he returns to his mansion, primed by Kisāgotamī's lesson. In the *Buddhacarita*, the women charged with providing him with comfort and pleasure fail miserably in distracting the prince with flirtations. Some quips flung in flirtation strike close to home, "Women have conquered you! Now, sir, conquer this earth!"[26] Another woman demands that he look at various trees that she imagines represent lovers—her insistent, vocative "Look . . . !"[27] peppering, pressuring him to sway his attention to look out there, beyond the palace. All of the sights of the seraglio intended to distract him only make him double down on his insight.[28] "Although seduced in this way, he wavered not, nor rejoiced, firmly guarding his senses, and perturbed at the thought: 'One must die.' "[29]

The scene of the female entertainers in *Lalitavistara* plays upon misaligned perceptions as well. The music produced by a bevy of female entertainers is meant to seduce and amuse the prince, but the gods again intervene and the instruments instead play quite a different tune. Instead of the beautiful music that might be heard by others not as advanced in the cultivation of insight, the prince hears a reminder that he has been on a long path through many lifetimes, and that it is time to leave for good:

> "Seeing the beings who are forever without protector,
> Hero, you made the following promise:
> 'I will awaken to the supreme state without old age or grief
> So that I can deliver all beings from death, old age, and other sufferings.'
> "Therefore, Virtuous One, quickly leave this fine city
> And practice the conduct of previous sages.
> When you reach the right place on the earth,
> You shall awaken to the incomparable wisdom of the victorious ones.
> "In the past you gave away your exquisite wealth and riches,
> And even your hands, feet, and dear body.
> Great Sage, now is your time;
> Open up the limitless river of Dharma for sentient beings."[30]

The Buddha-to-be hears what he needs to hear, much as he heard what he needed from Kisāgotamī.

In the *Jātakanidāna*, women make an effort to distract him from his detachment, only to grow bored when he fails to pay them attention. They fall asleep in all sorts of positions, "some of them with saliva pouring out of their mouths, some with bodies wet with saliva, some grinding their teeth . . . The large terrace of his mansion, magnificently decorated and resembling the abode of Sakka appeared to him as a charnel ground full of corpses scattered here and there."[31] Disgusted,[32] he immediately calls for his groom Channa (Chandaka) and announces, "I wish to set out on my Great Renunciation today."[33] The natural state of the women in disarray, reminding the Bodhisattva of the fleshy unsatisfactoriness of grounded, human existence leads to a sense of urgency for him to get on with his story.

The Great Departure

Returning to the frieze depicted at the beginning of the chapter, we see the moment the prince leaves the palace. We can follow the pointed attention of the citizens of Kapilavastu, and the gaze of the devas above them emphasizing the visual absence of the protagonist, Siddhārtha Gautama. They, like us, peer onto an absent presence. Much has been written on what is called an aniconic period in Buddhist art, where the Buddha is represented by surrogate symbols such as the bodhi tree or footprints.[34] In this image, the lack of the depicted personage does not mean the story is lacking—in fact, one might argue the story is more important because the blanks are filled in by an activated imagination. In this image we can "read" the Bodhisattva as present by the presence of the royal umbrella over the horse Kanthaka, led by his groom Chandaka, as they emerge from the city. A space is held visually and narratively for the Buddha-to-be. The blank space itself, the placeholder for the buddha-to-be, moves through the architrave, carrying the story forward just as Kanthaka carried the Bodhisattva.

Looking closely, we see that Kanthaka himself is also being carried—his hooves are lifted by the devas,[35] or in the case of the *Buddhacarita*, the *yakṣa*s. "*Yakṣa*s, then, bending their bodies low, supported the horse's hooves with the tips of their trembling hands, hands that resembled lotus buds, forearms adorned with golden bands, so that it seemed they were scattering lotuses."[36] In the *Lalitavistara*, a host of beings—gods, *nāgas*, *yakṣas*, and *gandharva*s—all conspire to make the prince's escape possible.[37] Siddhārtha's departure from the palace was not only inspired by others, but supported by others as well.

The image provides us with a view into the macrocosmic reverberations, the ripples of support that reach and carry along the Bodhisattva and his story. In this panel, the people of Kapilavastu jostle to catch sight of Siddhārtha as he departs, yet in many versions of the story, the gods put the residents of Kapilavastu to sleep to assist in the Bodhisattva's secretive escape (hence the need for the *yakṣa*s to muffle Kanthaka's hooves). A frieze can hardly present all versions of the narrative at once, contradictory as they are. But this window into Kapilavastu and the citizens' relationship to their prince and his quest may conflate several significant episodes in a productive way for the viewer "reading" it. We might more productively think about Kapilavastu's representation here as synoptic (where multiple episodes are shown in a single frame), as the residents appear wide awake and eager to catch a glimpse of the action.[38] Perhaps there is a visual conflation here to be more in line with their behavior in other episodes within the biographies where they yearn to see the Bodhisattva.

This observation on reading strategy provides us with an opportunity to consider the visual mode of narration on our architrave, which Vidya Dehejia has confidently identified as continuous[39] insofar as the various episodes unfold from left to right, from the (absent) prince leaving the palace, to leaving Kanthaka and Chandaka behind at the far right. It is true there is movement to follow—Kanthaka's image repeats four times moving left to right across the architrave, visually moving the absent Bodhisattva across the scene and out of the view of the city, and then you see Kanthaka in an abrupt, reversed direction, without the umbrella/Bodhisattva, heading back to Kapilavastu alone.[40] At the far upper right are a pronounced pair of *buddhapada* (footprints) where the Bodhisattva has apparently dismounted from his supportive friend and conatal Kanthaka, with the royal umbrella and fly whisk suspended above—a representation of Siddhārtha using his own two feet to find his place, even if it is preordained by the structured Buddha-life blueprint. We know where this story is going.

A Centered Tree

Figure 5.3 Detail of Figure 5.1 at the center: the tree embellished with a surrounding fence and garlands; the Great Stūpa at Sanchi, Eastern Gateway, middle architrave; courtesy of Kevin Standage.

Returning to what we can see on the image of the Great Renunciation on Sanchi's eastern gate, in the midst of the bustle and bifurcating the relief at the very center, we see a prominent tree, highlighted in Figure 5.3. It is embellished by the *vedika* (surrounding fence) and garlands that often demarcate the bodhi tree, which is both a stylized representation of the awakened Buddha as well as a fitting *caitya*, or place for remembering the Buddha.[41] But early archaeologist and interpreter Sir John Marshall identifies it as "a *jambu* tree (*Eugenia Jambu*), placed there by the sculptor, apparently as a reminder of the first meditation of the Bodhisattva and the path on which it subsequently led him."[42]

If we follow Marshall's identification, as I am inclined to do, the inclusion of this reminder of his past meditative experience brings another fabula, piece of the story, literally to the front and center. Several of the biographies place the Bodhisattva's meditation during the king's ploughing festival in his early childhood, well before the Great Departure.[43] With these versions of the event in mind, the placement of the *jambu* (rose apple) recalls the young Siddhārtha's first foray—a rehearsal—into meditation. But the Sanchi visual narrative might better be read in sync with the *Buddhacarita*, which places the meditation under the *jambu* after the Bodhisattva has already encountered three of the four sights (the old man, sick man, dead man, but not yet the renunciant).[44] That the *jambu* tree is placed here is a very significant example of penetrative synoptic visual narration, invoking the event when the Bodhisattva truly sees suffering for the first time.

The story goes like this. During a ploughing festival, Siddhārtha finds shade under a *jambu* tree and meditates. He enters the first level of meditative trance as he watches his father the king leading the other ploughmen driving suffering oxen, toiling with ploughs that slice through the soil homes, and the bodies, of insects and worms. He sees suffering in the midst of human labors, and attains the first *jhāna*, meditative state of absorption, contemplating the wretched, ignorant men "blinded by pride," unmoved by compassion for those who are afflicted—that which he had seen. "As thus he saw rightly the evils of the world, the evils of disease, old age, and death, pride of self in an instant departed from him, pride resulting from his strength, youth, and life."[45]

As if to highlight this important step toward renunciation and awakening, the sun participates in a miracle—the shade of the tree does not move naturally in the afternoon but stays over him. The *Jātakanidāna* places this episode in the Bodhisatta's childhood, enhancing the miraculous nature of his early meditative prowess. In that iteration, his nurses get the attention of the king to show him this miracle, and the king pays homage. Oblivious that he has become a highlighted spectacle for others, the Bodhisatta practices insight himself.[46]

In the *Buddhacarita*, however, this episode occurs well after three of the four sights, and after rebuffing the advances of the seraglio women. Instead of a festival scene, the Bodhisattva is dramatically moved to take leave of his father and head into the forest, "yearning to find peace."[47] He dismounts Kanthaka his horse and walks over the freshly turned soil scattered with bug parts, feeling a depth of grief as if his own family has been killed. He cries out at the wretchedness of the world; this awareness is the first step in the dress-rehearsal for his imminent Great Departure. Shedding the friends who had accompanied him—this is to be a solo quest, a rehearsal for the Great Departure—he sits under the rose apple (*jambu*) tree, contemplates the birth and death of all creatures, and enters into the first meditative state. Immediately afterward, he reiterates what he had learned from seeing the Four Sights: "How wretched that ignorant man, blinded by pride, who, though himself powerless and subject to the law or disease, old age, and death, should treat with contempt another who's sick, dead, or oppressed by old age!"[48] And he acknowledges he has come to know the "supreme dharma." This might be where the "germ of awareness and questioning" catalyzed by the first three sights takes actual root, the ploughing festival providing a fruitful field for cultivation. It also produces the opportunity for the fourth sight, for at the moment the bodhisattva commits to his awareness, a deity appears in the disguise of a renunciant. In this iteration, the meditation on suffering primes the prince to recognize his path forward.

The ploughing festival meditation can be understood as a trial run for the ultimate renunciation. Here, after the women in his harem failed to distract him from the perturbation of seeing an old man, sick man, and corpse, the prince ventures out on his horse Kanthaka and stumbles upon men ploughing in the fields, tearing up the soil. Notice that he strives for solitude, even amid the busy scene of a farming festival, pushing away his retinue and followers (like those in the gateway's architrave). "Getting rid of those friends who accompanied him, wishing to reach some clarity in his own mind, he reached the foot of a rose apple tree (*jambu*) in a lonely spot."[49]

But in this story, it isn't time for the full awakening. A distracting deity rouses him from his meditation, and the prince begrudgingly returns to the palace, recognizing he was returning for the sake of others although his heart was in the forest. This, too, seems to be a dry run for his renunciation and future return to the city for the sake of others.

In that very same episode, he is also a sight—a spectacle—himself. The miracle of the sun not moving draws the attention and awe of Śuddhodana (his father, the king) within the text, and the attention of the biographers outside it. They have used this episode illustratively, gesturing to the preordained, meditative, special nature of the prince, even when the prince seems unaware of his fate. This episode also functions as a scene of confirmation or affirmation for the reader/audience; the spectacle is a site for reflection and aspiration. Every telling is a retelling, refreshing the site for insight. Centrally represented on the architrave, this *Jambu* tree attracts attention just as the Buddha-to-be did, and prefigures the meditation and awakening that will be accomplished under the *bodhi* tree.

The Destination

Figure 5.4 Detail of Figure 5.1 at far right: Kanthaka moves the Buddha-to-be through throngs of people and gods to approach the destination; the Great Stūpa at Sanchi, Eastern Gateway, middle architrave; courtesy of Kevin Standage.

To the right of the central tree, Kanthaka moves the buddha-to-be through throngs of people and gods to approach the destination where he will stand on his own two feet. We do not see the scene captured in textual iterations of the Great Departure where the prince takes off the rest of his royal jewels and clothes and cuts off his hair. How could the frieze depict that dramatic gesture, as the Bodhisattva is not depicted in anthropomorphic form? New robes are provided, his top knot whisked away by the gods for future use as a relic, and the Bodhisattva is officially launched. The Buddha's footprints, the destination depicted in Figure 5.4, mark a palpable presence in the way the emptiness above Kanthaka's back cannot. Kanthaka is sent back toward Kapilavastu, dejected. That is the end of the story in our Sanchi gateway frieze.

What we do not get to see, but that is captured in the literary depictions of his time in the forest, away from Kapilavastu, are the Buddha-to-be's penultimate lessons from others. He seeks teachings from the ascetics Ārāḍa Kālāma and Udraka Rāmaputra, but ultimately finds them wanting and sets off on his own. He engages in another experience of mutual mistaken understanding when Sujātā gives him an offering of milk-rice. Sujātā was planning to honor the tree deity of the tree under which the Bodhisattva was sitting because her fervent wish for a child had come true. The Buddha-to-be accepted the gift of food after an extreme period of diet and preparation for his awakening, and the nourishment, arguably, is what helped him find the middle way. We will see more of the others in the next chapter; our frieze concludes with the solitary footprints of the Bodhisattva.

End Scene

In the Introduction to this book, we considered John Strong's caution regarding the "bias toward individualism in the study of sacred biography."[50] The path to awakening is often understood to be an inward, meditative process—a singular experience for a singular hero—but we have seen that in the events leading up to the awakening the star of the show had an extensive supporting cast, both in this final performance and in all the various dress rehearsals leading up to it. Cautioning against a fixation on the protagonist focalized by a "longitudinal" depth reading of a singular hero, John Strong argues for a "lateral expansion" as one reads through the expansive buddha life story. This lateral expansion includes the net of relationships that frame and support the Bodhisattva's experiences and life lessons. A good example of what a lateral expansion might reveal is in Sasson's preceding chapter; looking into the karmic depth of Gotama's relationship with Yaśodharā (through past lives, through various versions), she too observes that it is "not his story alone."[51]

What happens when we expand the lateral gaze, extend outward from the immediate *dramatis personae,* the named and recognizable members of Siddhārtha's community, and take stock of the others in the story? When reading various literary biographies, it can be difficult to see and appreciate the significant impact of others in the story. Strong suggests that an expanded, lateral vision, the point of the story shifts from the recognition of "significant biographical units," to an appreciation of "the multiple and collective dimensions of certain common biographical events."[52] As we have followed Kanthaka and his precious invisible cargo across the frieze at the beginning of this chapter, we have been applying a hermeneutical strategy we can call averted vision, which in astronomy refers to the practice of shifting or softening your gaze from the object you wish to perceive to rely more on peripheral perception. A star might be hard to see until you look indirectly, and then it pops into relief. The star of the Buddha biography is, of course, Siddhārtha Gautama, but by looking sideways at the cast of characters, and softening further to imagine the parts of the story that are not even visible in this form, we let our interpretive sight soften on the Bodhisattva to take in the actions of those around him, and his blueprint might snap into sharper focus.

The part of the Buddha biography we have considered here exceeds the Great Renunciation as depicted in the Sanchi Great Stūpa's eastern gateway frieze. We traced the prince's growing disenchantment with royal life, his encounters with others and experience of events that serve as incitements to renounce, and the Great Renunciation itself where he abandons the palace and his city, cuts his hair and changes clothes, sends his friends and horse back so he might find solitude. The panel presents selected fabulae of the story we want to cover, specifically the Great Departure, but not even close to all of it. A lateral look, an averted gaze, lets us take in and explore the fuller picture of the relationship between sights and insight, beginning with the spectacle of the Bodhisattva as seen through his (female) admirers, his own "Four Sights" (the sick man, old man, dead man, and renunciant) that catalyze his departure for ascetic life, and ending with the Bodhisattva choosing the most salient seat for the cultivation of insight according to the pattern established by all Buddhas before him.

It is possible even to extend a laterally expansive, averted vision to include the various ways the Buddha's story is read, seen, and reenacted within the realm of ritual. Strong says, "his Great Departure, even today, provides a mythic model for the ordination of Buddhist monks,"[53] who ask permission to leave home to join the monastery, shave their heads, don robes, and change behaviors and habits just like the Buddha did. Take a look at the image opening this chapter. How many pilgrims (and tourists, and scholars) have peered at this frozen tableau? Look closer. From the women peering over the balconies to catch a sight of the prince at the left, to the figure paying homage to footprints at the right, we see that the events leading up to the awakening, profoundly inward-turned insight all have to do with outward seeing and spectacle.

In this book, while retelling the story of the significant life of Siddhārtha Gautama, we have been thinking about what John Strong has called the "Buddha-life blueprint" in terms of the discrete events and accomplishments that must be experienced in order to become a buddha. Like traditional formulations, such as the list of "Twelve Great Acts" recognized in Tibetan tradition, a checklist is one way to think of the blueprint. Softening our gaze, however, from the vantage point of this book, we might also see that relationships conjured in the Buddha's life story are also building blocks for it, concretely providing context for his nascent renunciation and awakening. We might think about a blueprint as both a *model of* and a *model for* a building.[54] As a *model of*, it represents what exists so you can find the plumbing, electrical wiring, placement of windows and such—for a Buddha, a way to describe how he came to be and what he's made of. As a *model for*, a blueprint assures there may be buildings—and buddhas—in the future, and illustrates how they are made.

Just as the artists responsible for Sanchi's eastern gateway cast the story in a particular way,[55] so each literary rendition gathers the jewel-like fabulae, a kaleidoscopic creation. There are also events in the Buddha's life story that are not uniformly or explicitly articulated as requisite acts or events for a developing Buddha, but that circulate and carry the biography along. As John Strong has explained, "It should be remembered that in Buddhism, it is biography that makes a buddha and not the Buddha who makes his biography."[56]

Maybe it is because Siddhārtha's physical presence is removed from our vision that we are more able to see and interpret the supporting cast of characters and their agency in moving things along. Perhaps the omission of the physical representation of the star of the show in the material presentation of his story has less to do with anxieties over images, whether or not the Buddha can be represented, and more with reading strategies in general. This gateway, after all, opens onto a Great Stūpa, that inescapable, concrete reminder of the Buddha who is gone. This story is what carries him to the current day. Readers/hearers make an analogous effort to re-present Siddhārtha as he navigates his life, just as a viewer of this frieze sees the gestures and surrogate iconography characterizing the Buddha's presence even in his absence.

Notes

1. Sir John Marshall, *A Guide to Sanchi* (Calcutta: Superintendent, Government Printing, 1918), 62.
2. MN 26, see Bhikkhu Ñāṇamoli and Bhikkhu Bodhi, trans., *The Middle Length Discourses of the Buddha: A New Translation of the Majjhima Nikāya* (Boston: Wisdom, 1995), 253–268. Also see Jonathan S. Walters, "Suttas as History: Four Approaches to the 'Sermon on the Noble Quest' (Ariyapariyesanasutta)," *History of Religions* 38, no. 3 (1999), 247–284.
3. Or even before the vow—as he sat cross-legged in his mansion, Sumedha said, "O wise man, painful indeed is conception in a new existence, so is the dissolution of the body in whatever place one is born. And I am subject to birth, decay, disease and death. Being such as I am, it behooves me to seek for the great immortal state of Nibbāna, which is tranquil and free from birth, decay, disease and both pain and pleasure. Surely there must be a unique path that leads to Nibbāna, affording release from becoming." N. A. Jayawickrama, trans., *The Story of Gotama Buddha (Jātaka Nidānakathā)* (Oxford: The Pali Text Society, 2000), 5). See Chapter 1 in this volume.
4. N. A. Jayawickrama, trans. *The Story of Gotama Buddha (Jātaka Nidānakathā)*, 3.
5. John S. Strong, *The Buddha: A Short Biography* (London: Oneworld Publications, 2001), 23–24.
6. John Strong has also noted the critical "dry-run" or dress rehearsal for the Buddha's looming absence (*parinirvāṇa*) was his rains retreat in the Trāyastriṃśa heaven (John S. Strong, *Relics of the* Buddha (Princeton, NJ: Princeton University Press, 2004), 140, 177. For this story, see Chapter 7 in this volume. We might think of many instances that the Buddha life story provides for rehearsals, such as Siddhārtha's vision and repudiation of the dancing women prior to his Great Departure which could be understood as valuable practice for seeing and repudiating Māra's daughters (see this story in Chapter 6 of this volume), or when prior to his birth, from his vantage point in the

Tuṣita heaven, he is nudged by the gods to remember his goal of awakening and get on with it, and he surveys the world for the "five great considerations," in situating his birth—the time, country, family, mother, and her lifespan (see *The Story of Gotama Buddha (Jātaka Nidānakathā)*, 64–66, or Chapter 3 in this volume). This event (itself on the blueprint) parallels his search for the perfect seat for awakening, where he circumambulates the tree until he finds stable, established ground on the eastern side, as the "seat of meditation of all Buddhas is on the eastern side, it trembles not and shakes not." *The Story of Gotama Buddha (Jātaka Nidānakathā)*, 94.

7. *Buddhacarita* 3.22–23; all references to *Buddhacarita* refer to Patrick Olivelle, trans., *The Life of the Buddha by Ashvaghosha*. Clay Sanskrit Library (New York: New York University Press and JJC Foundation, 2008).
8. Strong, *The Buddha*, 51.
9. *The Story of Gotama Buddha (Jātaka Nidānakathā)*, 79. Embedded in the text, however, is the recognition of the various ways to retell the story: "But the Reciters of the Dīgha [-nikāya] say: 'He saw the Four Omens on the same day and went [forth].'"
10. The dramatic form of *Buddhacarita* is artfully addressed in Julie Regan, "Pleasure and Poetics as Tools for Transformation in Aśvaghoṣa's Mahākāvya." *Religions* 13 (2022): 578.
11. *Buddhacarita*, 3.10.
12. *Buddhacarita*, 3.18.
13. *Buddhacarita*, 3.25.
14. *Buddhacarita*, 3.26.
15. *Buddhacarita*, 3.27.
16. *Buddhacarita*, 3.34. Elsewhere, I have explored the explicitly preparatory work of *saṃvega* for concomitant *pasāda*, anxious thrill before calming peace. See Kristin Scheible, *Reading the Mahāvaṃsa: The Literary Aims of a Theravāda Buddhist History* (New York: Columbia University Press, 2016).
17. *Buddhacarita*, 3.35–6.
18. *The Story of Gotama Buddha (Jātaka Nidānakathā)*, 78. Note, too, that other elements of the Buddha-life blueprint are framed as clockwork; when the Bodhisattva sends his bowl upstream in the Nairañjanā river which confirms his impending Buddhahood, the bowl sinks in a whirlpool to land noisily atop the bowl used by previous buddhas, alerting the aptly named *nāgarāja* Kāla ("Time") there, who pronounced, "A Buddha was born yesterday, and again another today"(93). In *Buddhacarita*, Kāla awakens to the sound of the Bodhisattva's footsteps approaching the Bodhi tree (and *Lalitavistara* amplifies the "triumphant gait" after his bath in the Nirañjanā and meal from Sujāta), and pronounced that "surely you will become an Awakened One (Buddha) today." This is uttered just as the Bodhisattva sits down, mimicking a sleeping snake's coils with his folded leg posture. The snake "Time" has the last word before the awakening—the Bodhisattva responds, "I'll not break this posture on earth until I have fulfilled my task." *Buddhacarita* 12.116–121. See Kim and Lewis in this volume.
19. Pali sources list him as the nineteenth of twenty-four buddhas prior to Gautama. Gautama was born as a *nāga-rāja* at that time, ninety-one eons ago. See a helpful

table of the past buddhas correlated to the Bodhisattva's births in Strong, *The Buddha*, 26–29.

20. DN 14.2.1–14.2.14, see Maurice Walshe, *The Long Discourses of the Buddha: A Translation of the Dīgha Nikāya* (Boston: Wisdom Publications, 1995), 253–268.
21. Donald Swearer notes that the candle that is lit by chief sponsor at the outset of a Thai image consecration ceremony (where the buddha's biography is spoken *into* the Buddha image to bring it to life) is called the *tien vipassi.* Donald K. Swearer, "Hypostasizing the Buddha: Buddha Image Consecration in Northern Thailand," *History of Religions* 34, no. 3 (1995): 274.
22. While the Four Sights fabula predominates in extracanonical literature, the story featuring our Bodhisattva is notably absent in Pali canonical materials. However, the thrust of the story, the observability and didacticism of old age, illness, and death (*jarā, vyādhi, maraṇa*) is something that runs as a throughline in numerous suttas. As for the visual record, there are fairly early depictions of individual elements, such as the Bodhisattva "seeing the old man," or "seeing the sick man," on the walls of Borobudur, a colossal ninth century stūpa in central Java. Hajime Nakamura cites one "unusual" Gandhāran image of the newly married Gautama and Yaśodhara observing old age, sickness, and death together, at the same time. In a statement that supports Vanessa Sasson's argument in this book, Nakamura says this image means that "Siddhattha did not abandon his wife when he renounced the world, but that his act was based on a mutual understanding between them." He also shows how later Chinese materials correlate the excursions from the palace through each gate with the particular sights and offers a helpful list of legends concerning the "Excursions from the Four Gates." See Hajime Nakamura, *Gotama Buddha: A Biography Based on the Most Reliable Texts*, vol. 1 (Tokyo: Kosei, 2000), 95–99.
23. *The Story of Gotama Buddha (Jātaka Nidānakathā)*, 78–82.
24. Nibbutā nūna sā mātā nibbuto nūna so pitā, Nibbutā nūna sā nārī yassāyaṃ īdiso patī'ti; *The Story of Gotama Buddha (Jātaka Nidānakathā)*, 81.
25. *The Story of Gotama Buddha (Jātaka Nidānakathā)*, 81.
26. *Buddhacarita* 4.42.
27. *Buddhacarita* 4.44–50.
28. This anticipates a similar attempt to ensnare his attention by Māra's seductive daughters, see the following chapter in this book.
29. *Buddhacarita* 4.54.
30. *Lalitavistara* 13.19–21, Dharmachakra Translation Committee, *The Play in Full (Lalitavistara)* (84000: Translating the Words of the Buddha, n.d.).
31. *The Story of Gotama Buddha (Jātaka Nidānakathā)*, 82.
32. This recalls the disgust he felt in his birth as Sumedha when he first renounced the world: "And as men and women discharging their excrement on the depositing ground do not take it with them in their laps or wrapped in the folds of their garments, but depart discarding it with loathing, with no desire for it whatever, even so should I discard this putrid body with no attachment for it and enter the city of Nibbāna." *The Story of Gotama Buddha (Jātaka Nidānakathā)*, 7.

33. *The Story of Gotama Buddha (Jātaka Nidānakathā)*, 82.
34. See S. L. Huntington, "Early Buddhist Art and the Theory of Aniconism," *Art Journal* 49, no. 4 (1990): 401–408; and Vidya Dehejia, "Aniconism and the Multivalence of Emblems," *Ars Orientalis* 21 (1991): 45–66.
35. *The Story of Gotama Buddha (Jātaka Nidānakathā)*, 83; *Buddhacarita*, 5.80.
36. *Buddhacarita*, 5.81. Also see the discussion among the *yakṣas* about the merit they will make for having carried the prince in this way in *Lalitavistara*, 15.26 in Dharmachakra Translation Committee, *The Play in Full (Lalitavistara)* (84000: Translating the Words of the Buddha, n.d.).
37. *Lalitavistara* 15.23–28.
38. Vidya Dehejia, "On Modes of Visual Narration in Early Buddhist Art," *The Art Bulletin* 72, no. 3 (1990): 382.
39. Vidya Dehejia, "On Modes of Visual Narration in Early Buddhist Art," 387.
40. *The Play in Full (Lalitavistara)*, 15.150; Canto 6, *Buddhacarita*. In *Jātakanidāna*, Kanthaka moves away from the Bodhisattva and dies of his grief; *The Story of Gotama Buddha (Jātaka Nidānakathā)*, 87.
41. *Kāliṅgabodhi Jātaka* (479), in *The Jātaka or Stories of the Buddha's Former Births*, 6 vols., ed. E. B. Cowell, trans. Chalmers, Robert, W. H. D. Rouse, H. T. Francis, R. A. Neil, and E. B. Cowell (Cambridge: Cambridge University Press, 1895–1907), vol. IV, 142–148.
42. Sir John Marshall, *A Guide to Sanchi* (Calcutta: Superintendent, Government Printing, 1918), 61.
43. J. J. Jones, trans., *The Mahāvastu*, The Sacred Books of the Buddhists, vols. 16, 18, and 19 (London: Pali Text Society, 1949–1956 [1952]), 42–44. See also *The Story of Gotama Buddha (Jātaka Nidānakathā)*, 76–77.
44. Note that the blueprint list in the Pali commentarial tradition further affirms the Great Departure cannot occur until *after* the four sights. The Bodhisattva must be adequately primed by his sights to gain insight.
45. *Buddhacarita*, 5.14.
46. *The Story of Gotama Buddha (Jātaka Nidānakathā)*, 76–77.
47. *Buddhacarita*, 5.2.
48. *Buddhacarita*, 5.12.
49. *Buddhacarita*, 5.8.
50. John S. Strong, "A Family Quest: The Buddha, Yaśodharā, and Rāhula in the *Mūlasarvāstivāda Vinaya*," in *Sacred Biography in the Buddhist Traditions of South and Southeast Asia*, ed. Juliane Schober (Honolulu: University of Hawai'i Press, 1997), 114.
51. See Chapter 4 in this volume.
52. Strong, "A Family Quest," 114.
53. Strong, "A Family Quest," 122.
54. For a now-classic source to consult on the force of cultural patterns in religion, helpful to think about the reflective/descriptive and projective/constructive utility of a blueprint, see Clifford Geertz, "Religion as a Cultural System," in *Interpretation of Cultures* (New York: Basic Books, 1973), 93–95.

55. "The artist may also arrange his story in a series of more or less discrete episodes; if so, he must decide the manner in which he wishes to compose these episodes within the visual field. The sculptor or painter can also adopt a variety of modes to present the same or similar narratives to his viewers." Dehejia, "On Modes of Visual Narration in Early Buddhist Art," 374.
56. John S. Strong, *Relics of the Buddha*, 6.

6
Around the Tree of Awakening

Todd Lewis and Jinah Kim

Figure 6.1 View of the Bodhi tree during summer (left) Lay and monastic pilgrims paying homage to the bodhi tree (right), Mahabodhi temple complex, Bodhgaya. Photo by Jinah Kim (left) and Todd Lewis (right)

The great challenge for anyone (ancient or modern) wanting to convey what is meant by the awakening of the Buddha is that its ultimate meaning is beyond words, and well beyond the grasp of the unawakened audience. This moment nonetheless has had to be conveyed in words in the form of oral then written texts. Ancient (and modern) painters and sculptors tasked with representing this moment have faced the same problem. Textual narrative and symbolic art traditions were devised by Buddhist devotees to convey this greatest of human spiritual accomplishments. Artists (*citrakāra/raṅgakāraka*) and Buddhist preachers (*bhāṇaka*) rendered the Śākya-sage's awakening in visual/spoken narratives centered around the fig tree (*ficus religiosa*) where this momentous and cosmos-altering event occurred. In a world largely unable to read, preaching/lecturing

Todd Lewis and Jinah Kim, *Around the Tree of Awakening* In: *The Buddha.* Edited by: Vanessa R. Sasson and Kristin Scheible, Oxford University Press. © Oxford University Press 2024. DOI: 10.1093/oso/9780197649466.003.0007 along with the arts arrayed in monasteries and homes were the primary means of enculturating the beliefs and practices of the Buddhist tradition.

Our analysis of texts and imagery focuses on the event of the awakening and the first seven weeks in the life of the realized Siddhārtha, now a Buddha; it looks closely at the variety of illustrious beings (divine, demonic, human) and their paradigmatic, historically significant actions related to the newly realized sage, called "Sugata," "Tathāgata," or Śākyamuni. It is a remarkable story that begins with an extraordinary account of a man's complete spiritual awakening, in which we encounter gods, demons, serpent deities, dancing women, and devout men. And it all takes place under, and around, a sacred tree.

The site of the Buddha's awakening, Bodhgaya, is the most important pilgrimage site for Buddhists everywhere. During the winter months when the weather in north India is cool, throngs of Buddhists from all parts of the world visit the town now crowded with monasteries built by Buddhists from across the world. At the center of activity is a pipal tree (*Ficus religiosa*) or the Bodhi tree, pictured in Figure 6.1, the place where Siddhārtha reached awakening some 2,500 years ago. In the early morning and at sundown, pilgrims stream together doing continuous circumambulations, most chanting, some prostrating periodically, as they circle in a clockwise direction, the Indic (and Buddhist) ritual of *pradakṣiṇā*. Another focal point is the Mahābodhi temple next to the tree, in which a twelfth-century stone image of the Buddha is now enshrined. The temple with a soaring tower (*śikhara*, Sanskrit for "mountain peak") marks the main sanctum that was probably built after the fourth century CE. That this special tree (and not the temple) was the center of the site from the early centuries of Buddhist history is well attested in the depiction of King Aśoka; he visited the Bodhi tree, as seen in a sculpted scene that appears in one of the architraves of the eastern gateway to the Great Stūpa at Sanchi, a key monument datable to 50 BCE (Figure 6.2). In fact, the tree is not just the main object of pilgrimage but also the focal point in the Buddha's awakening experience and the center where other extraordinary events transpire over the next seven weeks.

Another Great Stūpa architrave on the western gateway reveals the main event of this chapter: the Buddha's defeat of Māra, the demon who is the quintessential incarnation of death and the poisonous *kleśas* (defilements): greed-lust-delusion. This moment is called *Māravijāya*, "Victory over Māra." It is depicted with a tree in the very center of the composition as we see in Figure 6.3.[1] Māra's attacking army, replete with hideous dwarfs, elephants, and horse riders and chariots, fails to elicit any fear in Siddhārtha and turns away in retreat. From the left side of the panel, a retinue of devotees, including adorants, musicians, and bearers of banner and pole standards (with symbols of the *triratna*, the three jewels of Buddhism), approaches the tree. The Bodhi tree at the center of the scene is marked by an umbrella and enshrined within what is probably a multistory temple building; inside, an empty seat marks the spot where the Buddha once sat to achieve awakening.

Figure 6.2 King Aśoka visits the Bodhi tree, architrave of the gateway, Great Stūpa at Sanchi, c. 50 BCE. Photo by Jinah Kim.

Figure 6.3 Aniconic representation of the Buddha's victory over Māra with a Bodhi Tree shrine, which has an empty throne (standing in for the Buddha) in the middle, architrave of the gateway, Great Stūpa at Sanchi, c. 50 BCE. Photo by Jinah Kim.

In what follows, as a method to explore the events around the Bodhi tree, we model an alternative way of narrative communication, one that is centered on the visual records in association with what we have now as written texts. We do so in part to express our appreciation to John Strong, whose scholarship creatively connected disciplinary boundaries, leading to many original insights about the Buddhist tradition and the faith's sociocultural history. As Strong points out, certain moments from the Buddha's life, which are later codified and remembered as the major events of the Buddha's life, are attested in the visual narratives of the Sanchi gateway (50 BCE) when no known text from such an early date records the incident. Just as there are many textual variations in the details of the Buddha's biography, as we have seen in previous chapters, there are many variations in the visual records, where the narrative diversity is even greater.[2]

The context of the production of stone and metal Buddhist sculpture must not be forgotten, when considering how narratives were passed down to artists and the nonliterate householders by word of mouth; as Joanna Williams has pointed out, there is a "likelihood that the Sarnath sculptors did not read at all and were familiar with such literary sources in oral form which can never be precisely reconstructed."[3] While there is no official canon of visual narratives, it is possible to discern a few major templates (or visual strategies) that mark the contours of ways in which people imagined and saw the Buddha's life stories.[4]

In early Buddhist art found at stūpa sites across South Asia, visual narratives are told in many different modes, from monoscenic to synoptic, from conflated to diachronic narrative networks.[5] The Buddha's life and birth stories are often told in a series of framed images whether in roundel or rectangle.[6] Overall, early Buddhist art shows much emphasis on the events leading up to the Buddha's arrival at the tree, and stories of his previous lives.

By the fifth century CE, we begin to see more images of the Buddha's long and illustrious career as a miracle-performing teacher in a few, common key episodes with similar iconographic features.[7] The Buddha's life stories usually get codified into eight great events; these are mapped onto the eight pilgrimage sites in the Buddhist heartland (mainly in today's Bihar, parts of Uttar Pradesh in India, and Lumbini in Nepal).[8] One of the earliest attempts to present the eight scenes of the Buddha's life as a set may be seen in a rectangular stele divided into eight equal compartments found at Sarnath, which may date to the sixth century or later.[9] The most long-lasting, impactful visual strategy for capturing the Buddha's life story occurred during the Pāla-dynasty (eighth through the twelfth century) in north India. The Buddha's attainment of awakening at Bodhgaya began to take center stage in pan-Asian Buddhist iconography: the event is epitomized by a central, enlarged image of the Buddha seated under the Bodhi tree in meditation with his outstretched right hand touching the ground, often with the earth goddess (*bhū devī*) holding up a water jar appearing under his seat. Just as the social and religious orders of this era took on more of a mandala organization with clear center-periphery relations, the key devotional images of Buddhism also use the template of a mandala, with the largest figure, an earth-touching Buddha under the Bodhi tree, as the central focus of the visual field.[10] In it, seven other scenes in miniaturized scale surround the central Buddha like satellites orbiting the earth: Birth, First Sermon, Śrāvastī Miracle, Descent from the Trāyastriṃśa ("The Thirty-three [gods]-) heaven, Taming of the mad elephant, Monkey's offering of honey, with the Parinirvāṇa in the apex.[11] All episodes are represented through cursory visual shorthand, the artist exercising extreme economy of detail with clear hierarchy, highlighting the awakening experience—in what we may call "the Māravijāya template" (Figure 6.4).

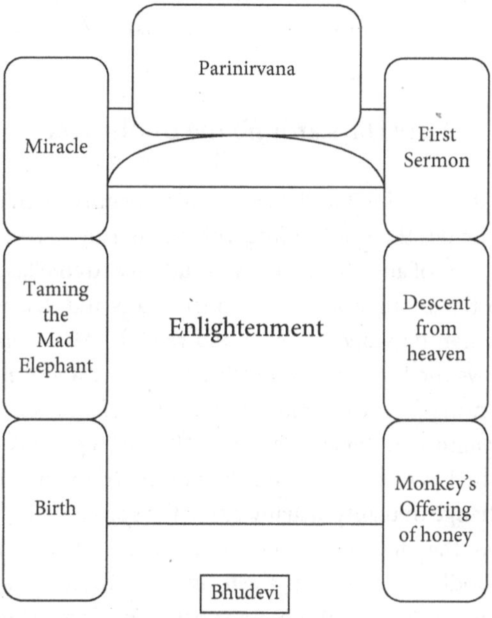

Figure 6.4 Māravijaya template. Diagram by Jinah Kim.

The Māravijāya template (or visual strategy) proved to be the most effective and popular, spreading as far as China (exemplified especially in the later Dunhuang caves) and also to Myanmar and across the Himalayan region until as late as the thirteenth or even fourteenth century.[12] As Janice Leoshko demonstrates, these images with the earth-touching Buddha in the center not only represent the crucial moment in the Buddha biography: they also stand for the spiritual and protective power found in Bodhgaya, the center of the faith.[13] Just as stories in textual sources may have more than one variation, innovations in the paintings and sculptures made using the Māravijāya template appeared occasionally, but none overturned the popularity and effectiveness of the Pāla original until today.

One effective variation may have been the addition of references to the seven weeks after the awakening by surrounding the Buddha with a double row of cursory events, many of which are seen in what is sometimes referred to as "*Andagu* plaques," like the example we see in Figure 6.17.[14] Here and elsewhere, the Buddha's defeat of Māra at Bodhgaya remained the quintessential moment of the life story in visual records throughout the long history of Buddhism, at times expressing cosmic meanings and at other times evoking very immediate, emotional responses. The events around the Bodhi tree have remained popular for illustration in temple murals in the regions of Pali Buddhism such as today's Sri Lanka and Thailand, and the defeat of the Māra's army remains one of the popular topics illustrated on murals in Thai Buddhist communities.

Fifty Days around the Bodhi Tree

This part of the story of the Buddha's awakening begins when a young woman named Sujātā provides the Bodhisattva with an offering of a bowl of rice-milk, breaking off six years of austere practices including extreme fasting. Siddhārtha then resolves to try another way to conquer death and discover the realities that underlie human bondage to death and rebirth. After consuming Sujātā's offering, he throws the bowl into the Nairañjanā river and it moves upstream, depicted in a painting from early modern Sri Lanka (Figure 6.5). This miracle is the result of Śākyamuni performing an "Act of Truth," a practice in ancient India in which a spiritual person calls upon the powers of the universe to effect an extraordinary change in reality, usually citing the speaker's high spiritual status or the recipient of the blessing's virtues. The *Jātakanidāna* recounts this Act of Truth, with the Bodhisattva making the formal declaration: "If I succeed in becoming a Buddha this day, let this bowl go upstream; if not, let it go downstream with the current."[15] It does move upstream, then sinks to the bottom where it lands on bowls of three previous Buddhas (who did the same, in the same place); this alerts a serpent deity named Kāla who had been there since first of three Buddhas.

Here is the first of a series of events when normal material causality gives way to supernatural occurrences, or "miracles" performed by the Buddha. To those who come to understand the full import and impact of a Buddha's appearance in the world, however, these miraculous displays in the Buddha biography will continue until his death, and then be manifested through his relics. Buddhas, in other words, by their appearance, alter the causal universe humans inhabit:

> Reality is always responsive to consciousness, but only a Buddha can exercise utter control over it. . . . As reality is linked to Buddhahood. The Buddha displays this truth through his command of the physical elements. . . . He offers a dramatic demonstration of matter being utterly malleable in the hands of a realized being.[16]

Figure 6.5 Buddha throws his begging bowl into the Nairañjanā river and it travels upward, c. early twentieth century, wall painting, Sri Lanka. Photo by Todd Lewis.

Figure 6.6 Buddha receives a bundle of *kuśa* grass from a grasscutter, c. early twentieth century, wall painting, Kelaniya Temple, Colombo, Sri Lanka. Photo by Todd Lewis.

Soon after this scene with Sujātā's bowl, the Bodhisattva walks toward his destined seat under the tree, meets a grasscutter and asks him to give a bundle of *kuśa* grass to sit on. *Kuśa* is a tall, tufted, leafy, perennial grass used in Vedic ritual and recommended as auspicious in later Hindu texts; Siddhārtha now intends to use it for a meditation seat. As in other details of the biography (e.g., *kṣatriya* education and training; wedding ceremony), the Bodhisattva follows preexisting Indic traditions. In the modern Newar epic of the Buddha's life, *Sugata Saurabha*, Kathmandu Valley poet Chittadhar Hridaya uses this request to introduce a moment of levity to move away from the ordeals of extreme asceticism and the Bodhisattva's swooning from the near-death experience of radical fasting. After seeing the brahmin grasscutter, he requests, "Give me a handful of straw." So the Brahmin lays his bundle to one side and asks, "Of what use is this straw to you?" Replies the Bodhisattva, "I will attain enlightenment sitting on it!" The brahmin laughs and replies, "How? Such knowledge has not come to us even though we sit on it every day!"[17] This same humorous sentiment is also reflected in the expression of the grass cutter's wife in a modern painting from Sri Lanka (Figure 6.6).[18]

Many traditions next show the Bodhisattva approaching the Bodhi tree.[19] He considers exactly where under its branches to take a seat with his back to the trunk. He considers all sides, following the norm of Indic clockwise circumambulatory worship called *pradakṣīṇā*. When he selects the south side, the earth quakes in protest; the same happens when he tries the west and north sides. But after he sits on the side that faces east, there is great peace and quiet, and there he places the *kuśa* grass. After sitting, he repeats the vow,

> Here on this seat my body may shrivel up,
> My skin, my bones, my flesh may dissolve,
> But my body will not move from this very seat
> Until I have obtained Awakening
> So difficult to obtain in the course of many kalpas.[20]

Entrance of Māra

The main antagonist of the Buddha stories appears prominently after the Bodhisattva first sits under the Bodhi tree: an evil, supernatural being named Māra. The earliest artistic representations of Māra show him as a regally adorned male figure carrying a weapon (spear or sword). He challenges the Buddha who sits cross-legged, peaceful, and resolute under the tree.[21] Māra's regal appearance is fitting for his stature as "a high-ranking god, one of the chief divinities of the realm of desire."[22]

This original confrontation of Māra's army and his defeat is seen in Cave 26 at the fifth century Buddhist cave temple site Ajanta (Figures 6.9 and 6.10), and is also found in the late eighth century relief sculpture at Borobudur (in Java, Indonesia) (Figures 6.7 and 6.8).

Figure 6.7 Scene of Māravijāya, first floor gallery, Candi Borobudur, Java, Indonesia, c. 780–850 CE, volcanic stone. Photo by Jinah Kim.

Figure 6.8 Detail of Figure 6.7 showing dejected Māra with his right hand on his chin being consoled by his retinue. Photo by Jinah Kim.

Close inspection of Figures 6.9 and 6.10 reveals a slender and regally adorned male figure seated looking dejected with his right hand propping up his face and with his sword on his lap on the bottom right side. Māra here is being consoled by his retinue.

Figure 6.9 Māra seated with his right hand on his chin being consoled by his daughters, detail of the Māravijāya panel, Cave 26, Ajanta, c. fifth century CE. Image courtesy of Regents of the University of Michigan, Department of the History of Art, Visual Resources Collections.

Māra is called both a *deva* ("divinity") and a *yakṣa* ("demon"). His name translates as "death" or "maker of death." Buddhist teaching regards him as a very powerful being who rules the world of mortals. Since all must die who at death have karma that leads to rebirth, Māra promotes the pursuit of *tṛṣṇa* ("thirst" or "desire") and blinds all in his realm from seeing that desire is the cause of suffering (as proclaimed in the Four Noble Truths). Māra foments false views, illusion, and distraction to confuse beings. In another doctrinal formulation, if individuals have been "poisoned" by the three *kleśas*[23]—as depicted in the very center of the

Figure 6.10 Māra's daughters dancing to seduce the Buddha while musicians play music, bottom half of the Māravijāya panel, Cave 26, Ajanta, c. fifth century CE. Image courtesy of Regents of the University of Michigan, Department of the History of Art, Visual Resources Collections.

wheel of life—they will continue to wander in Māra's domain, the six realms of rebirth. In other words, it is Māra who rules our mortal world.

But his unfettered dominion is threatened by the appearance of a bodhisattva who is about to become a Buddha. And Māra is a determined figure who wants to keep ruling unimpeded over mortals, most of whom have no clue about how to conquer their bondage to suffering and mortality. So he aggressively stalks, taunts, and interferes with the Bodhisattva in every way he can imagine.[24]

Predictably, his many attempts fail, and Māra soon feels there is no alternative but to attack the Bodhisattva directly. So Māra calls up his "Eightfold Army." Māra attacks and all the gods, including Indra and Brahma, flee in fear. Siddhārtha faces Māra's army alone.[25]

Māra's minions begin by sending swirling, destructive winds from the high Himalayas, but the gales never reach the Bodhi tree. Māra's armies then gather many hundreds of thousands of massed clouds that rain down torrents, so that the earth becomes soaked. But even as the mass of clouds rain destructively over the nearby forest groves and trees, not a single drop wets the Bodhisattva. Then, Māra sends a rain of stones, like those from a massive exploding volcano; these merely fall as bunches of divine flowers at the feet of the Bodhisattva.

After that, Māra sends a rain of all weapons—single edged, double edged swords, javelins, knives, and various others—that fall smoking and burning from the sky, but these turn into divine flowers and fall harmlessly before the Bodhisattva. Māra persists. He sends a rain of red-hot charcoal that falls from the sky, but these turn to divine flowers as they fall gently at his feet. White-hot ash likewise falls as fragrant pollen; fine smoking and flaming sand turns to divine aromatic powder. And smoking mud falls as a divine ointment. Māra next tries to frighten Siddhārtha by engulfing him in utter darkness. But the blackness transforms immediately into soothing sunlight.

Figure 6.11 Stone relief panel of Māravijāya showing the Buddha seated under the Bodhi tree with his right hand extended to touch earth while Māra challenges the Buddha with accompanying troop ready to attack, Gandhāra, c. second to third century CE. Photo by Jinah Kim.

Māra's mobilization of his troops to attack the Buddha is one of the most dynamic, action-packed moments in the Buddha's biography. In most textual records, Māra's army is rather graphically described as a vast assembly of monstrous creatures with animal faces and bizarre combinations of body parts. This moment lends itself to the fancies of the artists serving Buddhist communities, whether two thousand years ago or today, and countless examples survive in both painting and sculpture. In the *Mahāvastu*, for instance, the demon army includes beasts with faces of various animals, horses, buffalos, rams, tigers, and vultures; such animal-headed beasts frequent the scene in early Buddhist sculptures of the Gandhāra region (Figure 6.11).[26]

Figure 6.12 Hideous demons of Māra's army lunging with full force (to the Buddha who would have been in the central panel of the folio), a painted panel fragment of a palm-leaf manuscript folio, most likely of the Prajñāpāramitā, Nepal, c. 1100 CE. Image courtesy of Los Angeles County Museum of Art.

The fantastic minions of Māra painted in brilliant hues on a twelfth-century Nepalese palm-leaf manuscript (Figure 6.12) include snake-tongued demons hurling a skeleton and a mountain peak at the Bodhisattva, alongside a monster with snarling fire as his tongue, and a colorful four-armed demon with boar heads jutting out as his arms. This painting resembles a description in the *Mahāvastu*, where some in Māra's horde breathe "fire from their mouths, others snakes."[27] The army disturbs the serenity of the meditating Buddha not only with their demonic forms, but they are depicted as extremely loud, with blowing horns, screaming, and yelling.

Figure 6.13 Painted image of Māravijaya depicting the Buddha seated under the tree with his right hand extended downwards calling the earth while Māra's minions run a havoc around him, painted folio of a black paper manuscript of the Prajñāpāramitā, Nepal, c. mid to late twelfth century. Photo © The Trustees of the Chester Beatty Library, Dublin.

Māra's attempt to challenge the Buddha's right to be seated in that very spot under the tree is also conveyed through demons trying to lift and shake his seat. This can be seen in the delightful detail of frustrated demons in another late twelfth century Nepalese black paper manuscript of the *Prajñāpāramitā* (Figure 6.13). One of the two demons trying to lift the Buddha's seat looks up to the Buddha with an incredulous expression as if to say, "How is he making no single movement despite all my extreme physical exertions?" Against the frustrated and angry expressions of the demons, the Buddha sits with a serene smile and with his right hand stretched downward, signaling his call to the earth to witness his awakening. Such artistic representations of victory over Māra epitomize in one image the whole victorious experience of the Buddha that unfolds during the night of his awakening. Snake and fire-tongued demons visually capture the *āśravas* or "evil inclinations" that the Buddha destroys during the third watch of the night.

A common explanation for the Bodhisattva's ability to repulse these assaults has to do with the Bodhisattva's supernormal powers (*ṛddhi*). The Mahāyāna tradition also focuses on the natural protection afforded by his having "as a shield" the merit (*puṇya*, good karma) of completing the "Ten *Pāramitās*" that came to define the path to awakening over lifetimes for all bodhisattvas.[28]

The narrative traditions diverge with regards to when Māra's next assault occurs: either just now, or much later when Siddhārtha, now a Buddha, sits under the Bodhi tree. This second attack is by Māra's daughters. The texts imply that Māra is a family man who adores his daughters; the latter feel that their father's desperate request to defeat the Buddha will be useless, but they oblige him. They go scantily clad, then dance and vamp alluringly to try to elicit desire, even a twinge of any attachment to sensual life, in the Bodhisattva. Here, too, artists had a subject that called upon their ability to depict a lively and very human narrative.[29]

In the bottom half of the Māravijāya scene in the *pradakṣiṇā* path of Ajanta Cave 26, voluptuous female figures dance to the rhythms of the musicians around the Buddha's seat (see Figure 6.10). Later narrative traditions even have these daughters each multiply their form a hundred or more times, and specify that these women appear in the five stages of life, from children to elders. A Nepalese manuscript of the *Prajñāpāramitā* (dated 1682 CE) depicts the Buddha's victory over Māra with gusto (Figure 6.14).[30] Under the Buddha's seat, Māra's three daughters are represented twice, once as young ladies dressed in fine jewelry and dynamic dancing postures, and a second time, directly in front of the earth goddess as haggard and naked elderly ladies, paying homage to the Buddha with humility. Here, the unnamed artist likely seized an opportunity to illustrate what the Buddha really saw: beautiful maidens as shriveled hags. The Buddha ignores them, then dismisses them.

The pivotal moment in the Buddha's defeat of Māra is when he calls on the earth to witness his merit and affirm his imminent realization.[31] Māra had asserted that no one could affirm Siddhārtha's claim, but the Bodhisattva in

Figure 6.14 Detail of Māravijāya painting, Māra's daughters represented twice, once as beautiful dancing maiden and another as old haggard women, painted folio of a yellow paper manuscript of the Prajñāpāramitā, Nepal, dated 1682 CE. Harvard Art Museums/Arthur M. Sackler Museum, Francis H. Burr Memorial Fund, Photo © President and Fellows of Harvard College, 1965.553.

response touches the earth itself to be his witness: "the great earth, letting out a roar, with a hundred roars, with a thousand roars, with one hundred thousand great roars, said: 'I was then the witness.'"[32] The significance of the "Great Earth" quaking seven times in six ways,[33] "as far as the ocean, uttering a terrible sound"[34] is another instance of a Buddha's presence altering the entire cosmos that includes the human world. Māra's minions quickly disperse and flee.

In early depictions of the moment as seen in the circa third century Gandhāran relief in Figure 6.11, the earth's roaring and shaking is conveyed through soldiers falling and tumbling under the future Buddha's seat. It is unclear when the Buddhist tradition began to personify the earth as a goddess, but by the time the Buddha's biography was carved on volcanic rock at Borobudur (ninth-century Indonesia), the goddess appears with a pot of water (see Figure 6.7). A seventh-century metal image from Gilgit/Kashmir shows a kneeling female figure with a pot right under the Buddha's stretched right hand. A pot likely signals the role of water in this story of awakening; water became a crucial element in later

Southeast Asian depictions as seen in many murals in Thai and Cambodian Buddhist temples.[35] In these later renderings, the earth goddess wrings the water out of her long hair which creates a torrential deluge sweeping the evil creatures away.

After the defeat and retreat of Māra, all the gods and spirit beings that had fled in fear returned to the Bodhisattva and made vast offerings (*pūjā*).

Night of Achieving Complete Awakening (*Samyak-Sambodhi/Abhisaṃbodhi*)

The Bodhisattva settles under the tree and meditates, making discoveries: how human experience is constituted, why suffering occurs, and the spiritual causality in a twelve-fold sequence of dependent origination. The narrative tradition concludes that the defeat of Māra occurs near sundown so that the great achievement of awakening occurred at sunrise. So the Bodhisattva sits in the lotus position on the *kuśa* grass and begins meditating using a variety of methods, including trance practices he had learned from his teachers in the forest. He is also said to have remembered a natural experience he had as a child: while he watched his father do the year's "first plowing" ceremony, he experienced great bliss and clarity of mind by suspending self-centered thinking.[36]

The tradition divides this night into three watches.[37] During the first, he comes to understand "karmalogical knowledge," that is, how bodily, spoken, and mental human actions lead to specific consequences. During the second watch: he gains "cosmological knowledge," an understanding of the natural and supernatural world that humans inhabit. The third watch has him formulate "dharmalogical knowledge," when he sees the central doctrines that explain the world and the human experience of it.

At the moment the sun rises, with its light illuminating the dark world,[38] Siddhārtha experiences a new exalted mental state, blissful beyond words, with mind clear and serene as never before. Only now, properly speaking, can he be called a "Buddha" due to his experiencing *samyaksambodhi* ("complete, total enlightenment"). The doctrinal tradition will make it clear that it was not trance meditation (*samādhi*) that was essential in Siddhārtha's awakening but a practice utterly distinctive to all Buddhas: *sati* ("mindfulness") that perfects a critical discerning faculty, *prajñā*. He seals his awakening by uttering words for the beings assembled around the Bodhi tree:

> O house builder, you have been seen;
> You shall not build the house again.

Your rafters have been broken up,
Your ridgepole is demolished too.[39]

It is from this moment onward that Siddhārtha is properly called a "Buddha." One epithet that describes his extraordinary status— "neither human nor god"— is *daśabala* (Pali, *dasa bala,* "[One of/with] ten powers") that enables him (and only him, in full) his capacity to know ten facts of reality perfectly.[40] Only by defeating Māra is this possible.

The moment of transformation under the tree of awakening, and its impact in the cosmos, came to be understood, described, and depicted, according to the later schools' norms of doctrine and praxis. A new Buddha sets off vast supernatural eruptions throughout the cosmos, or Buddha-universe. The Pali tradition (*Jātakanidāna*) states that

> The ten thousand world systems revolved and remained like a wreath of garlands tossed about or like a well-arranged spread of flowers. The intervening regions of eight thousand yojanas between the world spheres which had not been lit before even with the radiance of seven suns shining together became one mass of light. The great ocean eighty-four thousand yojanas deep turned into sweet water. Rivers ceased to flow. Those blind from birth were able to see . . . Being thus honored . . . he gained penetrative insight into the knowledge of omniscience and made the ecstatic utterance customary with all Buddhas: . . . The mind that has gone beyond things composite has attained the destruction of cravings.[41]

The *Buddhacarita* has it that after awakening, to allay some of the gods' doubts about the Buddha's achievement, he performed the Twin Miracle. At the end of this first oration as a Buddha (that goes on summarizing the Bodhisattva's career), the text states, "the earth swayed like a woman drunken with wine."[42]

The Bodhi tree also remained as a symbolic center in Mahāyāna-Vajrayāna traditions that evolved in later Indo-Tibetan Buddhism. In painted palm-leaf manuscripts of the *Prajñāpāramitā Sūtra* prepared in the Pāla empire's domain (Bihar and West Bengal), the image of the Goddess Prajñāpāramitā, the quintessential epitome of the Mahāyāna doctrinal teaching of the *Prajñāpāramitā*, is most often paired together with the image of the Buddha represented at the moment of his awakening.[43] The directional Buddha adopting the *bhūmisparṣa* mudra becomes Akṣobhya, who symbolizes the embodiment of awakening facing east in the artwork associated with the tantric traditions.[44]

Seven Weeks

Figure 6.15 Miniature stele with Buddha's life scenes, with the Māravijaya event in the center (seven major moments with the Parinirvāṇa on top form the outer layer, and the seven stations are lined on either side of the Buddha forming the inner layer, on the bottom is the seven jewels of the cakravartin (*saptaratna*), which are common offerings included in medieval Buddhist images), Bagan, Myanmar, c. early thirteenth century CE. Harvard Art Museums/Arthur M. Sackler Museum, Louis Sidney Thierry Memorial Fund, Photo© President and Fellows of Harvard College, 1979.328.

The biographies of the Buddha have a wide variety of accounts on what happened after the awakening experience. Dwelling in the proximity of the place of *samyaksambodhi*, Siddhārtha savored the bliss of Buddhahood realized. Such a momentous achievement/transformation naturally made it necessary for the Buddha to put the internal, wordless experience of awakening into words and process the experience.

Most texts agree that the Buddha remained in the vicinity of the Bodhi tree for forty-nine days. This number is an important one in Indic religions and in the later formulation of Buddhist doctrine. Buddhist and non-Buddhist traditions hold that the "intermediate state" between death and rebirth is, at most, forty-nine days. As a result, one can interpret this narrative as signifying a liminal period separating the individual who had wandered in *samsāra* for many lifetimes seeking perfection, and the fully enlightened being no longer bound by karma or the *kleṣas*, now possessing a full understanding of reality and possessing extraordinary supernormal powers.[45]

In artistic rendering of the Buddha narrative, the events of the seven weeks were also significant. The Burmese Buddhists of Bagan incorporated them into the Māravijāya template as seen in the so-called Andagu plaque from today's Myanmar (Figure 6.15). It is clear even in miniature that the whole Buddha biography is anchored to the Bodhi tree.

Another Burmese example is a clay votive tablet that demonstrates the iconographic codification of the seven weeks following the Māravijāya template (Figure 6.16). The eight life scenes with the Buddha's awakening under the Bodhi tree in the center (now represented as the Buddha seated inside a towering shrine with a stūpa finial) are arranged in the typical manner of the Māravijāya template in this tablet with some delightful details of the narrative. On the bottom register represented in one row are seven Buddhas, each referencing the event of each of the seven weeks, again with extreme visual economy.[46]

If we look at the awakening narrative one week at a time, we learn that for the entire first week, immediately after awakening, the Buddha with unblinking eyes remained under the tree seated with legs crossed "feeling the bliss of deliverance."[47] The *Lalitavistara* adds[48] that the Buddha was "nurtured by the Joy of contemplation."[49]

During the second week, the Buddha got up and walked a short distance to the east, then turned to gaze joyfully but without blinking at the Bodhi tree in order to honor it. One account adds that he had the recurring thought, "At this place I exhausted the limitless suffering, in order to get rid of the heavy burden."[50] In Sri Lanka, this moment turned into a popular iconography of a standing buddha staring at a tree with his hands crossed in front of the chest.

Figure 6.16 Votive plaque with Buddha's life scenes, Bagan, Myanmar, c. early thirteenth century CE. Museum of Fine Arts, Boston Marshall H. Gould Fund 1976.62. Photograph © 2023 Museum of Fine Arts, Boston.

Most texts recount how the Buddha spent the third week walking up and down making a "long promenade" (*caṅkrama*), going from the tree to his standing place. This became renowned as "the cloistered walk" and became an architectural feature found at some Buddhist shrines that feature *stūpa*s and Bodhi trees (Figure 6.18). A *caṅkrama* is shown in two Bharhut scenes.[51]

For the fourth week, the Buddha ventured away from the tree. The *Mahāvastu* has him accepting the invitation of the nāga king Kāla to abide in his domain;[52]

Figure 6.17 Buddha standing and gazing at the Bodhi tree; wall painting in Kandy, Sri Lanka, c. nineteenth century. Photo by Todd Lewis.

by contrast, the Pali account describes the gods creating a "treasure house" where he focused his thought on formulating the advanced teaching, the *Abhidharma*. Yet another alternative is found in the *Lalitavistara*, where he spends a week staring at the awakening seat (*bodhimaṇḍa*) with unblinking eyes.[53] Whether standing or sitting, the textual traditions all have him doing intense meditation during this week.

Figure 6.18 View of the jeweled walkway (*caṅkrama*), Mahabodhi temple complex, Bodhgaya, December 26, 2023. Photo by Jinah Kim.

Figure 6.19 Buddha protected by the nāga Muchalinda when a torrential storm arose during the fifth week after the awakening, detail of painted wooden book cover, Kathmandu, Nepal, c. mid-eleventh century. Image courtesy of the Los Angeles County Museum of Art.

The connection between the Buddha (and early Buddhists) with the *nāgas* recurs in the fifth week: as torrential rains began falling, the *nāga* Mucalinda extends his coils around his body and his hoods above to provide shelter. The Pali texts assure that the experience of residing with a large serpent wrapped around his body for a week did not detract from being immersed in the bliss of deliverance and that he emerged "unharassed as if having resided in a fragrant chamber."[54] Unnamed Newar artists of the eleventh century depicted this moment as a center of the Buddha biography pictorial program on the wooden book covers (Figure 6.19). An impressively coiled snake with five hoods engulfs the Buddha while two *nāgas* approach him with food offerings, which may be conflating other narrative moments where *nāgas* appear in one scene.

Next the Buddha walks to the goatherd's *nigrodha* tree to spend the sixth week, where he again sat "immersed in the bliss of deliverance." A Pali tradition[55] and the *Lalitavistara* assert that it was during this week when Māra's daughters try to distract and divert the Buddha.[56]

Week seven has the Buddha still fasting, and moving to a grove of *kṣīrika* trees (or sitting under a *rajāyatana* tree) staying in "a shrine of many gods" again immersed in bliss feeding on the joys of deep meditation (*jhāna*) and the bliss of "completing the path and fruition."[57] At the end of this week, the Pali tradition has Indra direct two gods to offer the Buddha a medicinal fruit and betel stem tooth-stick to prepare him to break his seven-week fast.[58]

After the seventh week, the newly enlightened Buddha was still near the Bodhi tree when he was faced with the question of what to do next. Māra urges the Buddha to just enjoy his own bliss, or end his human existence by passing into final nirvāṇa, giving up on any urge to share his spiritual discoveries with other beings. Māra's suggestions have no effect, but the Buddha wrestles with a different concern: would his insight prove too difficult for others to understand? In some accounts, it is Māra pointing out the hopelessness and frustrations of teaching humans.[59]

The gods discern this and feel great dismay. First, the great god Brahma appears before the Buddha, kneels on his right knee, and says, "Venerable sir, let the Blessed One teach the Dhamma. Let the Sublime One teach the Dhamma. There are beings with little dust in their eyes who are wasting through not hearing the Dhamma. There will be those who will understand the Dhamma."[60] The Buddha then gazes about using his *ṛddhi*, superpowers. Once he sees that there are some beings "with little dust in their eyes" who would be capable of understanding his teachings, he announces his decision to share his Dharma with the world. The Buddha points out that Māra was trying to divert him to protect his sovereignty over all mortal beings and keep them circling in *saṃsāra*.

Two Merchants, The First Devotees, and Donors

The decision to teach now firmly rooted, the Buddha begins his engagement with the world. The first two humans who come upon the now fully awakened and resplendent Buddha are merchants, whose caravan passes near the Bodhi tree. (Some accounts add a back story that deceased relatives who are now deities nudged them in this direction, so they could make great merit through making offerings to the Buddha.) They show respect for him by their gestures, and are drawn to be his first disciples, so potent is the charisma of the newly enlightened Siddhārtha. These two merchants, Trapuṣa and Bhallika, are remembered as the first humans who "take refuge" in the Buddha and the Dharma, his teachings.[61]

Then the merchants do what devotees in South Asia have always done to express their reverence: they make offerings, in this case, of food such as honey and curds (some accounts add a "rice cake") to the solitary, seated Buddha. But there is a problem: the Awakened One knows that buddhas in earlier eras could not accept food directly in their hands, but must have a container to accept food offerings. Many accounts report that the onlooking gods had anticipated this issue beforehand, and four of them immediately manifested four bowls each made of a different precious metal, but the Buddha rejected these as unsuitable; then they offered stone bowls, and these too were deemed unsuitable.[62] After he turns all their manifested bowls into one, the Buddha finally accepts the first food that broke his forty-nine day postawakening fast.

Like merchants in later centuries who found the Buddha, Dharma, and Sangha a worthy refuge and focus for their patronage, Trapusa and Bhallika left "well-satisfied and filled with the greatest joy."[63] The Buddha intoned a long and effusive[64] series of verses zestfully willing these donors this-worldly success:

> May the blessing of the gods be with you!
> May success follow you always!
> May all your affairs go smoothly
> And according to your desire!
> . . .
> May well-being surround you
> like a garland around your head!
> . . . May the yakṣas, the great divine kings, and the Arhats,
> Together with Indra, be kind to you . . .
> May good fortune follow you everywhere.[65]

Once these merchants head off, the Buddha exits our chapter's frame: as a teacher, heading to the Deer Park at Sarnath, outside Varanasi.

Conclusions

The Buddha's long lingering at this site around the Bodhi tree highlights how, for devotees from the faith's origins, Bodhgaya should be the eternal, sacred center of Buddhism. And so it became for almost 2,500 years. As the scholar Haribhadra (eighth-century CE), in his commentary on the *Aṣṭasāhasrikā Prajñāpāramitā*, wrote: "The *bodhimaṇḍa*, the unsurpassed seat is a spot so named because the *maṇḍa*, the quintessence of awakening, is present there."[66] Pilgrims began visiting this place early, drawn by its historical importance and assured of its protective powers. The *Aṣṭasāhasrikā Prajñāpāramitā*, for example, declares that beings who go to the seat of awakening (*bodhimaṇḍa*) cannot be harmed there by men or ghosts, except as a result of the fruition of former deeds. The sacredness of the site is due to the power of the signature event of the whole Buddhist tradition, the Buddha's conquest over death through awakening to reality, and his promotion of fearlessness and nonenmity in all beings.[67]

Buddha images, especially those made in later centuries through the Pala era, commonly followed the Māravijāya template. But most depictions in this later period of Indic Buddhism clearly lacked narrative detail and emotional presence. Perhaps they were symbolizing something beyond Māravijāya, not simply the Sugata's last victory before awakening, but, as Janice Leoshko has suggested, an expression of how Buddhists came to regard "the power of enlightenment."[68] Māravijāya in image and narrative in this reading may have become a composite representation of all the Buddha's actions around the tree: an alms bowl moving upstream, the earth that quakes responsive to his actions, the earth goddess who appears as witness and ally, the first performance of the "Double Miracle," *nāga* and deity alliances affirming the supremacy of buddhas in the hierarchy of all divine beings. Here is the beginning of a new buddha's presence in our world. What touching the earth signifies is that through his Dharma, the Buddha reveals both the ultimate truth and the central cosmic power unleashed by a new Buddha's appearance. From these seven weeks onward, the Buddha will share this Dharma to benefit all living beings for matters transcendental and pragmatic. This is what makes Bodhgaya the powerful center of the tradition, the place most worthy of Buddhist pilgrimage.

Through this discussion, we can see less opaquely how the earliest Buddhist communities—led by devout merchants, artisans, and saṃgha reciters and ritualists—built Buddhism through their donations, craftsmanship, ritual praxis, and eventually their literate ability that by 100 BCE was directed to producing written texts. It is the art that reinforces a historical account indicating that rituals and festivals were underway at the beginning, with devotional traditions uniting householders and sangha. Present were sociocultural bonds that would foster the foundations of a great world religion, a tradition that would be adopted by both nomads and city dwellers, that could coexist with all manner of great gods, local tree spirits, serpent deities, and demons. These patterns, or historical blueprints can lead us to new insights about Buddhism in history. Examining what the tradition remembers occurring around the tree of awakening can open our cultural imagination, so we can view Buddhism more comprehensively, in three dimensions, going where texts alone cannot take us.

Notes

1. This tree as the center of the cosmos is a classic example of the *axis mundi* archetype highlighted by the noted religion scholar Mircea Eliade.
2. The diversity of style and iconography in the images of the Buddha around the globe certainly suggests that how people saw the Buddha varied greatly depending on the time and place.
3. Joanna Williams, "Sārnāth Gupta Steles of the Buddha's Life," *Ars Orientalis* 10 (1975): 186.
4. Simply stated, art is a powerful, distilled expression of religious culture. The more one understands the artistic tradition, the closer one sees faith and devotion through the eyes of a believer. See John Berger, *Ways of Seeing* (New York: Penguin Books, 1991).
5. Visual narratives provided flesh and fashion to the skeletal stories so people could see the Buddha's life stories in their own terms; they represent the Buddha in the garb of the lived world of the devotees in each epoch, making the stories more relatable and memorable. The Buddha's life scenes in stone or in painting might have in certain sites served as a basis for rituals, or a "visual liturgy," as is seen today.
6. Vidya Dehejia, *Discourse in early Buddhist art: Visual Narratives of India* (New Delhi: Munshiram Manoharlal Publishers, 1997).
7. Dehejia calls this phenomenon "narrative recess" or recess of visual narratives.
8. John Huntington, "Pilgrimage as Image: The Cult of the Astamahapratihariya—Part 1" *Orientations* 18, no. 4 (1987): 55–63; "Pilgrimage as Image: The Cult of the Astamahapratihariya—Part 2," *Orientations* 18, no. 8 (1987): 56–68.
9. Joanna Williams, "Sārnāth Gupta Steles of the Buddha's Life," *Ars Orientalis* 10 (1975): 171–192.
10. On the development of a *maṇḍala*-template social order, see Ronald M. Davidson, *Indian Esoteric Buddhism: A Social History of the Tantric Movement* (New York: Columbia University Press, 2002), 131–144.
11. Janice Leoshko, "Scenes of the Buddha's Life in Pala Period Art," *Silk Road Art and Archaeology* 3 (1993–1994): 28–52.
12. Elena A. Pakhoutova, "Reproducing the Sacred Places: the Eight Great Events of the Buddha's Life and their Commemorative Stūpas in the Medieval Art of Tibet (10th–13th century)" (ProQuest Dissertations Publishing, 2009); Ursula Toyka-Fuong, "The Influence of Pāla Art on 11th Century Wall-Paintings of Grotto 76 in Dunhuang," in *The Inner Asian International Style 12th–14th Centuries*, ed. Deborah

E. Klimburg-Salter and Eva Allinger (Wien: Verlag, 1998); Hiram W. Woodward Jr., "The Life of the Buddha in the Pāla Monastic Environment," *The Journal of the Walters Art Gallery* 48 (1990); Janice Leoshko, "About Looking at Buddha Images in Eastern India," *Archives of Asian art* 52, no. 1 (2001).

13. Janice Leoshko, "Time and Time Again: Finding Perspective for Bodhgayā Buddha Imagery." *Ars Orientalis* 50 (2021): 6–32.
14. This variation is mostly ascribed to Myanmar. See Hiram W. Woodward Jr., "The Indian Roots of the 'Burmese' Life-of the Buddha Plaques," *Silk Road Art and Archaeology* 5 (1997–1998): 395–407.
15. Gaffney, Sean, *Skyes pa rabs kyi gleṅ gźi (Jātakanidāna): A Critical Edition* (Oxford: Indica et Buddhica, 2018), 164. This is also found in the Pali *Nidāna-kathā*. See N. A. Jayawickrama, trans., *The Story of Gotama Buddha (Jātaka Nidānakathā)* (Oxford: Pali Text Society, 1990), 93.
16. Eviatar Shulman, "Buddha as the Pole of Existence, or the Flower of Cosmos," *History of Religions* 57, no. 2 (2017).
17. Todd Lewis and Subarna Man Tuladhar, trans., *The Epic of the Buddha: His Life and Teachings by Chittadar Hridaya* (Boulder: Shambhala, 2019), 177–178.
18. Although weighed down by the heavy load of grass on her head and under her left arm, the woman deftly carries a grass cutting knife and water pot. She looks at the unfolding exchange between the grass cutter and the Buddha incredulously.
19. In the Hindu tradition, the Bodhi tree is termed "*aśvattha*" in Sanskrit, and is regarded as sacred, linked to an incarnation of Vishnu as Vasudeva. See Eviatar Shulman, "Buddha as the Pole of Existence," 187.
20. Gwendolyn Bays, trans., *The Lalitavistara Sūtra* (Berkeley: Dharma Publishing, 1983), 2:439.
21. On representations of Māra in Buddhist art see Prithivi K. Agrawala, "The Depiction of Māra in early Buddhist Art," in *Function and Meaning in Buddhist Art*, ed. K.R. van Kooij & H. van der Veere (Groningen: Egbert Forsten, 1995), 125–134.
22. John S. Strong, *The Buddha: A Short Biography* (Oxford: Oneworld, 2001), 70.
23. Symbolized by a pig/rooster/snake found at the center of the "Wheel of Life/Rebirth" (*bhavacakra*): greed/lust/delusion) around which beings move repeatedly in *saṃsāra*. Because humans are poisoned by these *kleśas* they act in foolish ways and are reborn until they realize enlightenment.
24. Māra's interference in the Bodhisattva's life began even before Siddhārtha made his seat under the Bodhi tree. One Pali account has Māra starting his interference when Siddhārtha is about to leave home in the Great Renunciation (Pali Canon, *Paduna Sutta*). Māra tries to prevent the Great Departure by "flying into the air" and going to tell Prince Siddhārtha that if he stayed, in seven days he would become an ultimate king, or *cakravartin*. After the Bodhisattva ignores this, leaves the palace and reaches the forest, the stalking Māra says menacingly, "Wherever you get a thought of lust, malice, cruelty, I'll know it," and then follows him around for the next seven years, step by step. But in the end, Māra must testify, "I have found no entrance of lust, malice, cruelty to the Bodhisattva, a watchful one." Māra, however, persists. Once Siddhārtha gives up his extreme asceticism on the Nairañjanā River and begins to move toward his final efforts under the Bodhi tree, Māra urges

him to give it all up and return to a life of doing good and being a *cakravartin*, back to luxury and religious practice centered on Vedic fire offerings (*homa*). The Bodhisattva rejects this and denounces Māra again. For this story, see E. J. Thomas, *The Life of Buddha as Legend and History* (London: K. Paul, Trench, Trubner & Co., 1927), 54–73.

25. The following synthetic account is drawn from texts cited by E. J. Thomas, *The Life of the Buddha as Legend and History.*
26. J. J. Jones, trans., *The Mahāvastu: Translated from the Buddhist Sanskrit* (London: The Pali Text Society, 1952), 2, 365–366.
27. J. J. Jones, *The Mahāvastu*, 2:366.
28. These are: generosity, morality, forbearance, energy, one-pointed concentration, *prajñā ("insight; wisdom")*, skillful means, determination, strength, and spiritual knowledge.
29. For a discussion of Burmese examples depicting Māra's daughters, see Donald M. Stadner, "The Daughters of Māra in the Art of Burma," *Arts of Asia* 45, no. 2 (2015).
30. This powerful depiction is rendered despite its miniature size, measuring 4″ in height.
31. Less personalized is the account of the earth responding in *Jātakanidāna*: "And, drawing his right hand from beneath his robes, while stretching out his hand towards the great earth, he said: 'Are you, or are you not, witness to the event of my giving seven hundred and seven gifts during my existence as Vessāntara? Speak!'" The reference here is to his last life, when he showed his mastery over attachment by giving away all his wealth, his children, and his wife.
32. Sean Gaffney, *Skyes pa rabs kyi gleṅ gźi, Jātakanidāna*, 173.
33. Later commentators noted that these quakes were not destructive to living beings, though they did terrify and rout Māra's army.
34. Later Buddhist authors, as they did with so many topics, made a numbered list of the causes for the earth to quake in the Buddhist cosmos, including a naturalistic one: (1) natural (earth defined as earth resting on water resting on wind that rests on space; the wind moving upward causes quakes); (2) buddhists using *ṛddhi*; (3) done by the gods; (4) when a future Buddha first raises the conception of enlightenment; (5) future Buddha is born; (6) Buddha's moment of Awakening; (7) Buddha's first turning the wheel of Dharma; (8) Buddha declares the coming end of his life; and (9) *Parinirvāṇa*. E. J. Thomas, *The Life of Buddha as Legend and History* (London: K. Paul, Trench, Trubner & Co., 1927), 147.
35. The hair wringing iconography of the earth goddess grew out of an early auspicious motif of yakṣī or tree spirit figures, but the iconography's development and popularization happened in Southeast Asia rather than in India. For the history and significance of this iconographic development, see Elizabeth Guthrie, "A study of the history and cult of the Buddhist earth deity in mainland Southeast Asia" (Dept. of Philosophy & Religious Studies, University of Canterbury, 2004). This moment is sometimes represented in Gandhāran art.
36. As seen in the bottom left corner of the relief in Figure 6.11, a princely figure pensively sitting under a tree is often understood to be a reference to this moment. Also see Kristin Scheible's chapter.

37. We follow John Strong's useful terms for the insights the Bodhisattva gained; see Strong, *The Buddha*, 74–75.
38. Here there is an Indo-European connection that is relevant to the translation of this experience as "enlightenment:" (light in "enlightenment" resonates with the phrase "seeing the light" ≈ seeing/deep realization of the truth/Dharma. Some scholars prefer "awakening" as a translation of *samyaksambodhi*, with the useful connotation that finally he "woke up" to the clear understanding of reality.
39. From the Pali *Dhammapada*. See for example, Thomas Byron, *The Dhammapada*, Pocket Edition ed. (Boston: Shambhala 1993), 153–154.
40. (1) What is possible and impossible; (2) consequence of actions (*vipāka*); (3) abilities of other beings; (4) the direction of their lives; (5) the constituents of appearances; (6) the paths leading to the different realms of existence; (7) paths leading to purity and impurity; (8) states of meditation (*samādhi*) and absorptions (*dhyāna*); (9) deaths and reappearances; and (10) the eradication of all defilements (Skt. *āśrava;* Pali, *āsava*) due to the desire (kāma) or ignorance (*avidyā/avijja*).
41. Jayawickrama, trans., *The Story of Gotama Buddha (Jātaka Nidānakathā)*, 100–101.
42. XIV, 97 in E. H. Johnson, *The Buddhacarita*, 2nd ed. (New Delhi: Oriental Books Reprint Corporation, [1936] 1972), 213.
43. For further discussion of the iconographic program of the *Prajñāpāramitā* manuscripts, see Jinah Kim, *Receptacle of the Sacred: Illustrated Manuscripts and the Buddhist Book-Cult in South Asia* (Berkeley: University of California Press, 2013), 73–76. Characterized as "the mother of all Buddhas" in the *Prajñāpāramitā sūtras*, this profound philosophical reality is personified as a beautiful regally-bedecked goddess.
44. David L. Snellgrove, *Indo-Tibetan Buddhism: Indian Buddhists and Their Tibetan Successors* (New York: Shambhala, 1987), 171.
45. For a detailed account of the seven weeks, see Osmund Bopearachchi, *Seven Weeks after the Buddha's Enlightenment: Contradictions in Text, Confusions in Art* (New Delhi: Manohar Publishers & Distributors, 2016). This section follows the outline of events and utilizes the terms found there.
46. For instance, five snake hoods surrounding the Buddha in the far left corner references the event of the fifth week when the nāga king Mucalinda protected the Buddha from the torrential storm, while two standing Buddhas amongst the seven referenced two weeks during which the Buddha walked and stood in adoration of the tree (second and third weeks). These weeks are discussed in the following pages.
47. Bhikkhu Ñāṇamoli, *The Life of the Buddha: According to the Pali Canon* (Kandy: Buddhist Publication Society, 1992), 30.
48. Bays, *The Lalitavistara Sūtra*, 2: 559.
49. A Pāli narrative has it that the Buddha discerned that the gods were doubtful about his being truly enlightened. To allay their doubt, on the seventh day of this first week, he performed the "Double Miracle" a feat that he will repeat later in his life. (Art historical identifications often call this "the Miracle of Śrāvastī.) The "Double Miracle" consists of his rising up into the air to the height of "six coconut trees," then having flames/water issuing from his upper/lower body, the flames/water being switched,

then the display culminating in his multiplying his one body into a thousand bodies with the flames/water displayed. See the chapter by David Fiordalis.

50. This text and the Pali accounts state that a *stūpa* was built to mark this spot and it became known as "the shrine of steadfast gaze."
51. Minku Kim, "Where the Blessed One Paced Mindfully: The Issue of Caṅkrama on Mathurā's Earliest Freestanding Images of the Buddha," *Archives of Asian Art* 69, no. 2 (2019): 186.
52. Jones, *The Mahāvastu*, 2: 250.
53. Bays, *Lalitavistara Sūtra*, 2: 570.
54. Ñāṇamoli, *The Life of the Buddha*, 32.
55. Ñāṇamoli, *The Life of the Buddha*, 33
56. Bays, *The Lalitavistara Sūtra*, 2: 572.
57. The sole Buddha depicted inside a shrine structure among the seven in the clay tablet (third from the right) may depict this moment.
58. A Burmese narrative tradition has it that King Patanadi of Kośala (Skt. Prasenajit, Pali Pasenadi) later built seven stūpas around the Bodhi tree to mark the key event locations for each of the seven weeks. P. Bigandet, *Vie ou Légende de Gaudama: le Bouddha des Birmans* (Paris: E. Leroux, 1878), 104.
59. Ñāṇamoli, *The Life of the Buddha*, 19.
60. *Ariyapariyesanā Sutta*, MN 26; English translation from Bhikkhu Ñāṇamoli, trans., *The Middle Length Discourses of the Buddha: A Translation of the Majjhima Nikāya* (Boston: Wisdom, 1995), 57.
61. Later Buddhists will take the "Triple Refuge" once the third "jewel," the sangha (community of monastics), has been established.
62. These four gods are identified as four heavenly kings in later Mahāyāna and Vajrayāna traditions. They were popularly represented in East Asian Buddhist art and architecture as "world protectors" and stationed at the entrance to Buddhist monasteries.
63. Bays, *The Lalitavistara Sūtra*, 2: 589
64. This takes up four pages in English translation.
65. Bays, *The Lalitavistara Sūtra*, 584–588.
66. Translated in Daniel Boucher, "The *Pratītyasamutpādagāthā* and Its Role in the Medieval Cult of the Relics," *The Journal of the International Association of Buddhist Studies* 14, no. 1 (1991): 18.
67. Also discussed in Kim, *Receptacle of the Sacred.*
68. Leoshko, "Time and Time Again," 22.

7
The Buddha's Career
Teachings and Miracles

David Fiordalis

Figure 7.1 Eight episodes from the Buddha's life, clockwise from the top left: first sermon, great cessation, great miracle, taming the elephant, awakening, birth, monkey's gift, and descent from heavens. Sārnāth, fifth century. Photo by John C. Huntington, courtesy of the John C. and Susan L. Huntington Photographic Archive of Buddhist and Asian Art.

David Fiordalis, *The Buddha's Career* In: *The Buddha*. Edited by: Vanessa R. Sasson and Kristin Scheible, Oxford University Press. © Oxford University Press 2024. DOI: 10.1093/oso/9780197649466.003.0008

With his achievement of awakening and defeat of Māra, the Buddha has now finally become the Buddha, the "Awakened One." We have seen how his path to buddhahood began countless lifetimes ago with the vow he took as Sumedha, a path that continued through his many previous lives. His conception and final birth foreshadowed this achievement in important ways, and while his marriage and family bonds may have called it into question, these life experiences set the stage for his renunciation, which set into motion the series of events that culminated in his awakening. A widespread tradition tells us that the future Buddha leaves his home and family at the age of twenty-nine to seek an end to suffering. After six years practicing as a wandering ascetic, he finally achieves his goal. He has "done what must be done;" he has ended the cycle of future rebirth for himself.

At this point of the story, however, the Buddha—thirty-five years of age and newly awakened—still has so much life ahead of him.[1] "What, if anything, should I do now?" he may have wondered. The Buddhist narrative tradition also captures this important moment, and its answer to this question tells us something significant about the nature of a buddha, traditionally conceived. The story goes that, shortly after the Buddha's awakening, the great god, Brahmā Sahampati, becomes aware of his achievement and arrives on a mission to request that he teach what he has learned.[2] Thus prompted by Brahmā, the Buddha surveys the whole world with his newly opened "buddha-eye."[3] "Out of compassion for the world," he measures the capacity of others to understand his message and decides to teach, thus setting the stage for his long career.[4]

Storytellers, of both traditional and contemporary retellings, also reach a critical juncture at this point in the story, another opportunity to take stock and seek a broader vision, another "belvedere" moment, to use John Strong's apt term.[5] We face the dilemma of how to characterize the Buddha's long teaching career and provide the audience with a clear idea of a buddha's qualities. Truly, the entirety of the canonical literature, often traditionally characterized as the "word of the Buddha" (*buddhavacana*), many tens or even hundreds of thousands of pages in length, can be said to comprise or embody the Buddha's long teaching career. We need a principle to guide us to encapsulate so much material in a short narrative form.

In this volume, we have spoken several times about Strong's important notion of the "Buddha-life blueprint," a series of narrative episodes, sometimes called "mandatory events" or even "miracles," that constitute a template for telling the story of the Buddha's final lifetime.[6] We might compare it to what narrative theorists call the *fabula* or, more simply, the *story*, the basic chronological series of events in a story as distinct from how the story is told.[7] The Buddha-life blueprint can thus provide us with a method to solve the difficult problem posed above, but at the same time one must admit that there is no single solution, because there is no single blueprint. Different blueprints developed over time, expanding or contracting in different iterations, and we must chart a path through them.

There is a great deal of variety and complexity to the process of the blueprint's development over time. In the introduction to his excellent biography of the Buddha, in many ways the inspiration for this volume, Strong provides a good overview. Here, I will quote only a single passage from the fifth-century Pāli commentary on the *Discourse on the Great Story* (*Mahāpadāna Sutta*), itself a key early text for the development of the blueprint and the Buddhist narrative genre of past-life storytelling.[8] This commentarial passage lists a series of events in every buddha's life during which miracles are said to occur, and I have inserted numbers to highlight that they are eight:

> We will display miracles (*pāṭihāriya*) that will, among other things, shake the earth, which is bounded by the circle of ten thousand mountains, when (1) the all-knowing buddha-to-be enters his mother's womb, (2) is born, (3) attains awakening, (4) turns the wheel of Dharma, (5) performs the "twin miracle" (*yamaka-pāṭihāriya*), (6) descends from the realm of the gods, (7) releases his life-force, and (8) attains complete cessation.[9]

The commentary places this thought in the minds of Brahmā deities who gather from the various Brahmā heavens to bear witness when a buddha appears in the world, and the miracles these gods display seem to refer to the earthquakes and other miracles, which accompany these events, and not necessarily to the events themselves, only one of which, the twin miracle, is also explicitly called a "miracle" (*pāṭihāriya*).[10] The difference suggested here between two "types" of miracles has been noticed by Strong, who makes an insightful distinction between "testimonial miracles" and "display miracles."[11] The miracles the gods perform are "testimonial" and indicate the cosmic significance of the events. "Display" miracles, by contrast, show the Buddha displaying his own superhuman powers and knowledge.

For present purposes, we may note that the passage cited above lists three key events from the Buddha's teaching career: (1) the first sermon, when he first "turns the wheel of the Dharma," (2) the "twin miracle" or what some texts call the Buddha's "great miracle," and (3) the descent of the gods (and the Buddha) from the heavens. In Chapter 8 of this volume, Maria Heim discusses a fourth event mentioned above, releasing the life-force, a telling of which is found in the Pāli *Mahāparinibbāna Sutta* or *Discourse on the Buddha's Great Passing Away*. During this event, which is said to have occurred three months before the Buddha's death, the Buddha agrees to Māra's request that he enter final nirvāṇa now that he has established a Sangha capable of teaching the Dharma in his absence.[12] Thus, the event seems to indicate that his teaching career has nearly reached its end and that he is ready for his final death.

Other iterations of the Buddha-life blueprint, both textual and iconographic, list these and other significant events from the Buddha's teaching career. For example, the image in figure one that opens the chapter shows a relief also dated to the fifth century and found at the monastic complex at Sārnāth, where the Buddha is said to have taught the first sermon. In this relief, we see iconic representations of most of the same episodes. Only his conception and the release of his life force are replaced here by other events: the taming of the wild elephant, Nālagiri, and a monkey's gift of honey. So, we can tell that the process of expansion and contraction was not linear, but we also see evidence of the importance given to the three events mentioned above.

In the Tibetan tradition, we find another standardized list of twelve "great deeds" of the Buddha, a list found in the work of the Tibetan historian, Bu-ston, who was probably influenced by the *Lalitavistara*.[13] While this list expands on the Buddha's earlier life, his teaching career is compressed into a single event: the first sermon. At the same time, however, various eightfold lists have remained part of Tibetan Buddhist literature, material culture, and religious practice to this day. For example, two such lists reappear as part of the chapter on the Buddha's teaching career in a biography otherwise structured around the twelve deeds: Tenzin Chögyel's short retelling of the Buddha's life, composed in mid-eighteenth century Bhutan.[14] I have even seen eight small stupas representing these eight events constructed in a row along an outdoor passageway at Shechen Monastery in Boudha, Kathmandu, Nepal.[15]

The chapters on the Buddha's birth and death present us with a fundamental tension related to the nature of the Buddha, one that runs through the entire Buddhist tradition: he is born a human being among other humans and it is a basic truth that those who are born must die. Yet, the Buddha is an extraordinary being who experiences a wondrous birth unlike any normal human being, and as we will see in the next chapter, his death also takes on cosmic significance. In this chapter, therefore, we will continue to explore this tension between the human and the superhuman by focusing on the Buddha's ability to elicit wonder and generate insight among the characters who bear witness to his actions in the stories. He does so not only by displaying his superhuman powers and extraordinary knowledge, but also through the wondrous nature of his teachings. Taking our cue from the various Buddha-life blueprints in stone and text discussed above, we will focus our attention on the first sermon and the narrative cycle from the Buddha's great miracle at Śrāvastī to his descent alongside the gods at Saṃkāśya. These episodes from the Buddha's teaching career will allow us to reemphasize the connection between the human and cosmic dimensions of the story. They will help us draw connections between story, sacred place, and Buddhist practice, including ritual and pilgrimage, and they will provide us with a way to think about the nature of the Buddha who appears as such a charismatic figure throughout the vast expanse of Buddhist literature.

The First Sermon (at Sārnāth)

The Buddha's first sermon, often called "the discourse setting in motion the wheel of the Dharma" (Pāli: *Dhammacakkappavattana Sutta*), is perhaps the most iconic event of his entire teaching career, if not his whole life. Many versions of the first sermon are preserved in the different collections of Buddhist canonical literature in Pāli, Sanskrit, Chinese, and Tibetan.[16] It is famous for the content of the sermon, as well as for what the event represents: the Buddha teaching the Dharma and thereby beginning to establish his community (Saṅgha); that is, the three precious jewels often said to represent Buddhism as a whole.[17]

While justly famous for the way it condenses Buddhist doctrine into a tight presentation upon which teachers can expand, the different versions of the first sermon exhibit some important differences in both the content of the sermon and the narrative details surrounding the event. These differences have even led some scholars to suggest that one of the most famous doctrinal elements of the sermon, the explanation of the so-called "four noble truths" (of suffering, its origin, its cessation, and the path thereto) may have been a later development or addition.[18] Be that as it may, one finds a basic consistency between the four truths and other core concepts found in the different versions of the sermon, including the middle way and the noble eightfold path, as well as between these doctrinal elements and certain narrative details, such as the setting and audience of the sermon. With its well-crafted literary features and highly technical style of presentation, the whole story must have developed over time into the form(s) we have now.

In some of the longer canonical versions, the first sermon is part of a continuous narrative that tells of the period immediately following the Buddha's awakening and includes several other important episodes, including his conversions of a large group of rival Brahmin ascetics led by the three Kāśyapa brothers, a young man named Yaśas, as well as King Bimbisāra and two of the Buddha's most important disciples, Śāriputra and Maudgalyāyana. In the Pāli canon, this extended narrative forms a kind of introduction to the *Vinaya*; that is, the canonical collection that focuses on the rules and regulations of the Buddhist monastic order and tells stories of their formation and application.

Other versions found in the canonical collections of the Buddha's discourses, that is, the *Nikāyas* and *Āgamas*, often give the sermon with only a minimal narrative frame.

Yet, insofar as we are dealing here with a dialogue, every version, shorter or longer, contains at least some of the basic elements of a story: time, place, characters, plot, action and reaction. In the modern study (and practice) of Buddhism, however, these elements have too often been ignored in a search for the "true" (or "earliest") doctrine. One of the main arguments of this chapter and in this volume as a whole, an argument that has been made time and again by John Strong and other scholars, is that we should not ignore the narrative dimension.[19] In fact, the narrative often shapes the doctrine, as it does here.

In longer versions of the story, such as that found in the Pāli *Vinaya*, after the Buddha uses his "buddha-eye" and decides to teach, he must then decide to whom he will teach the Dharma. He first considers his two former teachers, but finds that each of them has recently died—one on the previous night, the other a week earlier. He then considers his five former companions in the ascetic life, whom he abandoned (or rather who abandoned him) when he decided to end his fasting regimen and other acts of extreme asceticism shortly before his awakening under the tree in Bodh Gaya. The Buddha determines that they should be the audience for his first sermon and sets out from Bodh Gaya to visit them at "Sages' Landing" (*Isipatana*) at Deer Park in Sārnāth.

Narratives form characters and place them in relation, and we find a number of important relationships and points of view in the story of the first sermon. As the Buddha approaches his former companions, the narrator deftly shifts our focus toward their perspective so that we can see how they view him. As they see him coming, they agree among themselves not to greet him, because he has given up his austerities. They seem determined not to offer him respect. We must remember that they are ascetics, after all, and they believe that only ascetic practice will bring true freedom from suffering. From their perspective, the Buddha has fallen from the correct path. They say to each other,

> Friends, here comes the ascetic Gotama, who lives in abundance, who has given up his efforts, and turned to a life of abundance. Let us not welcome him, or rise when he approaches, or take his bowl and robe, but let us put a seat there. He will sit, if he wishes.[20]

Yet, as the Buddha comes closer the five companions are unable to keep their agreement. They involuntarily rise and take his bowl and robe, prepare a seat for him, bring water for him to wash his feet, and greet him by his name and with the word, "friend." The Buddha admonishes them, however, saying that they should no longer address him in so familiar a fashion. He has become the perfect and fully awakened Buddha. He has achieved the deathless state. He will teach them the Dharma and show them a path by which they can also achieve the highest goal of the holy life, the goal for which young people leave home and become wandering ascetics like them. They should listen to his teaching, he tells them.[21]

Here we see the Buddha attempting to assert his newfound authority, and the ascetics initially express skepticism. They accuse him of giving up the ascetic life and living a life of abundance. They question how, by giving up his austerities and living such a life of abundance, he could have achieved powers beyond the capability of ordinary human beings. The Buddha responds by assuring them that he has not given up the path. He does not live a life of abundance. He repeats that he has become the perfect and fully awakened Buddha, and finally convinces them to listen to his teaching with an open mind.

The Buddha then begins his first sermon. It is only here that the shorter versions, such as the one found in the Pāli *Saṃyutta Nikāya*, take up the story, but even these shorter versions make reference to the particular time, place, and audience. Here, as with all the Buddha's discourses, context matters.[22] In several versions, the Buddha begins his sermon by explaining that there is a middle way between the lifestyles of extreme asceticism and a life of abundance. Many authors have suggested that the Buddha makes oblique reference here to his former abundant lifestyle as a prince, but for the five ascetics who are his direct audience in the story, even the austere lifestyle of a poor person who eats only one meal per day would likely count as a life of abundance. Many people living in the developed world today can and do recognize how much abundance they ordinarily enjoy, but even if we do not see ourselves reflected in the Buddha's earlier life of privilege, the context here can offer us another way to understand the Buddha's message and connect with it. When we pay close attention to the literary features of the story, we find new opportunities to place ourselves at the "scene of instruction."[23]

The Buddha goes on to explain to the five ascetics that the middle way between the extremes of ordinary abundance and intense asceticism will lead to wisdom, to direct knowledge, to awakening, and ultimately to cessation (of suffering as well as future rebirth). The middle way, he says, refers to the noble eightfold path. As Strong has pointed out, the middle way is a powerful and flexible metaphor in Buddhism.[24] Here, it refers to more than just a doctrine or correct belief, but to a total way of life that includes not only correct understanding of the nature of things, but also proper forms of living and the cultivation of certain physical and mental disciplines. Again, given that the five ascetics are his direct audience in the story, and their presumed beliefs, it makes sense that the Buddha would use the metaphor of the middle way and that it would involve such a total way of life. For those of us hearing or reading the story today, however, and who may consider that we actually do live in abundance, the Buddha's message may equally pose a challenge for us to reconsider our current ways of life in relation to the ideal practice of the middle way.

In some versions, the Buddha ends his sermon here. In others, he does not discuss the middle way at all. He begins instead with an explanation of the four noble truths, but such versions do not connect as precisely to the particular circumstances of the narrative's setting, as described above. This disconnect may be tacitly acknowledged by still other versions in which the Buddha pauses after explaining the middle way, allowing the five ascetics to digest his first message.[25] One such version even suggests that he waits until the next day before introducing them to the doctrine of the four noble truths.[26]

There is no time or space to offer an extended discussion of the four truths, the eightfold path, or their connection to the middle way, an analysis that can be expanded to encompass virtually all the key concepts of mainstream Buddhist doctrine.[27] My focus here on the connections between the literary features of the story and the core concepts of the sermon has shown that Buddhist canonical literature presents us with characters, settings, and circumstances to which we ourselves can connect, sometimes even in contrast. In these discourses, we see one character, the Buddha, whose nature and instruction we are trying to discern, and we see him engaged in dialogue with other human characters whose thoughts and motivations we can perhaps better understand, even if we are not ourselves wandering ascetics. Here, in this simple, unadorned dialogue form, we find an example of the basic narrative realism of this literature.

The literature also possesses a fantastic or cosmic dimension, as we have seen, and we find this dimension in the story of the first sermon, too. For instance, in one, probably later version preserved in Chinese, a wheel comes flying through the air and hovers spinning before the Buddha, who reaches out and stops it before beginning his sermon.[28] In many other versions of the story, however, several extraordinary events follow the completion of the sermon. The fantastic element most commonly found among the various versions is the immediate response of the earth-dwelling deities, who cry out that the Buddha has now turned the wheel of Dharma, a wheel that cannot be turned (or turned back) by any ascetic, brahmin, Māra, Brahmā or any other human being or god in the world! The cry is then taken up by the deities dwelling in the higher realms, beginning with the Heaven of the Four Great Kings, and proceeding through the Heaven of the Thirty-Three and the other heavens all the way up to the Heaven of the Brahmā Deities.

In the versions preserved in Pāli, we are told that the cry of the gods is followed by an earthquake that shakes the whole earth, a narrative element, we should recall, that is said to be common to all eight episodes in the Buddha's life listed in the Pāli commentarial passage quoted in the introduction to this chapter. A glorious light then appears in the world, surpassing the brilliance of the gods. In the *Mahīśāsaka-vinaya* version preserved in Chinese, there is no mention of an earthquake, but glorious light is mentioned and it is said to be accompanied by divine music and showers of flowers produced by the gods.[29]

If these miracles performed by the gods are "testimonial," as Strong suggests, then to what do they testify? We may say that they accentuate or give greater significance to the Buddha's teaching, but they also serve to highlight the effectiveness of the Buddha's performative act. The significance of the first sermon is not simply that the Buddha teaches the Dharma for the first time, but that his teaching is understood, and even more to the point, his sermon results in one of the five companions, Āññāta Koṇḍañña, the eldest of the five "who has now understood" (*āññāta*), becoming awakened himself. This is something the Buddha confirms in the story. In some versions, the narrator tells us that the Buddha even reads Koṇḍañña's mind before confirming his awakening. Thus, even though it might seem at first glance as though the agency to perform miracles belongs to the gods, we see that the Buddha retains the most significant agency in the story. However, the fact that the teaching is complete only when it has been properly understood does more than confirm the Buddha's agency. It signals the possibility that we, too, might understand the Buddha's teaching and achieve what the Buddha and Koṇḍañña have now achieved in the narrative. That, we might say, is the real "miracle" of the teaching.

The Buddha's "Great Miracle" (at Śrāvastī)

We move on now to the second of the events from the Buddha's teaching career listed in the Pāli commentarial passage on the *Mahāpadāna Sutta* with which we began this chapter: the Buddha's "twin miracle," sometimes called his "great miracle." If the first sermon is a short story of great significance, short enough for us to dwell on some of its literary details, but with the potential for one to expand exponentially on its doctrinal elements—and, indeed, it can stand for countless other teaching episodes recounted in the canonical discourses—then the story of the Buddha's "great miracle" is already a much more expansive tale. We encounter a much larger cast of characters, a more complicated plot structure, and multiple events, and we must somehow explain all the connections among them. The great miracle itself has an expansive character insofar as one miraculous display follows another, culminating in the Buddha's grand (or even somewhat grandiose) final performance, which in some versions leads directly into the account of subsequent miraculous events that form the next story or stories. The actions and responses of the characters drive the narrative as much as, or more than, the dialogue. The story possesses humor, irony, intrigue and even some violence!

As with the first sermon and many of the stories told in this volume, the Buddha's "great miracle" has many different versions.[30] For the most part, these different versions coalesce around different narrative traditions associated with distinct early Buddhist monastic lineages: Theravāda (i.e., the Pāli tradition), Mūlasarvāstivāda (preserved in original Sanskrit and Tibetan translation), Dharmaguptaka (preserved in Chinese translation), and so forth. This distribution of textual versions, along with the extensive art historical evidence, indicates the popularity of the story over a long period of time, and it is still commemorated today in Buddhist rituals and festivals from Tibet to Thailand and throughout the world.[31]

It will not be possible to tell the whole story in detail, and others, including Strong in his biography of the Buddha, have written excellent short, synthetic retellings. What I want to do here is give a sense of the narrative as well as some of the significant themes raised by the story, and consider its importance for understanding how the tradition came to conceive of the Buddha.

The basic plot of the story revolves around the question of whether or not the Buddha will perform a "miracle" or "wondrous display of his superhuman powers" (*iddhipāṭihāriya* in Pāli), and thereby defeat a group of six rival religious teachers, who appear throughout Buddhist narrative literature.[32] At least one version, the *Sūtra of the Wise and Fool*, even refers to the story as "the defeat of the rival teachers."[33] In some versions, including those associated with the Mūlasarvāstivāda tradition, the Buddha's rivals are first provoked by the god, Māra, who fools them into believing (falsely) that they actually possess superhuman powers to rival those of the Buddha; in others, particularly the ones associated with the Pāli tradition, they hear that the Buddha has recently made a monastic rule forbidding Buddhist monks from displaying their extraordinary powers to laypeople, and this prompts them to challenge him publicly, believing (again, falsely) that, being a monk himself, the Buddha will refuse to accept their challenge. They are sadly mistaken.

The story thus explores the ethics, the effectiveness, and the evidential value of performing miracles or displaying extraordinary powers, while offering another example of the "superhumanity" of the Buddha; that is, his status above ordinary human beings while still not being a god. In fact, his human birth together with the fact that he possesses such extraordinary powers is what makes him a wondrous being, whereas the gods, like Brahmā and Māra, possess such powers naturally, one might say.[34] In fact, the Buddha is regularly placed above the gods. He is commonly called "the teacher of gods and human beings," as well as "the unsurpassed leader of persons ready to be tamed."[35]

As we will see in the story, however, not all the witnesses to the Buddha's great miracle are ready to be tamed. This raises a question about the purpose of the miracle, but also whether the Buddha will consent to perform a miracle at all. The rival teachers do not approach him directly. Instead, they first ask the king, usually King Bimbisāra, the Buddha's longtime lay supporter, to make the request on their behalf.[36] In many versions, such as those of Mūlasarvāstivāda tradition, Bimbisāra refuses and the rival teachers must then ask King Prasenajit instead. In this way, the king's role in sponsoring the wonderworking contest mirrors the role of the king in hosting formal debates between rival religious philosophers in ancient India. Here, the purpose seems less about conversion than identifying who is superior to whom and thus more worthy of receiving royal support. In any case, we see here one possible response to the problem of religious diversity.

The Buddha offers different reasons for agreeing to the contest in different versions of the story. In the Pāli tradition, he explains that the precept he made forbidding the display of extraordinary powers does not apply to him, and offers an analogy of the king who may pick fruits from his own garden despite making the rule that his subjects may not. In this way, the Buddha compares himself to a king, an important analogy for thinking about the nature of a buddha and one that has been explored to some extent in recent scholarship.[37] In the Sanskrit tradition, however, he relies instead on the Buddha-life blueprint itself. He hesitates at first, arguing that he does not encourage his monks to display their superhuman powers, but then he considers what the buddhas of the past have done and sees that all of them have performed the great miracle as one of the five deeds (or ten, depending on the version of the story) that all buddhas must perform in their final lifetime. Thus, the story sometimes betrays a kind of circularity or reflexivity to justify the Buddha's performance of the miracle: he does it, because it is what buddhas do. In both cases, the reasoning gives us important information on what some, perhaps many, Buddhists have thought about the nature of a buddha.

The actual performance of the miracle (or miracles, since they are many) forms the main event(s) of the story, and primarily serves to demonstrate the Buddha's magnificence, his wondrous qualities. However, the miracles also inform us of the extraordinary power of his teachings (the Dharma) and of his community (the Saṅgha). Different versions of the story bring out this message in different ways. In the Pāli tradition, the Buddha's "twin miracle" is prefaced by a sequence of other wonders described by members of the Buddha's community, beginning with a young laywoman named Gharaṇī, who says that she will perform the miracle in the Buddha's stead. The Buddha asks her what miracle she will perform, and she says she will turn the whole earth into water and dive into it like a water bird and reappear at the various eastern, western, northern, and southern rims of the earth, and at its center. The Buddha confirms that she does possess such power, but assures her that he must take responsibility for the task. "This basket of flowers was not prepared for you," he says. What follows is a sequence of increasingly more detailed descriptions of increasingly more complicated wonders, which members of the Buddhist community with increasingly higher levels of status offer to perform on behalf of the Buddha. He declines all their offers, but the descriptions still work to heighten the suspense and accentuate the Buddha's own performance, as well as showing us the extraordinary capabilities of his community.[38] What kind of miracle will the Buddha perform?

In the Mūlasarvāstivāda tradition, some (but not all) of this sequencing is replaced by the episode of the unfortunate Prince Kāla, King Prasenajit's younger half-brother, who has his hands and feet cut off by the king, because he hears rumors that the prince has been soliciting one of the king's consorts.[39] As the prince is writhing in pain in the middle of the marketplace, he makes a plea in his mind to the Buddha, who hears it in his own mind and sends Ānanda to help the young man by performing an act of truth on his behalf. The act of truth is a common type of wonder found in classical Indian and Buddhist literature. It involves a kind of speech act with wondrous consequences if the statements are true. In this case, the Buddha tells his nephew and monastic attendant, Ānanda, to recite a long formula or sequence of poetic statements to the effect that if the Buddha is the best of all beings, and if his teaching on nonattachment is the best of all teachings, and if his community is the best of all communities, then by the truth of these statements, let Prince Kāla's body be restored. Ānanda does and says exactly as directed, and the prince is spontaneously healed. Apart from being a kind of opening act for the Buddha's great miracle, this act of truth expresses well the very point that I have been making here about the great miracle story as a whole: it serves to emphasize the cosmic supremacy of the Buddha, and by extension, that of his teachings and his community.

The Buddha's culminating miracle(s), whether it is the "twin miracle" of the Pāli tradition or the "great miracle" of other versions, would seem to support a similar conclusion. The former may refer to a demonstration of power such that the Buddha simultaneously transforms one half of his body into water and the other half into fire, and then does the reverse, and so forth, the fire blazing and water streaming out to cover the entire world, all while he is levitating above the pavilion. One possible interpretation, suggested by Strong, is that this miracle demonstrates the Buddha's power over the forces of nature.[40] Building on this interpretation, one may note the prevalence of fire and water imagery in the Indian poetics of sovereignty, which informed how Buddhists conceptualized the nature of a buddha.

In the Sanskrit versions, the Buddha performs the same miracle as above, but then remarks that the power to perform such a feat is common to all his disciples.

He then performs another miracle, the "great miracle," whereby he multiplies himself until an array of buddhas fills the entire cosmos up to the highest heaven. Two *nāgas* or divine serpents support him by creating an immense, jeweled lotus on which the Buddha sits and which branches and spreads as the buddhas multiply. We can see a depiction of this scene in Figure 7.1 with which we opened the chapter: in the righthand column in the second panel from the top the Buddha sits upon a lotus flanked by two more buddhas also sitting upon lotuses that branch from the main one. This performance has been interpreted in light of ancient Indian cosmology with the Buddha as the cosmic focal point akin to Prajāpati, the lord of beings. Yet, as Strong has pointed out, the great miracle also tells us something about the developing conception of a buddha. It provides a visual image of multiple buddhas appearing at the same time and place, an image developed in different ways in Mahāyāna Buddhist scriptures like the *Lotus Sūtra*.[41]

Like the first sermon and so many of the stories from the Buddha's teaching career, the great miracle story also features episodes of instruction. Buddhas teach the Dharma; that is what they do. In the Pāli narrative tradition of the twin miracle story, the Buddha teaches the Dharma to the audience during his fire and water miracle, and then afterwards he performs another act of instruction by duplicating himself and engaging in a dialogue on the Dharma with himself, a dialogue to which countless living beings, including humans and deities, bear witness. These teachings enable many of them to make further progress on the path, signaling the effectiveness of the Buddha's actions.

At the same time, the contrasting negative reactions and treatment of the rival teachers in the story is particularly noteworthy. In both stories, the rival teachers are physically attacked by gods who support the Buddha, although the place of this episode in the sequence of events differs depending on the version. In the Pāli tradition, it occurs after one of the early miracles in which the Buddha makes a mango tree grow to great size from seed in a matter of moments, an episode apparently depicted in stone from a relief at Sañci (see Figure 7.2).[42] Sakka, the king of the gods, then orders the wind-god to unleash a windstorm that destroys the pavilion constructed to host the miracle contest, and then the sun god stops his sun chariot in the middle of the sky and brings scorching heat down upon the rival teachers, who then scatter in search of shelter. One of the teachers, Pūraṇa Kāśyapa, even commits suicide by drowning himself in a nearby pond. So as mentioned above, the main purpose of the Buddha's great miracle(s) does not seem to be the conversion of the rival teachers so much as their defeat.

Figure 7.2 Various gods and people paying homage to an empty seat beneath a mango tree. Sañci, first century CE. Photo by John C. Huntington, Courtesy of the John C. and Susan L. Huntington Photographic Archive of Buddhist and Asian Art.

In the Sanskrit version found in the *Divyāvadāna*, a similar episode occurs later in the story after the Buddha performs the great miracle, but still before he teaches the Dharma to the multitude; whereas the closely related version in *Mūlasarvāstivāda-vinaya*, originally in Sanskrit and still preserved in Tibetan translation, places this episode at the end of the story even after the Buddha has instructed the assembly. In both these Sanskrit versions, the rival teachers are still dispersed violently by deities who support the Buddha: in the *Divyāvadāna* it is said to be Pāñcika, the general of the *yakṣa*s, who releases the storm of wind and rain upon them; in the *Mūlasarvāstivāda-vinaya*, it is Vajrapāṇi, the Buddha's famous superhuman strongman.[43] This episode not only underlines the magnificence of the Buddha, "the teacher of gods and men" and "unsurpassed leader of those ready to be tamed;" it also tells us that not everyone is at the same level of readiness and may indicate a reticence on the part of the traditional storytellers to ascribe responsibility for violent actions, or the consequences of such actions, to the Buddha himself.

We see that people encounter and respond to the Buddha and his message in different ways, and we learn that they must largely bear the responsibility for their own actions. Such are the implications of the central (but not uniquely) Buddhist doctrine of karma, the doctrine that (moral) actions have (real) consequences in this life or future lives, a doctrine that informs so much of Buddhist narrative literature. At the same time, however, this doctrine exists in a state of tension with the doctrine of the Buddha's superhuman power, his ability to effect changes in nature and individual beings through his teachings and miracles, a doctrine which gestures toward what Luis Gómez has called the Buddhist doctrine of grace.[44]

The Descent from the Heavens (at Saṃkāśya)

The final episode from the Buddha's teaching career that we will consider in this chapter is his descent alongside the gods, Brahmā and Indra (who is called Sakka in Pāli, Śakra in Sanskrit), from the Heaven of the Thirty-Three at the town of Saṃkāśya (Pāli: Saṅkassa). In the Pāli narrative tradition, this event follows the "twin miracle" performed at Śrāvastī and occurs after an intervening three-month period during which the Buddha resides in the Heaven of the Thirty-Three and teaches the Dharma—in the Pāli tradition, he teaches the entire Abhidharma—to his mother who has been reborn there as a god.[45] The "twin miracle" marks the Buddha's ascent, and the descent from the heavens marks his return to the earth at the end of the retreat. These three events, the importance of which is registered in multiple iterations of the Buddha-life blueprint, form a continuous narrative in the Pāli *Dhammapada* commentary, and taken together, they correspond to an important annual ritual and festival period, surrounding the three-month, rainy season monastic retreat, one that still occurs in many Buddhist cultures today.

As with the other narratives told here, the story of the descent has many different versions, both textual and visual.[46] While it may not appear among the earliest Buddhist textual sources concerning the Buddha's teaching career, the art historical record indicates that a narrative tradition concerning the descent was already established as early as the end of the second century BCE. For instance, in Figure 7.3 below, we see people paying homage to a throne beneath a tree, beside which is a triple ladder with the Buddha's footprint visible at the top and bottom of the central ladder.

Figure 7.3 The Scene of the Descent from the Heavens. Bharhut, late second century BCE. Photo by John C. Huntington, Courtesy of the John C. and Susan L. Huntington Photographic Archive of Buddhist and Asian Art.

We find many important themes in these stories. They feature multiple characters and several interlinking plotlines. For example, the Buddha's absence during his stay in heaven prefigures in some ways his absence after his final death. According to a story retold by the Chinese pilgrims, Faxian and Xuanzang (who visited Saṃkāśya and other important pilgrimage sites in the fifth and seventh centuries, respectively), the Buddha's absence prompts King Prasenajit to have the first Buddha-image carved out of sandalwood and placed on the seat where the Buddha normally sat, so that he could remember him.[47] Additionally, some versions feature a wondrous display of superhuman power by the Buddhist nun, Utpalavarṇā, who turns herself into a wheel-turning king in order to be the first to greet the Buddha upon his return only for him to reprimand her for her over-eagerness to see him in person.[48]

The theme of people's anxiety about the Buddha's absence and their urgent desire to see him again in the flesh also features in a short story related to the descent found in the *Avadānaśataka*, *The Hundred Buddhist Tales*.[49] Members of the Buddhist community here on earth request that the Buddha's disciple, Maudgalyāyana, use his superhuman powers to go to the Heaven of the Thirty-Three and ask the Buddha to return to earth out of compassion for them, because they do not have the power to travel to heaven and see him there themselves. Maudgalyāyana agrees, and when he reaches heaven and sees the Buddha teaching the Dharma to the multitude of deities there, he "smiles in wonder" at the scene, and a series of gods then explain to him how hearing and understanding the Buddha's teachings led to their rebirth in the heavens. Thus, we gain another sense that the story is foreshadowing a time when the Buddha will no longer be present in the world, except through his teachings and community, and there is also a message here about the power of hearing and understanding the Buddha's teachings, perhaps even in the absence of the living Buddha.

There is much more we could explore in the different versions of the descent story and related narratives, and once again we can scarcely do better than to start with John Strong's work on the subject from which I will draw below.[50] In what follows, I will focus briefly on two aspects of the story in order to bring this chapter to a close. First of all, I will discuss the connection between the human and cosmic dimensions of the Buddha evoked in the story by quoting a scene from the version in the Pāli *Dhammapada* commentary in which the Buddha sees the entire cosmos and the gods commune with humankind and vice versa. I will then conclude with a brief discussion of the connections between this story, sacred place, pilgrimage, and ritual.

As the Buddha is preparing for his descent from the Heaven of the Thirty-Three, which is located on the summit of Mount Meru, the central mountain of the world in traditional Buddhist cosmology, the narrator of the Pāli *Dhammapada* commentary version describes the scene for us:

> On the occasion of the descent of the gods, the teacher (i.e., the Buddha), standing on the summit of Mount Sineru (Meru, Sumeru), performed the twin miracle and looked up. There was a clear view as far as the Heavenly Realm of Brahmā. He looked down and there was a clear view as far as the Hell of Ceaseless Torture (Avīci). He looked to the four cardinal directions and the four intermediate directions, and there was a clear view of many hundreds of thousands of worlds. Gods looked upon men, and men looked upon gods, and everyone saw one another face-to-face. The Blessed One emitted rays of rainbow light. In the assembly, a circle thirty-six *yojanas* in circumference (approx. two hundred and fifty miles), not even one being looked upon the glory of the Buddha that day who did not desire to attain buddhahood.[51]

The cosmic dimension here is clear, and the Buddha is again at its center, as he is in the story of the "great miracle."[52] At this point, the Buddha descends from the heavens on a triple ladder or staircase made by Indra out of gold, silver, and precious jewels. He is flanked by Brahmā and Indra on his right and left side, the former holding a fan and the latter an umbrella, followed by their celestial retinues. We see Brahmā and Indra flanking the Buddha in the depiction of this scene in Figure 7.1, while other images, such as Figure 7.3, feature the triple staircase. The staircase connects the human realm to the heavens in a more mundane fashion, which allows the humans to see the gods and commingle with them. Ordinarily, of course, humans cannot see the gods or visit them in the heavens. Thus, Strong makes the point that the descent story results in a "levelling of the field between humans and deities and the Buddha," and he also points out that "religiously speaking, we have here an equating of humans and buddhas, at least in terms of their potential."[53] It is particularly noteworthy that the wish to become a buddha oneself, perhaps the central defining theme of the Mahāyāna Buddhist tradition, occurs here in an ostensibly mainstream Buddhist narrative.

We have thus reached yet another "belvedere" moment, another expansive and beautiful vision in the Buddha's life story as well as another clear vantage point from which to consider the powerful connections between the Buddha's life story, sacred place, pilgrimage, and ritual performance. As Strong points out, the descent (and, in fact, all the events discussed in this chapter and more besides) were connected in ancient times to specific places, which formed part of large pilgrimage routes perhaps even in the time of King Aśoka in the third century BCE.[54] He has also drawn attention to the fact that the story of the Buddha's descent is reenacted in ritual performances that still take place in modern times at the end of the rains-retreat. For evidence, he has quoted an excellent description by Kenneth Wells of one such event from twentieth century Thailand, which can help us to imagine the proceedings:

> Certain temples have traditional ceremonies at the time of *Ok Barnsa* [i.e., the end of the rains-retreat] such as bringing an image of Buddha down from a hill, or lowering an image from the top of a *cetiya* amid a fanfare of music, or conveying an image to the temple in a decorated cart followed by a procession of monks and worshipers. When food is given to monks walking in this procession it is an act of merit called *devorohana* or "Coming down from the deva world." This is in memory of the return of Buddha from Indra's heaven.[55]

In one of his articles, Strong cites another, more elaborate description of a similar ritual event from nineteenth century Burma.[56] Thus, the story of the descent not only teaches us how to think about the relationship between the Buddha (as a unique category of superhuman being), the gods (as divine beings), and ourselves as human beings; it also shows us how people use ritual, drama, and festival to transform the real world of their lived experiences so that it corresponds in some way to the story world created by the narratives. This, according to Gary Comstock, is what it could mean to speak of the truth of religious narratives.[57]

Conclusion

It is difficult to compress the Buddha's entire teaching career of more than forty years into a single chapter of a book, though it has, of course, been done before.[58] Here, as before, we have been guided by the Buddha-life blueprint, or certain iterations of it, which helped us to identify a series of events that have often been taken as emblematic of his teaching career: the Buddha's first sermon, his "great miracle" at Śrāvastī, and the descent from the heavens at Saṁkāśya. Of course, other iterations of the blueprint, such as the one seen in the Sārnāth relief in Figure 7.1 with which we began the chapter, would have prompted us to discuss more events (such as the time when the Buddha uses loving kindness to tame the rampaging elephant, Nālagiri, sent to kill him by his scheming cousin, Devadatta), but the three episodes considered here still represent important aspects of the Buddha as a character who appears throughout Buddhist literature. We see him as both charismatic teacher and wonderworker, and the various reactions of the audience in the stories are just as important for us to appreciate the significance of his actions.

Not only does the Buddha teach the Dharma. His teaching is understood, and this results in the establishment of the Buddhist community or Sangha. We thus encounter three key elements most cherished by Buddhists over time as the precious jewels or treasures of Buddhism. Even though what Buddhists may understand by the three jewels varies depending on the tradition, person, or context, they still form a reference point from which we can start to gain a sense of the broader significance of the Buddha and his teaching career.

In addition to the first sermon, we looked at the narrative cycle of events beginning with the Buddha's "great miracle" at Śrāvastī, continuing with his sojourn in the Heaven of the Thirty-Three, where he teaches the Dharma to his mother, and concluding with his descent from the heavens alongside the gods, Brahmā and Indra, at Saṃkāśya. Apart from being entertaining stories that showcase the magnificence of the Buddha, as well as the preeminence of the Dharma and the Sangha, these narratives can help us better understand the tension in Buddhist literature between the human and the cosmic dimensions of the Buddha by showing the complex relationships between him and an array of different characters who interact with him, including gods and human beings. Through the lens of these various relationships, the Buddha begins to come into focus as a unique category of superhuman being.

At the same time, one of the goals of retelling these stories has been to provide some sense of a method for engaging with the more expansive biography of the Buddha. Reading these stories with care and attending to their literary features can help us learn how to place ourselves at the countless scenes of instruction found throughout Buddhist literature, where we find the Buddha engaging in dialogue with so many different audiences. The stories also provide a window for us to see outside the literature at how Buddhists have engaged with these stories in their communities. They provide examples for us to see how the Buddha's life story has been made to correspond to the lived world of Buddhists through pilgrimage and ritual traditions. At this point in the Buddha's life story, we move on to the events surrounding his final death or "complete cessation" (*parinirvāṇa*), another crucial episode in which we will have the opportunity to observe the relationships between the Buddha and the various members of his community, and consider the range of complex emotional responses prompted by his passing.

Notes

1. The Pāli commentarial tradition lists the places where the Buddha spent the rains-retreat during the forty-five years of his teaching career, which assumes that he attained awakening at the age of thirty-five, since the Pāli tradition also says he died at the age of eighty. For the list, see John S. Strong, *The Buddha: A Short Biography* (Oxford: Oneworld, 2001; repr., 2009, as *The Buddha: A Beginner's Guide*), 133. Citations in this chapter are to the 2009 edition. Hajime Nakamura, *Gotama Buddha: A Biography Based on the Most Reliable Texts*, vol. 1 (Tokyo: Kosei, 2000), 271–277, reviews several sources that give differing chronologies.
2. There are several interpretations of this perplexing episode. One interesting theory is that Brahmā appears here because of his traditional role at the beginning of

great undertakings, for which see Monika Zin, *Ajanta Handbuch der Malereien, Handbook of the Paintings 2: Devotionale und ornamentale Malereien*, vol. 1 (Wiesbaden: Harrassowitz Verlag, 2003), 309. For a discussion of various theories, see Dhivan Thomas Jones, "Why Did Brahmā Ask the Buddha to Teach?" *Buddhist Studies Review* 26.1 (2009): 85–102, and Anālayo, "Brahmā's Invitation," *Journal of the Oxford Centre of Buddhist Studies* 1 (2011): 12–38.

3. The "buddha-eye" (*buddha-cakkhu*) is one of several types of eyesight mentioned in Buddhist literature. One early commentary found in the Pāli Canon, the *Cūlaniddesa*, list five types, all of which the Buddha is said to possess, and defines them: the physical or fleshy eye, the divine eye, the eye of wisdom, the buddha-eye, and the universal eye. For a translation of this passage, see Bhikkhu Bodhi, *The Suttanipāta: An Ancient Collection of the Buddha's Discourses Together with Its Commentaries* (Boston: Wisdom, 2017), 1174–1177.
4. Compassion is the reason given for the Buddha's decision to survey the world with his buddha-eye at the request of Brahmā in the versions of the story found in the Pāli *Vinaya* and the *Ariyapariyesana Sutta*. For the former in which the narrator voices the reason, see T. W. Rhys Davids and Hermann Oldenberg, *Vinaya Texts, Part I*, Sacred Books of the East, vol. 13 (London: Oxford University Press, 1885), 87; for the latter, which is given in first-person voice by the Buddha himself, see Bhikkhu Bodhi and Bhikkhu Ñāṇamoli, *The Middle Length Discourses of the Buddha: A Translations of the Majjhima Nikāya* (Boston: Wisdom, 1995), 261. See Anālayo, "Brahmā's Invitation," 30–32, for an argument that the whole episode might have been a later addition to an earlier iteration of the *sutta*.
5. For his use of this term, see John S. Strong, *The Legend and Cult of Upagupta* (Princeton, NJ: Princeton University Press, 1992), xii. I am grateful to Charles Hallisey for drawing my attention to this interesting concept in Strong's work.
6. Strong, *The Buddha*, 13–18.
7. See H. Porter Abbott, *The Cambridge Introduction to Narrative*, 3rd ed. (Cambridge: Cambridge University Press, 2021), 17–18 and 261, on story and fabula.
8. For a brief introduction to this important early discourse, see Sarah Shaw, *The Art of Listening: A Guide to the Early Teachings of Buddhism* (Boulder, CO: Shambhala, 2021).
9. William Stede, *The Sumaṅgala-vilāsinī: Buddhaghosa's Commentary on the Dīgha-nikāya, Part II* (London: Luzac and Co, 1931), 412. The translation is my own; there is no full English translation of this commentary.
10. In David V. Fiordalis, "Miracles in Indian Buddhist narratives and doctrine," *Journal of the International Association of Buddhist Studies* 33, nos. 1–2 (2011): 381–408, I cited this passage on p. 392, but interpreted it to be in the voice of the Buddha, when, in fact, the gods are speaking here. This is also helpful to note as we think about how best to translate the term, *pāṭihāriya*. Some may still hesitate to use the term, "miracle," in a Buddhist context, preferring perhaps "wonder" or "marvel" or "superhuman feat." I have no objection to these terms, which I also use myself. However, the context here clearly indicates divine agency: the gods perform the miracles. And the same term is applied here to the Buddha's own wondrous display of superhuman power. So, for this reason and others, I use the term miracle here and elsewhere in this

chapter. For the purposes of comparison and in order to see some of the difficulties of such an endeavor, even in an exclusively Judeo-Christian context, consider Yair Zakovich, *The Concept of the Miracle in the Bible* (Tel-Aviv: Mod Books, 1991).

11. Strong made this distinction in an unpublished presentation, entitled "Buddhist Miracles and the Hagiography of the Buddha," at the Triennial Meeting of the International Association of Buddhist Studies in Toronto, Canada, in August 2017.
12. For an English translation of this passage in the *Mahāparinibbāna Sutta*, see Maurice Walshe, *The Long Discourses of the Buddha: A Translation of the Dīgha Nikāya* (Somerville, MA: Wisdom, 1995), 246ff.
13. See Ernst Obermiller, *History of Buddhism (Chos-hbyung) by Bu-ston* (Heidelberg: Harrassowitz, 1931), 197ff.
14. Tenzin Chögyel, *The Life of the Buddha*, Kurtis Schaeffer, trans. (New York: Penguin, 2015), 74–76. Most of these same events are connected by the same author to the annual holiday calendar, emphasizing their connection to Tibetan ritual.
15. Further discussion of the rows of eight *chod rten* may be found in Pema Dorjee, *Stupa and its Technology: A Tibeto-Buddhist Perspective* (Delhi: Indira Gandhi National Centre for the Arts and Motilal Banarsidass, 1996).
16. For translations of the Pāli versions found in the *Saṃyutta Nikāya* and *Vinaya*, see respectively Bhikkhu Bodhi, *The Connected Discourses of the Buddha: A Translation of the Samyutta Nikāya* (Boston: Wisdom, 2000), 1843–1847; and Rhys Davids and Oldenberg, *Vinaya Texts*, 89ff. For translations of seven different versions extant in Chinese and a comparative analysis, see Anālayo, "Chinese Parallels to the Dhammacakkappavattana-sutta (1)," *Journal of the Oxford Centre of Buddhist Studies* 3 (2012): 12–46, and Anālayo, "Chinese Parallels to the Dhammacakkappavattana-sutta (2)," *Journal of the Oxford Centre of Buddhist Studies* 5 (2013): 9–41. Extant Sanskrit versions are found in the *Mahāvastu*, *Catuṣpariṣatsūtra*, and *Lalitavistara*, for English translations of which see, respectively, J. J. Jones, *The Mahāvastu, Vol. III* (London: Pali Text Society, 1978), 322–328; Ria Kloppenborg, *The Sūtra on the Foundation of the Buddhist Order* (Leiden: Brill, 1973), 21–29; and (translating the Tibetan translation thereof) Dharmachakra Translation Committee, *The Play in Full: Lalitavistara* (84000: Translating the Words of the Buddha, 2013). For a translation of another version of the first sermon preserved in the Tibetan Buddhist canon, see Dharmachakra Translation Committee, *Sūtra of the Wheel of Dharma: Dharmacakrasūtra* (84000: Translating the Words of the Buddha, 2018). N. Aiyaswami Sastri, "The First Sermon of the Buddha," *New Indian Antiquary* 1, no. 8 (1938): 473–492, includes a translation of another Chinese version deemed "late" and therefore not translated by Anālayo.
17. John Strong's excellent introductory textbook, *Buddhisms* (Oxford: Oneworld, 2015), xx–xxi, uses the three jewels as an organizing principle.
18. See André Bareau, *Recherches sur la biographie du Buddha dans les Sūtrapiṭaka et les Vinayapiṭaka anciens: De la quête de l'éveil à la conversion de Śāriputra et de Maudgalyāyana* (Paris: École Française d'Extrême-Orient, 1963), 172ff, an argument criticized by Lambert Schmithausen, "On some Aspects of Descriptions or Theories of 'Liberating Insight' and 'Enlightenment' in Early Buddhism," in K. Bruhn and A

Wezler, eds., *Studien zum Jainismus und Buddhismus, Gedenkschrift für Ludwig Alsdorf* (Wiesbaden: Franz Steiner, 1981), 199–250, and Anālayo, "The Chinese Parallels to the Dhammacakkappavattana-sutta (1)," 31ff. See also Strong, *Buddhisms*, 113–114.

19. Consider in this respect John S. Strong, *The Legend of King Aśoka* (Princeton, NJ: Princeton University Press, 1983); Charles Hallisey and Anne Hansen, "Narrative, Sub-Ethics, and the Moral Life: Some Evidence from Theravāda Buddhism," *Journal of Religious Ethics* 24, no. 2 (1996): 305–327; Luis Gómez, "On Reading Literature Literally," in *Special International Symposium on Pure Land Buddhism*, 5–30 (Kyoto: Otani University, BARC Research Center for Buddhist Cultures in Asia, International Symposium Series 1, 2011); Kristin Scheible, *Reading the Mahāvaṃsa: The Literary Aims of a Theravāda Buddhist History* (New York: Columbia University Press, 2016); Steven Collins, *Wisdom as a Way of Life*, edited by Justin McDaniel (New York: Columbia University Press, 2018); Eviatar Shulman, *Visions of the Buddha: Creative Dimensions of Early Buddhist Scripture* (New York: Oxford University Press, 2021); and Shaw, *Art of Listening*.
20. My translation modifies only slightly the one found in Rhys Davids and Oldenberg, *Vinaya Texts*, 92. The "efforts" or "ascetic practices" (*padhāna*) mentioned here are sometimes found as a list of four: (1) restraint of the senses; (2) abandonment of lustful, hateful, or cruel thoughts; (3) meditative cultivation of mindfulness and other mental conditions conducive to awakening; and (4) holding in the mind certain objects of meditation that will keep one on the right path, such as meditation on the stages of a decomposing corpse. For an example, see Walshe, *Long Discourses*, 490.
21. For a full translation of the Pāli *Vinaya* version on which I am mainly relying here, see Rhys Davids and Oldenberg, *Vinaya Texts*, 92–94.
22. On the importance of context for traditional understanding of a "discourse" (*sutta*), see Maria Heim, *Voice of the Buddha: Buddhaghosa on the Immeasurable Words* (New York: Oxford University Press, 2018).
23. For the notion of "scenes of instruction," see Mark D. Jordan, "Missing Scenes," *Harvard Divinity Bulletin*, 2010, http://bulletin.hds.harvard.edu/missing-scenes/ (Last accessed March 9, 2022).
24. This insight is, in fact, one of the particular contributions of Strong's introductory textbook, *Buddhisms*. See page xxiii and chapter 4 therein.
25. See Kloppenborg, *Sūtra on the Foundation of the Buddhist Order*, 23–24, for an example in which the Buddha gives the first part of the sermon in the morning and then waits until after the midday meal to give the second part.
26. For a translation of the *Mūlasarvāstivāda-vinaya* version in which the Buddha appears to wait until the next day, see Anālayo, "Chinese Parallels to the Dhammacakkappavattana-sutta (1)," 21ff.
27. For an introduction to such concepts, one can hardly do better than to read the chapter on the four truths in Strong, *Buddhisms*.
28. This version has been translated in Sastri, "First Sermon of the Buddha," and discussed briefly in Bart Dessein, "The First Turning of the Wheel of the Doctrine: Sarvāstivāda and Mahāsāṃghika Controversy," in A. Heirman et al., eds.,

The Spread of Buddhism, 15–48 (Leiden: Brill, 2007), and Anālayo, "Chinese Parallels to the Dhammacakkappavattana-sutta (1)." Another indication that it (or at least its opening frame story) may be later than other versions is the fact that it does not mention the five former companions as the direct audience for the sermon but refers instead to an audience of one-thousand monks and many gods.

29. Anālayo, "Chinese Parallels to the Dhammacakkappavattana-sutta (2)," 18–21.
30. Perhaps no one has done more to draw recent attention to this story than John Strong, who retells it in *The Buddha*, 140–147. David V. Fiordalis, "The Buddha's Great Miracle at Śrāvastī: a Translation from the Tibetan *Mūlasarvāstivāda-vinaya*," *Asian Literature and Translation* 2, no. 3 (2014): 1–33, and David V. Fiordalis, "The Buddha's Great Miracle, a Flowering Sprig from Kṣemendra's *Wish-Fulfilling Vine of Tales of the Bodhisattva* (*Bodhisattvāvadānakalpalatā*): English Translation with Editions of the Sanskrit Text and Tibetan Translation," *Korea Journal of Buddhist Studies* 67 (2021): 45–121, doi:10.21482/jbs.67..202106.45, contain references to many modern resources for exploring the various images, editions, and translations of the story. Natchapol Sirisawad, "The *Mahāprātihāryasūtra* in the Gilgit Manuscripts: A Critical Edition, Translation and Textual Analysis" (PhD dissertation, Ludwig-Maximilians University of Munich, 2019), 192ff, contains a helpful comparative analysis of the many different versions of the story, as well as an edition and annotated translation of two fragments recently identified from the Gilgit manuscript collection. Dieter Schlingloff, *Ajanta: Handbuch der Malereien, Handbook of the Paintings*. 3 vols. (Weisbaden: Harrassowitz Verlag, 2000), vol. 1, 488–515, and vol. 2, 100–105, also includes many references to textual versions as well as line-art renditions of various images by Monika Zin.
31. For example, an e-mail I received in early March, 2022, from Maitripa College in Portland, Oregon, announced the new year by noting the fact that Losar (Tibetan New Year) marks the beginning of the fifteen days leading up to the "Day of Miracles" in celebration of the Buddha's great miracle. This widespread Tibetan tradition apparently follows the narrative of the *Dharmagupta-vinaya* and the *Sūtra of the Wise and the Fool* wherein the sequence of miracles leading up to the Buddha "great miracle" takes place over a fifteen-day period. For English translations of these versions, see respectively Ju-hyung Rhi, "Gandhāran Images of the 'Śrāvastī Miracle': an Iconographic Reassessment" (PhD dissertation, University of California Berkeley, 1991), and Stanley Frye, *Sutra of the Wise and the Foolish* (Dharamsala: Library of Tibetan Works and Archives, 1981), 49–65. Rhi's dissertation contains the only English translations I know of several versions translated into Chinese.
32. This group includes Mahāvīra, the leader of the Jain religion, and thus bears some relation to actual religions of India. We might thus consider Buddhist literature as another form of "historicized prose fiction" or "fictionalized history," on which see Robert Alter, *The Art of Biblical Narrative: Revised and Updated* (New York: Basic Books, 2011), 27 and 47. He coins the latter term to describe the kind of narrative he finds in the Hebrew Bible.
33. See Frye, *Sutra of the Wise and the Foolish*; see also Sirisawad, "The *Mahāprātihāryasūtra* in the Gilgit Manuscripts," 194.

34. The Pāli Buddhist tradition contains reasoning quite similar to this. See, for instance, Phyllis Granoff, "The Ambiguity of Miracles: Buddhist Understandings of Supernatural Power," *East and West* 46 (1996): 79–96, who, on page 80, translates a passage from a medieval Pāli Buddhist text, the *Sārasaṅgaha*, for which I have found a close parallel in the earlier "sub-commentary" or *ṭīkā* on the *Mahāpadāna Sutta*. It may be possible to trace this line of thinking back to the canonical texts, as well.
35. On these common epithets for the Buddha, and especially the second one, see Monika Zin, *Mitleid und Wunderkraft: Schwierige Bekehrungen und ihre Ikonographie im indischen Buddhismus* (Wiesbaden: Harrassowitz Verlag, 2006), 4ff, as well as David V. Fiordalis, "The Buddha as Spiritual Sovereign," in Naomi Appleton, ed., *Narrative Visions and Visual Narratives in Indian Buddhism*, 213–237 (Sheffield: Equinox, 2022), 220–221.
36. In the Pāli tradition, they do not approach the king directly, but proclaim their challenge throughout town and King Bimbisāra hears of it and goes to see the Buddha. Sirisawad, "*Mahāprātihāryasūtra* in the Gilgit Manuscripts," 205ff, contains a detailed comparative analysis of this and other plot elements found in the various versions of the story.
37. See Natalie Gummer, "Speech Acts of the Buddha: Sovereign Ritual and the Poetics of Power in Mahāyāna Sūtras," *History of Religions* 61, no. 2 (2021): 173–211; David Fiordalis, "Buddhas and Body Language: The Literary Trope of the Buddha's Smile," in *The Language of the Sūtras*, ed. Natalie Gummer (Berkeley: Mangalam Press, 2021), 59–103; and Fiordalis, "Buddha as Spiritual Sovereign." For more on the relationship between kingship and religion in other South Asian religions, see the essays collected in Caleb Simmons, "Sovereignty and Religion in India: Negotiating Authority, Rule, and Realm in Premodern South Asia," *Religions* 12 (2021).
38. See Eugene W. Burlingame, *Buddhist Legend: Translated from the original Pali text of the Dhammapada Commentary Part 3*, Harvard Oriental Series, vol. 30 (Cambridge, MA: Harvard University Press, 1921), 38ff, for a translation of this episode.
39. See Sirisawad, "*Mahāprātihāryasūtra* in the Gilgit Manuscripts," 221ff, for a comparative analysis of this episode. Andy Rotman, *Divine Stories: Divyāvadāna, Part I* (Boston: Wisdom Publications, 2008), 253ff; and Fiordalis, "The Buddha's Great Miracle at Śrāvastī" and "The Buddha's Great Miracle," contain complete translations of relevant versions.
40. Strong, *The Buddha*, 145.
41. See Strong, *The Buddha*, 144–146, for a discussion of previous views and his own interpretation. I would add that this connection does not necessarily mean that this image or story of the "great miracle" is earlier than the *Lotus Sūtra*.
42. The "mango trick" is one of the stock tricks of the Indian magical performance tradition and one also attested in contemporary India. See Lee Siegel, *Net of Magic: Wonders and Deceptions in India* (Chicago: University of Chicago Press, 1991), as well as the entry for "mango trick" in the Sir Henry Yule, *Hobson-Jobson: A Glossary of Colloquial Anglo-Indian Words and Phrases, and of Kindred Terms, Etymological, Historical, Geographical and Discursive*, edited by William Crooke (London: J. Murray, 1903).

My thanks again to John Strong who shared with me an unpublished presentation he gave on this topic in Kyoto in 2009.

43. On the figure of Vajrapāṇi, see Monika Zin, "Vajrapāṇi in the Narrative Reliefs," in *Migration, Trade, and Peoples: Association of South Asian Archeologists, Proceedings of the Eighteenth Congress, London, 2005*, ed. Michael Willis (London: British Association for South Asian Studies, 2009), 73–88; and Étienne Lamotte, "Vajrapāṇi en Inde," in *Mélanges de Sinologie offerts à Monsieur Paul Demiéville*, 113–159 (Paris: Presses Universitaires de France, 1966).
44. See, for instance, the introductory material in Luis Gómez, *Land of Bliss: The Paradise of the Buddha of Measureless Light* (Honolulu: University of Hawai'i Press, 1996), as well as Luis Gómez, "Buddhism as a Religion of Hope: Observations on the 'Logic' of a Doctrine and its Foundational Myth," *The Eastern Buddhist, New Series* 32, no. 1 (2000): 1–21.
45. See Anālayo, "Teaching the Abhidharma in the Heaven of the Thirty-Three, The Buddha and his Mother," *Journal of the Oxford Centre of Buddhist Studies* 2 (2012): 9–35; and Peter Skilling, "Dharma, Dhāraṇī, Abhidharma, Avadāna: What was taught in Trayastriṃśa?" *Annual Report of the International Research Institute for Advanced Buddhology at Soka University* 11 (2008): 37–60.
46. Schlingloff, *Ajanta*, vol. 1, 476–487, and vol. 2, 95–99, includes an extensive list of textual sources and images of the story.
47. See Rongxi Li, *The Great Tang Dynasty Record of the Western Regions* (Berkeley, CA: Numata Center, 1996), 160; and James Legge, *A Record of Buddhistic Kingdoms* (Oxford: Clarendon Press, 1886), 56–57, both cited in Strong, *The Buddha*, 216.
48. Sonia Rhie Mace, "Localizing Narrative Through Image: The Nun Utpalavarṇā in a Stone Relief from Kaushambi," in *Narrative Visions and Visual Narratives in Indian Buddhism*, ed. Naomi Appleton (Sheffield: Equinox, 2022), 129–159, focuses attention on an image of Utpalavarṇā worshipping the Buddha from a relief dated to the first century BCE. She also discusses and provides images of the early iconography of the descent story and summarizes various textual accounts of this scene.
49. The story tells of a monk who has a wondrous birth by spontaneous generation, not through the normal means, and he goes to worship the Buddha at the time of the descent. The Buddha tells a brief story about the monk's past lives and the actions this monk performed in the past that resulted in his wondrous birth. See Léon Feer, *Avadâna-çataka: Cent Légendes (Bouddhiques)*, Annales du Musée Guimet 18 (Paris: Ernest Leroux, 1879), 326–332.
50. John Strong has written eloquently and in detail about these events and their connections to Buddhist ritual and pilgrimage traditions. In addition to his brief retelling and discussion in his Buddha biography, *The Buddha*, 146–154, and his introductory textbook, *Buddhisms*, 83–84, see John S. Strong, "The Triple Ladder at Saṁkāśya: Traditions about the Buddha's Descent from Trāyastriṃśa Heaven," in *From Turfan to Ajanta: Festschrift for Dieter Schlingloff on the Occasion of His Eightieth Birthday*, ed. Eli Franco and Monika Zin (Bhairahawa, Nepal: Lumbini International Research Institute, 2010), vol. 2, 967–978 ; and John S. Strong, "The Commingling of Gods and Humans, the Unveiling of the World, and the Descent from Trayastriṃśa

Heaven," in *Reimagining Aśoka: Memory and History*, ed. Patrick Olivelle et al., 348–361 (New York: Oxford University Press, 2012).

51. Here I am translating the Chaṭṭha Saṅgāyana edition of the text (Dhammagiri, Igatpuri, India: Vipassana Research Institute, 1995). I have also benefitted from Burlingame's translation in *Buddhist Legends*, 53, of the Pali Text Society edition of this passage, which appears to exhibit a couple of differences from the Chaṭṭha Saṅgāyana edition.
52. The theme of the cosmic vision, described as an "unveiling of the world" (*lokavivaraṇa*), also appears in ancient stories about King Aśoka. See Strong, "Commingling of Gods and Humans," 351–354.
53. Strong, "Triple Ladder at Saṁkāśya," 977 and 974.
54. See, for instance, Strong, "Triple Ladder at Saṁkāśya," 970; Strong, "Commingling of Gods and Humans," 349–351; and Strong, *Buddhisms*, 58–86. From 1985 to 1987, John Huntington published a series of articles on this topic in the Asian art magazine, *Orientations*, beginning with "Sowing the Seeds of the Lotus: A Journey to the Great Pilgrimage Sites of Buddhism, part I." *Orientations* 16, no. 11 (1985): 46–61.
55. Kenneth Wells, *Thai Buddhism: Its Rites and Activities* (Bangkok: Police Printing Press, 1960), 104, quoted in Strong, "Triple Ladder at Saṁkāśya," 973, and Strong, *The Buddha*, 153.
56. Strong, "Triple Ladder at Saṁkāśya," 973–974.
57. See Gary Comstock, "The Truth of Religious Narratives," *International Journal for Philosophy of Religion* 34, no. 3 (1993): 131–150, especially 146–147. For more on how stories create story worlds, see Abbott, *Cambridge Introduction to Narrative*, chapter 12.
58. Recall the example of Chögyel, *Life of the Buddha*, which has inspired this chapter.

8

Sorrow and its Ending in the Buddha's Last Days

Maria Heim

"'*Ānanda, I am tired and I will lay down.*' These words stir the emotion of the whole world."[1]

Figure 8.1 This image depicts the Buddha lying on his right side on his deathbed at his "final nirvana." Anguished kings have gathered above him, the monks Mahākassapa and Ānanda are present at his feet, and two women are seated below, one distraught and the other, in a nun's robe, serenely composed. The Buddha was said to have stretched out to die between two *sal* trees; one of them is visible in this Gandhāran image; second to third century CE, Gandhāra; courtesy of Victoria and Albert Museum

Maria Heim, *Sorrow and its Ending in the Buddha's Last Days* In: *The Buddha*. Edited by: Vanessa R. Sasson and Kristin Scheible, Oxford University Press. © Oxford University Press 2024. DOI: 10.1093/oso/9780197649466.003.0009

The inevitable end of the Teacher is an occasion for both joy and sorrow. On the one hand, the Buddha's "final nirvana" (*parinirvāṇa/parinibbāna*) is the culmination of his awakening under the Bodhi Tree forty-five years earlier when he awakened to the Dharma, transcended the human condition in all of its pain and loss, and ended his long sojourn in *saṃsāra*. His forty-five year teaching career thereafter is configured as "nirvana with substratum," as he continued to teach and work in the service of the Dharma. The substratum ends at his death, the moment of final release from the depredations of having a body in a transient world of old age, suffering, and loss. In this respect, the final nirvana is the final triumph, to be celebrated as the Buddha in fact does with a joyful utterance when he first sees the end come into view.

On the other hand, for those around him the loss of the Buddha is felt keenly. As much as the final nirvana is the immense "victory over sadness and death personified by Māra," as André Bareau puts it, it is also an occasion of great sadness and the acute awareness of death for his closest companions.[2] Despite the Buddha's many teachings on impermanence which might have prepared them for his loss, many of his disciples give way to anguish, as vividly caught in the Gandhāran sculpture opening this chapter (fig. 8.1). The ancient sculptor has captured the grieving faces and twisting bodies of the Buddha's followers, even while one figure has achieved meditative composure. The textual and artistic imaginings of the Buddha's death permit—and perhaps even invite—expressions of pathos and sadness at key junctures of the narrative.

In what follows I track the emotions of sadness and grief among the Buddha's followers, as well as the therapies the Buddha offers to ameliorate them. I will also note the way joy enters the story. People respond with different degrees and types of attachment and its concomitant loss; perspectives shift. The Buddha, for his part, addresses the sadness of his followers variously and strategically as he offers comforting balm in some cases, and harsh but effective medicine in others. The story of the final nirvana holds together multiple truths at once, where love means loss, and where grief and joy commingle.

Texts and Approach

The story of the last days of the Buddha is told in many sutras and commentarial traditions. Masahiro Shimoda suggests that the central narrative, the *Mahāparinirvāna Sūtra*, is really a "genre of more than 40 extant texts that purport to report on events and teachings associated with the Buddha's *parinirvāṇa* in the village of Kusinagarī."[3] The two earliest versions of the narrative still extant are the Pali *Mahāparinibbāna Sutta* and the Chinese (Dharmaguptaka) *Mahāparinirvāṇa Sūtra*, both in the "Long Discourses" of their respective collections, though elements of the story are found in their *vinayas* as well. We also have many other versions, ranging from commentarial expansions in the Pali tradition (chiefly, Buddhaghosa's commentary in his *Sumaṅgalavilāsinī*), to bits of the story found in Central Asian Sanskrit fragments and later tellings in Tibetan, Chinese, and other languages and media (the Buddha's deathbed scene was a favorite of sculptors and artists across Asia).[4] The versions tend to share a setting and an overall narrative arc, but often elaborate with additional supplements and extensions that deepen and enrich the emotional journey of the text.

I focus here on "tellings" of this narrative and avoid assuming an "original" text whereby "later" developments and versions are to be understood as "retellings." There is no way to determine the historical priority of the Pali and the Chinese versions, for example, and I treat them as literary tellings with many shared elements, but also with their own particular takes on what happened. I do not make a sharp distinction, at least from a literary point of view, between these canonical tellings and the commentarial elaborations of them by Pali commentators; in fact, there are places where the Pali commentators and the Chinese tellings share details not present in the Pali canonical account. Commentaries likely stretched back to the earliest days of the canonical sources and developed alongside them; they too purport to describe what happened and share literary practices with the *suttas* on which they comment.

My method is to tell the story according to many of the shared elements of the various versions we have—aware that I am adding yet another telling to the pile—while also pausing at particular moments of emotional richness and poignancy as told by one or another of the versions in front of us (but with a focus largely on the Pali tradition). The style of reading that I engage here is built on the insights of several astute readers of Buddhist biography.

I first acknowledge the work of John Strong who taught us how to read multiple versions of Buddha biographies, sometimes separately for their distinctive understandings, sometimes together in comparing the versions and marveling at the glimpses of a "whole"—the ever-expanding narrative across time and space, language and culture, of the Buddha's life. For my purposes, his insight that Buddha biographies provide both "lateral expansions" (where supplements are added to key moments of the text) and "longitudinal extensions" (where the tale gets longer over time at both ends, adding past lives and projecting future development of the relic cult after the Buddha's death), has emboldened me to linger over some of the lateral expansions that unfold below. Strong observes that lateral expansions indicate the collective nature of the Buddha's story and the many "ongoing karmic nexuses" of which he is a part;[5] in them, we come to know the *dramatis personae* who are inextricably part of his story. Also helpful to my thinking here is the work of Frank Reynolds, who, as the other contributors have noted, sees that Buddha biography is an ongoing "process," not a single, fixed text or story.

I also build on Charles Hallisey's insight about how Buddhist and Indian reading practices developed meaning through "the rich imagination of context." This idea describes literary practices very dear to the Buddhist sources, where narrating a "previously-unseen context" is regularly engaged in by both canon and commentary.[6] The Buddha is constantly urging a deeper imagining of a context that is only partially glimpsed at first by his interlocutors (we will see him do this below in the story of Kusinārā's past greatness, as just one example). Canonical tellings provide various expansions of contexts, with some embroidering details that are omitted by others. The practice continues in the hands of the commentators, Buddhaghosa and Dhammapāla. Their interpretative program fills in the previously unseen particularities of time, place, audience, and background of the events of *suttas* precisely to see how the Buddha's words spoken to their original narrative contexts, contexts that provide further meaning and subtlety when we come to know them more fully.[7] As he expands the story, Buddhaghosa takes himself to be giving details implicit in the canonical texts and carried forward in a huge body of lore that had grown up around them. To become a reader of this literature is to learn to anticipate previously unseen contexts that deepen the ways we can see the Buddha's words at work.

There are doctrinal and epistemological undercurrents at work with this style of literary elaboration. Just as Buddhist doctrine argues that events are caused and conditioned by myriad factors which themselves give rise to countless effects, nodes of a story are multiply conditioned by a nexus of causes. When we pause at any particular event or moment, we should expect to see a complex causal network of interconnected people, stories, details, and factors that have produced it.

Finally, attending to the rich imagining of context where narratives dive deep serves our focus on the experience of the emotions in the story with particular force. While emotions can be discussed and conveyed in general terms, they spring to life and come to be felt more movingly, I believe, in the *particular*, sometimes even the *singular*, ways they emerge in a specific scene, body, character, memory, gesture, or moment. Sorrow is known to us most vividly in the tears of an old woman falling on the Buddha's feet and the grief felt by Ānanda when it hits him that he will no longer be able to help wash the Buddha's face. Each of the followers gathered at the Buddha's deathbed in our Gandhāran image is depicted as singular and distinctive in his or her response. If I am right about the acute singularity of emotional experience, we must look closely at how grief and loss feel in the individual characters participating in the saddest moments of the Buddha's entire story, the last days of his long journey.

The Story

In what follows, I tell the story of the Buddha's death with an emphasis on the features that speak particularly to the emotional arc of the tale unfolding in the months leading up to and including the Buddha's final nirvana and its immediate aftermath. The story is long: it is told in the longest *sutta* in the book of the longest discourses in the Pali Canon, and the second longest *sūtra* in Chinese *Longest Discourses* (*Dīrgha Āgama*). One must be selective yet manage to convey something of the "whole" in describing the events associated with the Buddha's last days as he travels to various places before settling finally into Kusinārā, the "narrow and mean little town" where he lies down between a pair of Sal trees, head pointed to the north, and passes away. The narrative's pacing is sometimes deliberately slow to draw out time because it elaborates expansions and shifts of perspective; alternatively, the pacing sometimes speeds up to bring us inexorably to the death of the Buddha. Along the way, we will linger at several key moments, what I will call "close looks," that take us into the emotions of key figures in the narrative. These moments convey and evoke sorrow, terror, and sometimes joy. They do not necessarily pick up the "most important" events in the story (though who is to decide what is "most important," and according to what criteria?). Rather they are some of the "rich imaginings of context" that ancient authors cared about and that stopped me in my tracks when I encountered them.[8]

The story opens with the threat of war, with a bellicose king, Ajātasattu, preparing to invade and conquer the Vajjians, a neighboring kingdom. We will hear more about this king at the end of our tale. Upon hearing about Ajātasattu's campaign, the Buddha predicts that the Vajjians will be safe as long as they practice principles of harmonious, honest, and honorable statecraft. These same principles are then recommended to the monastic community as the key to continuing their institution: in his advanced age, the Buddha is looking to the future of his community and how it will thrive after his death. The narrative then relates the Buddha's excursions across north India with his devoted disciple Ānanda at his side, giving teachings that convey the key doctrines comprehensively in many settings.

The monsoon rains occur and after the rains the first signs of trouble appear when the Buddha is assailed by sharp abdominal pains. Yet he holds the distress in check with composure and equanimity. But Ānanda has noticed and becomes so distressed that he loses his bearings, reporting that, "my body seemed to be drugged and I did not know where to turn and things were not clear to me."[9] The Buddha gently counsels him that he, the Buddha, has achieved what he set out to do, and that he is now eighty years old, worn out, and reaching the end of his life's path, much like an old cart held together by straps. He has taught his followers everything, holding back nothing in a "closed fist." He instructs the monks to "live with yourselves as your island of refuge" and "with the Truth as your island of refuge."[10]

Shortly thereafter the Buddha drops several blatant hints to Ānanda to the effect that those with the Tathāgata's powers can choose to live out the rest of a *kalpa*, an eon, which is a vast amount of time.[11] But for the Tathāgata to do this, he must be entreated to do so. Sadly, Ānanda misses the hint and fails to beseech him to live longer, a blunder that reverberates throughout the ages. Ānanda will later feel sharp pangs of regret and will be eventually reprimanded by the Sangha for this.

The Buddha is then menaced by Māra, the Wicked One, who urges him to attain final nirvana now. The Buddha does not capitulate to Māra, of course, but he does announce that he will soon attain his final passing, in fact within three months' time. At this decision, there is a great and terrifying earthquake. Ānanda rushes to his side and learns of the significance of the earthquake and the terrible (as he sees it) resolution to pass away in three months. Now he begs the Buddha to live an eon, but it is too late, and the Buddha blames him for not having pleaded with him at the right time. The Buddha assembles a congregation of monks to convey his resolution.

A Close Look: A Terrible Earthquake, a Joyful Utterance, and a Therapy of Grief

Let us look more closely at these events. When the Buddha resolves to achieve final nirvana in three months there is an earthquake, one of the eight great earthquakes that mark the pivotal events of the Buddha's life, as we saw in Reiko Ohnuma's chapter. It is a terrifying earthquake, hair-raising, and full of thunder, with "the earth herself lamenting."[12] Ānanda is frightened and wonders what caused it. When he asks the Buddha the cause of the earthquake, the Buddha emits a "joyful utterance," an *udāna*:

> Comparing future-becoming with that which is incomparable, the Sage let go of the formative forces of future birth.
> Inwardly joyful and composed, he rent apart his own future-becoming as though it were a suit of armor.[13]

"Joyful utterances" are spontaneous exclamations of great happiness, and Pali commentators tell us that they can be uttered only "by the power of joy," never terror; he was not afraid of Māra.[14] The same event, the Buddha's resolution to finally abandon this life and future "becomings" (that is, births) brings at once sorrow, terror, and joy. What is terrifying and distressing for us in the world is a moment of "joy and happiness" for the Buddha.

Yet Ānanda is devastated, first at the news that the Buddha will soon be gone, and secondly at his own failure to take the hint and urge the Buddha to stay when he could have done so. The Buddha does not spare his feelings on this matter, telling him of the many occasions in fact when the hint was dropped and not picked up. Now it is too late, Ānanda has blundered, and the world shall soon lose the Buddha's living presence.

Buddhaghosa and Dhammapāla worry that we may consider this a harsh and painful rebuke to poor Ānanda. And it was not really even his fault, for he had been possessed by Māra. Māra, it seems, possesses people who are not fully free of the distortions of perception (and Ānanda is not yet an *arhat*). Māra does this by causing a frightening thing to occur and then when the person's mouth falls open, he inserts his hand and "kneads the heart," causing confusion.[15] This is what happened to Ānanda.

And further, the Buddha's decision to leave in three months was overdetermined: it was time to go, since there was no one else left to guide. And it was appropriate for him to go at this stage of life, Dhammapāla says, for *buddhas* attain final nirvana in the "fifth phase of their lifespan at a time when they are still dear and charming to the many folk," before "they have broken teeth and so on."[16] Moreover, his many contemporaries were dying off, and he was watching his closest disciples depart before him. (Indeed, his two chief disciples, Sāriputta and Moggallāna, had just died in the weeks before this, as Buddhaghosa recounts in detail; family members Gotamī, Yasodharā, and Rahula have all predeceased him, as well). Should the elders all die off, the Buddha would be left with only a retinue of child novices, a situation that could invite scorn.[17]

So if it was time to go, why then did the Buddha drop these hints, which he knew Ānanda would fail to catch, and then scold Ānanda for failing to do so? Because, both commentators argue, this would ameliorate his grief. Ānanda's annoyance with himself and his sense of regret would lessen his attachment and so interrupt his otherwise unbearable sorrow. This therapy of grief may strike us as unlikely. Masefield finds this "a rather odd psychology from a tradition otherwise noted for the subtleties of its psychological insights."[18] We might suppose that adding self-blame to the loss would surely only compound it. Regardless, the discussion shows that the commentators are worried about this moment and what it means for Ānanda.

The Story Continues

We resume the *via dolorosa*, as Strong likens the last journey—"a way of suffering that puts an end to suffering."[19] Ānanda and the Buddha continue their peregrinations to many towns and cities to teach for one last occasion. As the three months draw to a close, the smith Cunda secures the Buddha's presence at a meal.

The last meal has been the source of much debate due to ambiguity in what is meant by the fare served—"pig's delight"—which some sources take to be pork and others understand as a kind of mushroom or vegetarian food relished by pigs.[20] Regardless, after the meal the Buddha is ravaged with "severe sickness and bloody diarrhea and sharp pains as if he were about to die." The food is consequently buried so that no one else may eat it.[21] Still, the Buddha insists that Cunda is not to feel remorse, but that in fact his almsgiving is equal in merit to that of Sujātā, the young woman who fed him a meal on the eve of his awakening under the Bodhi Tree.

The Buddha demonstrates his composure and turns golden with the same radiance that he emitted on his awakening under the Bodhi Tree forty-five years earlier. He wishes to go to Kusinārā near a people called the Mallas, and to take a position lying between two Sal trees. Once there, he announces that he is tired and wants to lie down, and he does so in a lion posture, on his right side, one foot on the other. The Sal trees burst into blossom out of season. Divine music and song rain down in homage, and we become aware of vast hosts of deities who have gathered. At one point, the Buddha rather bluntly implores one of the stouter of the monks, Upavāṇa, who was fanning the Buddha, to please move aside so that the many deities in the outer rims of the heavenly crowd will be able to see him.

A Close Look: Happy Blood, the Frail Buddha, a Portly Monk, and a Divine Perspective

The Buddha is frail and in pain, ravaged by what must have been an enduring digestive complaint that we saw at the start of the tale exacerbated now by the unfortunate pigs' delight. But he turns golden and far outshines the yellow robe he wears. Buddhaghosa adds that when he bathes in a river even the fish and tortoises and the groves lining the river turn golden.[22] He attributes the Buddha's remarkable shine to the tremendous happiness (*pasāda*) achieved by nirvana. And when "his mind became happy, his blood became happy."[23] "Happy blood" makes his six faculties shine. Exactly what it is to have happy blood is unclear, but I can say that emotions in these texts are often known in the body, and the commentarial eye attends closely to the bodily experience of the Buddha in these last days, hours, and minutes.

When the Buddha says, "Ānanda, I am tired and I will lay down," a rush of emotion stirs the whole world. The emotion in question—*saṃvega*—is the acute shock of realizing the truth of impermanence; while alarming, it is nevertheless salutary in leading to a sense of religious urgency.[24] He is very ill at this point, Buddhaghosa recalls, making his way only with great difficulty and stopping twenty-five times to rest on this last segment of the journey from Pāvā to Kusinārā.[25]

What of the stout monk Upavāṇa who is nudged aside to let the deities politely gathered in the heavens see from the back? Was not the Buddha, who was never before known to utter a harsh word, a bit cursory with the good fellow? Ānanda is worried about this. Buddhaghosa points out that in fact Upavāṇa was the "size of a baby elephant," and his frame was blocking the view. The issue here is that the distant deities straining to see should get their chance. Deities can see through ordinary people, of course, but not through *arhats*, and Upavāna was an *arhat*.[26]

And we do need the gods to be able to see, because *we* need to see *them*. The close-up human frame of the story sometimes lets us forget that the gods, indeed the entire cosmos, are also bearing witness to these events. And their divine perspective is important. Some of the deities are in tremendous grief: "with disheveled hair they spread their arms wide and call out; they fall to the ground, broken, and roll back and forth: 'All too soon will the Blessed One attain final nibbana! All too soon with the Happy One attain final nibbana!'."[27] For all their comforts and pleasures, and the longevity of their lives, gods feel the impermanence and loss of the Buddha keenly.

Buddhaghosa takes us further into the perspective of the gods at the outer rim of these events straining to see. In the rear are deities who have extremely long life spans (at least from our perspective). These deities had heard one morning on one of their incredibly long days that a Buddha was soon to appear in the world. So they began to make a garland to honor his birth. But they don't manage to finish it in time for this birth, so they resolve to give it when he renounces the world. But he renounces the world as a young man without their finishing it. So they resolve to give their garland at each of the crucial moments of his life—his nirvana, his turning the wheel of the Dhamma, the twin miracle, his declaration renouncing his life, and now, the final nirvana—never managing to finish their garland in time for any of these monumental occasions. (Note how we see the Buddha's biography in full unfolding in the space of one of these deities' days.) So they show up at the final nirvana to offer their unfinished garland, only to find that they cannot secure a spot closer than the outermost rim of the world system. Yet from the outer rim they join up with linked arms in a circular chain and begin to sing of the "three jewels, the thirty-two marks of the great man, the six-colored rays, the ten perfections, the five hundred and fifty Jātakas, and the fourteen knowledges of the Buddha." At the end of each song, they utter, "O our helper, O our helper."[28]

These beautiful beings, for whom the events of the Buddha's life have passed in less than a day, fill the world with their songs. They open up space and time for us—we forget that our world is much bigger than it first appears and the events at Kusinārā are the center of a drama of grief rippling out into the furthest reaches of the cosmos. And we come to appreciate the impermanence of everything, when even in the long lives of the heavenly beings time passes much too quickly and a Buddha's time with us can only ever be fleeting.

The Story Continues

Back on earth beneath the Sal trees Ānanda presses the Buddha on details about what they should do with his remains, and is told that the matter will be looked to by householders, not monks. When pressed further, he says that his remains are to be treated as would those of a wheel-turning emperor and that a *stūpa* (a sacred relic mound) is to be erected at the crossroads. Then, in an extended and rather wrenching exchange between Ānanda and the Buddha, we see Ānanda move off from the scene in tears, weeping for the loss of the Buddha, who then calls him back to his side. The Buddha first reiterates the profound teachings of impermanence that should be recalled at times of death. And then he comforts and praises Ānanda. Ānanda then laments that the Buddha is dying in Kusinārā, a "miserable little town of wattle-and-daub."[29] The Buddha resists this notion, giving a story of this same town many eons ago when it was the opulent kingdom of a wheel-turning emperor named Mahāsudassana.[30] There is a much bigger context here, a context that Ānanda does not yet see.

A Close Look: Ānanda's Tears and an Ancient Kingdom

Ānanda's tears have been with us at various times of the journey. Ānanda, unlike so many of the close disciples of the Buddha, has not yet attained nirvana, held back by his deep affection for the Buddha. The narrative elements of these last days and months portray the Buddha's sometimes tender, sometimes blunt, management of Ānanda's attachment to him and its accompanying sadness. In this scene, the narrative gazes of both canon and commentary attend fully to the textures of Ānanda's grief.

Ānanda has moved off from the Buddha's side and stands leaning against a doorpost weeping. He laments that he still has work to do to attain nirvana, but his teacher "who shows me sympathy, is about to attain final nirvana."[31] Buddhaghosa sees more here. Ānanda will profoundly miss his daily companionship with the Buddha: "From tomorrow on, whom shall I give water to wash his face? Whose feet shall I wash? Whose lodging shall I take care of? Whose bowl and robe shall I carry around?"[32] Grief is felt most acutely, perhaps, in the abrupt ending of one's daily acts of care for another, and the gaping holes they leave in one's routine.

Indeed, Ānanda is prescient about how he will feel once the Buddha is gone. This episode foreshadows a later moment also caught by Buddhaghosa when, after the final nirvana, Ānanda will return along to Jeta's Grove at Savatthi (a central headquarters of the Buddha's movement and where the Buddha and Ānanda usually stayed when not wandering). There the townspeople will see him coming without the Buddha and will know something terrible has happened; they will ask him, "You have always come with the Blessed One. Where have you left the Blessed One today?" The great lamenting that ensues will be "just like it was on the day of the Buddha's final nirvana." Ānanda will have to teach them a teaching on impermanence and then make his way alone into the "fragrant hut," the Buddha's living quarters, and do the routine duties of opening the place up, dusting the room, sweeping thoroughly while moving and replacing the furniture, fetching water, and so on, much as he did daily when the Buddha was living. While doing so, he will be saying, "Come, Blessed One, now is the time for your bath, now is the time for teaching the Dhamma, now is the time for admonishing the monks, now is the time for lying down in the lion posture, now is the time for washing your face, and so on," weeping all the while. Buddhaghosa understands that these experiences of visceral loss are due to Ānanda's love (*pema*) for the Buddha, and the fact that Ānanda was not yet an *arhat*. Also, the tears come from "the softness generated in his mind from the help they had given one another for hundreds and thousands of lifetimes."[33]

We return to the present, where Ānanda stands at the doorpost weeping. The Buddha inquires where Ānanda has gone, and asks the monks to bring him forward. He then urges Ānanda to stop lamenting by first reiterating the bleak fact of impermanence: "Have I not warned about this before: we must lose everything pleasant and dear? So how else could it be?"[34] But then he shifts tone and message to remind Ānanda that Ānanda has for a long time attended him with loving care:

> Ānanda, you have attended the Tathagata for a long time with loving physical activities, and with loving verbal activities, and with loving mental activities, in ways that are beneficial, happy, consistent, and measureless.[35]

The Buddha knows that Ānanda is feeling the future loss of his daily acts of care, the concrete particulars that comprise love. Buddhaghosa expands on what is meant by loving physical, verbal, and mental activities in detail by considering the way that Ānanda had always washed the Buddha's face. Physically, he always brought water with great happiness, delight, and consistency; verbally, he would gently and kindly tell the Buddha that water had been brought; and mentally, after the morning face washings, Ānanda would sit quietly, and lovingly pray, "May the Teacher be healthy, peaceful, and happy."[36] Although it might seem that the daily gestures of helping the Buddha wash his face are rather small and routine, they are "measureless." That is to say, they are "without measure," and the world system is "too narrow" to contain their love.[37] Recalling to mind this intimate and concrete kind of love, the Buddha shows Ānanda that love can also be a source of comfort. We have grief because we love, but cherishing that love can be a balm to grief.

The Buddha then turns to the monks and praises Ānanda in lavish terms, as the very kind of caring attendant that all buddhas have. He notes that Ānanda is gifted with the quality that people of all kinds—monks, nun, laymen, and laywomen—love to see him and to hear his teachings.[38]

As we emerge from Ānanda's personal grief, we find him turning to the matter of the miserable little town of Kusinārā. Why die here? The Buddha counters that he has in fact labored hard to get here and has done so for several reasons: it is here that he will encounter his last disciple, Subhadda, and it is here that after his death the wise Doṇa can manage the royal competition for his relics without bloodshed.

But the chief reason for coming to Kusinārā is that it is a homecoming of sorts. The Buddha tells a story of Kusinārā having previously been the magnificent city of Emperor Mahāsudassana. Here the Buddha is giving more context—context about place, time, and the Buddha's own grand cosmic narrative. What looks to be a small and undistinguished place now was in the distant past the capital of a magnificent kingdom that ruled India for huge stretches of time, not once but six times over. This great king ruled righteously and justly and enjoyed the prosperity and symbolic jewels that righteous rule confers on wheel-turning emperors. What is more, it was none other than the Buddha-to-be himself who was the emperor in these six previous eras, ruling in glory and prosperity. In this way, the Buddha invites us to imagine the longer and larger spatial and temporal context of this place; what we see at first is never the whole story. When we are invited into the omniscient ken of the Buddha, we see a much greater whole, and Kusinārā becomes the final stop at a place that he had inhabited many times before when it—and he—reached the apex of what worldly life can offer.

This narrative of a cosmic timescape that the Buddha inhabited lifetimes ago as the world's greatest sovereign in those eras works to associate the Buddha both with royalty and the final renunciation of royalty. What is more, he has come back to the ruins of this distant great empire to complete his journey, although in the present time the limited human historical memory and imagination can see nothing, at first, but a "miserable little town."

The Story Continues

On his deathbed, the Buddha asks Ānanda to invite the local people, the Mallas of Kusinārā, to attend him on his final night, and they show up, weeping and tearing their hair. An aged wanderer, Subhadda, approaches to ask the Buddha to dispel his final doubts as to the doctrine, and becomes the Buddha's last personal convert and is ordained as a monk then and there. The Buddha gives some last pragmatic instructions. He tells them that after his death, the Dhamma and the Vinaya should be regarded as the teacher; the monks should no longer address one another as 'friend,' but rather in terms marking seniority; and a certain monk Channa is to receive a penalty. Most significantly, he instructs that after his passing, the Sangha may abolish "the minor rules." Unfortunately, Ānanda makes another omission for which he will also be later rebuked: he fails to ask the Buddha which rules are to be considered "minor." The Sangha later decides on this basis to abolish none of the rules.

The Buddha then invites the monks present to come forward with any doubts or uncertainties and to take advantage, this one last time, of the presence of the Teacher to clear up any unresolved matters. The monks remain silent, a silence that Ānanda takes to indicate their clarity and conviction regarding the Buddha's teaching. In the Chinese telling, the Buddha displays his golden skin by bearing his forearm to those present, noting the rareness of the sight of an actual Buddha and reminding them of the impermanence of all things.[39] The Buddha then utters his last words:

> Now monks, I declare to you: all conditioned things are of a nature to decay—strive on untiringly.[40]

And then, as he lies on his right side, the Buddha enters the eight spheres of meditative absorption from the first to the eighth, and then back through each down to the first, and then through the fourth absorption again until finally passing away.[41] A second great earthquake marks the moment. The Sal trees blossom out of season (though after the final nirvana, according to certain Chinese and Tibetan retellings, the Sal trees will then drop all fruits and leaves, turn "white as the wings of a white crane," and dry up and crumble away completely).[42]

Gods and monks and various interested parties ranging from Brahmā to Venerable Anuruddha utter verses of praise; the Chinese version also includes the verses of many others, such as the Buddha's mother Māyā observing from heaven, the spirits of the Sal trees between which he lies, and representatives of all the main heavens and the underworld.[43] It has been a cosmic event. Those who have not yet overcome their passions, however, weep and tear their hair, cast themselves upon the ground, writhing and fainting.

The Mallas arrive with garlands, music, and perfumes to honor the Buddha's body, and the gods offer their heavenly lotuses, sandalwood incense, and song until Kusinārā is knee-deep in flowers. The body is bathed and prepared as it would be for an emperor. But when it comes time to light the pyre seven days later, the fire cannot be made to touch the body. Why is this? The community realizes that there is one crucial person missing, the elder Mahākassapa. This great disciple has only just learned of the Buddha's final nirvana and is on his way to Kusinārā. While not his successor (the Buddha can have no successor), Mahākassapa will assume a leadership role after the Buddha's demise by convening a council to gather and consolidate the Buddha's teachings.

A Close Look: Mahākassapa and an Old Woman's Tears

Mahākassapa has been having a rough time of it. He was not present at the Buddha's death and in fact did not know of it, a detail that gives Buddhaghosa some trouble to explain, given that Mahākassapa is said to be an *arhat* and so should be capable of knowing such things as they occur. But the fact of the matter is that he had not attended to the matter, preoccupied as he was with his journey. He learns from a Jain ascetic that the Buddha has died. Shortly after this, he encounters a monk celebrating the Buddha's passing because now they need not be disciplined by the stern hand of the Teacher, and monastic life will ease up. Hearing this, "the elder felt it like a blow to the heart, like lightning from a dry sky striking his head." He feels "urgency" (*saṃvega*) for the Dhamma.[44] Mahākassapa realizes that this is a moment of great peril for the new religion, and what happens next will be of profound importance for the future survival of the dispensation. He must act to secure the teachings for the future. He hastens to Kusinārā where he finds everyone awaiting his arrival.

The Chinese telling lingers on a detail of Mahākassapa's worship of the Buddha's feet. Prior to Mahākassapa's arrival, Ānanda, ever solicitous to women, has ushered forward some Malla women who wish to pay their respects to the body, and one old woman's tears have stained the feet of the body. The body has then been wrapped and prepared for cremation. When Mahākassapa arrives he wishes to see the body, but Ānanda tells him it will be too difficult to make this happen, given that it is wrapped and prepared for cremation. Mahākassapa insists. Ānanda refuses. Just when the argument gets a bit heated, the Buddha's feet magically pop out for Mahākassapa to honor. But Mahākassapa is disturbed by the stains on the feet, and upon learning of the old woman's tears, is "downhearted and disappointed."[45] But he successfully lights the pyre.

The details here add the realism of character and personality to the story where even this steady *arhat* can be shaken. The realism is also evident in the sometimes fraught relationship between Ānanda and Mahākassapa.[46] We cannot go into details of the long relationship of these two very different personalities—Ānanda the tender but sometimes naïve attendant on the Buddha, and Mahākassapa, the stern meditation master, institution builder, and keeper of order—but here their differences nearly come to a head, though here too the Buddha manages to intervene in the crisis even after death in the miracle of the uncovering of the feet. The Buddha's story needs both of these closest disciples, and they serve the Buddha and Buddhism in very different ways. Here we see Ānanda untroubled by the stains of an old woman's tears adding to the palimpsest that is the Buddha's body. But Mahākassapa, with his sense of dignity and decorum, disapproves.

Another Close Look: Breaking the News to King Ajātasattu

The various tellings linger on how the news is delivered to and received by key figures in the Buddha's life. We may drop into the management of the grief of the belligerent king, Ajātasattu, whose rumblings of war against the Vajjians began our story. For all his martial prowess, Ajātasattu is fragile emotionally, even while mercurial and often cruel in his administration. His ministers are understandably cautious in broaching the news of the Buddha's death. He had, it seems, recently sought the Buddha's counsel to relieve his bad conscience concerning his patricide (he had had his father, the king, put to death in order to assume the throne), and received comfort and teachings from the Buddha. Now his ministers must deliver the news of the death.

The bad news could break him. So his ministers prepare a vat of four sweet drinks and ask the king to lie down in it fully submerged up to his nostrils. One brave minister makes his hair disheveled and removes his ornaments, and, turning in the direction of where the Buddha passed, breaks it to the king that the final nirvana has occurred. The king becomes unconscious, releasing his fever into the sweet bath. They set him upright and submerge him in another vat of four sweet drinks. When he comes to, he asks them what they are saying. Hearing again that the Buddha has died, he faints again and they submerge him in a third vat of sweet drinks. He regains consciousness, is washed, adorned, and set upright, but he weeps, clutching his breast, and flees the city. He goes straight to Jīvaka's mango grove, a place of profound significance for him, since it was here that he had approached the Buddha on the earlier occasion, seeking solace and wisdom, and it was here that the Buddha converted him from his wickedness and set him on the right course.[47] And it is here that we find him addressing the now absent Buddha:

> Did not the Blessed One, the omniscient one, sit here to teach me the Dhamma?
> You have got rid of the arrow of sorrow. You have taken out my arrow of sorrow.
> I took refuge in you. But now you, the Blessed One, give me no answer.[48]

The king finds his queries met only with silence. From there he resolves to get the relics of the Buddha, by force if necessary.

The Story Wraps Up

The story ends, as it began, with the specter of war. The narrative wraps up with an account of eight kings vying with one another for the relics, and the wise brahman, Doṇa, arbitrating between them to avoid bloodshed by sharing an equal distribution of the relics. War is averted with the building of ten great *stūpas*, eight containing the bodily relics, a ninth for the urn, and a tenth for the embers (the Chinese telling adds an eleventh containing the Buddha's hair). In Chapter 9, Stephen Berkwitz takes up the story of the relics, continuing the "longitudinal extension" of our story.

Conclusions

In my telling I have been drawn to moments of emotional poignancy in this narrative's various versions that give space for both joy and sorrow, and that do not allow the truth of impermanence to negate the truth of love. The story is the ultimate lesson in impermanence—even the Buddha must die—but despite this inevitability, and the many junctures in the story where the brutal truth of impermanence is reinforced, love is never entirely forsaken. We see this most vividly in the figure of Ānanda, but also in the final scenes with Mahākassapa that insist that a close disciple's personal needs to see and honor the Buddha's feet matter. And we see the Buddha working to manage his disciples' emotional needs with various therapies of grief.

The pacing of the narrative varies, and there are times that slow down with great sorrow. But the story never devolves into a dirge, or succumbs to the pathos. This is necessary, of course, because the Buddha taught detachment and freedom from the afflictions of grief and desire: if the Buddha's disciples, at least in the main, had not overcome grief, then his teachings would have been in vain. Still, it would be a hard and cold final journey indeed if impermanence were the only available lesson, and if his circle of followers greeted these events only with sublime and peaceful equanimity. So Ānanda—a disciple whose gift is that he is loved by many people and so we feel close to him—is permitted to break down and give voice to the love and the loss at stake.[49]

Smaller moments of narrative relief are made possible in the lateral expansions as we learn the richer context of the last days. We smile at the tubby *arhat* blocking the way, delight in the charming deities singing and swaying in locked arms around the outer rim of the cosmos, and savor the ludicrous as King Ajātasattu is plunged into his sweet baths. We are brought back to the urgency and folly of earthly matters as the kings prepare war over the relics.

Shifts of perspective allow us to glimpse the intimacy of the human scale of love and loss—Ānanda faces a tomorrow when he will not be able to help the Buddha wash his face—alongside much grander cosmic timescapes and perspectives. The events of the Buddha's life and death have passed through but a single day of the long-lived deities, a day even they found too short to make a proper garland for him.

Notes

1. As noted by both Pali commentators: Buddhaghosa (Yang-Gyu An, trans., *The Buddha's Last Days: Buddhaghosa's Commentary on the Mahāparinibbāna Sutta.* [Oxford: The Pali Text Society, 2005]: 134–135) and Dhammapāla (Peter Masefield, trans., *The Udāna Commentary by Dhammapāla*, vol. II. [Oxford: The Pali Text Society, 2003]: 1030).
2. André Bareau, "The Superhuman Personality of the Buddha and its Symbolism in the *Mahāparinrvāṇasūtra* of the Dharmaguptaka" In *Myths and Symbols: Studies in Honor of Mircea Eliade*, ed. Joseph Kitagawa and Charles Long (Chicago: The University of Chicago Press, 1969), 9.
3. Masahiro Shimoda, "Mahāparinirvāṇasūtra," in *Brill's Encyclopedia of Buddhism*, vol. I, ed. Jonathan A. Silk, Oskar von Hinüber, and Vincent Eltschinger (Leiden: Brill, 2015), 158.
4. For translations of the Pali Mahānibbānasutta, see Maurice Walshe, trans., *The Long Discourses of the Buddha: A Translation of the Dīgha Nikāya* (Boston: Wisdom, 1996), 231–277; Sister Vajira and Francis Story, trans. *Last Days of the Buddha: The Mahāparinibbāna Sutta* (Kandy: Buddhist Publication Society, 1998); and Rupert Gethin, trans., *Sayings of the Buddha* (Oxford: Oxford University Press, 2008), 37–97. For the Chinese version, see Shohei Ichimura, trans., *The Canonical Book of the Buddha's Lengthy Discourses*, vol. I. (Berkeley, CA: Bukkyo Dendo Kyokai America, 2015), 63–171. For Buddhaghosa's commentary, see An, *The Buddha's Last Days*, and for Dhammapāla's, see Masefield, *The Udāna Commentary by Dhammapāla*, vol. II, 851–862, 1024–1035. Ernst Waldschmidt, *Das Mahāparinirvāṇasūtra* (Berlin: Academie Verlag, 1950–1951) is a meticulous study of the Central Asian

Sanskrit fragments compared with Pali, Chinese, and Tibetan versions. Peter Skilling provides a useful overview of the genre and a short canonical Tibetan version (*Questioning the Buddha: A Selection of Twenty-Five Sutras* [Somerville, MA: Wisdom, 2021]: 25). Shimoda ("Mahāparinirvāṇasūtra") distinguishes between these narrative accounts of the Buddha's last days and the *Mahāparinirvāṇa-mahāsūtra* that develops Mahāyāna *tathāgatagarbha* doctrine; this text resolves the problem or loss of the Buddha at the time of his death with its teaching of a docetic Buddha, who is in fact eternal (see Mark Blum, trans., *The Nirvana Sūtra*, vol. I. [Berkeley: Bukkho Dendo Kyokai America, 2013]).

5. John Strong, "A Family Quest: The Buddha, Yaśodharā, and Rāhula in the Mūlasarvāstivāda Vinaya," In *Sacred Biography in the Buddhist Traditions of South and Southeast Asia*, ed. Juliane Schober (Honolulu: University of Hawai'i Press, 1995), 114.
6. Charles Hallisey, "Learning from Luis Gómez as a Reader of Buddhist Sūtras," in *The Language of the Sūtras*, ed. Natalie Gummer (Berkeley: Mangalam Press, 2021), xi, xvii.
7. On this interpretative program see Maria Heim, "Careful Attention and the Voice of Another," in *In Dialogue with Classical Indian Traditions*, eds. Brian Black and Chakravarthi Ram-Prasad. (London: Routledge, 2019): 181–196, and *Voice of the Buddha: Buddhaghosa on the Immeasurable Words*. (New York: Oxford University Press, 2018), ch. 3.
8. The story will be told with the Pali versions of names and terms, as the preponderance of my sources come from the Pali tellings.
9. Gethin, *Sayings of the Buddha*, 57.
10. Gethin, *Sayings of the Buddha*, 58.
11. Walshe, *The Long Discourses of the Buddha*, 246; see 569–70n400. The Chinese telling takes it to be an eon (Ichimura, *The Canonical Book of the Buddha's Lengthy Discourses*, 89–90), but Pali commentators understand a *kalpa* here to refer to a life span of a hundred years.
12. Buddhaghosa adds this detail suggesting the earth's impulse to lament, though he qualifies this to say he means the Goddess Earth, because of course the earth itself does not have a mind whereby it could lament (An, *The Buddha's Last Days*, 102).
13. *Dīgha Nikāya* ii.107, my translation, but see Walshe, *The Long Discourses*, 247, and Gethin, *Sayings of the Buddha*, 61, as the Pali admits of different possibilities. Ichimura, *The Canonical Book of the Buddha's Lengthy Discourses*, 91, has an image of a chick coming out of its shell rather than the rent armor. The Pali tradition takes this *udāna* and puts it in a collection of other joyful utterances called the *Udāna*. Dhammapāla then provides commentary on this verse (Masefield, *The Udāna Commentary*, 851–862).
14. An, *The Buddha's Last Days*, 95–96; Masefield, *The Udāna Commentary*, 859–860.
15. An, *The Buddha's Last Days*, 90; Masefield, *The Udāna Commentary*, 855.
16. Masefield, *The Udāna Commentary*, 853.
17. Masefield, *The Udāna Commentary*, 853.
18. Masefield, *The Udāna Commentary*, 909.

19. John Strong, *The Buddha: A Short Biography* (Oxford: OneWorld, 2001), 126.
20. The Pali commentators take it to be pork, while the Chinese sūtra takes it to be a vegetarian mushroom dish. There is considerable scholarship on this question (summarized by Strong, *The Buddha*, 134–136).
21. This is how the Pali canonical source puts it, as translated by Walshe (*The Long Discourses*, 257). There is considerable debate about whether the pig's delight actually caused the illness, and indeed, even what sort of illness the Buddha had, as he may have been vomiting blood—some of the recent work on this includes Peter Masefield and Nicolas Revire, "On the Buddha's 'Kammic Fluff': The Last Meal Revisited," *Journal of the Oxford Centre for Buddhist Studies* 20 (2021): 51–82; and John Strong, "Explicating the Buddha's Final Illness in the Context of his Other Ailments: The Making and Unmaking of some Jātaka Tales." *Buddhist Studies Review* 29, no. 1 (2012): 17–33.
22. An, *The Buddha's Last Days*, 128.
23. *Citte pasanne lohitaṃ pasīdati* (An, *The Buddha's Last Days*, 127).
24. As Charles Hallisey put it in our discussions, *saṃvega* is "fear of the inevitable" and the countering of it is *pasāda*, the happiness and composure that despite *saṃvega*, everything will be ok through the Buddhist answer to suffering. Ānanda's *saṃvega* is directly contrasted to the *pasāda* of the Buddha's mind and blood we just saw.
25. An, *The Buddha's Last Days*, 134–135.
26. An, *The Buddha's Last Days*, 147–148
27. Gethin, *Sayings of the Buddha*, 80. This utterance again contrasts the Buddha's happiness with divine and human grief.
28. An, *The Buddha's Last Days*, 1, 42–143.
29. Walshe, *The Long Discourses of the Buddha*, 266.
30. This narrative is told briefly in *Mahāparinibbāna Sutta*, but is given in full in the *Mahāsudassana Sutta* immediately following it in the Pali *Dīgha Nikāya*. The Chinese version tells the whole story in the course of the *Mahāparinirvāṇa Sūtra*.
31. Gethin, *Sayings of the Buddha*, 82.
32. An, *The Buddha's Last Days*, 160.
33. I am grateful to Charles Hallisey for catching this allusion to the *Sumaṅgalavilāsinī* (1.7). This is my translation of the textual passages, but see also H. C. Norman, "Gandhakuṭī—The Buddha's Private Abode." *Journal of the Asiatic Society of Bengal* 2 (1908): 2–3, and John Strong, "'Gandhakuṭī': The Perfumed Chamber of the Buddha" *History of Religions* 16, no. 4 (1977): 398–399.
34. Gethin, *Sayings of the Buddha*, 82.
35. *Dīgha Nikāya* ii.145, my translation.
36. An, *The Buddha's Last Days*, 161.
37. An, *The Buddha's Last Days*, 161.
38. Gethin, *Sayings of the Buddha*, 83.
39. Ichimura, *The Canonical Book of the Buddha's Lengthy Discourses*, 150.
40. Walshe, *The Long Discourses*, 270; cf. Ichimura, *The Canonical Book*, 150.
41. These spheres of absorption are called the *jhānas* and formless states; they involve increasingly rarified experiences. In this passage, the text is suggesting that he is inhabiting all reaches of meditative awareness front and back.

42. This is according to a short independent text that circulated in the Tang dynasty, and then also a Tibetan *Mahāparinirvāṇa Sūtra* (Skilling, *Questioning the Buddha*, 458–460). The Sal trees of the final nirvana thus counter the Bodhi Tree of the first awakening which lives on into the future while they crumble.
43. Ichimura, *The Canonical Book*, 152–155.
44. An, *The Buddha's Last Days*, 200.
45. Ichimura, *The Canonical Book*, 163. The Pali commentary does not recall the old woman's tears, but it does share with the Chinese telling the detail of the miracle of the feet emerging from the cloths in which they are wrapped so that Mahākassapa may worship them with his head (An, *The Buddha's Last Days*, 204).
46. Hellmuth Hecker, "Mahākassapa: Father of the Sangha." *Great Disciples of the Buddha*, edited by Bhikkhu Bodhi (Kandy: Buddhist Publications Society, 1997): 127–133.
47. These details of breaking the news to Ajātasattu are found in Buddhaghosa (An, *The Buddha's Last Days*, 209–212; cf. a Tibetan trace of the story in Woodville Rockhill, *The Life of the Buddha and the Early History of His Order*. [London: Kegan Paul, Trench, Trübner & Co., 1976]: 142). The story of the patricide Ajātasattu's encounter with the Buddha at Jīvaka's mango grove is told in the Sāmaññaphala Sutta, a *sutta* that occurs early in the *Dīgha Nikāya* (see Heim, "Careful Attention and the Voice of Another," 2019 for Buddhaghosa's expansion of this story). In a beautiful literary reading of the *Dīgha Nikāya*, Sarah Shaw argues that the book as a whole is centered on the "transience of the Buddha's human existence," as the "underlying bass note" of the whole collection; *The Art of Listening: A Guide to the Early Teachings of Buddhism* (Boulder, CO: Shambhala, 2021, 53). She sees the *Dīgha Nikāya* as a larger literary whole of which the Mahāparinibbāna is just a part, and the *sutta* should be read within and as part of the collection.
48. An, *The Buddha's Last Days*, 211.
49. The Tibetan telling by Tenzin Chögyel splits the role—and emotional release—of the bereaved and grieving disciple between Ānanda and the Buddha's son, Rāhula. Rāhula is losing not just the Teacher, but also his father and so we can hardly begrudge him his grief even if we know that the Buddha taught him to overcome it (Kurtis Schaeffer, trans., *Tenzin Chögyal's The Life of the Buddha* [New York: Penguin, 2015], 82–87).

9

The Buddha's Story Continues

Afterlives of the Relics

Stephen C. Berkwitz

Figure 9.1 The brahmin Doṇa distributes the Buddha-relics among the seven kings who arrived for the Buddha's funeral. Tradition holds that once the relics were divided in this manner, they were taken back and enshrined in stūpas, thus initiating the practice of relic veneration in the ancient Buddhist world. Pakistan, Gandhāra region, second to third century; public domain.

Buddhist traditions hold that the life story of the Buddha does not come to an end with the funeral rituals and cremation of his body. Instead, the Buddha's biography has been repeatedly extended by narrative accounts of the surviving relics associated with his physical body, objects he used, and images fashioned after his appearance. John Strong has made this very argument by demonstrating

Stephen C. Berkwitz, *The Buddha's Story Continues* In: *The Buddha*. Edited by: Vanessa R. Sasson and Kristin Scheible, Oxford University Press. © Oxford University Press 2024. DOI: 10.1093/oso/9780197649466.003.0010 how relics serve both as expressions and extensions of the Buddha's biography, since they retell stories told about his life and add on to his biography by appending tales told about the travels and actions of relics after his passing away in *parinirvāṇa* (P: *parinibbāna*).[1] In other words, objects associated with the Buddha have survived his death, and they refer back to his life story while allowing for virtually endless opportunities to draw out his story to incorporate more places and events into what is recalled about the Buddha. This extension of the Buddha-biography after his passing reflects what Frank Reynolds has described as the concerns of various Buddhist communities to relate the Buddha to their own topography and traditions.[2] As such, the life story of the Buddha has become repeatedly and variously extended by his followers in relic narratives to expand his dispensation (P: *sāsana*) across more space and time.

What Are Buddha-Relics?

Relics of the Buddha are objects that are understood to be traces of his existence that have survived his death. These objects are frequently endowed with significance by written and oral narratives that explain how the relic originated and traveled to its present location. Such accounts serve to authorize the power and importance of the relics, providing evidence of their pedigree for being understood and venerated as the material remains of the Buddha who has attained *parinirvāṇa*.[3] Relics of the Buddha must, in other words, be recognized as valid traces of the Buddha, and their validity is demonstrated and authorized by the same narratives that serve to connect these objects to the living Buddha who existed previously. As Robert Sharf has argued, relics require a *frame* in space and time to signal that they are sacred objects.[4] Narratives, caskets, and ritualized gestures all are examples of how relics of the Buddha are framed and thus identified as such. In most cases, Buddha-relics are described and viewed as powerful objects worthy of veneration and protection, objects that are capable of causing certain miraculous effects in the world.[5] The agency of Buddhist relics enables them to "make history," as it were, and thus they have become the subjects of Buddhist narratives that describe how those traces of the Buddha continue to act in ways that effect the welfare of devotees.

One influential way of categorizing Buddha-relics is to follow the threefold division: bodily relics, relics of use, and commemorative "relics" (in the sense of memorials described in some postcanonical Theravāda Buddhist texts). Bodily relics refers chiefly to remnants of the Buddha's body collected from his funeral pyre, although there are other examples such as hair relics and footprint relics that are said to have been given or left by the Buddha before he passed away.[6] The direct connection between bodily relics and the living Buddha allows his story to proceed by following the careers of various relics such as teeth, shoulder bone, neck bone, and smaller, broken bones that are carried to new lands and established in shrines for public worship.

Relics of use refer to objects that were used by the Buddha, and therefore had some direct contact with him. Examples of this type of relics include the Buddha's robe, bowl, and the Bodhi tree under which he sat when he attained his Awakening. In the case of the Bodhi tree, this particular relic of use serves to extend the Buddha's life story both beyond his lifespan and also back in time before he became a Buddha. The Pāli *Mahābodhivaṃsa*, for instance, explains how the Bodhi tree became established at a monastery in Sri Lanka in the very same spot as the Bodhi trees of the three previous Buddhas that existed eons before Siddhārtha Gautama, connecting the story of the most recent Buddha to those Buddhas whom the Theravāda tradition holds to have preceded him.[7] Textual accounts of previous Buddhas detail significant events that structure the life stories of virtually all Buddhas. The *Mahāvaṃsa* recalls a kind of Buddhist "prehistory," wherein the three Buddhas prior to Gautama (P: Gotama) visited an island much like Sri Lanka, preached and meditated, and arranged for relics in the forms of Bodhi trees and objects of use (i.e., a drinking vessel, a girdle, and a rain-cloak, respectively) to be established for devotees to venerate.[8]

Finally, so-called commemorative "relics" are typically images that represent the physical form of the Buddha such as statues fashioned to resemble him. Some Buddha images, particularly those that are attributed with legendary origins that stretch back to the time of the Buddha, may be perceived as being especially important and powerful.[9] Significantly, however, such images that commemorate or recall the Buddha, usually do so indirectly and without having been derived from contact with the Buddha himself.[10] As such, these images are more accurately described as a "memorial" or an "object of veneration" (P: *cetiya*) that nevertheless can also function to keep the Buddha's life story going.

As powerful objects that are associated with the Buddha, Buddha-relics generally require respectful veneration and storage by devotees. In the account of the Buddha's final days contained in the *Mahāparinibbāna Sutta* of the Pāli Canon and discussed in the previous chapter, we learn that the Buddha who has passed away is to be honored with funeral rites that are otherwise reserved for a Universal Emperor (P: *cakkavattin*). Being advised by the Sangha, the local rulers direct their men to wrap the Buddha's corpse in multiple layers of linen and cotton-wool, place it in an iron vat, and construct a pyre consisting wholly of fragrant substances in order to be cremated in an honorable fashion.[11] The same narrative closes with the assertion that the bodily relics of the Buddha should be honored above all others who are themselves honored, including the kings of all beings and the foremost of other people, stating, "Venerate him, folding one's palms together in respect, surely a Buddha is difficult to obtain through one hundred eons."[12] Implicit in this account is the sense that encountering and venerating a Buddha relic demands one's respect and appreciation. This devotional approach to Buddha-relics thus requires that they be established or installed in shrines where they may be properly encountered and venerated. The *Mahāparinibbāna Sutta* explains that upon the cremation of the Buddha's body, only bone-relics (*sarīra*) remained, and these became highly sought after by the kings who were his devotees.[13]

In this canonical account, we learn that the Buddha foresaw his own demise and instructed his disciples to treat his corpse as a *cakkavattin* or a "Universal Emperor," including depositing his cremains in a burial mound (*thūpa*) so that devotees may make offerings and give rise to serene joy.[14] The Buddha goes on to explain that those people who make offerings to the bodily remains of a Buddha and give rise to serene joy will be reborn in a heavenly realm after their own deaths. The Buddha's warrant for enshrining his relics in *thūpa*s (Sk: *stūpa*s) is followed by those who come into possession of a portion of his cremains near the end of the *sutta*. This account offers the formula for handling relics of the Buddha and other awakened beings (i.e., *arahant*s) in subsequent instances where they present themselves or are discovered by devotees. As such, the bodily relics obtained from the cremation of awakened beings who have passed into *parinirvāṇa* should be collected and deposited in relic shrines. These relics are deemed to be inherently valuable and powerful, and their worship carries strongly positive effects for devotees.

Collecting, Desiring, and Dividing Relics

The extension of the Buddha's story occurs in narratives that describe what happens to his bodily relics after his funeral and cremation. As depicted in Maria Heim's preceding chapter, the death and funeral of the Buddha are portrayed in Pāli, Sanskrit, and Chinese texts as deeply moving and sorrowful affairs for his unawakened followers. When the narrative proceeds to discuss his relics, the emotional tenor of the story changes markedly. The *Mahāparinibbāna Sutta* contains one version of this episode, and it portrays the Malla kings of Kusinārā, where the Buddha passed away, as protecting and venerating his bodily relics with dances, songs, music, garlands, and scents.[15] However, in a sign of how contentious the presence of Buddha-relics can be, other neighboring kings come to hear of the Buddha's *parinirvāṇa*, travel to Kusinārā, and demand to take possession of the relics in order to deposit them in a *thūpa* in their respective kingdoms. King Ajātasattu sends an envoy to claim the relics for his kingdom of Magadha, the Licchavis stake a claim for them to be enshrined in Vesālī, the Sakyans want them for their kingdom in Kapilvatthu, and other kings likewise demand to be given the Buddha's relics since they are of the warrior (*kṣatriya*) class like the Buddha was himself. Meanwhile, the Mallas of Kusinārā state their refusal to give up the relics to any other groups of kings. After all, as described in Maria Heim's preceding chapter, it was the Mallas who were invited to witness the Buddha's passing away and who were the first to honor his body at his cremation. This conflict over relics appears as a precursor to similar disputes over bodily relics and images that occur in later eras among Buddhists. Thus, from the very beginning, Buddha-relics have consistently been the objects of contention between those who wish to possess and profit from their immediate presence.[16] And later, as John Strong has shown, disputes over relics could involve non-Buddhists as well, including those who sought to remove and destroy them as symbols of "idolatry."[17] As objects of power and symbols of the Buddha, people have long desired to obtain relics for a variety of reasons.

The dispute over the Buddha's cremains in the *Mahāparinibbāṇa Sutta* becomes resolved through the intervention of a brahmin named Doṇa (Sk: Droṇa). As portrayed in the image at the beginning of this chapter (Figure 9.1), this event makes up a common motif in stone and pictorial representations of the Buddha's story. Therein, Doṇa reminds the quarreling parties that the Buddha was a teacher of forbearance (*khantivāda*), and thus it would be inappropriate to fight over possession of the relics. He suggests instead a resolution whereby they make eight equal shares of the relics for each royal clan so that they may be spread and enshrined in *thūpa*s in different directions where many people can have serene joy with respect to the Buddha.[18] This division of the relics into eight portions averts the potential loss of life and accentuates the beneficial effects of Buddha-relics by spreading them and increasing people's access to them. This dispersal of the relics initiates a pattern whereby kings and monks seek to make them more available "out of compassion for living beings," meaning that they give more people more opportunities to earn merit and obtain higher states of spiritual attainment, as well as offering supernatural protection to the kingdoms where people live.[19] Since Buddhist literature concerning relics consistently affirms that they are powerful objects that are conducive to earning merit and attaining good rebirths, Buddha-relics became highly desired and increasingly proliferated throughout the Buddhist world. The mobility of relics also facilitated the spread of Buddhism into new lands, often appropriating indigenous religious centers in the process.[20]

Thus, even the original apportionment of Buddha-relics was not the end of the division and dispersal of relics. The *Mahāparinibbāṇa Sutta* remarks that Doṇa the brahmin asked for the urn used to divide the relics, and that another group of kings who arrived late were given the ashes from the Buddha's funeral pyre. As result, at this stage in the Buddha's afterlife story, there are ten *thūpa*s built in kingdoms where the Buddha was known, enabling devotees to remember and venerate him. There are, however, different versions of this episode, including one where the brahmin Doṇa is said to have tried to conceal a tooth relic for himself before having it snatched away by a deity and having instead to settle for the urn.[21] This right canine-tooth from the Buddha's cremains is said by later texts to have been taken up by the god Sakka (Sk: Śakra) and enshrined in a heavenly *thūpa* for the deities to venerate. Once again, textual traditions hold that all devotees of the Buddha, even divine ones, desire to possess and venerate his relics. The closing section of the *Mahāparinibbāṇa Sutta* specifies that in addition to the ten *thūpa*s that were built to enshrine the Buddha's relics around Jambudīpa with one in the subterranean realm of the *nāga* kings, there were four tooth relics recovered from the pyre and enshrined for veneration. The text notes that these four relics were established in the Tāvatiṃsa Heaven, the city of Gandhāra, the Kālinga kingdom, and the *nāga* realm.[22] This early canonical account of the dispersal of relics and the different groups of beings that desired to possess and worship them sets the stage for accounts in later Buddhist narratives that identify even more relics to be possessed and venerated.

King Ajātasattu's Relics

As one of the original claimants of the Buddha's cremains, King Ajātasattu (Sk: Ajātaśatru) of Magadha plays an important role in the continuing story of the relics. A complicated figure in Buddhist literature, Ajātasattu appears variously as an ambitious prince who kills his father-king to gain the throne, a bellicose king who wishes to declare war against others for profit, and a devout follower of the Buddha whose piety led him to nearly expire at hearing the news of the Buddha's passing.[23] After the division of the relics and while returning to his capital city of Rājagaha, the king is said to have extended the roadway for a distance of twenty-five leagues and paid homage to the relics with flowers and festivities all along the journey.[24] In fact, Ajātasattu's display of veneration to his portion of the relics was so extensive—lasting a total of seven years, seven months, and seven days— that the god Sakka and some elder monks petitioned the king to hurry the procession along in order to finally reach the site where they would be enshrined.[25] The *Sinhala Thūpavaṃsa* describes how each time that the rear wheels of the chariot reached the spot where the front wheels had been, it was halted for more offerings to be made.[26] The extensive and prolonged offerings made by the king to the relics demonstrates the great lengths to which Buddhist kings could be expected to venerate Buddha-relics. After he hurries the relics along to Rājagaha, he enshrines them in a *thūpa*.

King Ajātasattu plays another important role in the narrative composed about relics. This king is enjoined by the Thera Mahākassapa to collect all the relics together and enshrine them into a single deposit in Rājagaha. The unspecified danger to the relics as mentioned in the Pāli *Thūpavaṃsa* is clarified in the Sinhala version as a danger posed by heretics that will harm the relics if they are spread across into eight different shrines.[27] The earlier contentious debate over ownership of the relics has apparently faded away, since there are no reports of the other kings resisting efforts to collect the Buddha's relics together into one shrine. The monks accepted the task of bringing the other relics to Rājagaha, with the exception of the portion guarded by *nāga*s in Rāmagāma. Once the relics have been brought, the king instructs his subjects to build a large relic house, wherein the relics are kept within a series of precious urns and *thūpa*s made of gems, sandalwood, and ivory.[28] The increasingly large relic houses built over all the structures protecting the relics are said to have been made entirely out of jewels and precious metals. Inside them, flowers and dust obtained from precious metals were spread across the floor, and reliefs depicting 550 Jātakas, the Eighty Great Disciples, and important figures from the Buddha's life were carved out of precious materials and established therein.[29] Large numbers of water pots, flags, and lamps with scented oil were added to the site. These extensive offerings made to the relics as they were enshrined, more or less, as one single deposit signals to the audience that these sacred objects are supremely valuable and worthy of devotion by all.

King Ajātasattu next makes the great sacrifice of offering his crown and the sixty-four royal ornaments to the relics, symbolically raising them to a position and status over his monarchy. Meanwhile, the Thera Mahākassapa is said to have made a prediction, whereby a prince named Piyadāsa will one day in the future become King Asoka, and he will take the relics from Rājagaha and spread them throughout the lands of Jambudīpa, coextensive with his empire.[30] This prediction is inscribed in a plate and left by the relics. Afterwards, the king and his men leave each chamber, locking each set of doors behind them. The deity Viśvakarma (P: Vissakamma) is then called upon to create a mechanical device of wooden figures holding swords that whirl around at great speeds to protect the relics within. This elaborate set of actions effectively demonstrate how pious kings like Ajātasattu are expected to collect, enshrine, and protect relics from those who might steal or destroy then. Numerous kings in subsequent eras decided to follow this model by proclaiming their efforts to collect and enshrine relics in their own kingdoms. Buddhist rulers are in this way closely linked with Buddha-relics, and possession of these powerful objects become indices of the righteousness of their reigns. Ajātasattu's collection and possession of relics become conspicuous signs of his power and piety. In this way, the extension of the Buddha's life story through obtaining and enshrining relics also serves to extend the power and reputation of certain kings.

Asoka's Diffusion of the Relics

If Ajātasattu appears as the earliest king to exhibit tremendous veneration to the relics of the Buddha, King Asoka appears as the king whose very reign is intimately tied to the worship, spread, and enshrining of relics. King Asoka (Sk: Aśoka) is renowned as the powerful, and apparently Buddhist, ruler of a large empire that stretched across most of the Indian subcontinent in the 3rd c. BCE. John Strong's study and translation of the *Aśokāvadāna* describes how before he converted to Buddhism, Aśoka was cruel to those who stood in his way to the throne and to those who refused to follow his commands.[31] Therein, this fierce king is said to have mercilessly executed five hundred of his ministers who balked at chopping down flower and fruit trees and later ordered five hundred of his concubines burned alive for dismembering a tree named after himself.[32] In this Sanskrit work, Aśoka continues in his violent reign until he is converted by a Buddhist monk who had been condemned to be boiled to death but had attained *arahantship* and could not be killed in that manner. The monk named Samudra displayed his supernormal powers and then realizes that King Aśoka would comprehend the Buddha's Dharma and would distribute the Buddha's relics in the future.[33] Preaching to the king about the Buddha's wondrous qualities, he explains that the Buddha also predicted that a king named Aśoka would become a righteous "King of Dharma" and spread his relics far and wide.[34] According to the *Aśokāvadāna,* this event sufficed to convert Aśoka to the teachings of the Buddha and to rule in a morally righteous manner, extending great efforts to spread the Dharma and relics throughout his empire and beyond.

The Pāli tradition offers a different account of King Asoka's decision to disperse the relics of the Buddha throughout his empire. His conversion is triggered not by a monk whom he has ordered to be boiled to death, but rather it is a young novice monk named Nigrodha who catches Asoka's eye with his guarded demeanor. The novice's restraint and deportment while walking makes the king realize that his morality is superior to all the other ascetics. The prediction of this king's role in spreading relics was made by the Elder Monk Mahākassapa to King Ajātasattu several generations before Asoka's birth. The *Thūpavaṃsa* states that Mahākassapa had the following message inscribed on a gold plaque and placed along with Ajātasattu's relic deposit: "In the future, a prince named Piyadāsa will raise the parasol of state and become a righteous monarch (*dhammarāja*) called Asoka. He will have these relics widely dispersed."[35] Later, when King Asoka uncovers the relics left by Ajātasattu, he is said to have discovered and read this prediction of the earlier monk that validates his desire to enshrine relics at each of the 84,000 monasteries he built across the ancient Indian subcontinent.

By spreading relics across his kingdom, King Asoka models some of the behavior that would become paradigmatic for Buddhist kings in later eras.

Righteous kings who are devotees of the Buddha often accepted the responsibility of promoting the Buddha's Dispensation (*sāsana*) far and wide. Building relic shrines and establishing relics became a central method for making the Buddha's Dispensation more widely known and venerated. In this way, Buddhist kings who enjoyed reputations for being a *dhammarāja* could obtain relics without being accused of stealing, since their purpose would ostensibly be to enshrine them so that devotees could venerate the relic and attain welfare in this life and the next. For example, when King Asoka breaks into the relic deposit established by King Ajātasattu, he is assisted by the gods and then praised by later authors for taking these relics and enshrining them throughout his empire.[36] The fact that Asoka was predicted to take the relics and spread them across his empire, along with the fact that he was given assistance by the gods, work to make his act of removing the relics from Ajātasattu's shrine a righteous one rather than mere theft.[37]

Likewise, when it comes time for King Duṭṭhagāmaṇī to build the Great Relic Shrine (Mahāthūpa) in Anurādhapura, Sri Lanka, the relics are obtained by an *arahant* novice monk who sees through the deceit of the *nāga*s to snatch them away from their shrine in the netherworld and bring them back to the surface of the earth where they can be venerated by human devotees. This act was again justified by a prediction first made by Ven. Mahākassapa, who explained to King Ajātasattu that the relics possessed by the *nāga*s ought to remain with them, since they will be enshrined in the island of Laṅkādvīpa (Sri Lanka) in the future, and then again repeated to King Asoka who also inquired of these relics and was told that the future King Duṭṭhagāmaṇī would enshrine them in his kingdom in Sri Lanka.[38]

While relics of the Buddha are material, usually portable, and therefore subject to damage or loss, their very movability made them prized treasures for kings who aspired to the power and righteousness attributed to King Asoka. Moreover, if an *arahant* or the Buddha himself made a prediction that such and such a relic would be enshrined in one or another location, obtaining and transporting the relic in question is an act that conforms to the will of someone who was awakened. The acquisition of a relic under these or similar circumstances amounts to following the word of an Awakened One and accomplishing the beneficent intention of the Buddha to have his relics venerated by others.[39] Aided by good intentions, divine assistance, and authoritative predictions, efforts to acquire relics and to enshrine them in one's own kingdom could be presented as a noble act. In some cases, it was enough for a king to request to receive relics of the Buddha rather than taking them by subterfuge or force. In the case of the Phra Sihing image, also known as the "Sinhala Buddha," the Thai King Ram Khamhaeng petitioned the king of Sri Lanka for this image, and that latter agreed to gift it to him. Made in Sri Lanka, the Phra Sihing was brought to Thailand, where it traveled and was taken to various kingdoms by kings who sought the relic while conquering various lands.[40] By acquiring relics, whether they are corporeal, objects used by the Buddha, or an image of the Buddha, kings could signal that they were like Asoka in possessing great righteousness and power. Their possession of relics also brought the story of the Buddha close to home, making the benefits and miracles popularly associated with relics immediately available to one's subjects, one's family, and oneself.

The Buddha's Relics and Stories Beyond India

For those who lived outside of the land of the Buddha's birth and after the period in which appeared in the human realm, relics could help to bridge the gaps between devotees and the recipient of their devotion. The stories told about the Buddha's relics not only served to extend the narrative of his life but also enabled it to spread to other lands. Stories about the proliferation of Buddha-relics came to include objects that preceded his *parinirvāṇa*.

One of the paradigms for establishing a relic as a substitute for the Buddha appears in the *Mahābodhivaṃsa*'s account of the Ānandabodhi tree. While the Buddha is away going on an alms-round, the tycoon Anāthapiṇḍika approached Ven. Ānanda to point out that the citizens of Sāvatthi were displeased by not having the Buddha around to receive their offerings of perfumes and garlands. Speaking on their behalf as well as his own, Anāthapiṇḍika tells the monk, "It would be good, Reverend, if the Meritorious [Buddha], having been informed of this need would permit a place suitable for offerings."[41] After explaining this problem of his absence to the Buḍdha and learning that a *bodhi* tree may be established for veneration even prior to the Buddha's *parinirvāṇa*, Ānanda receives permission from the Buddha to plant a seed from the Mahābodhi tree at the gateway to the Jetavana Monastery. The Buddha confirms that the planting of this tree would be "like my continuing abiding at Jetavana" (*jetavane mama nibaddhavāso viya*), even when he travels elsewhere.[42] Relics can thus stand in for the Buddha, and they can move around to be present for different communities much like the Buddha did when going on his alms-rounds.

Despite the Buddha's declaration in the *Mahābodhivaṃsa* that bodily relics could only be obtained after his *parinirvāṇa*,[43] there are other narrative accounts where the Buddha left parts of his body behind to be venerated. Starting shortly after he attained his Awakening, the Buddha is said in the commentary to the *Aṅguttara Nikāya* to have given some of his hairs to the merchants Tapassu and Bhalluka, who were the first lay disciples to give alms to the Buddha. The commentary goes on to say that these devotees took the hairs back to their city and built a shrine for them.[44] While on a trip to the island of Laṅkā, the *Mahāvaṃsa* describes how the Buddha gave some of his head-hair to a local deity to enshrine and worship after he returns to Jambudīpa or "India."[45] In a similar manner, a later Pāli text from Myanmar called the *Chakesadhātuvaṃsa* (History of the Six Hair Relics) relates how the Buddha, out of compassion for the beings who live in distant provinces, rubbed his head and gave six hairs to *arahant*s, who then arranged to have them enshrined and venerated.[46] In doing so, the *arahant*s then passed them on to a variety of devotees who are said to enshrine one hair apiece in six *thūpa*s placed in different directions. The text describes how these shrines are built in heavenly, *nāga*, and human realms, allowing for the physical absence of the Buddha to be remedied by his hairs that may remain behind to benefit his distant devotees after he has gone away.[47] Such acts performed by the Buddha at the request of others demonstrate, from a Buddhist perspective, that he cared for his devotees and wished to help them attain good rebirths as a result of venerating his relics when he was not around. The same logic applies to the Buddha's predictions and resolutions to have his bodily relics remain behind and be spread throughout the world for the benefit of all beings.[48]

Footprint relics of the Buddha, whereupon he is said to have trod and left an indelible mark upon the earth, function in a similar manner to his hair relics. In narratives where the Buddha is said to have traveled by air to distant lands that later become home to Buddhist communities, he occasionally left a footprint behind for people to venerate. Footprints associated with the Buddha are plentiful in ancient art and in contemporary monasteries, although these, as John Strong has noted, may usually be seen more as "commemorative" relics than actual footprints left by the Buddha himself.[49] Nevertheless, there are select footprint relics found across the Buddhist world that have special importance as places where the Buddha is believed to have stood and consciously left his mark. The Pāli *Samantakūṭavaṇṇanā* (Praise of Mount Samanta) contains an extended, poetic account of how the Buddha was said to have visited this mountain in Sri Lanka and left a footprint as a bequest to the deity Sumana.[50] Set upon a prominent mountain peak, his footprint is said to remain for beings to venerate long after he left the island and eventually left the world of *saṃsāra*. Similarly, the Burmese *Vaṃsadīpanī* (Treatise on the Lineage of Elders) describes how the Buddha, on a visit to Myanmar, left his footprints at some places in the country to allow his devotees to worship him after he had gone.[51] The implication behind the selective, durable appearance of Buddha footprints is that he willed them to appear and to remain to be worshipped, often containing remnants of the distinctive marks said to adorn the soles of his feet.[52] As such, these footprints were also left behind to benefit others and to extend the story of the Buddha to different locations long after his passing away.

Aside from those relics given by the living Buddha, most Buddha-relics were obtained and enshrined in the centuries after his *parinirvāṇa*. Stories told about these relics of the Buddha, often found in *vaṃsa* texts and other narrative genres, extend his biography into later eras and distant locations.[53] Aside from those accounts of miraculous Buddha visits whereby he, and sometimes select disciples, traveled by air to lands outside of Jambudīpa, the circulation of Buddha-relics offered another means for Buddhists in other lands to be closer to the Buddha. From early on, the notion of relics as being somehow equivalent to a living Buddha has led to the idea that venerating the former is just as meritorious as venerating the latter.[54] John Strong cautions us, however, not to see relics as the means by which the Buddha is perceived to be immanent or incarnated in his alleged physical remains, but rather as objects that continue the Buddha's presence—albeit in a different form—after his death.[55] It is not surprising, then, that devotees around the Buddhist world would want to obtain and venerate relics, as these inherently sacred remains afforded them with opportunities to encounter the Buddha directly and to obtain merit from giving offerings (*pūja*).

The devotional desire for relics is illustrated in an episode from the *Mahāvaṃsa* where the monk Mahinda tells King Devānampiyatissa that he wishes to see the Buddha again. The Sri Lankan king is at first confused, since he has been led to believe that the Buddha has passed away in *parinirvāṇa*. The *arahant* Mahinda, who also happens to be the son of King Asoka, explains that "When relics are seen, the Conqueror [of *saṃsāra*, i.e. the Buddha] is seen" (*dhātusu diṭṭhesu diṭṭho hoti jino*).[56] A more elaborate account of this scene in the *Sinhala Thūpavaṃsa* mentions that Mahinda and his fellow monks feel despondent, because they have not seen the Buddha for a long time and that there is no place in the island to venerate and make offerings.[57] The king, in turn, vows to build a *thūpa* (Sinh: *dāgäba*) if the *thera*s can obtain a relic. The *thera*s charge the novice Sumana, who possesses supernormal powers, with the task of obtaining the Right Collar Bone Relic from the god Sakka. When this task is done, the Right Collar Bone Relic becomes established in the Thūpārāma Relic Shrine in the Mahāmeghavana Park where the monks were residing. Sri Lankan *vaṃsa*s add further that this act to enshrine the first bodily relic in the island had been predicted earlier by the Buddha himself.[58] As a result of the Buddha's prediction for this relic, Mahinda's petition, and the king's construction of the shrine is that from then on, the residents of Sri Lanka would have access to a place where they can venerate and earn merit by honoring a relic of the Buddha.

This process of obtaining and enshrining relics of the Buddha, whether in the form of his physical remains or as other memorial objects closely associated with him, would be repeated frequently by his devotees in lands across Asia. Accounts from Sri Lanka portray King Devānampiyatissa following King Asoka's lead by taking relics and enshrining them in *thūpa*s at every league across the island for his subjects to venerate and obtain merit and good rebirths. Other narratives depict how particular relics of the Buddha were acquired and enshrined in various locations. Sri Lankan texts place greater emphasis on the Buddha's bodily relics and bodhi trees. Most of the former type of relics were designed to be sealed and interred out of sight, in contrast to bodhi trees and images of the Buddha.[59] This method of enshrining bodily relics makes the narratives composed about them even more crucial for establishing one's pious confidence (*saddhā*) in their authenticity and immediacy. Oral and written accounts of relics that extend the Buddha's biography beyond his death and extend his presence into Sri Lanka have determined that the Buddha's Neck Bone Relic was enshrined in the Mahiyaṅgaṇa Thūpa, his Forehead Bone Relic was enshrined in the Sēruvāvila Thūpa, his Right Tooth Relic in the Sōmāvati Thūpa, Hair Relics in shrines located at Kirivehera, Tiriyāya, and Dīghavāpi, a Finger Nail Relic in Dīghavāpi, and a large collection of smaller, broken relics in the Mahāthūpa in Anurādhapura. Similarly, a Burmese Buddhist tradition maintains that some of the Buddha's Hair Relics received by the merchants Tapassu and Bhalluka were subsequently brought back to the land now known as Myanmar and enshrined in the Shwe Dagon Pagoda in Rangoon.[60] As such, Buddha-relics in the forms of bones, hair, nails, and certain objects that he used were brought to lands far from India and sealed up in relic shrines to be venerated by the Buddhist faithful. Even if they cannot be seen, these relics remain accessible to devotees and allow for acts of merit that are said to yield great benefits for those who honor the Buddha's remains.

Other Buddha-relics that are visible still often have their own pedigrees and reputations that are established by written narratives. These visible relics are usually also transportable, and thus they too serve to spread Buddhist teachings and institutions to various locales. Tooth Relics of the Buddha were sometimes kept in movable reliquaries and presented for viewing. The Tooth Relic in Kandy, Sri Lanka is such an example, and its story of how it was brought to the island is found in the thirteenth-century *Dāṭhavaṃsa* (History of the Tooth Relic). Its association with Sri Lankan kingship meant that whenever the seat of power was moved in Sri Lanka, the Tooth Relic followed and was kept in proximity to the king. Tooth Relics tend to be enshrined in monastic buildings or palaces, able to be removed and carried in ceremonial processions or exhibited on special occasions.[61] Various accounts located Tooth Relics across the Buddhist world. Buddhist sources have noted Tooth Relics that were worshipped in Kashmir and Chang'an in ancient times. The Tooth Relic that allegedly was given by a deity to the Chinese Buddhist patriarch Daoxuan in the seventh century eventually came to be enshrined in Chang'an where Chinese devotees could venerate a relic without having to go to India and take part in the afterlife story of the Buddha.[62] Interestingly, the mobility of this particular Tooth Relic has led it to be claimed by several different temples in China, Japan, and Korea, which suggests that the desire to obtain and venerate Buddha-relics was comparably widespread in East Asia.

The End of the Relics?

The numerous accounts of relics that persist after the Buddha's *parinirvāṇa* and that extend his life story to later times and various locations suggest that he will *never*, in a sense, *not* be around or *not* be accessible to his devotees. As long as relics, in John Strong's words, "provide focal points for an ongoing relationship with the Buddha, even after his death," their resilient existence in multiple places across the Buddhist world might seem to offer comfort and confidence to adherents that the Buddha remains available to them.[63] However, Buddhist texts affirm that the Buddha's relics are impermanent like everything else in *saṃsāra*. Relics therefore also resemble the Buddha in that their presence in the world of *saṃsāra* must one day come to an end. Buddhist traditions hold that after the gradual but inexorable decline of the Buddha's *sāsana*, there will be a *parinirvāṇa* of the relics. The Theravāda textual tradition describes that after the slow disappearance of Buddhist practice, the knowledge of Buddhist texts and the life story of the Buddha, and monastic robes and bowls, Buddha-relics will no longer be venerated.[64] In other words, as people gradually begin to forget about the Buddha and his Dhamma, they will cease to guard their morality and observe the traditional rites and customs. Possessing the power of self-locomotion, relics are thought to leave those places where they do not receive appropriate and sufficient honor from devotees.[65]

Perhaps the fullest description of the "disappearance of the relics" (*dhātu-antaradhāna*) is found in the Pāli commentary to the canonical *Aṅguttara Nikāya*.[66] In accordance with the resolution of the Buddha, all the relics will assemble first at the Mahāthūpa in Sri Lanka, then move to the Rājāyatana Thūpa in the part of the island closest to India, before traveling to the site of the Bodhi tree where the Buddha obtained his Awakening.[67] There, the texts predict, all the relics will come together in the likeness of the Buddha, emitting the six-colored rays of light and displaying all the marvelous physical marks of the Great Man while sitting cross legged on the Seat of Awakening.[68] At that time, since all the humans will have forgotten the Buddha, only the gods will be present to lament the disappearance of the relics. A great fire will ignite from the relic-body and consume all the relics completely, leaving the gods to pay their respects. The bodily relics of Gotama Buddha—including bones, hairs, and other pieces of his cremated body—will forever be gone.

One might wonder why Buddhists would predict the disappearance of the very objects meant to sustain the bodily presence of the Buddha in the world in a future, tremendous conflagration. Beyond efforts to be consistent with the teaching of the impermanence of all things, the *parinirvāṇa* of the relics replicates the *parinirvāṇa* of the Buddha himself, thus further cementing the equivalence between the two. Indeed, for Buddha-relics to actually be like the Buddha, it is only appropriate that they would attain the same sort of ending as the living

Buddha once did. The *parinirvāṇa* of the relics also supply what Steven Collins, borrowing a phrase from Frank Kermode, called the "sense of an ending" to the life story of the Buddha.[69] In Collins' analysis, the Buddhist concept of *nirvāṇa* provides a full-stop in both Buddhist narrative and systematic thought. The idea of *nirvāṇa*, however abstract and incomprehensible it may seem to those who are unawakened, thus offers a moment of ending that gives structure to all the events that preceded it, while also giving a meaningful and satisfying resolution to an individual's life.[70] In the context of relics and the "nirvanized" Buddha's afterlife, the multilineal descendance of innumerable bodily relics gave rise to numerous narratives about bones, hairs, and other sacred objects that propelled his life story onward and outward. While these relics could be moved or stolen, they nevertheless are normally experienced as durable, physical remnants of the Buddha's presence in the world.

Textual accounts of the *parinirvāṇa* of the relics, however, serve to bring these multiple stories about relics to a necessary end. When Buddha-relics are forgotten and neglected, as Buddhist traditions hold, they disappear. As much as the disappearance of the relics represents an ending that devotees of the Buddha do not want, it is necessary to bring these stories to a close. Further, according to the Theravāda view of nonsimultaneous Buddhas, the *sāsana* of one Buddha must completely disappear before a new Buddha and his *sāsana* can arise anew.[71] The relics of previous Buddhas are identified in Pāli literature, but they are never found and venerated by devotees living during the time of the Buddha Gotama's *sāsana*. They are lost to time, as were the Bodhi trees of previous Buddhas, even though those trees are said to have been established in the same spot as Sri Lanka's Mahābodhi tree in the current eon.[72] In short, when the stories of the relics end, the story of Gotama Buddha will end. With this ending, however, an opportunity for a new life story of the Buddha may begin—that of Maitreya (P: Metteyya), the next Buddha prophesied to arise in the current world-period of cosmic history. This demonstrates, as John Strong reminds us in the next chapter, that stories can resemble Buddhas and relics, they always come to an end but somehow will begin again anew.

Notes

1. John S. Strong, *Relics of the Buddha* (Princeton, NJ: Princeton University Press: 2004), 7.
2. Frank E. Reynolds, "The Many Lives of Buddha: A Study of Sacred Biography and Theravāda Tradition," in *The Biographical Process: Studies in the History and Psychology of Religion*, ed. Frank E. Reynolds and Donald Capps (The Hague: Mouton, 1976), 48.

3. Kevin Trainor, *Relics, Ritual, and Representation in Buddhism: Rematerializing the Sri Lankan Theravāda Tradition* (Cambridge: Cambridge University Press, 1997), 78.
4. Robert H. Sharf, "One the Allure of Buddhist Relics," *Representations* 66 (1999): 81.
5. Stephen C. Berkwitz, "Narratives of Buddhist Relics and Images," in *Oxford Research Encyclopedia of Religion*, (https://doi.org/10.1093/acrefore/9780199340378.013.587), 1–2.
6. Similarly, the Burmese *Vaṃsadīpanī* describes how the Buddha, on a visit to Myanmar, left his footprints at some places in the country to allow his devotees to worship him after he had gone. See Patrick Arthur Pranke, "The 'Treatise on the Lineage of Elders' (*Vaṃsadīpanī*): Monastic Reform and the Writing of Buddhist History in Eighteenth-Century Burma" (PhD Dissertation, University of Michigan, 2004), 137–138.
7. S. Arthur Strong, ed., *The Mahā-Bodhi-Vaṁsa* (London: Pali Text Society, 1891), 159–160.
8. Wilhelm Geiger, *The Mahāvaṃsa: Or the Great Chronicle of Ceylon* (1912, reprint) (Oxford: Pali Text Society, 2001), 101–108.
9. The narrative composed about the "Sīhaḷa Buddha" in Thai is an example of an attempt to extend the Buddha's life-story in time and space into premodern Thailand. Camille Notton, trans., *P'ra Buddha Sihiṅga* (Bangkok: Bangkok Time, 1933), 27.
10. Strong, *Relics of the Buddha*, 19–20.
11. T. W. Rhys Davids and J. Estlin Carpenter, eds., *The Dīgha Nikāya*, vol. 2 (Oxford: Pali Text Society, [1903] 1995), 161–162.
12. Davids and Carpenter, *Dīgha Nikāya*, vol. 2, 167–168.
13. Davids and Carpenter, *Dīgha Nikāya*, vol. 2, 164–165.
14. Davids and Carpenter, *Dīgha Nikāya*, vol. 2, 142.
15. Davids and Carpenter, *Dīgha Nikāya*, vol. 2, 164.
16. Cf. Kevin Trainor, "When Is a Theft Not a Theft? Relic Theft and the Cult of the Buddha's Relics in Sri Lanka," *Numen* 39, no. 1 (1992): 1–26.
17. John S. Strong, *The Buddha's Tooth: Western Tales of a Sri Lankan Relic* (Chicago: University of Chicago Press, 2021).
18. Davids and Carpenter, *Dīgha Nikāya*, vol. 2, 166.
19. Strong, *Relics of the Buddha*, 47.
20. Sharf, "On the Allure of Buddhist Relics," 78.
21. N. A. Jayawickrama, trans. and ed., *The Chronicle of the Thūpa and The Thūpavaṃsa: Being a Translation and Edition of Vācissaratthera's Thūpavaṃsa* (London: Luzac & Company Ltd., 1971), 41, 178.
22. Davids and Carpenter, *Dīgha Nikāya*, vol. 2, 167.
23. G. P. Malalasekera, *Dictionary of Pāli Proper Names*, vol. I (1937, reprint) (New Delhi: Munshiram Manoharlal Publishers, 1995), 31–33.
24. Jayawickrama, *Chronicle of the Thūpa and the Thūpavaṃsa*, 42.
25. Note that the *Sinhala Thūpavaṃsa* mentions that the time spent by King Ajātasattu in conveying and worshipping the relics was only seven months and seven days in length. Stephen C. Berkwitz, *The History of the Buddha's Relic Shrine: A Translation of the* Sinhala Thūpavaṃsa (New York: Oxford University Press, 2007), 128.
26. Berkwitz, *History of the Buddha's Relic Shrine*, 127–128.

27. Berkwitz, *History of the Buddha's Relic Shrine*, 129.
28. Jayawickrama, *Chronicle of the Thūpa and the Thūpavaṃsa,* 45–46.
29. Berkwitz, *History of the Buddha's Relic Shrine*, 131.
30. Berkwitz, *History of the Buddha's Relic Shrine*, 131. As noted by Vanessa Sasson in a personal communication, predictions for relics work to advance their narratives in much the same way that dreams do for the living Buddha and his family in retellings of the Buddha's life-story. On the subject of relic predictions, see Strong's discussion of "predestined relics" in his *Relics of the Buddha,* 150–178, and Berkwitz, "Narratives of Buddhist Relics and Images," 7–10.
31. The Pāli name of King Asoka appears as Aśoka in Sanskrit sources. I have chosen to use the version of the name to match the source material being discussed in this chapter.
32. John S. Strong, *The Legend of King Aśoka: A Study and Translation of the* Aśokāvadāna (Princeton, NJ: Princeton University Press, 1984), 210–211.
33. Strong, *Legend of King Aśoka*, 216–217.
34. Strong, *Legend of King Aśoka*, 217.
35. Jayawickrama, *Chronicle of the Thūpa and the Thūpavaṃsa,* 46, 182.
36. Berkwitz, *History of the Buddha's Relic Shrine*, 142–143.
37. Trainor, "When Is a Theft Not a Theft?," 8–10.
38. Geiger, Mahāvaṃsa, 210–211; Jayawickrama, *Chronicle of the Thūpa and the Thūpavaṃsa,* 125; Berkwitz, *History of the Buddha's Relic Shrine,* 231–232.
39. Trainor, "When Is a Theft Not a Theft?," 14.
40. Stanley J. Tambiah, "Famous Buddha Images and the Legitimation of Kings: The Case of the Sinhala Buddha (Phra Sihing) in Thailand," *RES: Anthropology and Aesthetics* 4 (1982), 9–10.
41. Strong, *The Mahā-Bodhi-Vaṁsa*, 59.
42. Strong, *The Mahā-Bodhi-Vaṁsa*, 59.
43. Strong, *The Mahā-Bodhi-Vaṁsa*, 59.
44. Malalasekera, *Dictionary of Pāli Proper Names,* vol. I, 991.
45. The text *Mahāvaṃsa* describes an episode wherein the Buddha rubbed his head and gave some of his hair to a god on the Sumanakūṭa Mountain in Sri Lanka, and which subsequently was encased in a golden casket and deposited in a sapphire-made relic shrine. See Geiger, Mahāvaṃsa, 5.
46. H. V. Abhayagunawardana, ed., *Chakesadhātuvaṃsa* (Colombo: S. Godage and Bros., 1993), 26.
47. Strong, *Relics of the Buddha,* 84–85.
48. See, for example, Berkwitz, *History of the Buddha's Relic Shrine,* 119.
49. Strong, *Relics of the Buddha,* 86–87.
50. Vedeha Thera, *In Praise of Mount Samanta (Samatakūṭavaṇṇanā),* trans. Ann Appleby Hazelwood (London: Pali Text Society, 1986), 94.
51. See Patrick Arthur Pranke, "The 'Treatise on the Lineage of Elders' (*Vaṃsadīpanī*): Monastic Reform and the Writing of Buddhist History in Eighteenth-Century Burma" (Ph.D. Dissertation, University of Michigan, 2004), 137–138.
52. Strong, *Relics of the Buddha,* 87–88.

53. For more on this topic, see Stephen C. Berkwitz, "Vaṃsa: History and Lineage in the Theravāda," in *Routledge History of Theravāda Buddhism*, ed. Stephen C. Berkwitz and Ashley Thompson (London: Routledge, 2022), 245–248.
54. Peter Skilling, "Relics: The Heart of Buddhist Veneration," in *Relics and Relic Worship in Early Buddhism: India, Afghanistan, Sri Lanka, and Burma*, ed. Janice Stargardt and Michael Willis (London: The British Museum, 2018), 8.
55. Strong, *Relics of the Buddha*, 229.
56. Buddhadatta, A.P., ed., *The Mahāvansa: Pali Text Together with Some Later Additions* (Colombo: M.D. Gunasena & Co., 1959), XVII.3.
57. Berkwitz, *History of the Buddha's Relic Shrine*, 150.
58. See, for example, Geiger, *Mahāvaṃsa*, 120; Jayawickrama, *Chronicle of the Thūpa and the Thūpavaṃsa*, 67–68; Berkwitz, *History of the Buddha's Relic Shrine*, 153.
59. Skilling, "Relics," 10.
60. Strong, *Relics of the Buddha*, 76.
61. Strong, *Relics of the Buddha*, 180.
62. Strong, *Relics of the Buddha*, 188–189.
63. John S. Strong, *The Buddha: A Short Biography* (Oxford: Oneworld Publications, 2001), 147.
64. Strong, *Relics of the Buddha*, 222–223.
65. Trainor, "When Is a Theft Not a Theft?," 15.
66. Max Walleser, ed., *Manorathapūraṇī: Buddhaghosa's Commentary on the Aṅguttara-Nikāya*, vol. I, revised 2nd ed. (London: Pali Text Society, 1973), 88–91. Similar accounts of the extinction of the relics are found in other Pāli commentaries such as *Sumaṅgalavilāsini* (III.899) and *Sammohavinodani* (433).
67. As K. Arunasiri notes, the Pāli commentarial accounts do not mention any relics in Jambudīpa, apparently because the authors expected that all of the Buddha-relics would be in Sri Lanka, the *deva* worlds, and the *nāga* worlds by this time, but not in Jambudīpa anymore. See Arunasiri, "Relics," in *Encyclopaeḍia of Buddhism*, vol. VII, Fasc. 3, ed. W.G. Weeraratne (Colombo: Department of Buddhist Affairs, 2005), 538.
68. Strong, J. S., *Relics of the Buddha*, 224. Strong also notes a different, non-Theravādin account wherein all of the relics will be brought together by sixteen great *arhats* and deposited in a magnificent stūpa. After being venerated, this stūpa will disappear into the earth and descend all the way down to the base of the cosmos. See John Strong, *Relics of the Buddha*, 226.
69. Steven Collins, *Nirvana: Concept, Imagery, Narrative* (Cambridge: Cambridge University Press, 2010), 110.
70. Collins, *Nirvana*, 112–113.
71. Strong, *Relics of the Buddha*, 225.
72. Strong, *The Mahā-Bodhi-Vaṁsa*, 144–145.

10
Overstory
First There Is a Buddha, Then There Is No Buddha, Then There Is

John S. Strong

Figure 10.1 While the Malla strongmen struggle to unearth a great boulder blocking the path, the Buddha (in the guise of a monk) picks it up with ease. From a late fifteenth century illustrated Chinese life of the Buddha; courtesy of World Digital Library, Library of Congress.

John S. Strong, *Overstory* In: *The Buddha.* Edited by: Vanessa R. Sasson and Kristin Scheible, Oxford University Press.
 DOI: 10.1093/oso/9780197649466.003.0011

In 1967, the Scottish singer Donovan first performed a hit song that contained the refrain "First there is a mountain, then there is no mountain, then there is."[1] Whether he knew it or not, Donovan was here echoing the ninth-century Chinese Zen master, Qingyuan Weixin who famously declared, "Thirty years ago, before I practiced meditation, I saw that mountains are mountains and rivers are rivers. However, after having achieved intimate knowledge . . . I saw that mountains are not mountains and rivers are not rivers. But now that I have found rest, as before I see mountains as mountains and rivers as rivers."[2]

We have seen in this book something of the multiplicity, richness, and varied significances of the life stories of the Buddha. Chapter by chapter, the authors have insightfully traced some (though by no means all) of the factualized fictions and fictionalized facts by which Buddhists over the years have narrated the events of Śākyamuni's lives—from the start of his journey to buddhahood over four countless ages ago (see Chapter 1 by Andy Rotman) to his present ongoing existence embodied in the forms of relics and images (see Chapter 9 by Stephen Berkwitz).

As I read through all these accounts, I found myself wondering if there might be one story—one episode from the Buddha's life—that might serve to epitomize the course of his career as a whole in all its multifariousness and distinctiveness and give us a graphic idea of what kind of a person—what kind of a character—he was. Doubtless, many answers could be found in the tales already told in this volume, and readers may well wish to pick one of their own. We all have our "favorites." But, in searching for mine, I found myself thinking more and more of a story we have not yet touched upon and that comes toward the end of the Buddha's life. As illustrated above (Figure 10.1), it tells of him using his powers to remove a huge rock that was blocking the road to Kuśinagarī, the place of his *parinirvāṇa*. And that reminded me of the refrain from Donovan's song and of the Zen saying on which it is based, even though it does not really concern a mountain but a mountainlike boulder. The episode is not particularly well-known in that it does not figure in any biographical blueprint, but it is noteworthy because, coming toward the end of his life, it does prompt a kind of retrospective reflection on the question of what kind of an individual the Buddha was thought to be.

Variants of this tale may be found in a number of different texts as well as depicted in art.[3] In what follows, I will present a compounded narrative chiefly based on accounts found in three sources—the Sanskrit *Mahāparinirvāṇa sūtra* (*Discourse on the Great Extinction*),[4] the *Mūlasarvāstivāda Vinaya* (*Book of the Discipline of the Original Pan-Realists*),[5] and the *Ekottarāgama* (*Numerically Arranged Discourses*)[6]—with occasional references to other texts.[7] I realize that by using this methodology, I run the risk of not doing justice to each of these texts in their individuality, but I am a firm believer in the structuralist dictum that every variant of a narrative is a valid variant that can add insight and nuance to the thrust of the story as a whole.

First There Is a Boulder

Our story actually begins on the final day of the Buddha's life. Having recently suffered a bout of sickness after his dinner of "pig's delight" at the house of Cunda in Pāpā (Pali, Pāvā; see Chapter 8 by Maria Heim), the Blessed One is on the final leg of his journey to Kuśinagarī. He is now a frail, elderly man whose body, as he puts it, is creaking along like a broken-down cart held together with straps. The Mallas of Kuśinagarī, learning that he is coming, decorate the streets of their city in anticipation of his arrival. At the same time, they send some of their young men out to the countryside to clear and clean up the road so that his way will be made smooth and easy. They run into trouble, however, when they find a huge boulder (said to measure sixty by thirty cubits [*hasta*])[8] imbedded in the ground and blocking the path. At first, they attempt to dig it out themselves, but with no success. Then they try to uproot it with teams of camels, then oxen, then elephants; to break it apart by hitting it with diamond-hard wedges; to destroy it with medicinal herbs; to make it disappear by means of mantras; all to no avail. They merely succeed in exhausting themselves.[9]

At this point the Buddha arrives, together with Ānanda and a group of disciples, and asks them what they are doing. They explain: "We heard you were visiting the land of the Mallas and had reached Pāpā and were heading our way. We wanted to make ready the road for you, but we encountered this big boulder."[10]

It is clear that this rock is problematic in its materiality. It might as well be a mountain, for it is a major stumbling-block, not so much for the Buddha (as we shall see), but for the Mallas whose desire to honor him is being stymied by its immovability. But there is something else at work here. People who do great things to honor the Buddha (such as building *stūpas*, commissioning images, or, in this case, clearing and beautifying a road) do so not only out of devotion for him, but also out of a desire to magnify their own merit and be recognized for their own greatness. In the version just cited, the Malla youth affirm that they want to clear the road for the Buddha; in other texts, however, they declare that they want to dig the boulder out and set it upright by the side of the road so that it will stand as a monument to their greatness, and the magnitude of their devotion to the Blessed One will be remembered for generations to come.[11] Indeed, it appears that the Mallas of Kuśinagarī are in competition with their relatives, the Mallas of Pāpā, for they have heard that the latter received the Blessed One most splendidly when he was visiting them. "They treated him with the utmost esteem," they state, "with the highest reverence and the greatest respect, and bestowed on him the best, choicest foods, and magnificent gifts," and with this in mind they wish to outdo them in hospitality so that their own fame will win out.[12]

The word "Malla" is a tribal name, but it actually means "wrestler," or "strong man." The Mallas of Kuśinagarī are thus worried about their reputation as macho men, and embarrassed by their failure to budge the boulder, despite all their attempts. "For a whole month," they declare, "from the start of the day, we have been striving together with all our strength, but it never moves! We're ashamed, it's a disgrace; all under heaven are mocking us."[13] They are so distraught that when the Buddha first asks them what they are doing and hints that maybe he could be of some help, they do not respond, and then, when he repeats his question two more times, they get angry and snap back: "We're trying to dig up this stone! We've been working hard at it for a year; what makes you think you can do it single-handedly?"[14]

This, of course, is not the way one addresses the Buddha, especially when what one is doing is supposed to be in his honor. Perhaps because of this, in an apparent attempt to mitigate this faux pas, one of the late (fifteenth century) Chinese versions of the story specifies that before approaching the Mallas, the Buddha took on the form of an ordinary wandering monk—something that the illustration at the start of the chapter tries to depict. There we can see the Mallas, at the bottom of the picture, using a rope in a vain attempt to move the boulder, and, in a second scene, depicted right above, a monk and the Buddha side-by-side (though in the text, the Buddha is said to have been invisible), holding up the same rock with the greatest of ease.[15]

The Mallas, however, may have had other reasons (besides being embarrassed) to be irked at the Buddha. In one text, when the Blessed One first approaches them, he mocks them as "little boys" (*kumāraka*).[16] The same is true in another source where the Buddha taunts them with a question that Michael Radich translates as "Come on, you bunch of babies, what do you think you're doing?"[17] And in yet another text, the confrontation is even clearer: When the Buddha (in the guise of an old monk) asks the Mallas "what are you boys (*tongzi*) doing?" they angrily retort: "Monk, why do you call us boys?" The monk/Buddha answers: "You're a big group of three hundred thousand persons and are not able to move this boulder blocking the path; why shouldn't I call you 'boys'?" To which the Mallas say "okay, if you can move this rock, we'll know you're a great man."[18]

Whatever the relationship between the Buddha and the young Mallas, and whether he is asked to do so or not, the Buddha decides to help them out, and demonstrate his power. The scene is extraordinary but should not surprise us as it is illustrative of the kind of coexistence of humanity and superhumanity that we have witnessed in the Buddha since his birth, if not before (see chapters by Naomi Appleton and Reiko Ohnuma). Suddenly the sickness and frailty of this dying old man are forgotten, and he becomes a superhero! He pries up the boulder with his toe, picks it up with one hand (as depicted in the illustration) and then throws it up into the sky, as far as Brahmā's heaven (i.e., to the very top of the Buddhist universe), where it vanishes from sight.[19] This does not mean, however, that the thing is gone. Indeed, in the minds of the young Mallas, the rock is still very much present; knowing that what goes up must come down, they are naturally apprehensive and ask the Buddha when the boulder will return to earth. He explains that normally, if a man were up as high as Brahmā's heaven and dropped such a rock, it would take twelve years for it to fall down to our world, but he, using his Tathāgata's powers, can make it return right away. And immediately, the boulder reappears in the sky heading straight towards them! The young Mallas panic and start running away in every direction, but the Buddha tells them not to be afraid for "he knows the right moment." He then deftly catches the rock in one hand. The great trichiliocosm quakes in six ways in acknowledgement, and the gods, up in the sky, scatter myriads of lotus blossoms.[20]

Needless to say, the Mallas are impressed and immediately ask what power the Tathāgata used to move the stone? Was it by means of his supernormal power (*ṛddhi*)? Was it by the power of his wisdom? But the Buddha answers it was neither of these. He was able to pick up the boulder and toss it into the air by means of the innate "power that came to him from his father and mother" (*mā tāpaitṛkabala*),[21] or, more specifically, the "strength that came to him through being breastfed" (Ch., *rubu zhi li*)."[22] Generally speaking, this ordinary physical body "born of mother and father" is described as "material, made up from the four great elements, . . . fed on rice and gruel, impermanent, liable to be injured and abraded, broken and destroyed."[23] And here we come to a first important point this story makes about the Buddha: the Buddha is physically human; like the rest of us, he has a material, organic, body possessing its own physical strength. If his strength seems superhuman, it is only because it is greater than ours, but it is not qualitatively different. It is simply a matter of degree: we can all pick up a pebble and toss it into the air; the Buddha can do it with a huge boulder.

The Mallas, of course, want to know just how great this innate physical power is, and the Buddha obliges them with an elaborate simile: the power of ten ordinary oxen, he says, is equivalent to the power of a blue ox; that of ten blue oxen is equivalent to the power of a great bull; that of ten great bulls is equivalent to the power of a rhinoceros; that of ten rhinoceroses is equivalent to the power of an ordinary elephant; and so on and so forth through twenty-four more steps featuring elephants of various types both real and mythical, powerful legendary heroes, and deities, until, we are told, the power of many hundreds of Nārāyaṇas (Viṣṇus) is still less than the power the Buddha got from his mother and father.[24]

In sum, the boulder is a material thing, and the power that the Buddha uses to throw it into the air—though superlative—is, ultimately, a physical one.

Then There Is No Boulder

We left off our story about the Mallas at the point where the Buddha catches the boulder as it falls from Brahmā's heaven. He then blows on it and it breaks apart, atomized into tiny particles.[25] That is just one scenario, however. In other even more dramatic accounts, the boulder never makes it back to earth; as it rushes meteor-like on its collision course, the Buddha causes it to break up into fine dust particles while it is still in mid-air, and to float down to earth as a fine sprinkle of powder.[26] At one level, this is just an alternative way to allay the fears of the Mallas who are worried they will be crushed by the projectile when it hits the ground. More profoundly, however, it is intended as a doctrinal lesson. As David Fiordalis shows in his chapter, miracles can preach the Dharma, and here we have a clear instance of this, for, just before the boulder is pulverized, a voice resounds in mid-air, declaring: "All compounded things (*saṃskāra*) are impermanent—of that there is no doubt; all elements of existence (*dharma*) are without self."[27] This suggests that the tale can be read allegorically: that the stubborn stumbling-block of a boulder is symbolic of the false notion of the Self (*ātman*) and of the permanence of things. These beliefs will keep us in saṃsāra, until we realize—usually through meditation and Abhidharmic analysis but sometimes, as in this case, through a miracle—that the Self is nothing more than an impermanent conglomeration of its component parts (*dharma*s/dust particles), or, in Mahāyāna terms, that its form is empty. Until that happens, the road to nirvāṇa will be blocked.

This interpretation is reinforced by the story's assertion that this second feat of the Buddha's—the breaking up of the boulder—is due to a rather different power than was the first (his tossing it up to Brahmā's heaven). When the Mallas ask the Buddha what power he used to reduce the boulder to dust particles, he tells them it was by virtue of his power of meditative absorption (Skt., *dhyānabala*; Ch., *chanding li*),[28] or, more precisely, by virtue of his supernormal powers (Skt., *ṛddhi*; Ch., *shenzu*), which are commonly said to be attained by means of *dhyāna*.[29] And here again, he gives another simile to show his audience how his own buddha's supernormal powers are countless times greater than those of his disciple Mahāmaudgalyāyana who was renowned as being "foremost in *ṛddhi*."[30]

The explanation goes like this: Once upon a time, when the Buddha and his disciples were dwelling in the land of Verañjā, there was a great famine.[31] The monks, unable to get any almsfood, become emaciated, and, in their exhaustion, can no longer recite the Dharma. Mahāmaudgalyāyana, however, remembers that the Buddha once said that, at the beginning of this world cycle, there spontaneously arose a sweet nectar on the surface of the earth which the beings of that time fed on abundantly.[32] So, wanting to help out, he goes to the Buddha and proposes using his own supernormal powers, first, to overturn the earth in order to get at this primordial ghee-like savory essence that apparently still exists, buried deep underground. In this way, the monks will be able to nourish themselves and recite the scriptures. The Buddha, however, objects, telling his disciple that such a thing will injure the worms and moths and other creeping things that dwell in the earth, and, as a result, the monks eating this earth-essence will, by association, incur bad merit. Not one to be stymied, Mahāmaudgalyāyana then proposes, secondly, to magically create a replica of the earth in one of his hands, while he overturns the real earth with his other hand; in this way, the worms and creeping things will have a place to crawl to where they won't be injured. But to this the Buddha says, "Enough! Maudgalyāyana, if beings see this, they will be frightened to death, and besides, in overturning our earth, Buddhist monasteries and temples of the gods (and other things that cannot crawl to the replica world) will be destroyed." But Mahāmaudgalyāyana is still not ready to give up on his plan, and so, thirdly, asks the Buddha to allow the monks to fly to the Northern continent of Uttarakuru, where apparently there is no famine, and go on their begging rounds there. And for those who have not developed the magical power of flight—well, he will scoop them up and transport them there himself. But the Buddha objects again: "Stop it," he tells his disciple, and warns that if the monks fly to Uttarakuru, in future times, when there is another famine and the monks no longer have the supernormal power of flight and Maudgalyāyana is not around, they will be embarrassed by laypeople who will mock them saying "why don't you go and beg for food in Uttarakuru like you used to?"[33]

In this vignette, we can see some of the Buddha's concerns for the moral repercussions of the acts of his followers, the institutional structures of his religion, and the ultimate reputation of his monks, but the stated purpose of the story is to declare that the Buddha's supernormal powers are countless times greater than those of his disciple (and presumably those of other masters, whether Buddhist or not). The way it does this is not by showing the Blessed One actually performing a miraculous feat of his own that outshines those proposed by Mahāmaudgalyāyana, but by showing him to have a greater vision of the possible problematic ramifications of the exercise of supernormal powers. Mahāmaudgalyāyana's shortcomings are due to the fact that he is here depicted as a sort of "sorcerer's apprentice"—a figure much featured in world folklore (and made famous by Johann Wolfgang von Goethe in his poem "Der Zauberlehrling" and by Walt Disney in his animated film "Fantasia"). Basically, it is the story of a young magician, who, incompletely expert in the use of magical powers, loses control of what he sets in motion, and does not know how to reverse it (with comical, chaotic, and/or disastrous consequences).[34] This, of course, never happens to the Buddha, who, aware of all the possible negative outcomes of an action, either refrains from undertaking it, or, having undertaken it, has the necessary mastery to take corrective action.

Then There Is (a Boulder)

Returning to our story of the Mallas, we can see that the Buddha *is* able to take corrective action, for, having used his superpower to pulverize the boulder, he then gathers all the dust motes and presses them together to reconstitute them into a rock which has the same shape and size as the original; he then sets this new/old boulder down *by the side* of the path, and sits on it to talk to the Mallas.[35] Once again, they ask him what power he used in order to accomplish this feat. Was it his innate physical strength? Was it his supernormal abilities? Interestingly, he tells them that it was neither of these. Instead, he restored the boulder by means of the "power of his wisdom" (Skt., *prajñābala*; Ch., *zhihui li*).[36] And when they ask him to describe this, he gives them another "simile": everywhere, everyone knows that the wisdom of Śāriputra (the disciple recognized as being "foremost in wisdom)"[37] is deeper than the deepest ocean; if one were to pour it out, it would overflow the cosmos. But it is nothing next to the wisdom-power of the Buddha which is one hundred times, one thousand times, ten thousand times, one hundred million times, nay, many gazillion times greater, and which, like emptiness, is immeasurable.[38]

It is noteworthy that it is by means of this great wisdom that the Buddha undoes his earlier use of *ṛddhi* (the pulverization of the boulder). A miracle (or magic trick, or meditational attainment) may show us that reality is not as it seems, but wisdom allows us to live in the real world with that realization in mind. For it is the power of wisdom that shows the limits of *ṛddhi*—something already suggested in the story given above about Mahāmaudgalyāyana's shortcomings.

The question may be asked why the Buddha, having demonstrated the impermanence and insubstantiality of the boulder, proceeds to restore it. No immediate explanation is given in the text, but a number of reasons are imaginable. At a down-to-earth level, it may simply be that the Mallas are upset by the fact that the rock they had been hoping to erect as a monument to the greatness of themselves (and of the Buddha) is now gone, and they want it back. Indeed, in some versions of the story, the Buddha does not restore the boulder at his own initiative but in response to a request made of him by the Mallas. For, when they see particles of dust falling from the sky (rather than the rock), instead of being reassured that they will escape injury, they become distressed and say: "This is not good." The Blessed One then asks them "Do you want this dust to be put together into the original boulder?" and they answer, "yes, indeed."[39]

Doctrinally speaking, this is significant for it suggests that once the insubstantial nature of the world is shown, it need not remain in dissolution. Indeed, the Mallas clearly do not want it to be so left: having just seen the boulder pulverized and been told that all things are impermanent, they want something tangible back. And the Buddha, wisely, gives it to them: a "new/old" reconstituted boulder which does not differ from the first boulder except that its impermanence and insubstantiality have been realized so that it is now no longer an obstacle to liberation; it stands by the side of the path, and the way to Nirvāṇa is no longer blocked.

There is thus a dialectic pattern going on here: the "thesis" with which we started ("First there is a boulder") is contradicted by its "antithesis" ("then there is no boulder") resulting in a higher "synthesis" of sorts ("then there is [a new/old] boulder"). Put another way, we have here the gist of what the Buddha taught: the experienced permanence and substantiality of the things of the world—their inextricable physicality—is contradicted by miracles and meditation and doctrine that make us realize that the world is actually impermanent and unsubstantial, and the synthesis of these two results in the wisdom of liberation that allows us to live in the world and experience it as it truly is.

Conclusion

But what insights can we gain from this tale about the nature of the Buddha and his lifestory? Let me try to give one answer by focusing on two things: the various powers of the Buddha that are highlighted in his dealings with the boulder, and the just-mentioned dialectic progression implied in the story as a whole.

One of the epithets of the Buddha is that he is a "Daśabala" (a "Ten-powered One"), and the Buddhist scholastic tradition spent much energy enumerating and defining these.[40] None of these lists, however, includes the three powers that are featured in our story. In part for that reason, I prefer to think of them as indicating three characteristics or aspects of the Buddha. The first one—the "power that comes from his mother and father" (or from his mother's milk) reflects the fact that the Buddha is an extraordinary but *human* being, utterly superior to all other humans (and animals and gods) in dealing with the things of this world. Like all humans, he has parents, and so is deeply interconnected with others. The second "power that comes from meditation" reflects the fact that he is also a wonderworker, a miracle-maker possessed of superpowers (*ṛddhi*) that can magically change the appearance of the things of the world and thus demonstrate their lack of a constant self. The "power that comes from wisdom" shows that he is also a wise teacher who has realized the nature of the world but knows that he must live in it if only to help others to that realization. These three characteristics are present throughout the Buddha's life and can manifest themselves at any time, but they tend to be featured at different periods of his career, which, thanks to the chapters of my colleagues in this book, can easily be recapitulated here.

The first characteristic is especially emphasized during his time as a Buddha-to-be, prior to his awakening. We do not often think of the Buddha as a supreme strongman, but he was, not only in some of his past existences, but in the first part of his final life. The power he demonstrates in his initial "competition" with the Mallas is reminiscent of his besting his cousins in contests of martial arts (in order to win the hand of his wife), and his tossing of the boulder is akin to his throwing the corpse of an elephant that was blocking the city gate over the walls of hometown.[41] More generally, it can be said that the Buddha starts his final life as a very physical being (see chapter by Reiko Ohnuma). He has a superlative body in all respects. He possesses all the marks of the Great Man. He has a passionate relationship with his wife (as Vanessa R. Sasson makes clear in her chapter). In short, he is not only stronger, but also handsomer, smarter, and more virile than everyone else—a real "bull of a man."[42]

Despite all his perfections this is also a time of his life that is still marked by imperfections (as were his previous existences, as Naomi Appleton shows in her chapter). His mocking of the Mallas as weaklings when they cannot budge the boulder shows that, even though he is superior in all ways, he sometimes appears to suffer from a superiority complex. It should be remembered that during his early life, he is not yet awakened, not yet free from the "impurities" (*āśrava*) which Buddhist doctrine defines as sensual desire, clinging to existence, speculative views, and ignorance. He feels trapped by these, however, imbedded in the palace as surely as the boulder was buried in the earth of the road to Kuśinagarī. His solution is to extricate himself, to flee from the palace (see chapter by Kristin Scheible).

This Great Departure starts the transition towards his second identity. In his search for his true nature, he transforms his body through the practice of extreme asceticism, whittling it down to next to nothing. He then turns to the power of meditation, and soon achieves supernormal powers. Some of these are demonstrated in his encounter with Māra. In his awakening under the Bodhi tree, he overcomes the impurities and realizes for himself the truths of impermanence and non-self. Any lingering notion of a Self (*ātman*) has been destroyed just as surely as was the Mallas' boulder. During the weeks that follow, his meditation and trances and fasting continue (see the chapter by Jinah Kim and Todd Lewis). It seems he is content to not reenter the world.

But he is asked to come back by the god Brahmā (just as he was asked by the Mallas to restore the boulder), and this initiates the third phase of his career. He resumes eating. In his old/new body, as a "selfless person,"[43] he returns to the world to help others. He is no longer subject to the impurities. He becomes a teacher, an imparter of wisdom, a builder of community, an unblocker of the road to nirvāṇa (see chapter by David Fiordalis). "First there is a buddha, then there is no buddha, then there is a Buddha."

The Dialectic Continues

But, as we all know, "syntheses" in dialectics tend to become new "theses" which may need to be countered by new "antitheses." Boulders, even reconstituted ones whose ultimate insubstantiality has been realized, do not last forever. Neither do Buddhas, who, like boulders, are ultimately impermanent. Thus, our story ends on a different note. Following the Buddha's exposition of his three powers (his innate physical strength, his supernormal powers, and his wisdom),[44] the young Mallas ask further whether there is yet another power that surpasses all of these. The Blessed One answers that indeed there is: it is called the power of impermanence (Skt., *anityatābala*; Ch., *wuchang li*), and he tells them that, that very night, between the twin sal trees, pulled along by that power of impermanence, he will enter complete extinction.[45] This is evidenced not only by the Buddha's cremation, but by his own decision that his body will be pulverized into relics "as small as mustard seeds,"[46] that is, not much larger than the dust particles into which the boulder was transformed. "First there is a buddha, then there is no buddha, then there is. . . . And then there isn't."

This, of course, is not exactly true, for once a dialectic gets going, one cannot easily end it. Although the word *parinirvāṇa* is often understood to mean "complete extinction," we know from Stephen Berkwitz's chapter in this volume that the Buddha's life does not come to a full stop with his *parinirvāṇa*. Just as the scattered particles of the Mallas' boulder are put together into a new/old boulder, so too the scattered particles of the Buddha's body, after his *parinirvāṇa* can be put into a new/old buddha (his assembled relics). As Berkwitz points out, these relics are then collected by kings such as Ajātaśatru and Aśoka and are seen to make the Buddha's body present once again, in a new/old form. The most graphic example of this will happen in the future, when there will be a final coming together of the relics in Bodhgaya where they will once again take on the form of the Buddha's body. But even this will be subject to impermanence, for there will then occur a third extinction: "the nirvāṇa of the relics" when they will all be consumed by a final fire. "First there is a buddha, then there is no buddha, then there is, . . . then there isn't, . . . then there is, . . . then there isn't."

And *then*? Well, then, the next Buddha Maitreya will come, and another story (a new one, but also an old one) will begin.

Notes

1. "Donavan in Concert: There Is a Mountain." https://www.youtube.com/watch?v=lkLp9d7HKuA.
2. Urs App, *Master Yunmen* (New York: Kodansha, 1994), 111–112n.2 (slightly altered).
3. For representations in art from Gandhāra and Kucha, see Monika Zin, "About Two Rocks in the Buddha's Life Story," *East and West* 56 (2006): 351–55; and Monika Zin, "Sanskrit Literature and the Indian Pictorial Tradition in the Paintings of Kucha," in *Sanskrit and the Silk Route*, ed. Shashibala (New Delhi: Bharatiya Vidya Bhavan), 289-291 and 295 (fig. 3a–b). For a woodblock illustration from a Ming Dynasty Chinese biography of the Buddha, see Léon Wieger, "Les vies chinoises du Buddha: récit de l'apparition sur terre du Buddha des Sakya," in *Buddhisme*, vol. 2 (Sien-Hsien: Imprimerie de la Mission Catholique, 1913), pl, 164. See also Figure 10.1.
4. See Ernst Waldschmidt, "Wunderkräfte des Buddha. Eine Episode im Sanskrittext des Mahāparinirvāṇasūtra," *Von Ceylon bis Turfan* (Göttingen: Vandenhoeck & Ruprecht, 1967), 136–161, for an edition and Ger. trans. of the story. See also Claudia Weber, *Buddhistische Sutras: Das Leben des Buddha in Quellentexten* (Munich: Hugendubel Diederichs, 1999), 186–200. The episode is a Sanskrit *Sondertext* ("special text") with no corresponding parallels in the Pali, Tibetan, or Chinese versions of the sūtra. As a consequence, it was not included in Waldschmidt's 1950–1951 edition of the *Mahāparinirvāṇasūtra*. The manuscript contains a number of *lacunae* which, however, can be filled in by reference to other sources.
5. T. 1448, 24: 30c–31b (Ger. trans. in Waldschmidt, "Wunderkräfte," 121–124).
6. T. 125, 2: 749a–751b (Fr. trans. in André Bareau, "La fin de la vie du Buddha selon l'*Ekottara-āgama*," in *Hinduismus und Buddhismus. Festschrift für Ulrich Schneider*, ed. Harry Falk [Freiburg: Hedwig Falk], 14–19; sum. Ger. trans. in Ernst Waldschmidt, *Die Überlieferung vom Lebensende des Buddha: eine vergleichende Analyse des Mahāparinirvāṇasūtra und seiner Textentsprechungen* [Göttingen: Vandenhoeck & Ruprecht, 1944-48], 173–77).
7. These other sources include: (1) Story 15 of the *Avadānakalpalatā of Kṣemendra*, ed. P.L. Vaidya (Darbhanga: Mithila Institute, 1959), 1: 126–127; (2) T. 517, 14: 791a–c (= the *Foshuo moluowang jing* [Sutra of the Malla King]); (3) T. 135, 2:857c–859b (= the *Lishi yishan jing* [Sutra of the Mallas who Move a Mountain]); sum. Ger. trans. in Waldschmidt, *Überlieferung*, 172–186; (4) T. 193, 4, 103a–106b (= ch. 29 of the *Fo benxing jing* [Sutra on the Past Activities of the Buddha]); Eng. sum. trans. in Xi He, "Fo Benxing Jing: A comparative Study," unpublished paper given at the XVIIIth Congress of the International Association of Buddhist Studies, Toronto, August 24, 2017; (5) T. 1546, 28: 118c–119c (= *Abhidharmavibhāṣāśāstra*), and T.1545, 27: 155a–156b (= *Abhidharmamahāvibhāṣāśāstra*); sum. Ger. trans. of both in Waldschmidt, *Überlieferung*, 171–186. See also Michael Radich, "Embodiments of the Buddha in Sarvâstivāda Doctrine, with Special Reference to the **Mahāvibhāṣā*," *Annual Report of the International Research Institute for Advanced Buddhology at Soka University* 13 (2010): 129n.38; (6) Various editions of Baocheng's fifteenth century Chinese illustrated life of the Buddha. See Baocheng Shi and Bo Wang, *Shi Shi Yuan Liu Ying*

Hua Shi Ji: Si Juan (Account of Śākya Tathāgata's Origins and Manifestations, in four volumes), at https://www.loc.gov/item/2012402109/, vol. 2, no. 61; see also Ch. text and Fr. trans. in Wieger, "Vies Chinoises," no. 164 (facsimile edition at https://curiosity.lib.harvard.edu/chinese-rare-books/catalog/49-990080126080203941, vol. 4, seq. 25). On these and related texts, see also Emmanuelle Lesbre, "Une vie illustrée du Buddha (*Shishi yuanliu*, 1425), modèle pour les peintures murales d'un monastère du XVe s. (Jueyuan si, Sichuan)," *Arts asiatiques* 57 (2002): 69–101. For a discussion of many of these sources and the iconographic importance of the tale as a whole, see Zin, "Two Rocks," 340–347.

8. About twenty-seven meters by eighteen meters. In T. 135, 2: 857c26, the boulder is said to be sixty *zhang* (about 180 meters) square and 120 *zhang* (3,600 meters) high. In T. 517, 14: 791a28), it has grown to be ten li (c. five kilometers) in length!
9. Skt. text and Ger. trans. in Waldschmidt, "Wunderkräfte," 137–140.
10. Skt. text and Ger. trans. in Waldschmidt, "Wunderkräfte," 140–141. See also T. 1448, 24: 30c (Ger. trans. in Waldschmidt, "Wunderkräfte," 121).
11. T. 125, 2: 749a28–29 (Fr. trans. in Bareau, "La fin de la vie," 15). Bareau, always seeking to demythologize legends, would like to believe that there was some striking rock formation on the ancient road to Kuśinagarī that inspired this story. See also T. 135., 2: 858a19–20 (Ger trans. in Waldschmidt, *Überlieferung*, 174).
12. Skt. text and Ger. trans. in Waldschmidt, "Wunderkräfte," 141. The assertion that the Mallas of Pāpā fed the Buddha well is interesting in light of the fact that Cunda (who was from Pāpā) served him the meal of "pig's delight" (see chapter by Maria Heim). This reinforces the notion that that repast was actually a delicacy.
13. T. 135, 2:858a16–17.
14. T. 517, 14: 791b4–6. Note that, as the tale gets told, the amount of time the Mallas strive to unearth the boulder increases exponentially.
15. See also Wieger, "Vies Chinoises," 191 for another illustration of the same scene.
16. Skt. text and Ger. trans. in Waldschmidt, "Wunderkräfte," 140.
17. See T. 1545, 27: 156a16 (Eng. trans. in Radich, "Embodiments," 129n38). Radich describes the whole scene as a contest of strength between the Buddha and the Mallas.
18. Baocheng in https://www.loc.gov/item/2012402109/.
19. T 125, 2: 749b4–5 (Fr. trans. in Bareau, "La fin de la vie," 15). See also T. 1448, 24: 30c27 (Ger. trans. in Waldschmidt, "Wunderkräfte," 121).
20. T. 125, 2: 749b6–16 (Fr. trans. in Bareau, "La fin de la vie," 15).
21. T. 1448, 24: 31a8 (Ger. trans. in Waldschmidt, "Wunderkräfte," 121). In T. 135, 2:858b1, he declares that if he had used the power of *ṛddhi* instead of the power come from a nursing mother, he could have moved the whole trichiliocosm world system. For more on the Buddha's birth body, see Radich, "Embodiments," 127-34.
22. T. 135, 2: 858b4.
23. *Dīgha Nikāya*, 3 vols., ed. J. Estlin Carpenter (London, Pali Text Society, 1911), 1: 76 (Eng. trans, Maurice Walshe, *Thus Have I Heard: The Long Discourse of the Buddha* [London: Wisdom Publications, 1987], 104).
24. Skt. text and Ger. trans. in Waldschmidt, "Wunderkräfte," 142–144. Much the same simile is found in T. 125, 2: 749c (Fr. trans., in Bareau, "La fin de la vie," 16–17). See

also the list of comparisons in T. 135, 2: 858b4–16; and T.1545, 27: 155a8–b (Ger. trans., in Waldschmidt, "Wunderkräfte," 161–162).

25. T 193, 4: 103b19; T. 1545, 27:156a; and T. 135, 2: 858a25. Only in T. 125, 2: 749b17–22 (Fr. trans. in Bareau, "La fin de la vie," 15) does the Buddha not pulverize the boulder at this point, but, having caught it in his left hand, he puts it in his right hand and then sets it down on end.
26. T. 1448, 24: 31a1–3 (Ger. trans. in Waldschmidt, "Wunderkräfte," 121). See also *Avadānakalpalatā*, 127, and Wieger, "Vies Chinoises," No. 164, where he blows it apart in midair with a great gush of air from his mouth.
27. *Avadānakalpalatā*, 126. In T. 193, 4: 103b17, the declaration is "The world is impermanent, all dharmas are without self." In one of the editions of Baocheng, it is also announced that the rock is impermanent (see https://www.loc.gov/item/2012402109/, vol. 2, no. 61).
28. T. 1448, 24: 31a9 (Ger. trans. in Waldschmidt, "Wunderkräfte," 122).
29. T. 125, 2: 749c–750a (Fr. trans. in Bareau, "La fin de la vie," 17–18); T. 135, 2: 858b18–26 (sum Ger. trans. in Waldschmidt, *Überlieferung*, 182).
30. *Anguttara Nikåaya*, 5 vols., ed. R. Morris and E. Hardy (London: Pali Text Society, 1885–1900), 1: 23 (Eng. trans in Bhikkhu Bodhi, *The Numerical Discourses of the Buddha: A Translation of the Anguttara Nikāya* [Boston: Wisdom Publications, 2012], 109).
31. The first part of the tale of the famine in Verañjā is also found, in abbreviated form, in the Pali *Vinaya piṭakam*, 5 vols., ed. Hermann Oldenberg (London: Pali Text Society, 1969–1984), 3: 5–7 (Eng. trans. in I.B. Horner, 1938–1952. *The Book of the Discipline*, 6 vols. [London: Pali Text Society, 1938–1952], 1: 11–14).
32. On this nutritive edible essence of earth, see the "Aggañña Sutta" in *Dīgha Nikāya* 3, 85 (Eng. trans in Walshe, *Thus Have I Heard*, 410).
33. Skt. text and Ger. trans. in Waldschmidt, "Wunderkräfte," 151–156. See also T. 125, 2: 749c–750a; and T. 135, 2: 858b–c.
34. In Goethe's poem, the apprentice sorcerer, in his master's absence, animates a broomstick and gets it to carry buckets of water for him, but does not know the formula for putting a stop to this, resulting in a considerable flood, until the master comes back and rectifies the situation. See Jack Zipes, *The Sorcerer's Apprentice: An Anthology of Magical Tales* (Princeton, NJ: Princeton University Press, 2017), 97–100.
35. T. 1448, 24: 30c–31a (Ger. trans. in Waldschmidt, "Wunderkräfte," 121). See also *Avadānakalpalatā*, 127; T. 1545, 27: 156a.; Baocheng in https://www.loc.gov/item/2012402109/ vol. 2, no. 61.
36. T. 125, 2: 750a27 (Fr. trans. in Bareau, "La fin de la vie," 18–19). See also Waldschmidt, "Wunderkräfte," 149–151. Alternatively, the Buddha says he did it by his "power of emancipation" (Skt., *muktibala*, Ch., *jietuo li*); see T. 1448, 24, 31a10 (Ger. trans. in Waldschmidt, "Wunderkräfte," 122).
37. *Anguttara Nikāya* 1: 23 (Eng. trans. Bodhi, *Numerical Discourses*, 109).
38. T. 135, 2: 858c11–19 (sum. Ger. trans. in Waldschmidt, *Überlieferung*, 180).

39. T. 1448, 24: 30c–31a (Ger. trans. in Waldschmidt, "Wunderkräfte," 121). See also *Avadānakalpalatā*, 127; T. 1545, 27: 156a.; and Baocheng in https://www.loc.gov/item/2012402109/ vol. 2, no. 61.
40. For a listing and description of these ten powers, see A.G.S. Kariyawasam, "Dasabala," in *Encyclopaedia of Buddhism*, ed. Jotiya Dhirasekera (Colombo: Government of Sri Lanka Press, 1984), vol. 4, fasc. 2: 314–318.
41. See John S. Strong, *The Buddha: A Short Biography* (Oxford: Oneworld Publications, 2001), 45.
42. John Powers, *A Bull of a Man: Images of Masculinity, Sex, and the Body in Indian Buddhism* (Cambridge, MA: Harvard University Press, 2009).
43. See Steven Collins, *Selfless Persons: Imagery and Thought in Theravāda Buddhism* (Cambridge: Cambridge University Press, 1982).
44. It should be said that a number of our texts do not limit themselves to explaining just these three powers of the Buddha. T. 1448, 24: 31a26–28 (Ger. trans. in Waldschmidt, "Wunderkräfte," 122–123), and the Sanskrit *Mahāparinirvāṇa sūtra* (text and Ger. trans. in Waldschmidt, "Wunderkräfte," 145–149), for example, also describe the Buddha's "power of merit" (Skt. *puṇyabala*). T. 135, 2: 859a2–22 sees fit to add a listing of the Buddha's ten powers (*daśabala*) which have nothing to do with the story of the boulder.
45. T. 125, 2: 750b13–16 (Fr. trans. in Bareau, "La fin de la vie," 19).
46. T. 125, 2: 751a12 (Fr. trans. in Bareau, "La fin de la vie," 22).

Bibliography

Abbott, H. Porter. *The Cambridge Introduction to Narrative*. Third Edition. Cambridge: Cambridge University Press, 2021.

Abhayagunawardana, H. V., ed. *Chakesadhātuvaṃsa*. Colombo: S. Godage and Bros., 1993.

Agrawal, Prithivi K. "The Depiction of Māra in Early Buddhist Art." In *Function and Meaning in Buddhist Art: Proceedings of a Seminar Held at Leiden University, 21–24 October 1991*, edited by K.R. van Kooij and H. van der Veere, 125–134. Groningen: Egbert Forsten, 1995.

Alter, Robert. *The Art of Biblical Narrative: Revised and Updated*. New York: Basic Books, 2011.

Ambedkar, B. R. *The Buddha and his Dhamma: A Critical Edition*, edited by Akash Singh Rathore and Ajay Verma. New Delhi: Oxford University Press, 2011.

An, Yang-Gyu, trans. *The Buddha's Last Days: Buddhaghosa's Commentary on the Mahāparinibbāna Sutta*. Oxford: The Pali Text Society, 2005.

Anālayo. "Brahmā's Invitation." *Journal of the Oxford Centre of Buddhist Studies* 1 (2011): 12–38.

Anālayo. "Teaching the Abhidharma in the Heaven of the Thirty-three, The Buddha and his Mother." *Journal of the Oxford Centre of Buddhist Studies* 2 (2012): 9–35.

Anālayo. "The Chinese Parallels to the Dhammacakkappavattana-sutta (1)." *Journal of the Oxford Centre of Buddhist Studies* 3 (2012): 12–46.

Anālayo. "The Chinese Parallels to the Dhammacakkappavattana-sutta (2)." *Journal of the Oxford Centre of Buddhist Studies* 5 (2013): 9–41.

Anālayo. "Compassion in the *Āgamas* and *Nikāyas*." *Dharma Drum Journal of Buddhist Studies* 16 (2015): 1–31.

Anguttara Nikāya. 5 vols. Edited by R. Morris and E. Hardy. London: Pali Text Society, 1885-1900.

App, Urs. *Master Yunmen*. New York: Kodansha, 1994.

Apple, James. "Atiśa's Open Basket of Jewels: A Middle Way Vision in Late Phase Indian Vajrayāna." *The Indian International Journal of Buddhist Studies* 11 (2010): 134–176.

Appleton, Naomi. *Jātaka Stories in Theravāda Buddhism: Narrating the Bodhisatta Path*. Farnham: Ashgate, 2010.

Appleton, Naomi. "The Buddha as Storyteller: The Dialogical Setting of Jātaka Stories." In *Dialogue in Early South Asian Religions: Hindu, Buddhist, and Jain Traditions*, edited by Laurie Patton and Brian Black, 99–112. Farnham: Ashgate, 2015.

Appleton, Naomi, trans. *Many Buddhas, One Buddha: A Study and Translation of Avadānaśataka 1–40*. Sheffield: Equinox, 2020.

Appleton, Naomi. "The Story of the Path: Indian *Jātaka* Literature and the Way to Buddhahood." In *Mārga: Paths to Liberation in South Asian Buddhist Traditions*, edited by C. Pecchia and V. Eltschinger, 79–98. Vienna: Austrian Academy of Sciences Press, 2020.

Appleton Naomi, ed. *Narrative Visions and Visual Narratives in Indian Buddhism*. Sheffield: Equinox Publishing, 2022.

Appleton, Naomi, and Sarah Shaw, trans. *The Ten Great Birth Stories of the Buddha: The Mahānipāta of the Jātakatthavaṇṇanā*. Chiang Mai: Silkworm Press, 2015.

Arunasiri, K. "Relics." In *Encyclopaedia of Buddhism*, vol. VII, fasc. 3, ed. W.G. Weeraratne, 533–539. Colombo: Department of Buddhist Affairs, 2005.

Avadānakalpalatā of Kṣemendra. Edited by P. L. Vaidya. 2 vols. Darbhanga: Mithila Institute, 1959.

Avadānaśataka. Edited by J. S. Speyer. *Avadānaśataka: A Century of Edifying Tales Belonging to the Hīnayāna*. 2 vols. Bibliotheca Buddhica 3. St. Petersbourg: Commissionnaires de l'Académie Impériale des Sciences, 1902–1909.

Baker, Chris, and Pasuk Phongpaichit. *From the Fifty Jātaka: Selections from the Thai Paññāsa Jātaka*. Bangkok: Silkworm, 2019.

Baocheng, Bo Wang, and Chinese Rare Book Collection. *Shi Shi Yuan Liu Ying Hua Shi Ji: Si Juan*, at https://www.loc.gov/item/2012402109/.

Bareau, André. *Recherches sur la biographie du Buddha dans les Sūtrapiṭaka et les Vinayapiṭaka anciens: De la quête de l'éveil à la conversion de Śāriputra et de Maudgalyāyana*. Paris: École Française d'Extrême-Orient, 1963.

Bareau, André. "Le Dīpaṃkarajātaka des Dharmaguptaka." In *Mélanges de Sinologie offerts à Monsieur Paul Demiéville*, vol. 1, 1–16. Paris: Presses universitaires de France, 1966.

Bareau, André. "The Superhuman Personality of Buddha and its Symbolism in the Mahāparinirvāṇasūtra of the Dharmaguptaka." In *Myths and Symbols: Studies in Honor of Mircea Eliade*, edited by Joseph Kitagawa and Charles Long, 9–21. Chicago: University of Chicago Press, 1969.

Bareau, André. "Un personnage bien mysterieux: L'épouse du Buddha." In *Indological and Buddhist Studies, Volume in Honour of Professor J. W. de Jong on his Sixtieth Birthday*, edited by L. A. Hercus et al., 31–59. Canberra: Australian National University, 1982.

Bareau, André. "La fin de la vie du Buddha selon l'*Ekottara-āgama*." In *Hinduismus und Buddhismus: Festschrift für Ulrich Schneider*, edited by Harry Falk, 13–37. Freiburg: Hedwig Falk, 1987.

Bays, Gwendolyn, trans. *The Voice of the Buddha: The Beauty of Compassion (Lalitavistara)*. 2 vols. Berkeley, CA: Dharma Publishing, 1983.

Beal, Samuel, trans. *The Romantic Legend of Śākya Buddha: A Translation of the Chinese Version of the Abhiniṣkramaṇasūtra*. Delhi: Motilal Banarsidass, [1875] 1985.

Bechert, Heinz, ed. *When Did the Buddha Live? The Controversy on the Dating of the Historical Buddha*. Delhi: Sri Satguru Publications, 1995.

Behrendt, Kurt A. *The Art of Gandhara in the Metropolitan Museum of Art*. New Haven, CT: Yale University Press, 2007.

Berger, John. *Ways of Seeing*. New York: Penguin Books, 1991.

Berkwitz, Stephen C. *The History of the Buddha's Relic Shrine: A Translation of the* Sinhala Thūpavaṃsa. New York: Oxford University Press, 2007.

Berkwitz, Stephen C. "Narratives of Buddhist Relics and Images." In *Oxford Research Encyclopedia of Religion*, edited by John Barton. New York: Oxford University Press, 2019.

Berkwitz, Stephen C. "Vaṃsa: History and Lineage in the Theravāda." In *Routledge Handbook of Theravāda Buddhism*, edited by Stephen C. Berkwitz and Ashley Thompson, 243–256. London: Routledge, 2022.

Bhikkhu Bodhi, trans. *The Connected Discourses of the Buddha: A New Translation of the Saṃyutta Nikāya*, 2 vols. Somerville: Wisdom, 2000.

Bhikkhu Bodhi, trans. *The Numerical Discourses of the Buddha: A Translation of the Aṅguttara Nikāya*. Boston: Wisdom, 2012.

Bhikkhu Bodhi, trans. *The Suttanipāta: An Ancient Collection of the Buddha's Discourses Together with Its Commentaries*. Boston: Wisdom, 2017.

Bhikkhu Ñāṇamoli. *The Life of the Buddha According to the Pāli Canon*. Kandy: Buddhist Publication Society, 1991.

Bhikkhu Ñāṇamoli and Bhikkhu Bodhi, trans. *The Middle Length Discourses of the Buddha: A New Translation of the Majjhima Nikāya*. Boston: Wisdom, 1995.

Bigandet, P. *Vie Ou Légende De Gaudama: Le Bouddha Des Birmans*. Paris, 1878.

Bloss, Lowell W. "The Buddha and the Nāga: A Study in Buddhist Folk Religiosity." *History of Religions* 13, no. 1 (1973): 36–53.

Blum, Mark, trans. *The Nirvana Sūtra*, vol. I. Berkeley, CA: Bukkho Dendo Kyokai America, 2013.

Bodner, Carolina. "Depictions of the Narrative of the Buddha Dipankara and the Hermit Sumedha in the Art of Burma/Myanmar." MA thesis, Northern Illinois University, 2009.

Bopearachchi, Osmund. *Seven Weeks after the Buddha's Enlightenment: Contradictions in Text, Confusions in Art*. New Delhi: Manohar Publishers & Distributors, 2016.

Boucher, Daniel. "The Pratītyasamutpādagāthā and Its Role in the Medieval Cult of the Relics." *The Journal of the International Association of Buddhist Studies* 14, no. 1 (1991): 1–27.

Brown, Robert L. "Narrative as Icon: The *Jātaka* Stories in Ancient Indian and Southeast Asian Architecture." In *Sacred Biography in the Buddhist Traditions of South and Southeast Asia*, edited by Juliane Schober, 64–109. Honolulu: University of Hawai'i Press, 1997.

Buddhadatta, A. P., ed. *The Mahāvaṃsa: Pali Text Together with Some Later Additions*. Colombo: M. D. Gunasena & Co., 1959.

Burlingame, Eugene W., trans. *Buddhist Legends: Translated from the original Pali text of the Dhammapada Commentary Part 3*. Harvard Oriental Series, vol. 30. Cambridge, MA: Harvard University Press, 1921.

Buswell, Jr., Robert E., and Donald S. Lopez, Jr., eds. *The Princeton Dictionary of Buddhism*. Princeton, NJ: Princeton University Press, 2013.

Byron, Thomas. *The Dhammapada*. Pocket edition Boston: Shambhala 1993.

Cowell, E. B. "The Buddhacarita of Asvaghosa." In *Buddhist Mahāyāna Texts*, edited by F. Max Müller, 1–201. Delhi: Motilal Banarsidass, 1968.

Chakravarti, Uma. "Of Dasas and Karmakaras: Servile Labour in Ancient India." In *Chains of Servitude: Bondage and Slavery in India*, edited by Utsa Patnaik and Manjari Dingwaney, 35–75. Madras: Sangam Books, 1985.

Chögyel, Tenzin. *The Life of the Buddha*. Translated by Kurtis Schaeffer. New York: Penguin, 2015.

Cleary, Thomas, trans. *Entry into the Realm of Reality. The Text. A Translation of the Gandavyuha, the Final Book of the Avatamsaka Sutra*. Boston: Shambhala, 1989.

Collins, Steven. *Nirvana: Concept, Imagery, Narrative*. Cambridge: Cambridge University Press, 2010.

Collins, Steven, ed. *Readings of the Vessantara Jātaka*. New York: Columbia University Press, 2016.

Collins, Steven. *Wisdom as a Way of Life: Theravāda Buddhism Reimagined*. New York: Columbia University Press, 2020.

Comstock, Gary. "The Truth of Religious Narratives." *International Journal for Philosophy of Religion* 34.3 (1993): 131–150.

Cowell, E. B. ed.; Chalmers, Robert, W. H. D. Rouse, H. T. Francis, R. A. Neil, and E. B. Cowell, trans. *The Jātaka or Stories of the Buddha's Former Births*. 6 vols. Cambridge: Cambridge University Press, 1895–1907.

Cunningham, Alexander. *The Stûpa of Bharhut: A Buddhist Monument Ornamented With Numerous Sculptures Illustrative of Buddhist Legend and History in the Third Century B.C.* London: W. H. Allen and Co, 1879.

Das Gupta, Kabita. *Dharmaruci-avadāna*. Unpublished transliteration from Gilgit Manuscripts, 1984.

Davidson, Ronald M. *Indian Esoteric Buddhism: A Social History of the Tantric Movement*. New York: Columbia Uniersity Press, 2002.

Davidson, Ronald M. "Studies in Dhārāni Literature IV: A Nāga Altar in 5th Century India." In *Consecration Rituals in South Asia*, edited by István Keul, 123–170. Leiden: Brill, 2017.

Davis, Donald R., Jr. "Slaves and Slavery in the *Smṛticandrikā*." *The Indian Economic and Social History Review* 57, no. 3 (2020): 299–326.

Dehejia, Vidya. "On Modes of Visual Narration in Early Buddhist Art." *The Art Bulletin* 72, no. 3 (1990): 374–392.

Dehejia, Vidya. "Aniconism and the Multivalence of Emblems." *Ars Orientalis* 21 (1991): 45–66.

Dehejia, Vidya. *Discourse in Early Buddhist Art: Visual Narratives of India*. New Delhi: Munshiram Manoharlal Publishers, 1997.

Dehejia, Vidya. *Indian Art*. London: Phaidon Press, 1997.

Dessein, Bart. "The First Turning of the Wheel of the Doctrine: Sarvāstivāda and Mahāsāṃghika Controversy." In *The Spread of Buddhism*, edited by A. Heirman et al., 15–48. Leiden: Brill, 2007.

Dharmachakra Translation Committee. *The Play in Full (Lalitavistara)*. 84000: Translating the Words of the Buddha, n.d.

Dharmachakra Translation Committee. *The Sūtra of the Wheel of Dharma: Dharmacakrasūtra*. 84000: Translating the Words of the Buddha, 2018.

Dīgha Nikāya, 3 vols. Edited by J. Estlin Carpenter. London: Pali Text Society, 1911.

Divyāvadāna. Edited by E. B. Cowell and R. A. Neil. Cambridge: Cambridge University Press, 1886.

"Donavan in Concert: There is a Mountain." https://www.youtube.com/watch?v=lkLp9d7HKuA.

Dorjee, Pema. *Stupa and Its Technology: A Tibeto-Buddhist Perspective*. Delhi: Indira Gandhi National Centre for the Arts and Motilal Banarsidass, 1996.

Drewes, David. "The Problem of Becoming a Bodhisattva and the Emergence of the Mahāyāna." *History of Religions* 61, no. 2 (2021): 145–172.

Faure, Bernard. *Les mille et une vies du bouddha*. Paris, Seuil, 2018.

Fausbøll, V., ed. *The Jātaka Together with Its Commentary, Being Tales of the Anterior Births of Gotama Buddha*. 6 vols. and index. London: Trübner, 1875-97.

Feer, Léon, trans. *Avadana-Çataka: Cent légendes (bouddhiques)*. Annales du Musée Guimet 18. Paris: E. Leroux, 1891.

Finnegan, Damchö Diana. "'For the Sake of Women, Too': Ethics and Gender in the Narratives of the *Mūlasarvāstivāda Vinaya*." PhD dissertation, University of Wisconsin, 2009.

Fiordalis, David V. "Miracles in Indian Buddhist Narratives and Doctrine." *Journal of the International Association of Buddhist Studies* 33, nos. 1–2 (2011): 381–408.

Fiordalis, David V. "The Buddha's Great Miracle at Śrāvastī: A Translation from the Tibetan *Mūlasarvāstivāda-Vinaya*." *Asian Literature and Translation* 2, no. 3 (2014): 1–33.

Fiordalis, David V. "The Buddha's Great Miracle, a Flowering Sprig from Kṣemendra's *Wish-Fulfilling Vine of Tales of the Bodhisattva* (*Bodhisattvāvadānakalpalatā*): English Translation with Editions of the Sanskrit Text and Tibetan Translation." *Korea Journal of Buddhist Studies* 67 (2021): 45–121.

Fiordalis, David V. "Buddhas and Body Language: The Literary Trope of the Buddha's Smile." In *The Language of the Sūtras*, edited by Natalie Gummer, 59–103. Berkeley: Mangalam Press, 2021.

Fiordalis, David V. "The Buddha as Spiritual Sovereign." In *Narrative Visions and Visual Narratives in Indian Buddhism*, edited by Naomi Appleton, 213–237. Sheffield: Equinox, 2022.

Formigatti, Camillo A. "Walking the Deckle Edge: Scribe or Author? Jayamuni and the Creation of the Nepalese *Avadānamālā* Literature." *Buddhist Studies Review* 33, nos. 1–2 (2016): 101–140.

Frye, Stanley, trans. *Sutra of the Wise and the Foolish*. Dharamsala: Library of Tibetan Works and Archives, 1981.

Geertz, Clifford. "Religion as a Cultural System." In *Interpretation of Cultures: Selected Essays*, 87–125. New York: Basic Books, 1973.

Geiger, Wilhelm, ed. and trans. *The Mahāvaṃsa: Or the Great Chronicle of Ceylon*. Oxford: Pali Text Society, [1912] 2001.

Gethin, Rupert. *Sayings of the Buddha*. Oxford: Oxford University Press, 2008.

Gnoli, Raniero, ed. *The Gilgit Manuscript of the Saṅghabhedavastu, Being the 17th and Last Section of the Vinaya of the Mūlasarvāstivādin*. Serie Orientale Roma, vol. XLIX, 1. Rome: Istituto per il Medio ed Estremo Oriente, 1977.

Gómez, Luis. *The Land of Bliss, the Paradise of the Buddha of Measureless Light: Sanskrit and Chinese Versions of the Sukhāvatīvyūha Sutras*. Honolulu: University of Hawai'i Press, 1996.

Gómez, Luis. "Buddhism as a Religion of Hope: Observations on the 'Logic' of a Doctrine and its Foundational Myth." *The Eastern Buddhist, New Series* 32, no. 1 (2000): 1–21.

Gómez, Luis. "On Reading Literature Literally: Concrete Image Before Doctrine." In *Special International Symposium on Pure Land Buddhism*, 5–30. Kyoto: Otani University, BARC Research Center for Buddhist Cultures in Asia, International Symposium Series 1, 2011.

Granoff, Phyllis. "The Ambiguity of Miracles: Buddhist Understandings of Supernatural Power." *East and West* 46 (1996): 79–96.

Gummer, Natalie. "Sacrificial Sūtras: Mahāyāna Literature and the South Asian Ritual Cosmos." *Journal of the American Academy of Religion* 82, no. 4 (2014): 1091–1126.

Gummer, Natalie. "Speech Acts of the Buddha: Sovereign Ritual and the Poetics of Power in Mahāyāna Sūtras." *History of Religions* 61, no. 2 (2021): 173–211.

Guthrie, Elizabeth. "A Study of the History and Cult of the Buddhist Earth Deity in Mainland Southeast Asia." Dept. of Philosophy & Religious Studies, University of Canterbury, 2004.

Hallisey, Charles, and Anne Hansen. "Narrative, Sub-Ethics, and the Moral Life: Some Evidence from Theravāda Buddhism." *Journal of Religious Ethics* 24, no. 2 (1996): 305–327.

Hallisey, Charles. "Learning from Luis Gómez as a Reader of Buddhist Sūtras," in *The Language of the Sūtras*, edited by Natalie Gummer, vii–xx. Berkeley, CA: Mangalam Press, 2021.

Hanneder, Jürgen. "The Blue Lotus: Oriental Research between Philology, Botany and Poetics?" *Zeitschrift der Deutschen Morgenländischen Gesellschaft* 152 (2002): 295–308.

Hanneder, Jürgen. "Some Common Errors Concerning Water-Lilies and Lotuses." *Indo-Iranian Journal* 50 (2007): 161–164.

Hara, Minoru. "A Note on the Buddha's Birth Story." In *Indianisme et bouddhisme: mélanges offerts à Mgr Étienne Lamotte,* 143–157. Louvain-la-Neuve: Université Catholique de Louvain, Institut Orientaliste, 1980.

He, Xi. "Fo Benxing Jing: A Comparative Study." Unpublished paper presented to the XVIIIth Congress of the International Association of Buddhist Studies, Toronto, August 24, 2017.

Hecker, Hellmuth. "Mahākassapa: Father of the Sangha." *Great Disciples of the Buddha*, edited by Bhikkhu Bodhi, 107–136. Kandy: Buddhist Publications Society, 1997.

Heim, Maria. *Theories of the Gift in South Asia: Hindu, Buddhist, and Jain Reflections on Dāna*. New York: Routledge, 2004.

Heim, Maria. *Voice of the Buddha: Buddhaghosa on the Immeasurable Words*. New York: Oxford University Press, 2018.

Heim, Maria. "Careful Attention and the Voice of Another." In *In Dialogue with Classical Indian Traditions*, edited by Brian Black and Chakravarthi Ram-Prasad, 181–196. London: Routledge, 2019.

Horner, I. B., trans. *Buddhavaṃsa Commentary (Madhuratthavilāsinī)*. London: Pali Text Society, 1946.

Horner, I. B., trans. *The Book of the Discipline*. 6 vols. London: Pali Text Society, 1938–1952.

Horner, I. B., trans. *The Minor Anthologies of the Pali Canon, Part III: Basket of Conduct (Cariyāpiṭāka)*. London: Pali Text Society, 1975.

Horner, I. B., trans. *The Clarifier of the Sweet Meaning (Madhuratthavilāsinī), Commentary on the Chronicle of Buddhas (Buddhavaṃsa) by Buddhadatta Thera*. London: Pali Text Society, 1978.

Huntington, John. "Sowing the Seeds of the Lotus: A Journey to the Great Pilgrimage Sites of Buddhism, Part I." *Orientations* 16.11 (1985): 46–61.

Huntington, John. "Pilgrimage as Image: The Cult of the Astamahapratihariya, Part 1." *Orientations* 18, no. 4 (1987): 55–63.

Huntington, John. "Pilgrimage as Image: The Cult of the Aṣtamahapratihariya, Part 2." *Orientations* 18, no. 8 (1987): 56–68.

Huntington, S.L. "Early Buddhist Art and the Theory of Aniconism." *Art Journal* 49, no. 4 (1990): 401–408.

Ichimura, Shohei, trans. *The Canonical Book of the Buddha's Lengthy Discourses*, vol. I. Berkeley, CA: Bukkyo Dendo Kyokai America, 2015.

Jaini, Padmanabh S. "The Story of Sudhana and Manoharā: An Analysis of the Texts and the Borobudur Reliefs." *Bulletin of the School of Oriental and African Studies, University of London* 29.3 (1966), 533–558.

Jaini, Padmanabh S. "Buddha's Prolongation of Life." In *Collected Papers on Buddhist Studies*, edited by Padmanabh Jaini, 191–199. Delhi: Motilal Banarsidass, 2001.

Jamison, Stephanie. *Sacrificed Wife/Sacrificer's Wife: Women, Ritual, and Hospitality in Ancient India*. New York: Oxford University Press, 1996.

Jamison, Stephanie. "Women 'Between the Empires' and 'Between the Lines.'" In *Between the Empires: Society in India 300 BCE to 400 CE*, edited by Patrick Olivelle, 191–214. New York: Oxford University Press, 2006.

Jātaka Together with Its Commentary. 6 vols. Edited by Viggo Fausböll. London: Pali Text Society, 1877–1896.

Jayawickrama, N. A., trans. and ed. *The Chronicle of the Thūpa and the Thūpavaṃsa: Being a Translation and Edition of Vācissaratthera's Thūpavaṃsa*. London: Luzac & Company, 1971.

Jayawickrama, N. A., trans. *The Story of Gotama Buddha (Jātaka-Nidāna)*. Oxford: Pali Text Society, 1990.

Johnston, E. H., ed. and trans. *The Buddhacarita or Acts of the Buddha, by Aśvaghoṣa*. New enlarged ed. Delhi: Motilal Banarsidass, 1984. Orig. pub. 1936.

Jones, Dhivan Thomas. "Why Did Brahmā Ask the Buddha to Teach?" *Buddhist Studies Review* 26, no. 1 (2009): 85–102.

Jones, J. J. *The Mahāvastu: Translated from the Buddhist Sanskrit*. 3 vols. London: Pali Text Society, 1949–1956.

Jongeward, David, Timothy Lenz, with Jessie Pons. "The Buddha's Previous Births: Gandhāran Stories in Birchbark and Stone." Unpublished Manuscript, n.d.

Jordan, Mark D. "Missing Scenes." *Harvard Divinity Bulletin* (Summer/Autumn 2010).

Jyväsjärvi, Mari Johanna. "Fragile Virtue: Women's Monastic Practice in Early Medieval India." PhD dissertation, Harvard University, 2011.

Kariyawasam, A.G.S. "Dasabala." In *Encyclopaedia of Buddhism*, edited by Jotiya Dhirasekera, vol. 4, fasc. 2, 314–318. Colombo: Government of Sri Lanka Press, 1984.

Khoroche, Peter, trans. *Once the Buddha Was a Monkey: Ārya Śūra's Jātakamālā*. Chicago: University of Chicago Press, 1989.

Khoroche, Peter, trans. *Once a Peacock, Once an Actress: Twenty-Four Lives of the Bodhisattva from Haribhaṭṭa's Jātakamālā*. Chicago: University of Chicago Press, 2017.

Kim, Jinah. "Iconography and Text: The Visual Narrative of the Buddhist Book-Cult in the Manuscript of the Ashṭasāhasrikā Prajñāpāramitā Sūtra." In *Kalādarpaṇa: The Mirror of Indian Art*, edited by Devangana Desai Arundhati Banerji, 255–272. New Delhi: Aryan Books International, 2008.

Kim, Jinah. *Receptacle of the Sacred: Illustrated Manuscripts and the Buddhist Book-Cult in South Asia*. Berkeley, CA: University of California Press, 2013.

Kim, Minku. "Where the Blessed One Paced Mindfully: The Issue of Caṅkrama on Mathurā's Earliest Freestanding Images of the Buddha." *Archives of Asian Art* 69, no. 2 (2019): 181–216.

Kinnard, Jacob N. "Māra." In *Encyclopedia of Buddhism*, edited by Robert E. Buswell, 512–513. New York: Macmillan, 2004.

Kloppenborg, Ria, trans. *The Sūtra on the Foundation of the Buddhist Order*. Leiden: Brill, 1973.

Konczak, Ines. "Praṇidhi-Darstellungen an der Nördlichen Seidenstraße: Das Bildmotiv der Prophezeiung der Buddhaschaft Śākyamunis in den Malereien Xinjiangs." PhD Dissertation, Ludwig-Maximilians-Universität, 2014.

Kritzer, Robert. "Life in the Womb: Conception and Gestation in Buddhist Scripture and Classical Indian Medical Literature." In *Imagining the Fetus: The Unborn in Myth, Religion, and Culture*, edited by Vanessa R. Sasson and Jane Marie Law, 73–89. American Academy of Religion Cultural Criticism Series. Oxford: Oxford University Press, 2009.

Kudo, Noriyuki, ed. *Gilgit Manuscripts in the National Archives of India Facsimile Edition, vol. 3: Avadānas and Miscellaneous Texts*. New Delhi: National Archives of India and Tokyo: The International Research Institute for Advanced Buddhology, Soka University, 2017.

Lamotte, Étienne. "Vajrapāṇi en Inde." *Mélanges de Sinologie offerts à Monsieur Paul Demiéville*, 113–159. Paris: Presses Universitaires de France, 1966.

Langenberg, Amy Paris. *Birth in Buddhism: The Suffering Fetus and Female Freedom*. London: Routledge Press, 2017.

Legge, James. *A Record of Buddhistic Kingdoms*. New York: Paragon, [1886] 1965.

Leoshko, Janice. "About Looking at Buddha Images in Eastern India." *Archives of Asian Art* 52, no. 1 (2001): 63–82.

Leoshko, Janice. "Scenes of the Buddha's Life in Pala Period Art." *Silk Road Art and Archaeology* 3 (1993–1994): 251–276.

Leoshko, Janice. "Time and Time Again: Finding Perspective for Bodhgayā Buddha Imagery." *Ars Orientalis* 50 (2021): 6–32.

Leoshko, Janice. "Tracing Buddhist Devotion in South Asia." *Orientations (Hong Kong)* 41, no. 2 (2010): 89–94.

Lesbre, Emmanuelle. "Une vie illustrée du Buddha (*Shishi yuanliu*, 1425), modèle pour les peintures murales d'un monastère du XVe s. (Jueyuan si, Sichuan)." *Arts Asiatiques* 57 (2002): 69–101.

Lewis, Todd T. "Contributions to the Study of Popular Buddhism: The Newar Buddhist Festival of Gumla Dharma." *The Journal of the International Association of Buddhist Studies* 16, no. 2 (1993): 309.

Lewis, Todd T., and Subarna Man Tuladhar, eds. *The Epic of the Buddha: His Life and Teachings by Chittadar Hridaya*. Boulder, CO: Shambhala, 2019.

Li, Rongxi, trans. *The Great Tang Dynasty Record of the Western Regions*. Berkeley, CA: Numata Center, 1996.

Mahāvastu. 3 vols. Edited by Emile Sénart. Paris: Imprimerie Nationale, 1882–1897.

Malalasekera, G. P. *Dictionary of Pāli Proper Names*, 3 vols (1937, reprint). New Delhi: Munshiram Manoharlal Publishers, 1995.

Mānava-Dharmaśāstra. Manu's Code of Law: A Critical Edition and Translation of the Mānava-Dharmaśāstra, edited and translated by Patrick Olivelle. New York: Oxford University Press, 2005.

Marshall, Sir John. *A Guide to Sanchi*. Calcutta: Superintendent, Government Printing, 1918.

Masefield, Peter, trans. *The Udāna Commentary by Dhammapāla*, vol. II. Oxford: The Pali Text Society, 2003.

Masefield, Peter, and Revire, Nicolas, "On the Buddha's 'Kammic Fluff': The Last Meal Revisited." *Journal of the Oxford Centre for Buddhist Studies* 20 (2021): 51–82.

Matsumura, Junko. "The Sumedhakathā in Pāli Literature and Its Relation to the Northern Buddhist Textual Tradition." *Journal of the International College for Postgraduate Buddhist Studies* 14 (2010): 101–133.

Matsumura, Junko. "The Story of the Dīpaṃkara Prophecy in Northern Buddhist Texts: An Attempt at Classification." *Journal of Indian and Buddhist Studies* (*Indogaku bukkyōggaku kenkyū*) 59, no. 3 (2011): 1137–1146.

Matsumura, Junko. "An Independent Sūtra on the Dīpaṃkara Prophecy: Tibetan Text and English Translation of the *Ārya-Dīpaṃkara-vyākaraṇa nāma Mahāyānasūtra*." *Journal of the International College for Postgraduate Buddhist Studies* 15 (2011): 81–141.

Matsumura, Junko. "The Formation and Development of the Dīpaṃkara Prophecy Story: The *Ārya-Dīpaṃkaravyākaraṇa-nāma-mahāyānasūtra* and its Relation to Other Versions." *Journal of Indian and Buddhist Studies* (*Indogaku bukkyōggaku kenkyū*) 60, no. 3 (2012): 1204–1213.

Morrison, Toni. "The Dancing Mind," National Book Award Acceptance Speech. 1996. https://www.nationalbook.org/tag/the-dancing-mind/

Murnane, Gerald. *Last Letter to a Reader*. New York: And Other Stories, 2021.

McClintock, Sara. "Ethical Reading and the Ethics of Forgetting and Remembering." In *A Mirror is for Reflection: Understanding Buddhist Ethics*, edited by Jake H. Davis, 185–202. New York: Oxford University Press, 2017.

Nakamura, Hajime. *Gotama Buddha: A Biography Based on the Most Reliable Texts*. Volume 1. Tokyo: Kosei, 2000.

Nāradasmṛti. Edited and translated by Richard W. Lariviere. Philadelphia: University of Pennsylvania, 1989.

Nasim Khan, M. *The Sacred and the Secular: Investigating the Unique Stūpa and Settlement Site of Aziz Dheri, Peshawar Valley, Khyber Pakhtunkhwa, Pakistan*. 3 vols. Peshawar: M. Nasim Khan, 2010.

Nasim Khan, M. and M. A. Durrani. "Playing with Rings—Siddhārtha and Yaśodharā: A Relief Panel from Aziz Dheri Revisited." *Ancient Pakistan* 21 (2021), 35–47.

Nattier, Jan. "Dīpaṃkara." In *Encyclopedia of Buddhism*, edited by R. E. Buswell, vol. 1, 230. New York: Macmillan, 2004.

Neelis, Jason. "Making Places for Buddhism in Gandhāra: Stories of Previous Births in Image and Text." In *The Geography of Gandhāran Art*, edited by Wannaporn Rienjang and Peter Stewart, 175–185. Proceedings of the Second International Workshop of the Gandhāra Connections Project, University of Oxford, 22nd–23rd March, 2018. Oxford: Archaeopress Publishing, 2019.

Neelis, Jason. "Aspiring Narratives of Previous Births in Written and Visual Media from Ancient Gandhāra." *Postscripts* 10 (2019): 103–121.

Nichols, Michael D. *Malleable Māra: Transformations of a Buddhist Symbol of Evil*. Albany: State University of New York, 2019.

Norman, H. C. "Gandhakuṭī—The Buddha's Private Abode." *Journal of the Asiatic Society of Bengal* 2 (1908): 1–5.

Notton, Camille, trans. *P'ra Buddha Sihiṅga*. Bangkok: Bangkok Time, 1933.

Obermiller, Ernst, trans. *History of Buddhism (Chos-hbyung) by Bu-ston*. Heidelberg: Harrassowitz, 1931.

Obeyesekere, Gananath. "The Goddess Pattini and the Lord Buddha: Notes on the Myth of the Birth of the Deity." *Social Compass* 20, no. 2 (1973): 217–229.

Obeyesekere, Gananath. *Medusa's Hair: An Essay on Personal Symbols and Religious Experience*. Chicago: University of Chicago Press, 1981.

Ohnuma, Reiko. *Ties That Bind: Maternal Imagery and Discourse in Indian Buddhism*. Oxford: Oxford University Press, 2012.

Ohnuma, Reiko. *Head, Eyes, Flesh, and Blood: Giving Away the Body in Indian Buddhist Literature*. New York: Columbia University Press, 2007.

Olivelle, Patrick. *The Āśrama System: The History and Hermeneutics of a Religious Institution*. New York: Oxford University Press, 1993.

Olivelle, Patrick. "Ascetic Withdrawal or Social Engagement." In *Religions of India in Practice*, edited by Donald Lopez, 533–546. Princeton, NJ: Princeton University Press, 1995.

Olivelle, Patrick. "Hair and Society: Social Significance of Hair in South Asian Traditions." In *Hair: Its Power and Meaning in Asian Cultures*, edited by Alf Hiltebeitel and Barbara D. Miller, 11–49. New York: State University of New York Press, 1998.

Olivelle, Patrick, trans. *Life of the Buddha by Aśvaghoṣa*. Clay Sanskrit Library. New York: New York University Press and JJC Foundation, 2008.

Pakhoutova, Elena A. "Reproducing the Sacred Places: The Eight Great Events of the Buddha's Life and Their Commemorative Stūpas in the Medieval Art of Tibet (10th–13th Century)." ProQuest Dissertations Publishing, 2009.

Péri, N. "Les femmes de Cākya-muni," *Bulletin de l'École française d'Extrême Orient* 18, no. 2 (1918): 1–37.

Powers, John. *A Bull of a Man: Images of Masculinity, Sex, and the Body in Indian Buddhism*. Cambridge, MA: Harvard University Press, 2009.

Pollock, Sheldon. "How We Read." In *Sensitive Reading: The Pleasures of Reading South Asian Literature in Translation*, edited by Yigal Bronner and Charles Hallisey, 44–51. Oakland: University of California Press, 2022.

Pranke, Patrick Arthur. "The 'Treatise on the Lineage of Elders' (*Vaṃsadīpanī*): Monastic Reform and the Writing of Buddhist History in Eighteenth-Century Burma." Ph.D. Dissertation, University of Michigan, 2004.

Radich, Michael. "Embodiments of the Buddha in Sarvâstivāda Doctrine: With Special Reference to the **Mahāvibhāṣā*." *Annual Report of the International Research Institute for Advanced Buddhology at Soka University* 13 (2010): 121–172.

Radich, Michael. *The Mahāparinirvāṇa-mahāsūtra and the Emergence of Tathāgatagarbha Dotrine*. Hamburg Buddhist Studies, No. 5. Hamburg: Hamburg University Press, 2015.

Ramanujan, A. K. "Three Hundred Rāmāyaṇas: Five Examples and Three Thoughts on Translation." In *Many Rāmāyaṇas: The Diversity of a Narrative Tradition in South Asia*, edited by Paula Richman, 22–49. Berkeley: University of California Press, 1991.

Rank, Otto. *The Myth of the Birth of the Hero: A Psychological Interpretation of Mythology*. Translated by F. Robins and S. E. Jelliffe. New York: Johnson Reprint Incorporation, [1914] 1970.

Raymond, Catherine. "The Seven Weeks: A 19th-Century Burmese Palm-Leaf Manuscript." *The Journal of Burma Studies* 14, no. 1 (2010): 255–267.

Regan, Julie. "Pleasure and Poetics as Tools for Transformation in Aśvaghoṣa's Mahākāvya." *Religions* 13 (2022): 578.

Reynolds, Frank E. "The Many Lives of the Buddha." In *The Biographical Process: Studies in the History and Psychology of Religion*, edited by Frank E. Reynolds and Donald Capps, 37–61. The Hague: Mouton, 1976.

Reynolds, Frank E. "Rebirth Traditions and the Lineages of Gotama: A Study in Theravāda Buddhology." In *Sacred Biography in the Buddhist Traditions of South and Southeast Asia*, edited by Juliane Schober, 19–39. Honolulu: University of Hawai'i Press, 1997.

Rhi, Ju-hyung. "Gandhāran Images of the 'Śrāvastī Miracle': an Iconographic Reassessment." PhD dissertation: University of California Berkeley, 1991.

Rhie Mace, Sonya. "Localizing Narrative Through Image: The Nun Utpalavarṇā in a Stone Relief from Kaushambi." In *Narrative Visions and Visual Narratives in Indian Buddhism*, ed. Naomi Appleton, 129–159. Sheffield, UK: Equinox, 2022.

Rhys Davids, C. A. F., ed. *The Visuddhi-Magga of Buddhaghosa*. 2 vols. London: Pali Text Society, 1920–1921.

Rhys Davids, T. W., and Hermann Oldenberg, trans. *Vinaya Texts, Part I*. Sacred Books of the East, Vol. 13. London: Oxford University Press, 1885.

Rhys Davids, T. W., and William Stede, eds. *The Dīgha Nikāya*. 3 vols. London: Pali Text Society, 1890-1911.

Rocher, Ludo. "In Defense of Jimutavahana." *Journal of the American Oriental Society* 96, no. 1 (1976): 107–109.

Rockhill, W. Woodville. *The Life of the Buddha and the Early History of His Order*. London: Kegan Paul, Trench, Trübner & Co., 1976.

Rotman, Andy. *Divine Stories: Translations from the Divyāvadāna, part 1*. Classics of Indian Buddhism Series. Boston: Wisdom Publications, 2008.

Rotman, Andy. *Thus Have I Seen: Visualizing Faith in Early Indian Buddhism*. New York: Oxford University Press, 2009.

Rotman, Andy. "The Power of Proximity: Creating and Venerating Shrines in Indian Buddhist Narratives." In *Buddhist Stūpas in South Asia: Recent Archaeological, Art-Historical, and Historical Perspectives*, edited by Jason Hawkes and Akira Shimada, 51–62. Delhi: Oxford University Press, 2009.

Rotman, Andy. *Divine Stories: Translations from the Divyāvadāna, part 2*. Classics of Indian Buddhism Series. Boston: Wisdom Publications, 2017.

Rotman, Andy. *Hungry Ghosts*. Somerville: Wisdom Publications, 2021.

Sasson, Vanessa R. "A Womb with a View: The Buddha's Final Fetal Experience." In *Imagining the Fetus: The Unborn in Myth, Religion, and Culture*, edited by Vanessa R. Sasson and Jane Marie Law, 55–72. American Academy of Religion Cultural Criticism Series. Oxford: Oxford University Press, 2009.

Sasson, Vanessa R. "A Buddhist Love Story: The Buddha and Yaśodharā." *Buddhist Studies Review* 37, no. 1 (2020): 53–72.

Sasson, Vanessa R. "Jeweled Renunciation: Reading the Buddha's Biography." In *Jewels, Jewelry, and Other Shiny Things in the Buddhist Imaginary*, edited by Vanessa R. Sasson, 65–85. Honolulu: University of Hawaiʻi Press, 2021.

Sasson, Vanessa R. *Yasodhara and the Buddha*. London: Bloomsbury Academic, 2021.

Scheible, Kristin. *Reading the Mahāvaṃsa: The Literary Aims of a Theravāda Buddhist History*. New York: Columbia University Press, 2016.

Schopen, Gregory. *Bones, Stones, and Buddhist Monks: Collected Papers on the Archaeology, Epigraphy, and Texts of Monastic Buddhism in India*. Honolulu: University of Hawaiʻi Press, 1997.

Schopen, Gregory. *Buddhist Nuns, Monks, and Other Worldly Matters: Recent Papers on Monastic Buddhism in India*. Honolulu: University of Hawaiʻi Press, 2014.

Schlingloff, Dieter. *Ajanta: Handbuch der Malereien, Handbook of the Paintings*. 3 volumes. Weisbaden: Harrassowitz Verlag, 2000.

Schmidt, Hanns-Peter. *Some Women's Rites and Rights in the Veda*. Poona: Bhandarkar Oriental Research Institute, 1987.

Schmithausen, Lambert. "On some Aspects of Descriptions or Theories of 'Liberating Insight' and 'Enlightenment' in Early Buddhism." In *Studien zum Jainismus und Buddhismus, Gedenkschrift für Ludwig Alsdorf*, edited by K. Bruhn and A Wezler, 199–250. Wiesbaden: Franz Steiner, 1981.

Senart, Émile, ed. *Mahāvastu avadānaṃ. Le Mahāvastu: Texte sanscrit publié pour la première fois et accompagné d'introductions et d'un commentaire*. 3 vols. Paris: Société Asiatique, 1882–1897.

Schaeffer, Kurtis, trans. *Tenzin Chögyal's The Life of the Buddha*. New York: Penguin, 2015.

Sharf, Robert H. "On the Allure of Buddhist Relics." *Representations* 66 (1999): 75–99.

Skilling, Peter. "Relics: The Heart of Buddhist Veneration." In *Relics and Relic Worship in Early Buddhism: India, Afghanistan, Sri Lanka, and Burma*, edited by Janice Stargardt and Michael Willis, 4–17. London: The British Museum, 2018.

Shaw, Sarah. "And that was I: How the Buddha Himself Creates a Path between Biography and Autobiography." In *Lives Lived, Lives Imagined: Biography in the Buddhist Traditions*, edited by Linda Covill, Ulrike Roesler, and Sarah Shaw, 15–47. Boston: Wisdom Publications, 2010.

Shaw, Sarah. "Yaśodharā in *Jātakas*." *Buddhist Studies Review* 35, nos. 1–2 (2018): 261–278.

Shaw, Sarah. *The Art of Listening: A Guide to the Early Teachings of Buddhism*. Boulder: Shambhala, 2021.

Shi Huifeng (Matthew Orsborn). "Chiastic Structure of the *Vessantara Jātaka*: Textual Criticism and Interpretation Through Inverted Parallelism." *Buddhist Studies Review* 32, no. 1 (2015): 143–159.

Shimoda, Masahiro. "Mahāparinirvāṇasūtra." *Brill's Encyclopedia of Buddhism*, vol. I, edited by Jonathan A. Silk, Oskar von Hinüber, and Vincent Eltschinger, 158–170. Leiden: Brill, 2015.

Shinohara, Koichi. "The All-Gathering Mandala Initiation Ceremony in Atikuta's Collected Dharani Scriptures: Reconstructing the Evolution of Esoteric Buddhist Ritual." *Journal Asiatique* 298, no. 2 (2010): 389–420.

Shulman, Eviatar. "Buddha as the Pole of Existence, or the Flower of Cosmos." *History of Religions* 57, no. 2 (2017): 164–196.

Shulman, Eviatar. "Contemplating the Buddha in the *Jātakas*." *Religions of South Asia* 12, no. 1 (2018): 9–33.

Shulman, Eviatar. *Visions of the Buddha: Creative Dimensions of Early Buddhist Scripture*. New York: Oxford University Press, 2021.

Siegel. Lee. *Net of Magic: Wonders and Deceptions in India*. Chicago: University of Chicago Press, 1991.

Simmons, Caleb, ed. "Sovereignty and Religion in India: Negotiating Authority, Rule, and Realm in Premodern South Asia." Special Issue, *Religions* 12 (2021).

Silk, Jonathan. "The Story of Dharmaruci: In the *Divyāvadāna* and Kṣemendra's *Bodhisatt vāvadānakalpalatā*." *Indo-Iranian Journal* 51, no. 2 (2008): 137–185.

Silk, Jonathan. *Riven by Lust: Incest and Schism in Indian Buddhist Legend and Historiography*. Honolulu: University of Hawai'i Press, 2009.

Simpson, Bob. "Impossible Gifts: Bodies, Buddhism and Bioethics in Contemporary Sri Lanka." *The Journal of the Royal Anthropological Institute* 10, no. 4 (2004): 839–859.

Sirisawad, Natchapol. "The *Mahāprātihāryasūtra* in the Gilgit Manuscripts: A Critical Edition, Translation and Textual Analysis." PhD Dissertation: Ludwig-Maximilians University of Munich, 2019.

Skilling, Peter. "Dharma, Dhāraṇī, Abhidharma, Avadāna: What Was Taught in Trayastriṃśa?" *Annual Report of the International Research Institute for Advanced Buddhology at Soka University* 11 (2008): 37–60.

Skilling, Peter. *Questioning the Buddha: A Selection of Twenty-Five Sutras*. Somerville, MA: Wisdom, 2021.

Snellgrove, David L. *Indo-Tibetan Buddhism: Indian Buddhists and Their Tibetan Successors*. New York: Shambhala, 1987.

Stadtner, Donald M. "The Daughters of Māra in the Art of Burma." *Arts of Asia* 45, no. 2 (2015): 93–106.

Stede, William, ed. *The Sumaṅgala-vilāsinī: Buddhaghosa's Commentary on the Dīgha-nikāya, Part II*. London: Luzac and Co, 1931.

Strong, Arthur, ed. *The Mahā-Bodhi-Vaṁsa*. London: Pali Text Society, 1891.

Strong, John S. "'Gandhakuṭī': The Perfumed Chamber of the Buddha." *History of Religions* 16, no. 4 (1977): 390–406.

Strong, John S. "The Buddhist Avadānists and the Elder Upagupta" In *Tantric and Taoist Studies in Honor of R.A. Stein*, edited by Michel Strickmann. 862–881. Mélanges Chinoises et Bouddhiques 22. Brussels: Institut belge des hautes études chinoises, 1985.

Strong, John S. *The Legend of King Aśoka (Aśokāvadāna)*. Princeton, NJ: Princeton University Press, 1989.

Strong, John S. *The Legend and Cult of Upagupta: Sanskrit Buddhism in North India and Southeast Asia*. Princeton, NJ: Princeton University Press, 1992.

Strong, John S. "A Family Quest: The Buddha, Yaśodharā and Rāhula in the Mūlasarvāstivāda Vinaya." In *Sacred Biography in the Buddhist Traditions of South and Southeast Asia*, edited by Juliane Schober, 113–128. Honolulu: University of Hawai'i Press, 1997.

Strong, John S. *The Buddha: A Short Biography*. Oxford: Oneworld, 2001. Reprinted as *The Buddha: A Beginner's Guide*, 2009.

Strong, John S. *The Experience of Buddhism: Sources and Interpretations*. 2nd ed. Belmont, CA: Wadsworth/Thomson Learning, 2002.

Strong, John S. *Relics of the Buddha*. Princeton, NJ: Princeton University Press, 2004.

Strong, John S. "The Triple Ladder at Saṁkāśya: Traditions about the Buddha's Descent from Trāyastriṃśa Heaven." In *From Turfan to Ajanta: Festschrift for Dieter Schlingloff on the occasion of his eightieth birthday*, vol. 2, edited by Eli Franco and Monika Zin, 967–978. Bhairahawa: Lumbini International Research Institute, 2010.

Strong, John S. "The Buddha as Ender and Transformer of Lineages." *Religions of South Asia* 5, nos. 1–2 (2011): 171–188.

Strong, John S. "Explicating the Buddha's Final Illness in the Context of his Other Ailments: the Making and Unmaking of some *Jātaka* Tales." *Buddhist Studies Review* 29, no. 1 (2012): 17–33.

Strong, John S. "The Commingling of Gods and Humans, the Unveiling of the World, and the Descent from Trayastriṃśa Heaven." In *Reimagining Aśoka: Memory and History*, edited by Patrick Olivelle et al., 348–361. New York: Oxford University Press, 2012.

Strong, John S. *Buddhisms: An Introduction*. Oxford: Oneworld, 2015.

Strong, John S. "Buddhist Miracles and the Hagiography of the Buddha." Unpublished paper presented to the XVIIIth Congress of the International Association of Buddhist Studies, Toronto, August 24, 2017.

Strong, John S. *The Buddha's Tooth: Western Tales of a Sri Lankan Relic*. Chicago: University of Chicago Press, 2021.

Strong, John S. "Relics and Images." In *The Oxford Handbook of Buddhist Practice*, ed. Kevin Trainor and Paula Arai, 131–147. Oxford: Oxford University Press, 2022.

Swearer, Donald K. "Hypostasizing the Buddha: Buddha Image Consecration in Northern Thailand." *History Of Religions* 34, no. 3 (1995): 263–280.

Taishō shinshū daizōkyō. 55 vols. Edited by J. Takakusu and K. Watanabe. Tokyo: Taishō Issaikyō Kankōkai, 1924–1929.

Tambiah, Stanley J. "Famous Buddha Images and the Legitimation of Kings: The Case of the Sinhala Buddha (Phra Sihing) in Thailand." *RES: Anthropology and Aesthetics* 4 (1982): 5–19.

Tatelman, Joel, trans. *Heavenly Exploits (Buddhist Biographies from the Dīvyavadāna)*. Clay Sanskrit Library. New York: New York University Press and JJC Foundation, 2005.

Thomas, E. J. *The Life of Buddha as Legend and History*. New York: A.A. Knopf, 1927.

Tournier, Vincent. *La formation du "Mahāvastu" et la mise en place des conceptions relatives à la carrière du "bodhisattva."* Paris: École française d'Extrême-Orient, 2017.

Toyka-Fuong, Ursula. "The Influence of Pāla Art on 11th Century Wall-Paintings of Grotto 76 in Dunhuang." In *The Inner Asian International Style 12th–14th Centuries*, edited by Deborah E. Klimburg-Salter and Eva Allinger, 67–95. Wien: Verlag 1998.

Trainor, Kevin M. *Relics, Ritual, and Representation in Buddhism: Rematerializing the Sri Lankan Theravāda Tradition*. Cambridge: Cambridge University Press, 1997.

Trainor, Kevin M. "When Is a Theft Not a Theft? Relic Theft and the Cult of the Buddha's Relics in Sri Lanka." *Numen* 39, no. 1 (1992): 1–26.

Trenckner, Vilhelm, ed. *The Majjhima Nikāya*. 4 vols. London: Pali Text Society, 1888–1925.

Vaidya, P. L., ed. *Lalitavistara*. Buddhist Sanskrit Texts, No. 1. Darbhanga: Mithila Institute, 1958.

Vaidya, P. L., ed. *Gaṇḍavyūhasūtra*. 2nd ed. Buddhist Sanskrit Texts, vol. 5. Darbhanga, India: Mithila Institute, 2002.

Vajira, Sister and Francis Story, trans. *Last Days of the Buddha: The Mahāparinibbāna Sutta*. Kandy: Buddhist Publication Society, 1998.

van Kooij, Karek R. "Remarks on Festivals and Altars in Early Buddhist Art." In *Function and Meaning in Buddhist Art: Proceedings of a Seminar Held at Leiden University, 21–24 October 1991*, edited by K. R. van Kooij and H. van der Veere, 33–43. Groningen: Egbert Forsten, 1995.

Vedeha Thera. *In Praise of Mount Samanta (Samatakūṭavaṇṇanā)*. Translated by Ann Appleby Hazelwood. London: Pali Text Society, 1986.

Vinaya piṭakam. 5 vols. Edited by Hermann Oldenberg. London: Pali Text Society, 1969–1984.

Waldschmidt, Ernst. *Die Überlieferung vom Lebensende des Buddha: eine vergleichende Analyse des Mahāparinirvāṇasūtra und seiner Textentsprechungen*. 2 vols. Abhandlungen der Akademie der Wissenschaften in Göttingen, Philologish-historische Klasse, nos. 29–30. Göttingen: Vandenhoeck & Ruprecht, 1944–1948.

Waldschmidt, Ernst, ed. *Das Mahāparinirvāṇasūtra*. Berlin: Academie Verlag, 1950–1951.

Waldschmidt, Ernst, ed. "Wunderkräfte des Buddha. Eine Episode im Sanskrittext des Mahāparinirvāṇasūtra." In *Von Ceylon bis Turfan*, 120–163. Göttingen: Vandenhoeck & Ruprecht, 1967.

Walleser, Max, ed. *Manorathapūraṇī: Buddhaghosa's Commentary on the Aṅguttara-Nikāya*, Vol. I. Revised 2nd edition. London: Pali Text Society, 1973.

Walshe, Maurice, trans. *The Long Discourses of the Buddha: A Translation of the Dīgha Nikāya*. Boston: Wisdom Publications, 1987.

Walters, Jonathan S. "The Buddha's Bad Karma: A Problem in the History of Theravāda Buddhism." *Numen* 37, no. 1 (1990): 70–95.

Walters, Jonathan S. "Stūpa, Story and Empire: Constructions of the Buddha Biography in Early Post-Aśokan India." In *Sacred Biography in the Buddhist Traditions of South and Southeast Asia*, edited by Juliane Schober, 160–192. Honolulu: University of Hawai'i Press, 1997.

Walters, Jonathan S. "Suttas as History: Four Approaches to the 'Sermon on the Noble Quest' (Ariyapariyesanasutta)." *History of Religions* 38, no. 3 (1999): 247–284.

Walters, Jonathan S. "*Apadāna: Therī-apadāna*: Wives of the Saints: Marriage and Kamma in the Path to Arahantship." In *Women in Early Buddhism: Comparative Textual Studies*, edited by Alice Collett, 160–191. Oxford: Oxford University Press, 2014.

Walters, Jonathan S. *Legends of the Buddhist Saints (Apadānapāli)*. Walla Walla, WA: Jonathan S. Walters and Whitman College, 2017. Also available digitally at http://apadanatranslation.org.

Wayman, Alex, and Ferd Lessing, eds. *Fundamentals of the Buddhist Tantras: Rgyud Sde Spyihi Rnam Par GźAg Pa Rgyas Par Brjod*. The Hague: Mouton, 1968.

Wayman, Alex, and Ferd Lessing, eds. *Introduction to the Buddhist Tantric Systems*. 2nd ed. Delhi: Motilal Banarsidass, 1978.

Weber, Claudia. *Buddhistische Sutras: Das Leben des Buddha in Quellentexten*. Munich: Hugendubel Diederichs, 1999.

Wells, Kenneth E. *Thai Buddhism: Its Rites and Activities*. Bangkok: Police Printing Press, 1960.

Wieger, Léon. "Les vies chinoises du Bouddha: récit de l'apparition sur terre du Buddha des Sakya." *Buddhisme*, vol. 2. Sien-Hsien: Imprimerie de la Mission Catholique, 1913.

Willemen, Charles, Bart Dessein, and Collet Cox. *Sarvāstivāda Buddhist Scholasticism*. Leiden: Brill, 1998.

Williams, Joanna. "Sārnāth Gupta Steles of the Buddha's Life." *Ars Orientalis* 10 (1975): 171–192.

Wilson, Liz. *Charming Cadavers: Horrific Figurations of the Feminine in Indian Buddhist Hagiographic Literature*. Chicago: University of Chicago Press, 1996.

Woodward Jr., Hiram W. "The Life of the Buddha in the Pāla Monastic Environment." *The Journal of the Walters Art Gallery* 48 (1990): 13–27.

Woodward Jr., Hiram W. "The Indian Roots of the 'Burmese' Life of the Buddha Plaques." *Silk Road Art and Archaeology* 5 (1997–1998): 395–407.

Wu, Juan. "The *Cīvaravastu* of the Mūlasarvāstivāda *Vinaya* and Its Counterparts in Other Indian Buddhist Monastic Law Codes: A Comparative Survey." *Journal of Indian Philosophy* (2020): 1–38.

Yājñavalkya Dharmaśāstra. Yajnavalkya: A Treatise on Dharma. Edited and translated by Patrick Olivelle. Murty Classical Library of India, vol. 20. Cambridge, MA: Harvard University Press, 2019.

Yule, Henry, Sir. *Hobson-Jobson: A Glossary of Colloquial Anglo-Indian Words and Phrases, and of Kindred Terms, Etymological, Historical, Geographical and Discursive*, edited by William Crooke. London: J. Murray, 1903.

Zakovich, Yair. *The Concept of the Miracle in the Bible*. Tel-Aviv: Mod Books, 1991.

Zin, Monika. *Ajanta Handbuch der Malereien, Handbook of the Paintings 2: Devotionale und ornamentale Malereien*. Volume 1. Wiesbaden: Harrassowitz Verlag, 2003.

Zhu, Tianshu. "Reshaping the Jātaka Stories: From Jātakas to Avadānas and Praṇidhānas in Paintings at Kucha and Turfan." *Buddhist Studies Review* 29, no. 1 (2012): 57–83.

Zhu, Tianshu. "Revisiting the Dīpaṃkara Story in Gandharan Buddhist Art." In *Connecting the Art, Literature, and Religion of South and Central Asia: Studies in Honour of Monika Zin*, edited by Ines Konczak-Nagel, Satomi Hiyama, and Astrid Klein, 415–429. New Delhi: Dev Publishers and Distributors, 2022.

Zin, Monika. *Mitleid und Wunderkraft: Schwierige Bekehrungen und ihre Ikonographie im indischen Buddhismus*. Wiesbaden: Harrassowitz Verlag, 2006.

Zin, Monika. "About Two Rocks in the Buddha's Life Story." *East and West* 56 (2006): 329–358.

Zin, Monika. "Vajrapāṇi in the Narrative Reliefs." In Michael Willis, ed., *Migration, Trade, and Peoples: Association of South Asian Archeologists, Proceedings of the Eighteenth Congress, London, 2005*, 73–88. London: British Association for South Asian Studies, 2009.

Zin, Monika. "Sanskrit Literature and the Indian Pictorial Tradition in the Paintings of Kucha." In *Sanskrit on the Silk Route*, edited by Shashibala, 99–111. New Delhi: Bharatiya Vidya Bhavan, 2016.

Zipes, Jack. *The Sorcerer's Apprentice: An Anthology of Magical Tales*. Princeton, NJ: Princeton University Press, 2017.

Index

For the benefit of digital users, indexed terms that span two pages (e.g., 52–53) may, on occasion, appear on only one of those pages.

Figures are indicated by *f* following the page number

Abhidharma, xix, 139–40, 164
Act of Truth, 124, 161
Ajanta, 84, 126, 128*f*, 129*f*, 133
Ajātasattu, King, 181, 191–92, 193, 196n.47, 200–1, 202–3, 204–5
Ānanda, 50, 69–70, 76–77, 161, 177*f*, 180–85, 206–9
  tears of, 186–89
Ānandabodhi tree, 206
Anāthapiṇḍika, 206
Andagu plaques, 123–24, 138
Aṅguttara Nikāya, 206–7, 210
Anurādhapura, Sri Lanka, 205, 208–9
arhats/arahants (awakened beings), 15–16, 27, 28–31, 143, 183, 185, 187, 190–91, 193, 200, 204–7, 214n.68
Ariyapariyesanasutta, 99–100
asaṅkheyya (immeasurable time period), 5–6, 99–100
Aśoka, King, 99, 120, 121*f*, 167, 208
  diffusion of relics by, 204–6
Aśokāvadāna, 204
Aṣṭasāhasrikā Prajñāpāramitā, 144
avadāna, 17, 28–29, 33–34n.12, 50
Avadānaśataka, 31, 46–47, 166
Avataṃsaka Sūtra, 66–67
awakening story, Buddha's
  fifty days around the Bodhi tree in, 124–26
  first devotees in, 143
  first seven weeks after awakening in, 120, 123–24, 137–42
  Mara's attack in, 129–32
  Mara's defeat in, 132–35
  night of achieving complete awakening in, 135–36
Aziz Dheri stūpa settlement, 82–83, 82*f*

Bagan, 138–39
Bareau, André, 178
belvedere, xiii–xviii, 67, 151, 167
Bhalluka. *See* merchants, the two (Tapassu and Bhalluka)
Bharhut stūpa, 40*f*, 40–41, 48, 54, 139, 165*f*
Bimbisāra, King, 69–70, 154–55, 160
biography. *See* Buddha's biography, the study of the
birth story, Buddha's final, 4–5, 36–37n.41, 42–43, 56, 60–62, 99–100, 104, 114–15n.6, 185–86
  and cosmic time, 67–69
  foreshadowing, 70, 151
  impossibility of, 76–77
  as a jewel in Indra's Net, 67, 73–76
  as miraculous, 7, 61, 65–66
  as a perfect birth, 63–66
  and space, 71–73
  as suffering, 61, 63–64, 92–93
blueprint, the Buddha-life, 9, 11, 216
  Buddha's birth in, 73–75
  conceptual overview of, xvii–xviii, 3–6, 113, 151–53
  the Four Sights in, 103–4
  the Great Departure in, 99–100
  marriage's role in, 88
  teaching career in, 160, 164–65, 168
Bodhgaya, 119*f*, 120–23, 141*f*, 144, 155, 225
bodhimaṇḍa (seat of awakening), 4, 120, 126, 132–35, 139–40, 144, 163*f*, 210
Bodhisattva/Bodhisatta, the (Buddha-to-be), 4, 15, 27–29, 36–37n.41, *See also* birth story, Buddha's final; Buddha-to-be; Great Departure story, the; jātaka stories; Sumati/Sumedha; Yaśodharā and the Bodhisattva's love story
  career of, 44, 61–62, 68–69, 75, 80n.45
bodhisattvas/bodhisattas, 57n.4, 64–68, 133
  birth of, 36–37n.41, 61–62, 75–76

bodhi tree, (cont)
bodhi tree, 69–70, 99, 108–9, 110, 135–36, 138, 140*f*, 142–44, 178, 184, 199, 206, 210, 224
  Buddha's approach and sitting under the, 124–26
  in Buddhist iconography, 121–24, 121*f*
  Mara's army, 126, 130, 133
  as pilgrimage site, 119*f*–20
Borobudur stūpa, 84, 126, 127*f*, 134–35
Brahmā Sahampati, 71, 104, 130, 142, 151, 167, 169, 224–25
Brown, Robert, 55
Buddha-to-be, 4–7, 14*f*, 15–16, 28–30, 40*f*, 41–44, 46–50, 51–53, 57n.4, 84–85, 98–99, 104–7, 110–11, 152, 188. *See also* Bodhisattva/Bodhisatta, the (Buddha-to-be)
Buddha, Gautama/Gotama
  Dispensation of (see *sāsana* [Buddha's Dispensation])
  final birth of (*see* birth story, Buddha's final)
  final death of (*see* death story, Buddha's final)
  footprints of (see *buddhapada* [Buddha's footprints])
  as human, 61, 223–25
  relics of (*see* relics)
  as superhuman (see *iddhipāṭihāriya* [Buddha's superpowers])
Buddha's biography, the study of the, 1–6. *See also* blueprint, the Buddha-life; lateral expansion of Buddha's biography; narrative dimensions of Buddha's biography; Strong, John
Buddha's life stories. *See* awakening story, Buddha's; birth story, Buddha's final; death story, Buddha's final; Great Departure story, the; jātaka stories; Mallas and the boulder story; relic stories, Buddha's; teaching career stories, Buddha's; vow story, Buddha's; Yaśodharā and the Bodhisattva's love story
Buddhacarita, 27, 91–92, 101–3, 105–6, 107, 109–10, 136
Buddhaghosa, 63, 180, 183–88, 190
buddhapada (Buddha's footprints), 26, 107–8, 111–13, 207
Burmese Buddhist tradition, 123, 138, 149n.58, 168, 207, 208–9, 212n.6

caitya (shrine), 26, 108–9
cakravartin (Universal Emperor), 64–65, 69, 140*f*, 146–47n.24, 199–200
Chakesadhātuvaṃsa, 206–7
Channa/Chandaka, 69–70, 92, 106–8, 189
Chinese Buddhist tradition, 33n.7, 44, 67, 154, 157–59, 166, 178–79, 181, 189–91, 209, 215*f*, 216, 218
Collins, Steven, 49, 53, 210–11
compassion, 28, 109, 151, 166, 170n.4, 201, 206–7
Comstock, Gary, 168
conatals *(sahajāta)*, 69–70, 89–90, 98–99
constellations. *See* Uttarāsāḷha; Visākha
crocodiles, 45–47, 53
Cunda, 184, 217

Daoxuan, 209
Dāṭhavaṃsa, 209
death story, Buddha's final, 181–83, 192–93. See also *parinirvāṇa*
  Ānanda's anticipatory tears for, 186–89
  earthquake and joyful utterance before, 182–83
  King Ajātasattu's reaction to, 191–92
  last journey before, 184–86
  Mahākassapa's reaction to, 190–91
  moment of, 189–92
Deer Park, 143, 155
Dehejia, Vidya, 107–8
Departure story, the Great. *See* Great Departure story, the
Devadatta, 8, 50, 52–53, 168
Dhammacakkappavattana Sutta, 154
Dhammapada, 164–65, 166–67
Dhammapāla, 180, 183
dharma/dhamma, 3–4, 10, 70–71. *See also* teaching career stories, Buddha's
  a companion in the (see *sahadharmacāriṇī*)
  miracles and the spreading of the, 220–21
  relics and the spreading of the, 204
  wheel of, 61, 88, 152–53, 154, 157, 185–86
Dharmaguptaka tradition, 159, 178–79
Dharmaruci-avadāna, 15–17, 24, 28–29, 31, 33n.10
dharmatā khalu ("now it is the rule that"), 74
dhyāna, 220
dialectic pattern, 223–25
Dīgha Nikāya, 55, 104
Dīpa, King, 17–18, 22–24
Dīpaṅkara Buddha, 5–6, 14*f*, 15–18, 20–26, 28–31, 38n.53
Dīpāvatī (Full of Light), 17–19, 22–23, 24, 28
Dispensation, Buddha's. See *sāsana*
Divyāvadāna, 15–17, 21–22, 25, 84, 164
Doṇa, 188, 192, 197*f*, 201–2
Donovan, 216

duḥkha (suffering), 6–7, 53
the Bodhisattva's first true seeing of, 109–10, 135
and the Buddha's last journey, 184
as a primer for awakening, 98–99, 104, 151 (*see also* Sights, the Four)
solving the human problem of, 76, 92
as used by Māra, 128–29
of the womb, 61, 63–64, 65–66
of Yaśodharā, 92–93
dung beetles, 47–48
Duṭṭhagāmaṇī, King, 205
dvadaśa-buddha-kārya (twelve deeds of a Buddha), 75, 113, 153

earthquakes, 22–23, 27–28, 72–73, 157–58, 182, 189
Ekottarāgama, 216–17
elephants, xvii–xviii, 42–43, 47–48, 52, 64–65, 88, 91, 122–23, 150*f*, 153, 168–69, 185, 219–20, 224
emotions, xvii, 178–80, 192–93, 200–1. *See also* grief; *pasāda* (happiness, composure); *pema* (love); *saṃvega* (shock, distress); *udāna* (a joyful utterance)

fabula, xvii–xviii, 100–1, 109, 151–52
Faure, Bernard, 8
Faxian, 166
footprints, Buddha's. See *buddhapada*
Forster, E. M., xviii
Four Noble Truths, the. *See* Noble Truths, the Four
Four Sights, the. *See* Sights, the Four

Gaṇḍavyūha Sūtra, 7, 75
Gandhāra, 201–2
art of, 16, 29–31, 65–66, 83, 116n.22, 130*f*, 131, 131*f*, 134–35, 177*f*, 180
literature of, 16, 28–29
gandharva, 63
Garbhāvakrānti Sūtra, 64
generosity. See *pāramitā*; Strong, John
Gharaṇī, 160–61
Ghosts. *See* hungry ghosts
Goethe, Johann Wolfgang von, 221–22, 228n.34
Gómez, Luis, 164
Great Awakening, the. *See* awakening story, Buddha's
Great Departure story, the, 6–7, 51–52, 70–71, 90–92, 224
as depicted on a Sanchi Stūpa gateway, 10, 98–102, 98*f*, 107–9, 111
finding shade under a *jambu* tree, 108–10
footprints as the destination, 111–12, 111*f*
the Four Sights as precursors, 102–4
leaving on and then leaving behind Kanthaka, 107–8
priming by Kisāgotamī for, 104–6
Great Man, marks of a. See *mahāpuruṣa*
Great Miracle, the. *See* Twin Miracle
Great Relic Shrine, the. *See* Mahāthūpa
Great Renunciation, the. *See* Renunciation, the Great
Great Stūpa at Sanchi, the, 54–55, 54*f*, 98–99, 101, 114, 120
gateway friezes of, 43*f*, 54*f*, 98*f*, 101*f*, 102, 108*f*, 111, 111*f*, 121*f*, 122
grief, 92, 109–10, 178, 180–82, 185–88, 191
therapy of, 183, 192–93
Gūthapāṇa Jātaka, 41–48

Hair. *See also* relics; Sumati/Sumedha
cutting of, 111, 113
tearing of, 189–90
wringing of, 134–35, 147n.35
Hallisey, Charles, 180
happiness. See *pasāda*
Haribhadra, 144
Heaven of the Thirty-Three, 122–23, 157, 164–65, 166, 169
Hindu traditions, 126, 146n.19
Brahmanical Hinduism, 19–20
horse, Buddha's. *See* Kanthaka
Hridaya, Chittadhar, 126
hungry ghosts, 68–69, 71

iddhipāṭihāriya (Buddha's superpowers), 152–54, 159–60, 168, 170–71n.10, 219–20
imperfection
of Buddha's past lives, 45–47
of others, 47–48
and perfection, 42–49
impermanence, 11, 178, 185 --87, 189, 192–93, 210–11, 222–25
India, 181, 188. *See also* Ajanta; Bodhgaya; Great Stūpa at Sanchi, the; Jambudīpa
Indra's Net *(indrajāla),* 66–68, 73–76
Indra/Sakka, 67, 106, 130, 142–43, 162, 164–65, 167, 169, 202, 208. *See also* Indra's Net *(indrajāla)*
indrajāla. See Indra's Net *(indrajāla)*

jackal, 40*f*, 41, 48
Jain tradition, 173n.32, 190
Jambudīpa, 201–3, 206–8, 214n.67

Janaka, 45, 48–49
jātaka stories, 15, 27, 40–42, 44, 49–53, 83–87
of the attempts of the Buddha-to-be to escape from Māra, 53
of the dung beetle, 47, 48
of the monkey and the crocodile, 45–47
of Vessantara, 42–49, 43*f*
of Yaśodharā and the Buddha-to-be, 52
Jātakanidāna, 90–92, 102–6, 109, 124, 136
Jātakatthavaṇṇanā, 41, 44–48, 50
Jeta's Grove, 187
Jetavana Monastery, 206
jhāna, 109, 142
joyful utterance. See *udāna*

Kāla, 115n.18, 124, 139–40, 161. *See also* nāgas
Kāḷudāyī, 69–70
Kanthaka, 7–8, 69–70, 92, 107–8
Kapilavastu/Kapilvatthu, 71, 98*f*, 101, 104, 107–8, 111
karma, 17, 20–21, 28, 45–47, 49–50, 63–64, 128–29, 133, 138, 164
Kermode, Frank, 210–11
Kinnarī Jātaka, 84–87
Kisāgotamī, 104–6
Koṇḍañña, Āññāta, 158
Krakucchanda Buddha, 28–29
kṣatriya (warrior class), 104–5, 126, 200–1
kuśa grass, 125*f*, 126, 135
Kusinagarī, 178–79
Kusinārā, 181, 184–86, 188–90, 200–1

Lakkhaṇa Sutta, 54–55
Lalitavistara, 61, 62, 76, 87–90, 93, 102, 106–7, 138, 139–40, 142, 153, 179–80, 193
Langenberg, Amy, 61
Laṅkādvīpa. *See* Sri Lanka
lateral expansion of Buddha's biography, 7–8, 112–13
Leoshko, Janice, 123, 144
Licchavis, 200–1
light, 17, 23, 61–62, 65, 70, 72–74, 135–36, 148n.38, 157–58
lions, 41, 52, 87
Liudu ji jing, 44
lokapāla (World Guardian deities), 68, 72, 74
Lotus Sūtra, 161–62
Lumbinī Grove, 4–5, 65–66, 69, 71, 75

Magadha, 200–1, 202
Mahabodhi temple complex, 119*f*, 141*f*
Mahābodhivaṃsa, 199, 206–7
Mahākassapa, 177*f*, 190–92, 196n.45, 202–5
Mahāmaudgalyāyana, 220–22
Mahāmāyā, xix
Mahāmeghavana Park, 208
Mahāpadāna Sutta, 3–4, 74, 104, 152, 158–59
Mahāparinibbāna Sutta, 152–53, 178–79, 199–202
Mahāparinirvāna Sūtra, 178–79, 196n.42, 216–17
mahāpuruṣa, 54–55, 64–65, 68–69, 104, 184–85, 210, 224
Mahāsāṃghika-Lokottaravādins, 15–16, 52
Mahāsudassana, Emperor, 186, 188
Mahāthūpa (the Great Relic Shrine), 205, 208–10
Mahāvaṃsa, 199, 206–8, 213n.45
Mahāvastu, 15–16, 38n.53, 52–53, 84, 86–87, 89–90, 92, 131–32, 139–40
Mahinda, 208
Mallas, the, 184, 189–92, 200–1, 215*f*, 217–20, 222–23
Mallas and the boulder story
boulder as obstruction, 217–20
boulder broken up, 220–22
boulder reconstituted, 222–23
Manoharā, 52, 84–85, 94–95n.8
Māra, 7–8, 53, 120, 121*f*, 123–24, 135–36, 142, 151, 159, 178, 182–83, 224. See also *Māravijāya*
attack on the Bodhisattva by, 129–32
defeat by the Bodhisattva of, 132–35
Māravijāya (Victory over Māra), 120, 127*f*, 128*f*, 129*f*, 130*f*, 132*f*, 133–35, 134*f*, 138, 140*f*, 144
Māravijāya template, 122–23, 123*f*
marriage, 18, 20–22, 26–27, 37n.46, 88, 151
Brahmanical rules of, 19–20
Marshall, Sir John, 108–9
Masefield, Peter, 183
Mati, 17, 23–24
Maudgalyāyana, 154–55, 166, 221–22
Māyā, Queen, 7, 60*f*, 64–66, 71–72, 75, 189–90
merchants, the two (Tapassu and Bhalluka), 143, 206–7, 208–9
Meru, Mount, 166
methodology, 8–10
middle way, the, 111–12, 154, 156–57
miracles. See also *pāṭihāriya*; Twin Miracle
display, 152
testimonial, 152, 158
Morrison, Toni, xvi
mountains, 71, 132, 166, 207, 213n.45, 216, 217–18
Muchalinda/Mucalinda, 141*f*, 142, 148n.46

Mūlasarvāstivāda tradition, 15–16, 25, 31, 36–37n.41, 159–61. See also *Mūlasarvāstivāda Vinaya*
Mūlasarvāstivāda Vinaya, 62, 91, 164, 216–17
Murnane, Gerald, xiii
Myanmar. *See* Burmese Buddhist tradition

nāgas, 41, 98–99, 107, 142, 161–62, 201–3, 205, 206–7. *See also* Kāla; Muchalinda/Mucalinda
Nairañjanā river, 115n.18, 124, 125*f*, 146–47n.24
Nālagiri, 153, 168
narrative dimensions of Buddha's biography, xvii–xix, 1–10, 51, 100–1, 151–52, 181, 186, 197–98, 210–11, 216–17
  acceptance of the conflicts within the, 76–77
  Buddha portrayed as human in the, 47
  community aspects of the, 92–93
  complex causal networks within, 180
  conflated mode of, 29
  cosmic timescape in the, 188–89
  cultural imagination in the, 144–45
  dialectic within the, 223–25
  emotions role in the, 178–80, 192–93
  and his teaching career, 168–69
  images and, 30, 107–8, 109, 121–23, 138
  mandatory events or miracles as a template, 151–52
  the possibilities alive within the, 31
  presence in absence, 112–14
  relics' role in the continued existence of Buddha stories in, 210–11
  tensions within, 42, 56
Nepal, 122, 131*f*, 132*f*, 134*f*, 141*f*, 153
Nigrodha, 204
Nimi, King, 45
nirvana, 53, 64, 210–11, 220, 223, 224–25
Buddha's final, 16, 71, 142, 152–53, 177*f*, 178 (*see also* death story, Buddha's final)
Noble Truths, the Four, 61, 128–29, 154, 157

offerings. See *pūja*
Omens, the Four. *See* Sights, the Four
omnipresence, 72
otters, 40–41, 48

Pāli/Pali tradition, 12n.9, 15, 41, 44–45, 48, 53, 74, 99–100, 116n.22, 123–24, 136, 142, 158–59, 160, 162, 164–65, 178–79, 199–200, 204, 211
pañcavaggiya (Group of Five), 70–71
Pāñcika, 164
pāramitā/*pāramī*, 43–45, 48–49. *See also* generosity
parinirvāṇa, 70–71, 99, 100, 123*f*, 125*f*, 169, 178–79, 197–98, 200–1, 206–9, 210–11, 216, 225. *See also* death story, Buddha's final
pasāda (happiness, composure), 103, 115n.16, 184–85, 195n.24
pāṭihāriya (miracles), 152, 170–71n.10
pema (love), 187–88
perfection, 17, 138. See also *pāramitā*
  of the Bodhisattva's birth, 63–66
  of the Buddha, 45–47, 51, 55–56
  and imperfection, 42–49
  as a karmic nexus, 28, 49–50, 180
  as a path vs. a destination, 48–49
Phra Sihing image (Sinhala Buddha), 205–6
pilgrimage traditions, xvii, 8–9, 30, 120, 122, 144, 153–54, 166–67, 169
Piyadāsa, Prince, 203, 204
pradakṣiṇā (offering circumambulation), 120, 126, 133
Pradyota, King, 69–70
Prajāpati, 161–62
prajñābala (power of his wisdom), 135, 222
Prajñāpāramita Sūtra, 131*f*, 132*f*, 133, 134*f*, 136, 144
praṇidhāna (fervent aspiration), 22
Prasenajit, King, 69, 160, 166
pūja (offerings), 17–22, 28, 30, 50–51, 55, 111–12, 122–24, 135, 140*f*, 143, 202–3, 206, 207–8
Pūraṇa Kāśyapa, 162

Qingyuan Weixin, 216

Radich, Michael, 61, 218
Rāhula, 69–70, 99–100, 183, 196n.49
Rājagaha, 202–3
Ramanujan, A. K., 62
Rāmāyaṇa, 62
Ram Khamhaeng, King, 205–6
ṛddhi (superpowers), 24, 133, 142, 219–20, 222–23, 227n.21
rebirth, 18–19, 22, 25–26, 28–29, 51–53, 56, 64, 67, 71, 89–90, 124, 128–29, 138, 151, 156–57, 166
relic stories, Buddha's
  collecting, desiring and dividing of, 200–2
  diffusion beyond India, 206–9
  diffusion by Asoka, 204–6
  King Ajātasattu's role in, 202–3

relics, 2, 10–2, 26, 30–31, 54–55, 66, 99, 111, 124, 188, 192–93, 197*f*, 210–11, 225. *See also* relic stories, Buddha's
Buddha's bones, fingernails and teeth as, 208–9
Buddha's footprints as, 26, 198–99, 207, 212n.6
Buddha's hair as, 198–99, 206–7, 208–9, 213n.45
disputes over, 200–1
Great Relic Shrine, the (*see* Mahāthūpa)
as impermanent, 210–11
introduction to, 198–200
role in dispensation, 197–98 (see also *sāsana*)
veneration of, 197–200, 202, 204, 206–7
Renunciation, the Great, 69, 106, 108–9, 112–13, 146–47n.24
Reynolds, Frank, 4, 179–80, 197–98

sahadharmacāriṇī (companion in the dharma), 26–27, 37n.46, 94n.3
sahajāta. *See* conatals
Sakka/Indra. *See* Indra/Sakka
Śākyamuni Buddha, 15–17, 23, 24, 26, 28–29, 60, 67–68, 73–75, 91, 120, 124
Sakyans, 200–1
Samantakūṭavaṇṇanā, 207
Saṃkāśya/Saṅkassa, 153–54, 164–68
saṃsāra, 3, 53, 61, 72, 93, 103, 138, 142, 178, 207–8, 210, 220
Samudra, 204
saṃvega (shock, distress), 103, 104, 185, 190, 195n.24
Saṃyutta Nikāya, 156
Sanchi. *See* Great Stūpa at Sanchi, the
Saṅgha, 3, 10, 143, 144–45, 152–53, 154, 160–61, 168–69, 182, 189, 199–200
Saṅghabhedavastu, 62, 91–93
Sanskrit tradition, 12n.9, 15–16, 41, 44, 61, 160, 161–62, 164, 204
Śāriputra, 154–55, 222
Sarnath, 122–23, 143, 150*f*, 153–55, 168
sāsana (Buddha's Dispensation), 69–70, 190, 197–98, 204–5, 210–11
Savatthi, 187
Seat of Awakening. See *bodhimaṇḍa*
Sharf, Robert, 198
Shimoda, Masahiro, 178–79
shock. See *saṃvega*
shrines, 23–24, 26, 30–31, 121*f*, 200, 202–3, 204–5. See also *caitya*
Mahāthūpa; *stūpas/thūpas*; Thūpārāma Relic Shrine
Siddhārtha Gautama, xvii, 1–2, 60, 82–83, 98–99, 100–2, 107–9, 112, 114, 120, 124, 126, 130, 133, 135–36, 138, 143, 146–47n.24, 199
Sights, the Four, 90–91, 92–93, 102–4, 109–10, 112–13, 116n.22
Sinhala Thūpavaṃsa, 202–3, 207–8, 212n.25
Sivi/Śibi, King, 48–49, 68–69
space, xiv–xv, 6–7, 61–62, 67, 71–73, 75–76, 107, 185–86, 197–98
Śrāvastī, 24, 69–70. *See also* Twin Miracle
Sri Lanka (Laṅkādvīpa), 2, 123–26, 125*f*, 138, 140*f*, 199, 205–10, 214n.67
stories. *See* Buddha's life stories
Strong, John, 54–55, 93, 100, 112–14, 121–22, 152, 155, 156–57, 158–59, 161–62, 167–68, 179–80, 184. *See also* blueprint, the Buddha-life
on bias towards individualism, 4, 7–8, 112
The Buddha: A Beginner's Guide, xvii, 2
generosity of, xvi, 10
on lateral expansions, 7–8, 112, 179–80, 193
mandatory events as narrative templates, 151–52
on relics, 197–98
scholarly contributions of, 2
study and translation of *Aśokāvadāna*, 204
on ways of reading Buddha's life stories, xv–xvii
stūpas/thūpas, 16, 43*f*, 139, 149n.58, 197*f*, 214n.68, *See also* Aziz Dheri stūpa settlement; Bharhut stūpa; Borobudur stūpa; Great Stūpa at Sanchi, the; relics
Subhadda, 52–189
Śuddhodana, King, 64–65, 110
Sudhana, Prince, 52, 84–85
suffering. See *duḥkha*
Sugata Saurabha, 126
Sujātā, 111–12, 124, 184
Sukhamalasutta, 87
Sumati/Sumedha, 5–6, 17–22, 28, 36–37n.41, 99–100, 151
matted hair of, 15, 22–24, 34n.17, 36n.40
as schooled in Brahmanical Hinduism, 19–20
superhuman powers. See also *ṛddhi*
of Buddha (see *iddhipāṭihāriya*)
of others that are not Buddha, 24, 159, 164
svayaṃvara (choosing for oneself), 19–20

Tapassu. *See* merchants, the two (Tapassu and Bhalluka)
Tatelman, Joel, 85
Tathāgata, 10–11, 75–77, 120, 182, 187, 219

teaching career stories, Buddha's
decision to teach in, 142–43, 151, 155–56
Descent from the Heavens in, 164–69
first sermon in, 150*f*, 154–58, 168
the Great Miracle at Śrāvastī, 158–64 (*see also* Twin Miracle)
tears, 91–92, 180
of Ānanda, 186–89
of an old woman, 190–91, 196n.45
Temiya, Prince, 45
Thailand, 123–24, 134–35, 159, 167, 205–6, 212n.9
theras, 208
Theravāda. *See* Pāli/Pali tradition
Thūpārāma Relic Shrine, 208
Tibetan Buddhist tradition, 113, 153–54, 159, 164, 189, 196n.49
time, 3–6, 39n.57, 61–62, 67–69, 71, 73, 100, 115n.18, 179–80, 188 See also *asaṅkheyya*
Trāyastriṃśa (heaven of the thirty-three gods), 11, 122–23
trees. See also *bodhi* tree
jambu trees, 102, 108–10
kṣīrika trees, 142
mango trees, 162, 163*f*, 191–92
nigrodha trees, 142
pipal trees *(Ficus religiosa)*, 119–20
Sal trees, 177, 181, 184, 186, 189–90, 196n.42, 225
Tuṣita Heaven, 24, 36–37n.41, 64, 67–68, 71, 75, 99–100
twelve deeds of a Buddha. See *dvadaśa-buddha-kārya*
Twin Miracle, 4, 11, 70–71, 122–23, 136, 144, 152–53, 158–64, 167

udāna (a joyful utterance), 182–83, 194n.13
Udayana, King, 69–70
Universal Emperor. See *cakravartin*
Upavāṇa, 184–85
Uppallavaṇṇā, 50
Uttarakuru, 220–21
Uttarāsāḷha, 70–71

Vajjians, 181, 191
Vaṃsadīpanī, 207
Vāsava, King, 17–18, 20–24, 28
veneration, 29–30, 72
of relics, 197*f*–200, 201–2, 204, 206
Vesālī, 200–1
Vessantara, Prince, 42–43, 43*f*, 45, 48–49, 51–52, 68–69
Vidhura, 41
Vinaya, 155, 189. See also *Mūlasarvāstivāda Vinaya*
Vipassī, Buddha, 3–4, 74, 104
Visākha, 68, 70–71
Visuddhimagga, 63
Viśvakarma/Vissakamma, 203
vow story, Buddha's. *See also* Sumati/Sumedha
in Gandhāran art and practice, 29–31
"The Story of Dharmaruci," 15–17
Sumati getting waterlilies from the young woman, 17–19
Sumati offering waterlilies to Dīpaṅkara, 22–24

Walters, Jonathan, 55
warrior class. See *kṣatriya*
waterlilies, 18–19, 20–26, 29, 34n.15
Wells, Kenneth, 167–68
Williams, Joanna, 122

Xuanzang, 166

yakṣas, 98–99, 107, 164
Yaśodharā and the Bodhisattva's love story, 27, 52, 82–87, 82*f*, 89–93, 94n.4